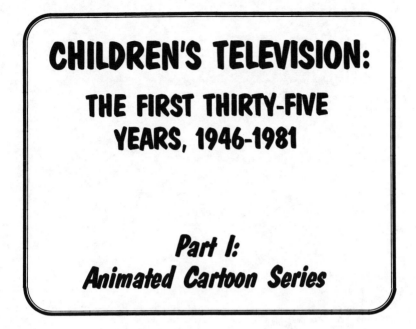

# CHILDREN'S TELEVISION:
## THE FIRST THIRTY-FIVE YEARS, 1946-1981

## Part I:
## Animated Cartoon Series

by

GEORGE W. WOOLERY

The Scarecrow Press, Inc.
Metuchen, N.J., & London
1983

**Library of Congress Cataloging in Publication Data**

Woolery, George W., 1937-
   Children's television, the first thirty-
five years, 1946-1981.

      Includes index.
      Contents: pt. 1. Animated cartoon series.
      1. Television broadcasting of motion
picture cartoons--United States--History.
I. Title.
PN1992.8.M6W6   1982   791.45'75        82-5841
ISBN 0-8108-1557-5 (pt. 1)              AACR2

For my parents, George C. Woolery and Leotia P. Sutton,
eternally supportive whatever my aspiration or folly,
and in memory of Robert "Bobe" Cannon and Pete Burness,
two of the noble directors of film animation.

# CONTENTS

# ACKNOWLEDGMENTS

For the resources that made this book possible, former Ambassador Walter K. Annenberg, and for their support and encouragement, Dr. Frederick Williams, Dr. Richard B. Byrne, Dr. Thomas H. Martin and Carolyn Spicer, Annenberg School of Communications, University of Southern California.

For their assistance in supplying information and materials, Squire Rushnell, Peter Roth, Dolores Moers and particularly Noel Resnick, ABC Television; Jerry Golod, Faith Frenz-Heckman and Kevin McDonald, CBS Television; George A. Heinemann, Margaret Loesch and Irwin "Sonny" Fox, NBC Television; Ivette M. Alemar, PBS; Alan Press, Columbia Pictures Television; Peter M. Piech, Filmtel International; Joe Dowling, King Features Syndicate; Joseph E. Ondrick and Kathy Fenus, MCA-TV; Patricia Stiphout, Metromedia Producers Corporation; Sybil Coen, National Telefilm Associates; Jay Rizick, Sandy Frank Film Syndication; Helen Killeen and Jack McLaughlin, United Artists Television; Debbie Peck, Viacom International; and Barry Zajac, Worldvision Enterprises.

For their helping hand and recollections, Dick Brown, Animation Filmakers; Dan Enright, Barry and Enright Productions; Bob Clampett, Bob Clampett Productions; Bob Gillis, Depatie-Freleng Enterprises; Joe Barbera, Art Scott, John Michaeli and Sarah Baisley, Hanna-Barbera Studios; Bill Hurtz, Jay Ward Productions; Ken Snyder and Duane Busick, Ken Snyder Enterprises; Bill Melendez, Phil Roman, Bernie Gruver and Sandy Arnold, Bill Melendez Productions; Joe Ruby, Ken Spears and Ericka Grossert, Ruby-Spears Enterprises; Bill Weiss, Terrytoons; Hal Geer, Warner Brothers Television and Daws Butler, Les Goldman, Mark Kausler, Al Kouzel, Herb Klynn, Steve Leiva, Bill Scott and especially Adrian Woolery, Playhouse Pictures.

For their research assistance, Maureen Wieczorek, Broadcast Information Bureau; James B. Poteat, Television Information Office; David R. Smith, Walt Disney Archives; Fred Patten; and the Orange Library Reference Staff, particularly Linda Cucovatz, Barbara Poff and Randall A. Robb.

Also helpful were The American Animated Cartoon (E. P. Dutton 1980) by Danny and Gerald Peary, Of Mice and Magic (McGraw-Hill 1980) by Leonard Maltin, The Warner Brothers Cartoons (Scarecrow 1981) by Will Friedwald and Jerry Beck, the magazines Funnyworld, Box 1633, New York, NY 10001, edited by Mike Barrier, and Animania (formerly Mindrot), 3112 Holmes Ave. S., Minneapolis, MN 55408.

# INTRODUCTION

If you like animated cartoons, are curious about them or watched them on television as a child, within this filmography you can savor the heady nostalgia of your favorite programs. From Felix the Cat, Bugs Bunny and Popeye the Sailor to Fat Albert, The Pink Panther and Scooby-Doo, all the cartoon series seen on television are profiled from the early uncensored theatrical films to the pro-social mode of the new. The flamboyant caricatures from Rocky and His Friends, Beany and Cecil and George of the Jungle are re-echoed for their avid cult followers, the epic struggles against evil by Courageous Cat, Astro Boy, Hong Kong Phooey, Superman, Batman and Spider-Man for the legion of heroic fantasy buffs, and the enchanting whimsy of Dr. Seuss, Peanuts and Winnie-the-Pooh for those who cherish some of the finest folk and animal tales ever animated. Wrapped in historical perspective, this volume has been carefully researched for the aficionado, the scholar and the professional who want to know the roots, who did it, what happened and when. But like its subject matter, the animated cartoon series televised during the first thirty-five years, it is also purely for enjoyment.

Despite those who see in an occasional animated film a renaissance of the classic art made for theaters, television has altered the focus and form of the film cartoon and in large part its destiny. Excluding production of TV commercials, which kept hundreds of artists working between 1955 and 1965 during the last gasp of the theatrical cartoon, in twelve months the TV-oriented industry employs more craftsmen and turns out more footage than did all the major Hollywood cartoon studios in one of their heyday years. In the artistic and economic transition to the electronic age, datemarked to the split-second, naturally there are differences in production methods, budgets and standards. Compared to the painstaking pace of the Golden Years, when studio-owned theaters assured repeated distribution for their affiliated cartoon stars, the fickle TV appetite for fresh characters and content seems insatiable. For several reasons, not the least pro-social concerns and a respectable audience-share, the concept overrides the production handicaps for all but a few TV Specials. Of course, all the freedom and resources in the world cannot guarantee meaningful visual ingenuity. No matter the technique, the art of breathing film life into an inanimate form is still boundless, literally, limited only by the wispy fancies of the mature mind. Most on television, unfortunately, belong to that ambiguous adolescent twilight that Keats described. Yet perhaps we should be grateful that animated cartoons, as a film art undergoing electronic translation, provide at least a few hours of childish imagination each week.

# ANIMATED CARTOONS AS TELEVISED PROGRAMMING:
## A BRIEF CHRONICLE

As part of television's infinite kaleidoscopic panorama, animated cartoons have been around far longer than most people realize, probably because their evolution was a collateral development of children's programming. On May 3, 1939, NBC presented its first full-scale evening of telecasting on experimental station W2XBS, now WNBC, New York. Helen Lewis served as mistress of ceremonies for the program, which represented just about everything in the way of entertainment, including music, songs, a film and a play, and a preview of Walt Disney's Donald's Cousin Gus (May 19, 1939), the first film cartoon shown on television. During the Second World War, when the New York stations offered sporadic experimental programs, WRGB, The General Electric Company station in Schenectady, New York, devoted about half its programming between 1942 and 1944 to full-length features, short subjects and cartoons. Following the war, in the decade between 1946 and 1955, when the major Hollywood studios were still jealously guarding their well-stocked vaults from the new in-home competition, several distributors of vintage cartoons enjoyed a modest windfall. Among the first to appear regularly were some black-and-white films made in the thirties by Van Beuren Studios, seen in Spring 1947 on Movies for Small Fry, Tuesday evening on DuMont's WABD, New York. At the January 19, 1948 meeting of the Small Fry Club, a weekday evening network continuation of the show, Big Brother Bob Emery screened a film from the Van Beuren series "Cubby Bear" (1931-1933), and in 1950-1951 before the program ended, featured early Walter Lantz films. The Van Beuren cartoons also appeared on TV Tots Time on WENR, Chicago and the ABC Network between 1950 and 1952 along with the silent "Aesop's Fables" (1921-1929) from Fables Studios, produced by Paul Terry. Also during the period, Ub Iwerks' "Flip the Frog" (1930-1933) and "Willie Whopper" (1933-1934) were programmed locally as weekly fare. Although most of the vintage films were retired from distribution in the early sixties, replaced by more recent color cartoons, the rudimentary theatrical films televised exceptionally well on small, low-definition black-and-white receivers.

If in theaters the short cartoon was developed for a general audience, after the graphic films were leased for television programming the focus changed. By the early fifties, the film cartoon was scheduled almost exclusively on children's shows, usually those hosted by an adult. Routinely dropped in a multipurpose format, which fused many elements too costly to produce locally as separate programs, the cartoons were seen between the games, songs, storytelling, crafts and contests. From the sandbox set to the bubblegum brigade, the simply defined characters, broadly played slapstick, fantasy action and visual pizazz enthralled juveniles in droves. Nothing that would unduly tax the interest or attention span of the viewer, cartoons were staple programming throughout the country on such programs as the Captain Bob Show in Buffalo, Banjo Billie's Funboat in Miami, Uncle Willie's Cartoon Show in Beaumont, Texas and Uncle

Dudley, Uncle Don and Uncle Al programs by the score. With only a few animated film packages in distribution, the cartoons were repeated again and again. But programmers soon discovered children derived very real pleasure encountering something recognizable by its repetition and, moreover, were apt to stay with it.

Long before network executives succumbed to the maxim, program managers of local stations were unswayable converts to the philosophy that "cartoons were for kids." The concept was reinforced in later years by audience measurement. In 1953, one industry survey showed 20 to 25 stations regularly running cartoon shows, the majority of which were receiving high ratings. Some of the vintage films were of poor print quality and of questionable taste for a juvenile audience by today's standards. But despite their age and content few could deny animated films were a potent children's programming device and in the fifties the demand and price for cartoons began to escalate, stimulated by television's growth to over 400 operating stations by January 1, 1955.

To finance large screen spectacular entertainment and induce customers to return to the theaters, the struggling film industry began the proliferation when the economic rewards became attractive in 1955-1956. Among the larger packages, the pre-1948 library from Warner Brothers and films from Paramount-Fleischer-Famous Studios deluged local daytime and early evening hours with Bugs Bunny, Daffy Duck, Porky Pig, Betty Boop, Popeye the Sailor, Superman, Little Lulu and other cartoon stars enjoying new life entertaining children. While the earlier "Terry Toons" were seen on Barker Bill's Cartoon Show (CBS, 1953-1956), the first weekday afternoon network animated program, the more recent cartoons released through Twentieth Century-Fox Films arrived in late 1955, when CBS bought producer Paul Terry's Studio. That year, they launched Mighty Mouse Playhouse (CBS, 1955-1966), the initial Saturday morning network cartoon show, and in Summer 1956, CBS Cartoon Theater hosted by Dick Van Dyke, the first prime time network series with animated fare. Retaining control over his library, Walt Disney debuted in 1954 with Disneyland, ABC's first major hit, periodically presenting some of his films, like "Alice in Wonderland" (Nov. 3, 1954), the first animated feature, and the first shorts on "The Donald Duck Story" (Nov. 17, 1954). The following season, The Mickey Mouse Club (ABC, 1955-1959) burst onto home screens weekdays featuring his most tenured cartoon star. With the exception of portions of the Disney library, MGM's Tom and Jerry package and several theatrical series still in production, by the end of 1960 nearly all the major and independent studios had released their films to television.

Largely a story of syndication, the first made-for-TV cartoons debuted in 1949 with the trail-blazing, serialized Crusader Rabbit, whose format was copied by producers into the sixties. Even more significant were Hanna-Barbera's Huckleberry Hound, Quick Draw McGraw and Yogi Bear, which introduced the half-hour all-cartoon program between 1958-1963, attracting national sponsors. For the next ten years, almost every subsequent development for the syndicated market was implicit in the format, characters and style of the three series. Since the characters did not have to be paid, except for limited voice residuals, the all-cartoon show in part sealed the fate of the local hosted children's programs. Another contributor in the late sixties were such Japanese series as Marine Boy, Speed Racer and Kimba, the White Lion which filled local hours with economical imports. By the early seventies, spiraling production costs and wages, the availability of off-network packages, and pressure by Action for Children's Television, which resulted in a new code addition by the National Association of Broadcasters, banning commercials delivered by both live and cartoon children's show hosts, nearly ended the genre after more than a quarter century.

Notable also among the network pioneers were The Gerald McBoing-Boing Show (CBS, 1956-1958), which presented children in part with the first new cartoons including some educational films made for the network by UPA, a major cartoonery, The Ruff and Reddy Show (NBC, 1957-1964), the first hosted all-new Saturday morning show, Tennessee Tuxedo and His Tales (CBS, 1963-1966 ... ), the first entertaining-educational series and The Flintstones (ABC, 1960-1966 ... ), the first and last series to invade prime time viewing hours successfully. Yet, almost from the start, adolescents and children under twelve saved the caveman comedy from cancellation, providing the show's largest block of viewers, a fact ABC recognized when it moved the program from 8:30-9:00 PM Friday to 7:30-8:00 PM Thursday in 1963. Ironically, even before the end of its nighttime run, The Flintstones' demographics validated that old adage about cartoons being the paramount province of children and hardened the philosophy among network hierarchy. Of the eleven animated series introduced in the faddish rush to network prime time between 1960 and 1966, only four lasted more than one season and of the total, three entered syndication and eight were rescheduled on Saturday mornings. The ripple effects continue unabated. Since 1966, there has not been a cartoon series scheduled during a regular season after 7:30 PM on network television. Instead, web programmers have preferred periodic animated specials always telecast during the earliest prime time hours, which affords a large juvenile audience. With few exceptions, the cartoon specials adhere to subjects drawn from juvenile literature or are built around purely children's themes and holidays, utilizing adaptions of popular TV cartoon, comic book and newspaper comic characters. And shortly after the fanciful Stone Age comedy was rerun solely for children, viewers could watch Saturday mornings and scarcely see a living soul, except in the commercials.

In the mid-sixties, the networks discovered finally what local children's show hosts had known for years, that juveniles and some adults too, love animated cartoons. They had long been devoted, unanimously, to a variety of adolescent and pre-adolescent entertainment, even though largely repeats of vintage theatrical cartoons and programs like The Lone Ranger, Fury, My Friend Flicka, Sky

King and Dennis the Menace, with a handful of new variety and educational programs. Encouraged by Kellogg's and General Mills, foremost among the early sponsors using the syndicated all-cartoon show's tremendous pulling power, CBS broke with tradition in 1963-1964. The network block programmed two hours of cartoons on Saturday morning for the advertisers, "hammocking" the new Tennessee Tuxedo and His Tales and Quick Draw McGraw from the syndicated ranks between popular holdovers, The Alvin Show and Mighty Mouse Playhouse. In the following two seasons another hour was added, introducing among the repeats, Linus, the Lionhearted in 1964-1965 and after re-editing, The Tom and Jerry Show in 1965-1966. ABC followed suit in 1964 and NBC in 1965. In the latter season, ABC premiered The Beatles and NBC its hour-long package The Atom Ant/Secret Squirrel Show, two landmark series which decimated all competition and affected cartoon content and programming formats into the seventies.

At age 26 in 1963 the CBS daytime programmer Fred Silverman, who expanded the network's cartoon programming, reacted by wangling a $8 million kitty with which to purchase new shows. In a wholesale shake-up in 1966-1967, the wunderkind almost single-handedly revolutionized the structure of children's programming. Among nine cartoon half-hours, back-to-back, the newly appointed vice president scheduled six new, hard-action, derring-do fantasies featuring The New Adventures of Superman and Space Ghost, an original hit, launching the superhero vogue. The overhauled line-up hit the air with a ratings explosion, catapulting CBS into first place in the Saturday morning ratings, a position it has seldom relinquished since. Variety chronicled his amazing exploit with the headline "Hi-Yo Silverman!" and TV Guide credited him with putting "Zing" and "Profit" in Saturday mornings.

Among the several lessons learned was that the old shibboleth that children liked repeats and watched anything that moved was no longer valid. Growing ever more sophisticated with time and exposure, juveniles were responsive to new programming and the new cartoons delivered the largest audience. For the first time in the late sixties, Saturday mornings became "a jungle of competition from 8:00 AM to 1:00 PM," as ABC vice-president Edwin T. Kane characterized it. At prices ranging from $48,000 to $62,000 per half-hour, the networks began fierce bidding for new animated cartoon shows. Generally, ABC and CBS bought 16 episodes over two years rerunning each cartoon six times while NBC usually purchased 13 episodes of a series over one year, repeating it four times, totaling 52 weeks. The practice continued virtually unchanged through the seventies, while costs mushroomed from $70,000 to $100,000 per thirty-minute program. But while much of the early success had to do with Silverman's professed maxim, "familiarity breeds acceptance," and his use of some popular, well-known properties, the rival networks joined the cartoon bandwagon sometimes relying on any new animated product. In 1967-1968, thirty million Americans, largely juveniles, had their pick of twelve-and-one-half hours of cartoons on the three networks and the top-rated shows pulled in fourteen million viewers. On Saturday mornings alone, the combined web take was $50 million and by 1970 the weekend juvenile take totaled $66.8 million. Animated cartoons were on Saturday mornings to stay.

Silverman scheduled the first all-cartoon line-up of six hours on Saturday morning in 1968-1969 and subsequently introduced some novel animated programming concepts. The Messiah of the Saturday morning rating wars in the sixties, and paterfamilias of animated comic book stars, minority characters and pro-social programs, Silverman not only changed the look of children's programming but the destiny of the TV film cartoon. Except for new standards and formats, which toned down violence and provided greater diversity, since his changes Saturday morning network schedules remain much the same. Still populated by hundreds of curious creatures, androgynous talking animals, flying heroes and caricatures from prime time shows, the animated cartoon series dominates weekend children's television.

## WHAT THIS BOOK CONTAINS

This is a compendium of animated cartoon series programmed on the commercial networks and public television or syndicated extensively to local stations in the United States, since the beginning of regular telecasting by connected Eastern stations in 1946. With few exceptions, they were normally seen between 8:00 AM and 8:00 PM and ran for at least four consecutive weeks in the same time period. Also included are several animated special series containing three or more related programs. All entries are arranged alphabetically by their titles. In some instances, generic names, like The Archies, Mr. Magoo and Peanuts, are used to group conveniently all the programs featuring the same characters and interrelated content under a single heading. Many of the syndicated theatrical cartoons were used for multipurpose entertainment programs for both adolescents and pre-adolescents. The made-for-TV cartoon series range from pre-school focus through teen orientation, with the majority intended for eight- to fourteen-year-olds. Omissions generally include those series without sufficient documentation, mainly vintage theatrical and a few imported cartoons, and purely academic or instructional films programmed largely on closed-circuit or Educational TV. Over 300 network programs and syndicated packages, including hundreds of sub-series and components, are profiled. They contain a wealth of features and valuable cross-references are included to assist identification.

This is the first book to trace the origins, growth and development of animated TV series through descriptive profiles. It details only one aspect, however, of the recorded account of widespread programming for the young viewer. Cross-references are made also to the companion volume, Children's Television: The First Thirty-Five Years, 1946-1981, Part II: Live, Film, and Tape

Series (Scarecrow 1983).  These cross-references are differentiated from others by use of an asterisk (*).

Under each series title are the following:

## Network History

Includes the date each series premiered, the network, inclusive months and years, the day or days and the time it was shown. AM or PM refer in all cases to Eastern Standard Time unless otherwise noted as Central (CST), Mountain (MST) or Pacific (PST) Standard Time.  Generally, the first run is indicated by the inclusive months and years on the originating network.  Dates of network changes are mentioned in the description.  The date of the last program on the network is exclusive of the program's syndication.

## Syndicated History

Includes the year or date the series premiered, sometimes followed by the TV station, city and the day or days and the time. The distributor is followed by the first year the series was circulated and the last year if the films were withdrawn or changed representatives.  The syndicated title is listed if different from the network designation.

## Production Credits

Includes the Executive Producer, Producer and Director as appropriate.  Credits for important contributors are provided in the description.  The Production Company is followed by the number of films produced in the series, in color, unless specified in black-and-white (B&W), and sometimes the inclusive years.  The length in minutes is given if the running time is shorter or longer than the standard thirty-minute program.

## Principal Characters and Voices

Generally, only the recurring characters are listed, those that appeared in all episodes.  If the performer did not voice the role for all films in the series, the inclusive years are given. Important supporting characters and voice imitations are covered in the description.

## Description

Each series is summarized to delineate the theme and component segments, and explain the relationship of the main characters.  Frequently, episodic titles and examples are given.  Pioneer and landmark series, origins and relationships to others of the genre are identified.  Significant craftsmen, awards, programming practices and other information is contained in the narrative.

## Sources

The Los Angeles, Chicago and New York editions of TV Guide since April 1953 were the principal sources of scheduling information. For programs between 1946 and 1953, the local editions of the New York TV Guide and Los Angeles Radio/TV Life plus The New York Times, The Los Angeles Times and The Chicago Sun-Times were consulted. Information from network sources, Broadcasting Magazine, Radio/TV Age, Television Digest, Broadcast Information Bureau--TV Series Source Book and program distributors were used to cross-check various data. Character and content description were drawn from the same references, supplemented by production company records, network and syndicated press material, reviews in Variety and interviews and correspondence with producers, directors, writers, performers and others. Extensive use was made of the author's personal collection of video and audio tapes. A list of persons who shared in this work is contained in the acknowledgments.

The purpose of this book is to provide an accurate account of televised animated cartoon series within the context of their use as scheduled programming. Work began on this study in 1975 at the Annenberg School of Communications, University of Southern California, an outgrowth of academic and professional interest. Since no reference is as exact in every detail as it can be, and bygone events are often obscure, comments are encouraged and welcome.

George W. Woolery
P. O. Box 3804
2683 N. Orange-Olive Road
Orange, CA 92665

# ABBREVIATIONS

AAP     - Associated Artists Productions (UA-TV, 1959)
ABC     - American Broadcasting Company
AIP     - American International Pictures
AIT     - American International Television (Filmways, 1979)
BBC     - British Broadcasting Corporation
BV     - Buena Vista Distributions Company (Walt Disney films)
CBC     - Canadian Broadcasting Corporation
CBS     - Columbia Broadcasting System
CNS     - Chicago Tribune--New York News Syndicate
COL     - Columbia Pictures Industries
CPT     - Columbia Pictures Television (Screen Gems, 1951-1974)
DTN     - DuMont Television Network (1946-1955)
ETV     - Educational Television (PTV, 1967)
FAW     - Fawcett Publications
FCC     - Federal Communications Commission
KFS     - King Features Syndicate
MCA     - Music Corporation of America
MCA-TV - MCA-TV Film Syndication
MGM     - Metro-Goldwyn-Mayer Pictures
MGM-TV - Metro-Goldwyn-Mayer Television
MON     - Monogram Pictures Corporation (Allied Artists, 1952)
MUT     - Mutual Broadcasting System
NBC     - National Broadcasting Company
NEA     - Newspaper Enterprise Association
NHK     - Japanese Broadcasting Corporation
NP     - National Periodicals (National and D.C. Comics)
NTA     - National Telefilm Associates (NBC Films, c1955-1971)
NTI     - Nielsen Television Index
O&O     - Owned and Operated Stations
PAR     - Paramount Pictures Corporation (Gulf and Western, 1966)
PAR-TV - Paramount Television
PBS     - Public Broadcasting Service (network supplier to PTV, 1970)
PTV     - Public Television (successor to ETV, 1967)
REP     - Republic Pictures Corporation (Republic, 1960)
REV     - Revue Studios/Productions (UTV, 1964)
RKO     - RKO Radio Pictures Corporation (RKO General, 1959)
SYN     - Syndicated (programs supplied to local stations)
TCF     - Twentieth Century-Fox Film Corporation
TCF-TV - Twentieth Century-Fox Television
UA     - United Artists Corporation (Transamerica, 1967)
UA-TV  - United Artists Television
UFS     - United Feature Syndicate

| | |
|---|---|
| UP | - Universal Pictures Corporation (MCA, 1964) |
| UPA | - United Productions of America/UPA Pictures |
| UTV | - Universal Television |
| VCI | - Viacom International (CBS Films, c1955-1971) |
| WB | - Warner Brothers Corporation (Warner Communications, 1969) |
| WB-TV | - Warner Brothers Television |
| WD | - Walt Disney Productions |
| WVE | - Worldvision Enterprises (ABC Films, c1960-1972) |

ANIMATED CARTOON SERIES

# ANIMATED CARTOON SERIES

## ABBOTT AND COSTELLO CARTOONS

Syndicated History
    Premiere: Fall 1967

Distributor: Gold Key Entertainment, King World Productions/1967-
Executive Producer: Lee Orgel
Producers: William Hanna, Joseph Barbera
Company: Hanna-Barbera Studios for RKO-Jomar/156 films, 5 minutes

Principal Characters and Voices

Bud Abbott                         Bud Abbott
Lou Costello                       Stan Irwin

    Abbott and Costello Cartoons recaptured the slapstick burlesque routines of the most successful comedy team in motion picture annals. The graphic comedy series was produced eight years after the death of Lou Costello (1906-1959), christened Louis Francis Cristillo, and Stan Irwin voiced the part with William "Bud" Abbott (1895-1974). Produced by Lee Orgel, the films were influenced by the team's earlier TV boarding house comedy, The Abbott and Costello Show (SYN, 1952-   ), that remained popular in repeats through the early sixties. Pure hokum, the telefilms debuted December 5, 1952 and were seen through 1954, mainly on CBS, distributed by Revue Productions (MCA-TV), and sponsored by Chevrolet. Their juvenile potential was realized in 1954-1955 when CBS repeated the episodes at 11:30-12:00 AM, Saturday. Orgel may have had hopes of a network time-slot for the cartoons as well, as they could be strung together as thirty-nine half-hours. But the series arrived at the beginning of the superhero proliferation.
    Presented as episodic comedy-adventures, the only thing interesting about the films was the voice of Abbott. In modernizing the characters, Bud was depicted with a perpetual glowering expression, be-hatted as usual, but without his conventional double-breasted suit. Abbott always left the dirty work to his partner, and was the typical city slicker alert to any money-making scheme or easy mark. Constantly trying to defend himself against verbal and physical assaults, Lou was the dumpy fall-guy, the butt of the jokes. Given a loud striped coat but bereft of his traditional baggy pants, he was portrayed as a wistful little fellow, struggling to comprehend and

3

animated with a hint of pathos. Costello's apologetic cry, "I'm a bad-d-d-d-d boy!," was the catch-call of the show, but coming from a different voice it seemed pathetically out of place. Laboring for laughs, the episodes were sadly silly and carried such titles as "The Little Fat Boy Cried Wolf," "Merry Misfits," "Eskimo Pie-Eyed," "Yankee Doodle Dudes," "Hey, Abbott!" and "Bully for Lou."

In 1942 and 1943, Abbott and Costello were the number one box office attraction in the United States. After they were placed under contract in 1939, the comics almost single-handedly bailed financially troubled Universal Pictures out of the red, starring in twenty-eight films for the studio out of the thirty-seven they made between 1940 and 1951. They met in 1936 at the Eltinge Theatre on West Forty-Second Street in New York. Bud was working with Harry Evanson and Costello's partner was John Grant, but they decided to team up and Grant became their writer for the next twenty years.

Abbott and Costello became permanently identified with the hilarious "Who's On First?" routine, partly written by Grant and perfected during their radio appearance on The Kate Smith Show (CBS, 1931-1937). The funny baseball skit was featured in three of their movies, their radio and TV programs and in the cartoons. "Who's On First?" is filed in the Smithsonian archives under classic Americana and since 1956 a gold record and text have been displayed at the Baseball Hall of Fame, Cooperstown, New York.

Always opening with Costello's famous cry, "Heyyyy Abbot-t-t-t-t!," The Abbott and Costello Program (NBC/ABC, 1941-1951) premiered October 8, 1941 on radio. Later they hosted a Saturday morning Abbott and Costello Children's Show (ABC, 1947-1949), which awarded $1,000 savings bonds to "outstanding youngsters of the week" and spotlighted juvenile talent. Their TV bow came on January 7, 1951 on The Colgate Comedy Hour (NBC, 1950-1955), reprising their "Who's On First?" routine. Starring Harvey Korman and Buddy Hackett as the pair, a two-hour NBC TV movie, Bud and Lou (Nov 15, 1978), dramatized the backstage lives and tumultuous careers of the comedy team, which broke up in 1957.

Abbott was partnered in the ownership of the cartoons and continued to profit from them until his death. But it was not the first time the pair were "animated." Voiced by Tedd Pierce and Mel Blanc, Babbit and Catstello appeared as a pair of conniving alley cats in a "Merrie Melodies" film, A Tale of Two Kitties (Nov 14, 1942), attempting to catch a cute little "boid" named Tweety, that upon seeing them first exclaimed, "I tawt I saw a Puddy Tat!"


ABC HEALTH AND NUTRITION COMMERCIALS

Network History
    Premiere: September 10, 1977
    ABC/Sep 1977-    /Saturday, Sunday, Various AM

Producers: David DePatie, Friz Freleng
Company: DePatie-Freleng Enterprises/14 films, 60 & 30 seconds

    ABC Health and Nutrition Commercials dispensed advice on

good eating habits and dental hygiene. Presenting Lynn Ahrens' lyrics and music, the animated spots described elements of foods and how they make the body grow in "You Are What You Eat," and in "The Chopper" explained how teeth work. "Make a Saturday," not a sundae, encouraged youngsters to eat a healthful snack, and "Sunshine on a Stick" instructed them on how to make orange juice popsicles. The network's initiative was prompted in part by an attempt to balance information about nutritional foods with commercial advertising of sugar-coated breakfast cereals and snacks. Dr. Joan Cussow, Chairman, Program on Nutrition, Columbia Teacher's College, served as consultant. The public service messages were seen on the children's weekend schedule, increased to two-and-one-half minutes on Saturday and three minutes on Sunday in 1979-1980.

## ABC SATURDAY SUPERSTAR MOVIE, THE

### Network History
Premiere: September 9, 1972
ABC/Sep 1972-Sep 1973/Saturday 9:30-10:30 AM

### THE NEW SATURDAY SUPERSTAR MOVIE
ABC/Sep 1973-Aug 1974/Saturday 12:00-1:00 PM
Last Program: August 31, 1974

### Syndicated History

ANIMATED SPECIALS

Distributor: Taft H-B Program Sales/1976-1979
Company: Hanna-Barbera Productions, Rankin-Bass Productions, Filmation Productions, King Features Syndicate Television/20 films, 60 minutes

### Principal Characters and Voices

| | |
|---|---|
| Phoebe Figalilly | Juliet Mills |
| Hal Everett | David Doremus |
| Butch Everett | Trent Lehman |
| Prudence Everett | Kim Richards |
| Professor Harold Everett | Richard Long |
| Gidget | Kathi Gori |
| Rink/Steve | Denny Evans |
| Bull | Bob Hastings |
| Jud | David Lander |
| Ann Marie | Marlo Thomas |
| Tabitha Stephens | Cindy Eilbacher |
| Adam Stephens | Michael Morgan |
| Max | John Stephenson |
| Julie | Shawn Shepps |
| Ernie | Gene Andrusco |
| Sue | Judy Strangis |
| Mike | Frank Welker |

| | |
|---|---|
| Dr. Zachery Smith | Jonathan Harris |
| Craig Robinson | Mike Bell |
| Linc Robinson | Vince Van Patten |
| Deana Carmichael | Sherry Alberoni |
| Robon | Don Messick |
| Robin Hoodnik / Alan Airdale / | |
|     Friar Pork / Little John / | |
|     Lord Skurvy | Lennie Weinrib |
| Oxx | Joe E. Ross |
| Donkey | Hal Smith |
| Scrounger / Richard | Daws Butler |
| Sheriff / Carbuncle | John Stephenson |
| Marion | Cynthia Adler |
| The Dodger | Mike Bell |
| Oliver | Gary Marsh |

The ABC Saturday Superstar Movie conjured up sundry characters that had already entertained youngsters, in one way or another, in hour-long animated features made for television. Seventeen films were telecast in the first season, each repeated four or
five times to amortize the $300,000 per film production cost. Al-
though the name was changed in 1973-1974 to The New Saturday
Superstar Movie, only three new features were presented with the
reruns. While sixty-minute cartoon programs with several components had debuted eight years earlier with The Atom Ant/Secret
Squirrel Show (q.v.), together with the CBS entry, The New Scooby-
Doo Comedy Movies (q.v.), the Superstar Movies were the first
one-hour TV graphic series of their kind. Not all were entirely
fresh. Some were padded with prior films and others expanded
from hapless TV pilots. They were tied together with wraparound animation by Hanna-Barbera Productions and there were
some inspired moments.

    Largely comedy-mysteries, nearly one-third were adapted
from prime-time programs, like the premiere, "The Brady Kids
on Mysterious Island" (Sep 9, 1972). The story found the six
youngsters from The Brady Bunch (ABC, 1969-1974) ferreting out
a fake spook or two and performing as a rock group, a prelude to
their weekly series, The Brady Kids (q.v.). The original cast
was caricatured for "Nanny and the Professor" (Sep 30, 1972), a
1970-1971 ABC show about an uncanny English governess. Hal,
Butch and Prudence found a mysterious microdot and Phoebe Figa-
lilly struggled to protect and deliver it to the proper authorities.
In a sequel, "Phantom of the Circus" (Sep 15, 1973), the Everett
household was mixed-up with acrobats and a disgruntled high-wire
performer. With different voice characterizations, "Gidget Makes
the Wrong Connection" (Nov 18, 1972) was adapted from the ABC
"Teencom," Gidget* (q.v.), and presented some new friends of the
perky teenager, who had a run-in with gold smugglers on the high
seas. Marlo Thomas, the struggling actress Ann Marie in That
Girl (ABC, 1966-1971), was animated as "That Girl in Wonderland"
(Jan 13, 1973), preparing a book of fairy tales and visiting with
Snow White, The Wizard of Oz and Sleeping Beauty to gather some
first-hand advice.

Three other unsuccessful TV pilots were the "Mini-Munsters" (Oct 27, 1973), based on The Munsters (CBS, 1964-1966), in which the clan discovered that their hearse-dragster ran on music instead of gas; "Tabitha and Adam and The Clown Family" (Dec 2, 1972), which introduced the Stephens' off-spring from Bewitched* (q. v. ) as a teenage witch and warlock in a circus setting; and a science-fiction adventure adapted from Lost in Space* (q. v. ), which opened the second season, September 8, 1973.

In "The Adventures of Robin Hoodnik" (Nov 4, 1972), the bowman's jolly band of animals was pursued by the evil Lord Skurvy. The characters from Charles Dickens' 1838 novel were adapted for "Oliver Twist and the Artful Dodger" (Oct 21 & 28, 1972), a two-part feature. From the comics, "Popeye Meets the Man Who Hated Laughter" (Oct 7, 1972) introduced in animation for the first time Steve Canyon, The Phantom, Tim Tyler, and the epic space hero Flash Gordon, with such Sunday oldtimers as Blondie and Dagwood, The Katzenjammer Kids, The Little King, Beetle Bailey, and Jiggs and Maggie. And "Daffy Duck and Porky Pig Meet The Groovie Goolies" (Dec 18, 1972) was a comic tale of sabotage by The Phantom at a movie studio. "Lassie and The Spirit of Thunder Mountain" (Nov 11, 1972) was later telecast as two episodes on Lassie's Rescue Rangers (q. v. ), and "Yogi's Ark Lark" (Sep 16, 1972) was the successful pilot appearing on Yogi's Gang (q. v. ). "The Banana Splits in Hocus Pocus Park" (Nov 25, 1972) engaged in a bit of tom-foolery with a witch.

Other entries included "The Red Baron" (Dec 9, 1972), "Luv-cast" (Jan 6, 1972), and "The Mad, Mad Monsters" (Sep 23, 1972). One of the more original was "Willie Mays and the Say-Hey Kid" (Oct 14, 1972), featuring the voice and likeness of the baseball great. It was about an Angel who granted Mays a wish that would mean winning the pennant--but there was a catch: he had to take care of a mischievous youngster who had been named his Godchild.

## ADDAMS FAMILY, THE

### Network History
Premiere: September 8, 1973
NBC/Sep 1973-Dec 1973/Saturday 9:00-9:30 AM
NBC/Jan 1974-Aug 1974/Saturday 8:30-9:00 AM
NBC/Sep 1974-Aug 1975/Saturday 8:00-8:30 AM
Last Program: August 30, 1975

Executive Producers: William Hanna, Joseph Barbera
Producers: John Halas, Joy Batchelor
Company: Halas & Batchelor, London for Hanna-Barbera Productions/17 films

### Principal Characters and Voices

| | |
|---|---|
| Gomez Addams | Lennie Weinrib |
| Morticia Addams/Granny Addams | Janet Waldo |
| Uncle Fester | Jackie Coogan |

| | |
|---|---|
| Lurch | Ted Cassidy |
| Pugsley Addams | Jodie Foster |
| Wednesday Addams | Cindy Henderson |

   The Addams Family showed a humorous household of horrific
humans, created by cartoonist Charles Addams for the New Yorker
magazine.   The caricatures somewhat resembled the live-action
cast of The Addams Family (ABC, 1964-1966), an engaging situation
comedy from which the program was adapted.   Two members voiced
their original roles:  former child screen star Jackie Coogan as
Morticia's portentous Uncle Fester, and Ted Cassidy as the towering Lurch, the Frankenstein-like family butler.   Unaffected by their
own ghoulish abnormalities, the eccentric and piercing-eyed Gomez
and his beautiful but somber wife Morticia were the proud parents
of two equally strange children, their son Pugsley and daughter
Wednesday.   Together with Granny, the only normal looking relative, the Addams motor-toured the country in their two-story
castle-like recreational vehicle, a haunted home complete with a
moat, bats, and an ominous dark cloud that followed it everywhere.
Along for the weird happenings was The Thing, a severed right
hand that kept popping out of a black box to pay tolls.   During
their trip to regional locales, from the wild west to the swampy
south, they continually had to cope with sundry con men and scoundrels, who pegged them as an easy mark in such stories as "Ghost
Town," "The Mardi Gras Story," "Addams Go West" and "Aloha
Hoolamagoola."

ADVENTURES OF BATMAN, THE   See   BATMAN AND ROBIN

ADVENTURES OF GULLIVER, THE

Network History
   Premiere:   September 14, 1968
   ABC/Sep 1968-Aug 1969/Saturday 9:30-10:00 AM
   ABC/Sep 1969-Dec 1969/Saturday 11:30-12:00 AM
   ABC/Jan 1970-Sep 1970/Saturday 8:00-8:30 AM
   Last Program:   September 5, 1970

Syndicated History

BANANA SPLITS AND FRIENDS

Distributor:   Taft H-B Program Sales/1971-1979; Worldvision
   Enterprises/1979-
Executive Producers:   William Hanna, Joseph Barbera
Company:   Hanna-Barbera Productions/17 films

Principal Characters and Voices

| | |
|---|---|
| Gary Gulliver | Jerry Dexter |
| Tagg | Herb Vigran |

| | |
|---|---|
| Thomas Gulliver/Captain Leech/King Pomp | John Stephenson |
| Flirtacia | Ginny Tyler |
| Egger/Glumm | Don Messick |
| Bunko | Allan Melvin |

The Adventures of Gulliver borrowed a setting and the family name of the young hero in Gulliver's Travels (1726), and little else from the classic satiric novel by Dr. Jonathan Swift (1667-1745). Except for the premise, the fantasy adventures roamed far afield. Setting sail with a copy of a treasure map to find Thomas Gulliver, his missing father, Gary's ship was caught in a tropical storm and the boy marooned in the Land of Lilliput, ruled by King Pomp. There he awoke to find himself held captive by the little people, who were only six inches tall. But the Lilliputians' initial fear of the strange new giant soon turned to trust and friendship when Gulliver was released and saved them from annihilation by a dreaded foe.

Told that his father was on the island seeking the hidden cache, together with his dog Tagg and his tiny new friends, Egger, Glumm, Bunko and Flirtacia, the teenager began a search. Following the map's landmarks, the group were beset at every turn by the evil Captain Leech, a treasure-seeking scoundrel who coveted Gulliver's map for himself. Constantly in jeopardy, marked by such dialogue as "They're right behind us, keep running gang!," Gary and his pals were threatened by Leech and other hazards they encountered. One time Leech sealed them in the Caves of No Return, and while attempting to escape they entered the "Valley of Time," where they were menaced in a stone age continuum by prehistoric reptiles and a tribe of cavemen. Gulliver continued his search in such episodes as "The Forbidden Pool," "Mysterious Forest" and "The Missing Crown," scripted in part by Joe Ruby and Ken Spears.

## ADVENTURES OF HOPPITY HOOPER, THE

Component Series
  FRACTURED FAIRY TALES, PEABODY'S IMPROBABLE HISTORY, Others

Network History
  Premiere: September 26, 1964
  ABC/Sep 1964-Oct 1965/Saturday 12:30-1:00 PM
  ABC/Oct 1965-Sep 1967/Saturday 1:00-1:30 PM
  Last Program: September 2, 1967

Syndicated History

UNCLE WALDO
  Premiere: Fall 1965

Distributor: Filmtel International/1965-1979; DFS Program Ex-

change/1979-
Producers: Jay Ward, Bill Scott
Directors: Bill Hurtz, Pete Burness, Ted Parmelee
Company: Jay Ward Productions with Producers Associates for
    Television/52 films

Narrator
    Paul Frees

Principal Characters and Voices

| | |
|---|---|
| Hoppity Hooper | Chris Allen |
| Professor Waldo Wigglesworth | Hans Conried |
| Fillmore | Bill Scott |

The Adventures of Hoppity Hooper involved a naive little
jumping frog and his cronies, Professor Waldo Wigglesworth, a
sharp fox, and Fillmore, a dim-witted, good-natured bear. Continually stumbling or badgered into some ridiculous scheme, often
goaded into the mess out of avarice, the gullible Hooper and the
bugle-blowing bear were the foils of Waldo, a boastful con-artist.
Naturally, things never went as expected when they tried to sell
patent medicine out west in "Wottabongo Corn Elixir" or when they
rented out a pair of spectres, Wilbur and Clair, to haunt houses
or individuals in "Ghost." One time the fox turned his frog pro-
tegé into another Girl of the Year. Overnight, by skillful promo-
tion, Hoppity became "Baby Hooper," in "Rock 'n' Roll Star," and
a sensation with his new dance, the Croak. But when he was faced
with a rival, Susan Swivelhips, and her dance, the Boing, there
was a merger, creating "Croak and Boingenanny," which immediately became the rage with the college campus crowd. Hailing
from the town of Foggy Bog, Wisconsin, the trio appeared in such
other serialized stories as "The Dragon of Eubetcha," "Giant of
Hootin' Holler" and the "Masked Martian." Although the episodes
featured a normal complement of explosions, booby-traps and fire-
arms, and placed Hoppity and his friends in jeopardy, the satirized
situations lifted the series above the usual frenzied cartoons with
punning good fun.
    Written mainly by Bill Scott, two installments of the four-
part cliff-hangers were the wrap-around segments for repeat components of Rocky and His Friends (q. v.), initially Edward
Everett Horton's "Fractured Fairy Tales" and "Peabody's Improbable History." To further expose the property, after the first
twenty-six shows were run on ABC in 1964-1965, they were re-
edited with different components and introduced in syndication as
Uncle Waldo, adding the remainder of the episodes when the network show ended. Since 1965, only Uncle Waldo, in many repackaged versions, sometimes known as Uncle Waldo's Cartoon
Show, has continued in national distribution. Hoppity Hooper was
the second Jay Ward repackaged series, following the popular
muddle-headed moose, Bullwinkle (q. v.). The Hoppity films were
seen also in Fall 1965 as part of Cartoon Fun (q. v.).

ADVENTURES OF JONNY QUEST, THE

Network History
    Premiere:  September 18, 1964
    ABC/Sep 1964-Dec 1964/Friday 7:30-8:00 PM
    ABC/Dec 1964-Sep 1965/Thursday 7:30-8:00 PM
    CBS/Sep 1967-Sep 1969/Saturday 12:30-1:00 PM
    CBS/Sep 1969-Sep 1970/Saturday 1:30-2:00 PM
    ABC/Sep 1970-Sep 1971/Sunday 10:00-10:30 AM
    ABC/Sep 1971-Sep 1972/Saturday 12:00-12:30 PM

GODZILLA POWER HOUR
    NBC/Sep 1978-Nov 1978/Saturday 9:30-10:30 AM

GODZILLA SUPER 90
    NBC/Nov 1978-Sep 1979/Saturday 9:00-10:30 AM

JONNY QUEST
    NBC/Sep 1979-Nov 1979/Saturday 12:00-12:30 PM
    NBC/Apr 1980-Sep 1980/Saturday 11:00-11:30 AM
    NBC/Sep 1980-Sep 1981/Saturday 12:00-12:30 PM
    Last Program:  September 6, 1981

Syndicated History

Distributor:  Taft H-B Program Sales/1972-1979; DFS Program Exchange/1979-
Executive Producers/Directors:  William Hanna, Joseph Barbera
Company:  Hanna-Barbera Productions/26 films

Principal Characters and Voices

| | |
|---|---|
| Jonny Quest | Tim Matthieson |
| Dr. Benton Quest | (1964) John Stephenson |
| | (1964-1965) Don Messick |
| Roger Bannon | Mike Road |
| Hadji | Danny Bravo |
| Bandit | Don Messick |

    The Adventures of Jonny Quest began as a prime-time series
on ABC and later appeared on the Saturday morning schedule of all
three networks.  An episodic adventure in science and intrigue, the
show dramatized the worldwide exploits of a quartet of life-like
characters, searching for answers to unexplained mysteries.  Young
tow-headed Jonny was the son of the group's leader, Dr. Benton
Quest, a bewhiskered scientist working in secret intelligence.
Traveling aboard a supersonic plane, they were accompanied by
muscular, blond-headed Roger "Race" Bannon, the pilot of the jet
and Dr. Benton's assistant, Jonny's turbaned East Indian friend,
Hadji, and everybody's pal Bandit, a miniature black-eyed bulldog.
Alerted to mysterious happenings, reports of mythical creatures,
and unresolved disappearances of ships at sea and explorers in

strange lands, Dr. Quest and Jonny repeatedly encountered unearthly phenomena and menacing danger in their investigations. More
often than not, the quest uncovered a bug-eyed monster or two, as
in the "Mystery of the Lizard Men," in the premiere. The scenarios explained scientific principles behind various natural and
man-made phenomena and incorporated an educational reminder for
younger viewers in such episodes as "The Curse of Anubis," "Werewolf of Timberland" and "A Small Matter of Pygmies."

A durable series, considerably better than the average science fiction adventure, Jonny Quest was carefully researched and
written by Doug Wildey, the fourth network evening program developed by Hanna-Barbera after the success of The Flintstones
(q. v.). After the ABC first run ended September 9, 1965, the
series was repeated from September 9, 1967 until September 5, 1970
on CBS, and on ABC from September 13, 1970 to September 9,
1972. Again rerun on NBC starting September 9, 1978, the program appeared as a segment of the Godzilla Power Hour (q. v.),
which was expanded to a ninety-minute show, November 4, 1978.
Featured in its own timeslot, Jonny Quest was seen on NBC beginning September 8, 1979.


ADVENTURES OF LARIAT SAM, THE

Network History

CAPTAIN KANGAROO
    Premiere:  September 10, 1962
    CBS/Sep 1962-Aug 1965/Monday-Friday 8:00-9:00 AM
    Last Program:  August 27, 1965

Syndicated History

Distributor:  CBS Films/1965-1971; Viacom International/1971-
Producer:  Bill Weiss
Directors:  Arthur Bartsch, Robert Kuwahara, Connie Rasinski,
    Dave Tendlar
Company:  CBS Terrytoons with Robert Keeshan Associates/65
    films, 5 minutes or 13 films, 15 minutes

Principal Characters and Voices

Lariat Sam/Tippytoes/Badlands
    Meeney                            Dayton Allen


    The Adventures of Lariat Sam was a mock-western geared
to preschoolers. Believing there was nothing mean or unfriendly
about the Old West, Sam was a pure, honest and friendly cowpoke
who never carried a gun. His ally, Tippytoes, was a derby-hatted,
poetry-reading steed known as the "Wonder Horse." Badlands
Meeney was the recurring, not-so-nasty villain. The characters
appeared in three-part serials with such titles as "Below the Water
Lion," "Horse Opera Hoax," "Mark of Zero," "Rock-a-bye Bad-

lands" and "Bushwack in Toyland. " Created by Robert Keeshan
Associates, the series was initially seen on Captain Kangaroo* (q. v. ).


ADVENTURES OF MUHAMMAD ALI, THE  See  I AM THE GREAT-
    EST:  THE ADVENTURES OF MUHAMMAD ALI


ADVENTURES OF POW WOW, THE

Network History

CAPTAIN KANGAROO
    Premiere:  1957

Syndicated History
    Return:  May 3, 1958
    WRCA, New York/Saturday 9:00-10:00 AM

Distributor:  Screen Gems/1957-1960; Tele-Features/1960-
Producer:  Sam Singer
Company:  Tempe Toons/39 B&W films, 5 minutes

Principal Character
    Pow Wow

    The Adventures of Pow Wow, a young Indian boy, were re-
counted in this very limited graphic series.  In 1957, twenty-six
films were telecast on Captain Kangaroo* (q. v. ), and syndicated by
Screen Gems to the eleven Western states where the program was
not seen.  The stories were based on Indian folklore and related
fables like "How the Fox Got His White Tipped Tail, " "How the
Turtle Got His Shell, " "Pow Wow and Playing Possum" and "How
the Rabbit Got His Hop. "  Off-network the films were syndicated
for local programming, introduced in 1958 by Ray Forrest on Saturday mornings in New York as a weekly segment on his Children's
Theater (WNBT/WRCA/WNBC 1949-1961).  Perhaps one of the
earliest televised children's series, although it is not known whether
on film or narrated panel drawings, The Adventures of Pow Wow
first appeared locally as a fifteen-minute program, January 30 to
March 13, 1949 at 11:30-11:45 AM, Sunday on WNBT, New York.


ADVENTURES OF SINBAD, JR. , THE  See  SINBAD JR. , THE
    SAILOR


ADVENTURES OF SUPERMAN, THE  See  SUPERMAN


ADVENTURES OF TIN TIN, THE  See  TIN TIN


ALL-NEW PINK PANTHER SHOW, THE  See  PINK PANTHER

ALL-NEW POPEYE HOUR, THE  See  POPEYE THE SAILOR


ALL-NEW SUPERFRIENDS HOUR, THE  See  SUPERFRIENDS


## ALVIN SHOW, THE

Component Series
  THE ADVENTURES OF CLYDE CRACKUP

Network History
  Premiere:  October 4, 1961
  CBS/Oct 1961-Sep 1962/Wednesday 7:30-8:00 PM
  CBS/Sep 1962-Sep 1963/Saturday 10:00-10:30 AM
  CBS/Sep 1963-Sep 1965/Saturday 9:00-9:30 AM

ALVIN AND THE CHIPMUNKS
  NBC/Mar 1979-Sep 1979/Saturday 8:00-8:30 AM
  Last Program:  September 1, 1979

Syndicated History

Distributor:  CBS Films/1966-1971; Viacom International/1971-
Executive Producer:  Ross Bagdasarian
Producer:  Herb Klynn
Directors:  Rudy Larriva, Osmond Evans
Company:  Format Films for Bagdasarian Films/104 films

Principal Characters and Voices

Alvin/Simon/Theodore/David
  Seville                                   Ross Bagdasarian
Clyde Crackup                              Shepard Menken
Leonardo (non-speaking)

      The Alvin Show featured three mischievous, falsetto-singing
chipmunks in the first all-new cartoon series on CBS.  One of ten
animated shows which failed to duplicate the success of The Flintstones (q. v.), the program was seen in prime time before moving
to Saturday morning, September 29, 1962.  Its origins date from a
1958 recording, "The Chipmunk Song," a sensational hit selling over
four million copies, created by song writer Ross Bagdasarian (1920-
1972) under his professional name, David Seville.  Searching for a
name for the voices, initially he thought of butterflies, but after his
three children heard his experiments they suggested chipmunks.
Walt Disney's Chip 'n' Dale (Nov 28, 1947) used a similar technique and they probably prejudiced the children's imagination.  Seville followed his hit with Chipmunk albums and singles, dolls and
puppets, a game called "The Big Record" and other merchandise,
and adapted them for the TV series.  Alvin was named after Al
Bennett, vice president of Liberty Records, Seville's releasing
label; Simon for Si Waronker, a company executive, and Theodore

for Ted Keep, the engineer on the first Chipmunk record.

Depicted as the life-like manager of the famous singing group, Seville was a song-writing bachelor with whom they lived, shocked by their impulsive and unpredictable activities. He showed his displeasure with Alvin's antics by emitting a long drawn-out yell, "Al-l-l-l-l Vin-n-n-n!," the catch-call of the series. Wearing a baseball cap and completely engulfed by a sweatshirt with a big "A" on the front, Alvin was egotistical and clever, proud of his success, a harmonica player and idol of young girls. Daisy Mae, a neighborhood girl voiced by June Foray, had a crush on him. More interested in eating than girls, Theodore was the tubby member of the trio, who giggled a lot. A bookworm, Simon was the brain, distinguished by hornrimmed glasses, and often dragged into mischief by his brothers. Instigated by Alvin, the aggressive and foolhardy leader, in various episodes they plagued their disliked middle-aged baby sitter, tied their complaining neighbor to a sky-rocket, and tried to push off a steeple-top a reluctant eagle that did not know how to fly. The stories were built around their rehearsals, trips to such locations as Scotland or Miami Beach and simple domestic situations. Each program opened and closed with one of their ill-fated adventures, with one based on an original or well-known song. Also, they appeared in a brief vignette and conducted a sing-a-long with such tunes as "Oh Where, Oh Where Has My Little Dog Gone?"

In a separate comedy, "The Adventures of Clyde Crackup" documented the attempts of the famous inventor to perfect such discoveries as the safety match and the wheel. One time Crackup tried to invent soap, but invented swimming instead, because the bathtub he invented to test the soap did not have a drain. His assistant, the bald-headed Leonardo, communicated by whispering in his ear.

A first cousin of playwright William Saroyan, Bagdasarian was from the Armenian-American community in Fresno, California, where his family owned vineyards associated with Sierra Wines. Using hand-puppet Chipmunks, he guested on The Ed Sullivan Show (CBS, 1948-1972) and others, assisted by Bob Clampett. Ending September 18, 1965 on CBS, the series was syndicated through the sixties as Alvin and The Chipmunks and NBC repeated the program under this title, beginning March 17, 1979.


AMAZING CHAN AND THE CHAN CLAN

Network History
    Premiere: September 9, 1972
    CBS/Sep 1972-Sep 1973/Saturday 9:00-9:30 AM
    CBS/Sep 1973-Sep 1974/Sunday 7:30-8:00 AM
    Last Program: September 1, 1974

Syndicated History

Distributor: Taft H-B Program Sales/1974-1979; Worldvision Enterprises/1979-

Executive Producers:  William Hanna, Joseph Barbera
Producer:  Alex Lovy
Director:  Charles A. Nichols
Company:  Hanna-Barbera Productions/16 films

Principal Characters and Voices

| | | |
|---|---|---|
| Charlie Chan | | Keye Luke |
| Henry Chan | | Bob Ito |
| Alan Chan | | Brian Tochi |
| Stanley Chan | (1972) | Stephen Wong |
| | (1972-1974) | Lennie Weinrib |
| Suzie Chan | (1972) | Virginia Ann Lee |
| | (1972-1974) | Cherylene Lee |
| Mimi Chan | (1972) | Leslie Juwai |
| | (1972-1974) | Cherylene Lee |
| Anne Chan | (1972) | Leslie Kumamota |
| | (1972-1974) | Jodie Foster |
| Tom Chan | (1972) | Michael Takamoto |
| | (1972-1974) | John Gunn |
| Flip Chan | (1972) | Jay Jay Jue |
| | (1972-1974) | Gene Andrusco |
| Nancy Chan | (1972) | Debbie Jue |
| | (1972-1974) | Beverly Kushida |
| Scooter Chan | (1972) | Robin Toma |
| | (1972-1974) | Michael Morgan |
| Chu Chu | | Don Messick |

   Amazing Chan and the Chan Clan spent a lot of time tripping
over one another, trying to unravel puzzling mysteries and expose
notorious crooks.  Beset by a precocious brood of ten children and
their dog, Chu Chu, the venerable Chinese sleuth, Charlie Chan,
made his first appearance in an animated cartoon series.  The role
was voiced by Chinese actor Keye Luke, remembered as the wise
monk-mentor, Master Po, on Kung Fu (ABC, 1973-1975).  Intimately
acquainted with the proverb-preaching detective since the feature
film Charlie Chan in Paris (TCF 1935), Luke was ten times Chan's
number one son Lee, in movies based on the mysteries created by
novelist Earl Derr Biggers (1884-1933).  An inauspicious graphic
debut, the scenarios, built around clever robberies and thefts, pitted
Chan and his offspring against colorful and cunning master criminals,
in such episodes as "The Crown Jewel Case," "The Bronze Idol,"
"Captain Kidd's Doubloons" and "The Phantom Sea Chief."
   Manufacturing humor through the interplay of contemporary
children with their more traditional and reserved parent, the episodes suffered from the clutter of speaking parts--six Chan boys
and four girls, some with unintelligible oriental dialects.  After
the first few segments, all the voices were replaced with the exception of Luke, Bob Ito as Henry, and Brian Tochi as Alan.
Throughout it all, however, the patient and sagacious sleuth still
expounded a profound axiom or two, such as "Insignificant mole-
hill sometimes more important than conspicuous mountain."
   Despite the fact that the methodical investigator appeared in

just six novels between 1925-1930, after his introduction as a member of the Honolulu Police in The House Without a Key (1925), Charlie Chan has been featured in virtually all media. Philip N. Krasne and James S. Burkett purchased the film rights from Twentieth Century-Fox Films in 1944. Subsequently acquiring sole ownership, Krasne produced six features for Monogram Pictures between 1947 and 1949, starring Roland Winters (1904-   ), and then introduced the master detective to television in The New Adventures of Charlie Chan (SYN, 1957-   ), starring J. Carroll Naish (1900-1973).

During a span of twenty-three years, the inscrutable oriental was portrayed by six actors in forty-seven movies, beginning with three silent films, starring Japanese actors George Kuwa (1926) and Kamiyama Sojin (1928), followed by English actor E. L. Parks (1929). Biggers' character, however, did not become widely popular until Warner Oland (1881-1938), a Swedish actor, essayed the role in Charlie Chan Carries On (TCF, 1931), the first of his sixteen sound portrayals between 1931 and 1937. Sidney Toler (1875-1947) was seen in twenty-two features between 1938 and 1947. In the ABC TV movie, subtitled "Happiness Is a Warm Clue," Charlie Chan (Jul 17, 1979) was played by Ross Martin (1920-1981), better known as Artemus Gordon, the master of disguise on The Wild Wild West (CBS, 1965-1970). Peter Ustinov became the ninth actor to portray the fictional detective when he was cast in a new feature, Charlie Chan and the Curse of the Dragon Queen (American-Cinema, 1980).

The wily Chinese lawman was played on radio by Walter Connelly (NBC, 1932-1933/MUT, 1937-1938), Ed Begley (ABC, 1944-1947), and Santos Ortega (MUT, 1947-1948). Fighting international crooks, saboteurs and spies, Charlie Chan (McNaught, 1938-1942) was also a newspaper comic, drawn by Alfred Andriola. The famous detective appeared in comic books by Prize Publications (1948-1949), and Charlton and National Periodicals (1955-1959), briefly revived by Dell (1965-1966). And Charlie Chan is still one of the most distinguished investigators of baffling crimes in mystery fiction, worldwide.


AMAZING 3, THE

Syndicated History
    Premiere: September 6, 1967
    WPIX, New York/Monday-Friday 3:00-3:30 PM

Distributor: Modern Programs/1967-
Producer: Osamu Tezuka
Company: Mushi Productions, Japan; Erika Productions (owner)/52
    films

Principal Character
    Kenny Carter

    The Amazing 3, a trio of aliens from outer space who arrived on Earth and disguised themselves as animals, formed the premise for this Japanese fantasy series with a strong anti-war theme. A Galactic Congress debated whether to destroy Earth before warlike humans could spread their destruction among the galaxies or wait in the hope that mankind would end its fighting before it developed space flight. Three galactic patrolmen were sent to Earth to gather information, and operating incognito they appeared as a very long-eared, enormous-eyed rabbit, a comical Daffy-like duck, and a long-legged, swift-running horse. Soon after their arrival, they befriended a jean-clad boy named Kenny Carter. Although they were only supposed to observe and report to their superiors, they banded together with the young boy, using their advanced technology to secretly battle deranged despots, criminals, military dictators and the quirks of nature.

The cartoons were edited and re-dubbed by Joe Oriolo Productions for English-speaking audiences. Originally titled W 3, for "Wonder Three," the science-fiction series premiered June 6, 1965 and ended June 26, 1977 on Japanese television.


ANIMATOONS

Syndicated History
    Premiere: 1967

Distributor: Radio and Television Packagers/1967-
Company: Animatoons Productions/22 films, 6-8 minutes

Narrator
    Nancy Berg

Animatoons was a package of narrated children's films, largely original stories and fairytales. Included were several well-known classics, "Peter and the Wolf," "Goldilocks and the Three Bears" and "Ali Baba and the Forty Thieves." The series was distributed with teacher's guides, which recapped the story or moral and provided collateral reading sources.


AQUAMAN

Network History

THE SUPERMAN/AQUAMAN HOUR OF ADVENTURE
    Premiere: September 9, 1967
    CBS/Sep 1967-Sep 1968/Saturday 11:30-12:30 PM

AQUAMAN
    CBS/Sep 1968-Sep 1969/Sunday 7:30-8:00 AM
    Last Program: September 7, 1969

Syndicated History

SUPERMAN/AQUAMAN/BATMAN

Distributor: Warner Brothers Television/1970-
Executive Producer: Allen Ducovny
Producers: Louis Scheimer, Norman Prescott
Director: Hal Sutherland
Company: Filmation Studios for Ducovny Productions/17 films

Principal Characters and Voices

Aquaman                                    Ted Knight
Aqualad                                    Jerry Dexter
Mera                                       Diana Maddox
Storm (Aquaman's seahorse)
Imp (Aqualad's sea pony)
Tusky (Aqualad's pet walrus)


   Aquaman, known to his comic book fans as "The King of the
Seven Seas," was the second invincible superhero from print media
adapted for the CBS Saturday morning schedule. The aquatic star
had been preceded for one year by Superman (q. v. ), and was first
combined with the world's most famous superbeing in The Superman/
Aquaman Hour of Adventure. This combo-concept, attributed to
Fred Silverman, furthered the comic book explosion on television.
In the hour show, six seven-minute cartoons were alternated, including four of the superheroes' and two with "Superboy" and rotated
"guests" from different National Periodicals' features in their own
episodic adventures. Also making their television debut were "The
Atom," "Flash," "The Green Lantern," "Hawkman and Hawkgirl,"
"The Teen Titans," and the "Justice League of America," which
included Aquaman, revived in 1973 as Superfriends (q. v. ).
   Born of an Atlantian mother and marine scientist, Aquaman's
fantasies were a cross-section of derring-do, battling versatile villains both human and beast. Created by writer Mort Weisinger and
artist Paul Norris, Aquaman debuted in More Fun Comics Number
75 (Nov 1941) as National's answer to Timely/Marvel Comics' popular Sub-Mariner (q. v. ). He was the leader of the lost continent
of Atlantis, who swam forth "to keep the freedom of the seas in
tropic and arctic waters alike." His son, Aqualad, was born
March 6 in Aquaman Number 23, the result of his marriage with
Mera in issue 19, one of the infrequent comic book weddings.
Mera also appeared in the cartoons, once as a hostage held for
ransom by the vicious Captain Cuda. Aquaman was terrestrial,
but more deftly an underwater hero who summoned sea creatures
through his telekinetic powers when he needed help to fight menacing terror in the briny deep.
   Aquaman often rode into action on his seahorse, Storm, and
Aqualad on his sea pony, Imp, accompanied by Tusky, the lad's pet
walrus. Aqualad, whose favorite expression was "Jumping Jelly-
fish!," was headquartered in an aquacave and bore no relation to
the golden-haired hero in the cartoons. Uttering such expletives
as "Suffering Sailfish!," Aquaman was challenged by Black Manta,
a sea pirate, and vanquished The Reptile Men, a horde of lizard-
like creatures in the premiere. As defender of the Atlantian kingdom, the practiced hero fended off the plundering "Sea Raiders,"
the invading "Fire Demons" and the "Volcanic Monsters" that

threatened to erupt a sea volcano, leveling the city.    Also, he was locked in struggles with the Ice Dragon, The Brain, Mephisto, the Goliaths of the Deep Sea Gorge, the Sinister Sea Scamp, the Mirror Men from the planet Imago, The Torpedo Man, the evil mermaid Vasa, and the Trio of Terror, Torp, Magneto and Claw.    Most of the villains were voiced by Marvin Miller.

Beginning September 15, 1968, Aquaman was repeated in half-hour episodes containing two of his adventures and one with the guest superheroes.


ARCHIES, THE

Component Series
ALLEY OOP, BROOM HILDA, THE CAPTAIN AND THE KIDS, DICK TRACY, EMMY LOU, MOON MULLINS, NANCY AND SLUGGO, SMOKEY STOVER (1971-1973)

Network History

THE ARCHIE SHOW
Premiere:  September 14, 1968
CBS/Sep 1968-Sep 1969/Saturday 10:00-10:30 AM
Last Program:  September 6, 1969

THE ARCHIE COMEDY HOUR WITH SABRINA, THE TEENAGE WITCH
Premiere:  September 13, 1969
CBS/Sep 1969-Sep 1970/Saturday 11:00-12:00 AM
Last Program:  September 5, 1970

ARCHIE'S FUNHOUSE
Premiere:  September 12, 1970
CBS/Sep 1970-Sep 1971/Saturday 11:00-12:00 AM
CBS/Sep 1972-Sep 1973/Sunday 7:00-7:30 AM
Last Program:  September 2, 1973

ARCHIE'S TV FUNNIES
Premiere:  September 11, 1971
CBS/Sep 1971-Sep 1972/Saturday 10:30-11:00 AM
CBS/Sep 1972-Sep 1973/Saturday 12:00-12:30 PM
Last Program:  September 1, 1973

EVERYTHING'S ARCHIE
Premiere:  September 8, 1973
CBS/Sep 1973-Jan 1974/Saturday 12:00-12:30 PM
Last Program:  January 26, 1974

THE U.S. OF ARCHIE
Premiere:  September 7, 1974
CBS/Sep 1974-Jan 1975/Saturday 12:00-12:30 PM
CBS/Jan 1975-Sep 1976/Sunday 7:00-7:30 AM
Last Program:  September 5, 1976

THE NEW ARCHIE/SABRINA HOUR
    Return:   September 10, 1977
    NBC/Sep 1977-Nov 1977/Saturday 8:30-9:30 AM
    Last Program:  November 19, 1977

THE BANG-SHANG LALAPALOOZA SHOW
    Return:   November 26, 1977
    NBC/Nov 1977-Jan 1978/Saturday 10:00-10:30 AM
    Last Program:  January 28, 1978

Syndicated History

Sponsor:  Mattel Toys, Continental Baking (1977-1978)
Distributor:  Vitt Media International/1977-

Executive Producers:  Louis Scheimer, Norman Prescott
Producer:  Hal Sutherland
Creative Director:  Don Christensen
Directors:  Don Towsley, Lou Zukor, Rudy Larriva, Bill Reed
Company:  Filmation Productions/104 films

Principal Characters

    Archie Andrews
    Jughead Jones
    Betty Cooper
    Veronica Lodge
    Reggie Mandell
    Moose
    Carlos
    Sabrina
    Mr. Weatherby
    Miss Grundy
    Hot Dog (the gang dog)

Voices

    Dal McKennon
    Howard Morris
    Jane Webb
    John Erwin
    Jon Flores

        The Archies survived a staggering succession of title changes
to become one of the longest running network cartoon series, enjoying eight consecutive years on CBS and another on NBC.   The films
introduced the teenagers popularized and conceived by Bob Montana
(1920-1975) who had debuted in Pep Comics Number 2 (Dec 1941).   Retaining some of the charm and flavor of the original comics,  and
all of the innocence,  The Archies Show featured a gang of stereotyped high school youngsters from Riverdale, U. S. A.   From their
neatly trimmed haircuts right down to their penny loafers,  the
teenagers were an anachronism.   They represented youth in the

late sixties, as adults would have liked to see them.

Straightforward and popular Archie Andrews was the pivot of the fun, a typical well-mannered redhead about sixteen years old, the picture of consummate all-American youth. His close friends were the bumbling but lovable Jughead, always rumpled-haired and wearing a serrated-edged beany, the blond crew-cut gridiron hero Moose, a muscled numskull, and his rival Reggie Mandell, the bumptious know-it-all with the slicked-down black hair. Veronica Lodge and Betty Cooper were Archie's girlfriends who vied for his attentions. The rich and somewhat spoiled brunette Veronica was originally modeled after sultry movie actress Veronica Lake, and the blond Betty after one of Montana's old girlfriends. A gang pet named Hot Dog, a large white shaggy dog, and Latino boy, Carlos, were added to the group. Other regulars were Mr. Weatherby, the harried high school principal, and the frumpy spinster teacher Miss Grundy. In the 1968-1969 show, the high school hijinks of the gang were featured in two ten-minute sketches, each containing a moral on such topics as cheating and proper manners. With Archie as the lead guitar, the group appeared briefly as a rock band, The Archies, in a dance-of-the-week selection.

Incubated and nurtured by the head of CBS daytime programming Fred Silverman, in part The Archies was conceived to answer mounting criticism of the violent superhero cartoons glutting network schedules, which he introduced in 1966-1967. The series began a comedy-variety formula that would predominate CBS Saturday cartoon programming beginning in 1969-1970. One of Silverman's favorite shows, The Archies initiated a change that presented wholesome comedy interwoven with pro-social themes, a concept that would be copied and refined in the seventies. And it boosted The Archies into one of the top-rated children's shows on television.

When the program returned in 1969-1970 as the expanded Archie Comedy Hour, it ousted NBC's 1968 ratings leader The Banana Splits Adventure Hour (q. v.). Following Silverman's practice of combining cartoon stars, the show merged repeats of The Archie Show with a new feature, Sabrina, The Teenage Witch (q. v.), separated by rock tunes and humorous vignettes. The young sorceress was created and introduced as a new gang member who tried to lead a normal life, constantly beset by her magical powers. Borrowing a principal from nighttime programming, Silverman adapted the spin-off concept for children's shows in 1969, beginning with characters from The Wacky Races (q. v.) and, similarly, Sabrina appeared in her own hit series beginning in 1970-1971.

Archie's Funhouse, with the giant juke box, was a slick fast-paced music-comedy-variety series between 1970 and 1973, incorporating some repeats. Archie became an on-stage host with his pals, and the program intercut clips of an actual studio children's audience responding to the skits, jokes, and music. Silverman brought in a writer from Rowan and Martin's Laugh-In (NBC, 1968-1973) to help script the show, which included "Lightning Bolts" with fast one-liners, comedy vignettes such as smart-aleck Reggie trying to teach the fellows how to surf, and "Knock Knock" jokes. To a visual display of pulsating psychedelic art, rock tunes were performed by The Archies, who in 1969 had a number one hit,

"Sugar Sugar," followed by two best sellers, "Jingle Jangle" and "Who's My Baby." A CBS special musical preview, Archie and His New Friends (Sep 14, 1969), appeared in prime time, and was repeated as The Archie, Sugar, Sugar, Jingle, Jangle Show (Mar 22, 1970).

In a convoluted format between 1971 and 1973, Archie's TV Funnies depicted the group as real teenagers, producing a television show featuring their favorite cartoon characters. Actually a budget-shaving scheme, some of the films, like Dick Tracy (q. v. ), had been seen before and several of the others were unsuccessful TV pilots. But some new animated comedies were produced, and the eight segments also included "Moon Mullins," "Smokey Stover," "Emmy Lou," "The Captain and The Kids," "Alley Oop," "Nancy and Sluggo," and "Broom Hilda." The last four cartoons were resurrected on NBC as The Fabulous Funnies (q. v. ). In 1973-1974, Everything's Archie returned with repeats of the original programs plus some new wraparounds.

In anticipation of the bicentennial, U. S. of Archie represented Archie, Jughead, and Veronica in the roles of great Americans, acting out various accomplishments from the annals of history. It was the CBS colossal ratings failure of 1974-1975. Children switched away from it in droves because the series was more educational than entertaining. In mid-season, January 18, 1975, it was slotted on Sunday mornings, where the series finally ended in 1976, inauspiciously.

As a stopgap to bolster its weak 1977-1978 Saturday schedule, NBC repeated thirteen episodes of The Archie Comedy Hour as the first half of The New Archie/Sabrina Hour. But even a change of name in November 1977 to Bang-Shang Lalapalooza, opposite the expanded ninety-minute version of The Bugs Bunny/Roadrunner Show on CBS, could not alter the time-worn content and dismal ratings. The Archies fared better in syndication under two primary sponsors for a time, on about fifty stations in 1978-1979.

As a comic book character, Archie was not particularly original. Montana's teenager was inspired by Henry Aldrich, the crackly-voiced star of NBC radio's popular "Teencom" which was transferred to television in 1949, The Aldrich Family* (q. v. ). On radio, Archie Andrews (MUT/NBC 1946-1963) was almost a carbon copy of the program, voiced by Jack Grimes and Bob Hastings, first seen on TV regularly in Atom Squad* (q. v. ). Even before its CBS cartoon heyday between 1968 and 1972, the characters had been extensively merchandised, but the exposure expanded the licensed novelties into a multi-million dollar business and made The Archies a smash recording bubblegum rock group. An ill-fated ABC live-action pilot, Archie (May 18, 1977), featured Dennis Bowen in the title role of the hour special.

The Archies was one of the most successful animated programs in weekend network history and much of the credit belongs to Silverman. Though he may not have realized it, he lifted the property from the comic pages into a new niche as pure Americana.

AROUND THE WORLD IN 80 DAYS

Network History
    Premiere:  September 9, 1972
    NBC/Sep 1972-Sep 1973/Saturday 12:00-12:30 PM
    Last Program:  September 1, 1973

Syndicated History

Distributor:  D. L. Taffner/1973-1979; DFS Program Exchange/
    1979-
Producer:  Walter J. Hucker
Director:  Richard Slapezynski
Company:  Air Programs International, Australia/16 films

Principal Characters and Voices

Phileas Fogg                        Alistair Duncan
Jean Passepartout                   Ross Higgins
Mr. Fix                             Max Obistein

        Around the World in 80 Days followed the race against time
of the consummately British Phileas Fogg, who overcame forbidding
obstacles with aplomb and endless resourcefulness.    The series adhered to the 1873 novel of French author Jules Verne (1825-1905),
with adventure piled on adventure and a few new escapades to fill
sufficient episodes.    Set at the beginning of the industrial revolution
in the late nineteenth century, when steam power was replacing sails
on ocean-going vessels and trains were beginning to run on schedule,
Fogg accepted Lord Maze's challenge to circle the globe.    His mo-
tive was to prove himself worthy of his fiancée, Balinda Maze, because their wedding plans were cancelled when her uncle objected.
Wagering twenty thousand pounds that he could not complete the
journey in eighty days, Maze hedged his bet by secretly hiring Mr.
Fix, an unscrupulous detective, to foil the attempt.    But the unflappable, methodical Englishman and trusting, skitterish Jean
Passepartout, his French valet, overcame all the ingenious schemes
and diversions of the crafty Mr. Fix along the way.    Each episode
concentrated on one of these nasty plots, interwoven with geographic
educational elements, during their travels in Africa, China, India,
and other exotic locales.    Naturally, the cool and intrepid Englishman returned in time, in the last episode, after traveling the globe
by ship, train, balloon, elephant, and nearly everything that moved.
        The cartoon series was the first produced in Australia to be
seen on network television.    It was influenced greatly by the humorous treatment in the movie, Around the World in 80 Days (1956),
starring David Niven.    An Oscar-winning film spectacular, it was
produced by Mike Todd and seen on several prime time special
telecasts.

ASTRO BOY

Syndicated History
  Premiere: September 7, 1963
  WPIX, New York/Saturday 6:00-6:30 PM
  Distributor: NBC Films-Screen Gems (CPT)/1963-1971
  Producer: Osamu Tezuka
  Company: Mushi Productions, Japan/104 B&W films

Principal Characters and Voices

Astro Boy/Astro Girl          Billie Lou Watt
Doctor Elefun                 Ray Owens

  Astro Boy was the first successful Japanese cartoon series
shown in the United States. It starred a super-robot youngster who
could fly through space and had the atomic strength to move mountains. The episodes opened with a four-stanza theme song that began,
          There you go, Astro Boy!
          On your flight into space
          rocket high,
          through the sky,
          What adventures soon you will face....
  The creation of Dr. Boynton ("Dr. Tenma" in the Japanese
version), head of the Institute of Science, Astro Boy was built as a
surrogate for his son Astor, who was killed in a traffic accident.
When the boy failed to mature normally, the disappointed scientist
sold him to a circus. Rescued from his plight as a side-show attraction by the kindly Dr. Elefun ("Dr. Ochanomizu"), the new head
of the Institute, the adopted mechanical boy began to display human
feelings in return, and was imbued with a sense of purpose. With
Dr. Elefun, and later his robot sister Astro Girl, the youngster
became a friend of humanity, fighting such fiendish villains as the
Phoenix Bird, Sphinx, Long John Floater, Crooked Fink, the Mist
Men and Zero, the invisible. In one episode which was a notch above
the norm, Astro Boy used his remarkable powers to thwart Dr. I.
Q. Plenty, an agent from the planet Xenon, who was recruiting
children for special tutoring to help the aliens rule a conquered
Earth. A one-stanza version of the theme closed the half-hour
show:
          Astro Boy's A-OK!
          On your flight into space,
          What can I do,
          to be like you,
          and become a real Astro Boy!
  The cartoon's genesis was the comic strip Tetsuwan-Atom
("Mighty Atom"), a popular action feature and the longest-running
strip in Japanese history, appearing in the monthly Shōnen between
1951-1958. For a time called Atom-Taishi ("Ambassador Atom"),
it was created in April 1951 by Osamu Tezuka, recognized as "The
King of Japanese Comics" since the Second World War. Mighty
Atom was the initial production of Tezuka's Mushi Productions

(1960-1972) and the 193 episodes debuted on Fuji TV, January 1, 1963. Concurrently, they began in April on the NHK network, ending their three-year run on December 31, 1966.

Astro Boy, which appeared in more than twenty other countries, was known as Mighty Atom throughout the world except in the United States. Having the same title, Mighty Atom was a mouse character appearing in Tick Tock Tales, an American comic book published in January 1948 and periodically until about 1958. In May 1963, when NBC Films acquired one hundred and four of the cartoons for American audiences, the series was retitled to avoid copyright infringement. After nine years on local stations, the films were withdrawn in 1972 due to complications arising from the bankruptcy of Mushi Studios.

## ASTRONUT SHOW, THE

Component Series
   HASHIMOTO, SIDNEY, LUNO THE FLYING HORSE (1965-1971)
   JAMES HOUND, POSSIBLE POSSUM, SAD CAT (1971-   )

Syndicated History
   Premiere: August 23, 1965
   KHJ, Los Angeles/Monday-Friday 5:00-5:30 PM PST
Distributor: CBS Films/1965-1971; Viacom International/1971-
Executive Producer: Bill Weiss
Directors: Arthur Bartsch, Robert Kuwahara, Connie Rasinski,
   Dave Tendlar
Company: CBS Terrytoons/26 films

Principal Characters and Voices

| | |
|---|---|
| Astronut/James Hound | Dayton Allen |
| Oscar Mild/Sad Cat/Gadmouse/ | |
| Impressario/Latimore/Feni- | |
| more/Luno/Timmy | Bob McFadden |
| Possible Possum/Billy Bear/ | |
| Owlawishus Owl/Macon | |
| Mouse | Lionel Wilson |

The Astronut Show starred a friendly but nutty character from outer space, with no visible body, just all feet and a large head with antennae on top. The little alien first appeared in an episode of Deputy Dawg (q. v. ), then in ten CBS Terrytoons theatrical cartoons between 1964 and 1966, initially Brother from Outer Space (1964), directed by Connie Rasinski. Like a guardian angel, Astronut arrived on Earth as a do-gooder from somewhere out in the great Universe. Befriended by Oscar Mild, a meek and timid human caricature, for the most part he helped his new pal out of his ordinary troubles, performing amazing feats with his extraordinary powers. In the late sixties, the program's component comedies included "Hashimoto" and "Sidney, " which were first introduced on The Hector Heathcote Show (q. v. ), and "Luno the

Flying Horse," also a prior theatrical series of six films between 1963 and 1964, debuting with The Missing Genie (Apr 1963). New episodes were made featuring the winged white-stallion, the magical steed of Timmy, a young boy. The fantasy adventures took them to Baghdad, out west to battle the Gold Dust Bandit, and to a remote island where Jungle Jack tried to capture the giant ape Ding Dong. But in execution, the fine premise turned out to be something less than mediocre. The syndicated package was telecast in 1965 on Bill Stulla's Shake Shop, a weekday show on KHJ, Los Angeles.

Viacom repackaged the program in the seventies with three later theatrical series. Written by Eli Bauer and Al Kouzel, "Sad Cat" debuted in Gadmouse, The Apprentice Good Fairy (Jan 1965), directed by Ralph Bakshi. A dreary character, the lamentable feline was seen in spoofs on modern man stereotypes, incorporating such characters as Impressario, Latimore and Fenimore, and Gadmouse, exaggerated personalities depicted in humorous social commentaries. A more topical figure, "James Hound," the canine counterpart of Ian Fleming's fictional hero James Bond, made his bow in Dr. Ha Ha Ha (Feb 1966). The pooch found his thrills in cases where he matched wits with sundry fanatics in crazy schemes like "The Phantom Skyscraper" and "The Monster Maker." "Possible Possum" helped prove that nothing's impossible even in the hills of ol' Tennessee, at first in Freight Fright (Mar 1965). A cute family of animals that inhabited Happy Hollow, loyal friends of the carefree guitar-playing minstrel included Billy Bear supplying the brawn, Owlawishus Owl the ideas, and Macon Mouse along for the fun of it. They usually combined to find a way out of their humorous predicaments in typical backwoods comedies.


ATOM ANT/SECRET SQUIRREL SHOW, THE

Component Series
    THE HILLBILLY BEARS, PRECIOUS PUPP, SQUIDDLY DIDDLY, WINSOME WITCH

Network History
    Premiere: October 2, 1965
    NBC/Oct 1965-Jan 1967/Saturday 9:30-10:30 AM

THE ATOM ANT SHOW
    NBC/Jan 1967-Sep 1967/Saturday 9:30-10:00 AM

THE SECRET SQUIRREL SHOW
    NBC/Jan 1967-Sep 1967/Saturday 11:00-11:30 AM

THE ATOM ANT/SECRET SQUIRREL SHOW
    NBC/Sep 1967-Aug 1968/Saturday 11:30-12:00 AM
    Last Program: August 31, 1968

Syndicated History

BANANA SPLITS AND FRIENDS

Distributor: Taft H-B Program Sales/1971-1979; Worldvision Enter-
prises/1979-
Executive Producers/Directors: William Hanna, Joseph Barbera
Company: Hanna-Barbera Productions/26 films, 60 & 30 minutes

Principal Characters and Voices

| | |
|---|---|
| Atom Ant | Howard Morris/Don Messick |
| Secret Squirrel | Mel Blanc |
| Morocco Mole | Paul Frees |

THE HILLBILLY BEARS

| | |
|---|---|
| Paw Rugg | Henry Corden |
| Maw Rugg/Floral Rugg | Jean Vander Pyl |
| Shag Rugg | Don Messick |

PRECIOUS PUPP

| | |
|---|---|
| Precious Pupp | Don Messick |
| Granny Sweet | Janet Waldo |

SQUIDDLY DIDDLY

| | |
|---|---|
| Squiddly Diddly | Paul Frees |
| Chief Winchley | John Stephenson |

WINSOME WITCH

| | |
|---|---|
| Winsome Witch | Jean Vander Pyl |

The Atom Ant/Secret Squirrel Show smothered its network
competition with a pair of anthropomorphic heroes, each with two
separate supporting comedies fused to fill an hour. It was the
initial "packaged" program, concentrating on holding viewer interest by offering a number of elements from the same production
source under an umbrella title. When modified and extended, the
format would drastically alter children's cartoon programming in
the mid-seventies. A forerunner of the paired concept, followed
by the first human caricatures in The Superman/Aquaman Hour of
Adventure (q. v.), it was a combined treatment that was successfully exploited with both comic book and original characters.
Endowed with superpower by a pair of atomized eyeglasses,
Atom Ant was the smallest but mightiest defender of law and order
on television and mocked Mighty Mouse (q. v.). Quartered in his
secret laboratory, far beneath the earth's surface, even under the
underworld, the invincible hero answered urgent pleas for help with
cases too tough for the police. After reading up on the modus
operandi of the evildoers in "The Crook Book," Atom Ant leaped
into action with his catch-cry, "Up and at 'em!" The world's
strongest insect flew to the scenes of crime everywhere to tame
such public enemies as Godzilla Termite, Crankenshaft's Monster,
Killer Diller Gorilla, Dragon Master, the Rambling Robot and the

wily oriental Mr. Moto, a karate expert.  In "Ferocious Flea," he
even investigated skullduggery at a flea circus, where the owner
had given his performers a day off, suggesting they take in a dog
show.

Mollycoddled by a Billie Burke-like Granny Sweet, "Precious
Pupp" was the cunning nemesis of all around him, unbeknown to the
kindly millionairess.  The beguilingly clever hound tricked the "Butterfly Nut" and "The Bird Watcher," outsmarted a plan to abduct
him for ransom in the "Doggone Dognapper" and ensnared Sawed-
Off Sawyer, the Baby Bandit, who stole the priceless Tanganese
Royal Scepter in "Precious Jewels."  If not the prototype, the
tricky, snickering canine had a lot in common with Muttley, the
honor-seeking mutt in Dastardly and Muttley in their Flying Machines (q. v. ).

A hickish, backwoods family, "The Hillbilly Bears" carried
on in such rustic romps as "Goldilocks and the Four Bears,"
"Courtin' Disaster" and "My Fair Hillbilly."  Lazy, muttering Paw
was the patriarch of the Rugg clan, which included Maw and his
progeny, Floral and young Shag.  In "Rickety-Rockety-Raccoon,"
the Ruggs tried to horn in on the act of Ricky Raccoon, a guitar-
playing singer resembling Ricky Nelson.

Another intrepid agent inspired by Ian Fleming's James
Bond, himself a parody, "Secret Squirrel" was clad in a traditional
trench coat and fedora, and teamed with Morocco Mole, a fez-
wearing, puerile partner with a voice like Peter Lorre's (1904-
1964).  Working undercover for Double Q, their secret government
boss, their arch foe was Yellow Pinkie.  Their assignments were
mainly in English locales and had titles such as the "Scotland Yard
Caper," "Captain Kidd's Not Kidding," "Robin Hood and His Merry
Muggs" and "Jester Minute."

An octopus, "Squiddly Diddly," tried a succession of new oc-
cupations in "Naughty Astronaut," "Clowning Around" and "Hollywood Folly," much to the consternation of Chief Winchley.  A star-
struck hopeful at an aquatic amusement park, Squiddly constantly
escaped to pursue careers in the outside world.

A friendly sorceress whose magic was used to solve human
problems, "Winsome Witch" appeared in such stories as "Ugly
Duckling Trouble," "The Hansel and Gretel Case" and "The Little
Big League."

An hour-long preview on NBC, The World of Secret Squirrel
and Atom Ant (Sep 12, 1965) was one of the earliest network promotions for a Saturday morning children's program.  A surprise
success, the Saturday show topped the ratings and caused an up-
heaval in rival programming, particularly on CBS, which in 1966
launched the superhero vogue.  As individual programs, Atom Ant
and Secret Squirrel were separated beginning January 7, 1967, but
they were coupled again on September 9, 1967 for a thirty-minute
program.


BAGGY PANTS AND THE NITWITS

Network History
    Premiere:  September 10, 1977

NBC/Sep 1977-Jan 1978/Saturday 9:00-9:30 AM
NBC/Feb 1978-Sep 1978/Saturday 11:00-11:30 AM
NBC/Sep 1978-Oct 1978/Saturday 12:30-1:00 PM
Last Program: October 28, 1978
Executive Producers: David DePatie, Friz Freleng
Directors: Gerry Chiniquy, Robert McKimson, Sid Marcus
Company: DePatie-Freleng Enterprises/13 films

Principal Characters and Voices

Baggy Pants (non-speaking)
Tyrone                                  Arte Johnson
Gladys                                  Ruth Buzzi

Baggy Pants and The Nitwits featured a fanciful revival of a pantomime prankster and an elderly pair of misfits turned crime-fighters in separate comedies. A Chaplinesque cat, Baggy Pants was dressed like the British comedian, recapturing the mannerisms and mime theatrics of the screen actor in a short silent film. Animated with a touch of pathos, the forlorn feline appeared in stories emphasizing delicate visual comedy, backed by a dandy musical score and effects. In the premiere, "Lost Dog," the little hobo character recreated several of Chaplin's more familiar schticks while attempting to befriend a stray canine, a loner that neither wanted or needed help. Rebuffed and ridiculed by the mongrel and others, Baggy Pants' unruffled affection and continued resolve to be a friend of mankind, even though unwanted, was the crux of such stories as "The Painter's Helper," "Hobo and Forgetful Freddie," and "A Pressing Job."

The Nitwits also resurrected the amorous oldster Tyrone and the frumpy old maid Gladys, from Rowan and Martin's Laugh-In (NBC, 1968-1973), re-teamed as man and wife and voiced by Arte Johnson and Ruth Buzzi, the original stars. Tyrone was a retired superhero with an ebbing power to fly, who accepted, "for a limited time, crime-fighting engagements." Faster than a butterfly, agile as a caterpillar and powerful as a bulldog, the former "Guardian of the People" was actually an old fogy, too weak to vie physically with his foes. Known by his code name, Agony Nine, Tyrone was aided in his hapless assignments by his flying cane Elmo, that acted like a pet dog. The walking stick bounced about magically at his command and purpose, with a coiled-spring "boing-boing" effect. Singing in his monotone baritone a few bars from his favorite tunes, "When Johnny Comes Marching Home," "Lucky Lindy" and "Josephine," the decrepit superhero matched wits in the premiere with Hole-in-the-Wall Harry and Big Boomer Bob, a pair of diamond thieves, and lost. Invariably at the close, the purse-wielding throttler Gladys, his "sweet Gladiola," "beloved pet" and "double love," saved the day in "The Evil Father Nature," "False Face Filbert," "Genie Meanie" and other episodes.

Slow-paced in contrast to the usual slam-bang cartoon fare, the humor of the uncommon characters in this series, created and written mainly by Arte Johnson and Bob Ogle, was a refreshing interlude.

BAILEY'S COMETS

Network History
Premiere: September 8, 1973
CBS/Sep 1973-Jan 1974/Saturday 8:30-9:00 AM
CBS/Feb 1974-Aug 1975/Sunday 7:30-8:00 AM
Last Program: August 31, 1975
Executive Producers: David DePatie, Friz Freleng
Directors: Robert McKimson, Sid Marcus, Spencer Peel, Brad Case
Company: DePatie-Freleng Enterprises with Viacom International/16 films

Principal Characters and Voices

| | |
|---|---|
| Barnaby Bailey | Carl Esser |
| Dude | Bob Holt |
| Bunny | Sarah Kennedy |
| Wheelie | Jim Begg |
| Pudge | Frank Welker |
| Sarge | Kathi Gori |
| Dooter Roo | Daws Butler |
| Gabby | Don Messick |

Bailey's Comets, who shared a love of roller skating, were a team of six teenagers with distinctively individual characteristics. They were led by the unflagging Barnaby. In a continuing race around the world for hidden treasure, reported on by Gabby from a helicopter piloted by Dooter Roo, the Comets were aligned against sixteen other teams of skaters with descriptive names. In a sort of combination of Roller Derby and Wacky Races (q.v.), their competitors included The Black Hats, The Broomer Girls, The Cosmic Rays, The Doctor Jekyll/Hydes, The Duster Busters, The Gargantuan Giants, The Gusta Pastas, The Hairy Madden Red Eyes, The Mystery Mob, The Ramblin' Rivets, The Rock 'n' Rollers, The Roller Bears, The Roller Coasters, The Stone Rollers, The Texas Flycats and The Yo Ho Hos.

The clues to the million-dollar cache, the object of their hunt, were presented in a series of poetic rhymes which the youngsters had to unscramble. In episodes like "To Win or Toulouse," "Philippine Flip Flop" and "Madagascar Mix-Up," the Comets relentlessly rolled toward the finish and fortune, overcoming devious plots by their rivals to eliminate them from the race. With dozens of characters the program was all rather involved and difficult for young viewers to unravel. The series was created by Joe Ruby and Ken Spears and two episodes were seen in each program. It lasted only four months on the Saturday line-up.


BANANA SPLITS ADVENTURE HOUR, THE

Component Series
THE ARABIAN KNIGHTS, DANGER ISLAND, THE HILLBILLY BEARS, THE MICRO VENTURES, THE THREE MUSKETEERS

Network History
  Premiere: September 7, 1968
  NBC/Sep 1968-Sep 1970/Saturday 10:30-11:30 AM
  Last Program: September 5, 1970
Sponsor: Kellogg's Cereals

Syndicated History

BANANA SPLITS AND FRIENDS

Distributor: Taft H-B Program Sales/1971-1979; Worldvision Enter-
  prises/1979-
Executive Producers: William Hanna, Joseph Barbera
Company: Hanna-Barbera Productions/18 films, 60 minutes

Narrator
  Gary Owens

Hosts and Voices

Fleegle                          Paul Winchell
Bingo                            Daws Butler
Drooper                          Allan Melvin
Snorky                           Don Messick

Principal Characters and Voices

THE ARABIAN KNIGHTS

Bez                              Henry Corden
Fariik                           John Stephenson
Raseem                           Frank Gerstle
Prince Turhan                    Jay North
Princess Nida                    Shari Lewis
Evil Vangore                     Paul Frees

THE MICRO VENTURES

Professor Carter                 Don Messick
Jill Carter                      Patsy Garrett
Mike Carter                      Tommy Cook

THE THREE MUSKETEERS

D'Artagnan                       Bruce Watson
Porthos                          Barney Phillips
Aramis                           Don Messick
Athos                            Jonathan Harris
Tooly                            Teddy Eccles
Queen Anne/Constance             Julie Bennett

THE HILLBILLY BEARS  See  ATOM ANT/SECRET SQUIRREL
  SHOW, THE

Cast

DANGER ISLAND

| | |
|---|---|
| Professor Irwin Haydn | Frank Aletter |
| Leslie Haydn | Ronne Troup |
| Link Simmons | Michael Vincent |
| Morgan | Rockne Tarkington |
| Chongo | Kahana |
| Mu-Tan | Victor Eberg |
| Chu | Rodrigo Arrendondo |

The Banana Splits Adventure Hour departed from the usual Saturday fare with a quartet of animal-costumed actors as wrap-around hosts for the component series. They cavorted on-stage and off with all the slapstick hijinks of an anthropomorphic version of The Monkees* (q. v.), miming their parts to pre-recorded sound tracks. The Splits were Fleegle, a guitar-strumming and lisping Bassett Hound, a hip bongo-playing gorilla named Bingo, a smart-aleck lion called Drooper, and Snorky, a cutesy runt elephant. The foursome doubled in brass as a rock group, and in each show sang their simple theme:

> One banana, two banana, three banana, four,
> Four bananas make a bunch and so do many more.
> Four bananas, three bananas, two bananas, one,
> All bananas playing in the bright warm sun.

Featured in their own comedy sketches, sometimes the Splits raced about in their "Banana Buggies," the action punctuated by an off-camera announcer and cornball jokes. "The bananas are in a bunch." "Wait a minute," he would pause, "They're about to split." For several appearances in the 1968-1969 season, they were teamed in songs and dances with the "Sour Grape Girls," a rocking neighborhood gang aged ten to eleven. The set included a number of strange props, a letter-grabbing mailbox, and a trash can that would not accept trash. A regular feature was the "Dear Drooper." "Who," he would ask, "invented spaghetti?" Answering himself, the wiseacre lion replied, "Spaghetti was invented by a guy who used his noodle." The comedy vignettes provided continuity between the rotated cartoons and the filmed adventure serial.

In the animated segments "The Arabian Knights," a trio of sand dune heroes named Bez, Fariik and Raseem, sallied forth in ancient Araby to save the fair Princess Nida and Prince Turhan from the clutches of the Evil Vangore in such stories as "The Ransom," "Isle of Treachery" and "The Desert Pirates." Actors were superimposed with animated micro-organisms and phenomena to create another trio's microanalytical journey in "The Micro Ventures." In the same vein as Fantastic Voyage (q. v.), four serialized episodes found Professor Carter and his progeny, Jill and Mike, threatened by deadly peril in "The Dangerous Desert," "The Backyard Jungle," "The Tiny Sea" and "Exploring an Ant Colony."

"The Three Musketeers," loosely adapted from Alexandre Dumas' 1844 pseudo-historical novel, added Tooly, a young lad, to the familiar cast of swashbucklers. As loyal swordsmen of the Queen, the quartet clashed with "The Evil Falconer," foiled "The

Plot of the Puppet Master" and engaged in "Tooly's Treasure Hunt."
Featuring the farcical Rugg family, "The Hillbilly Bears" were re-
cycled comedies first seen on The Atom Ant/Secret Squirrel Show
(q. v. ).

In the only live-action serial, after they were attacked by
cutthroats while scuba-diving for a lost city, Professor Irwin Haydn
and his daughter, Leslie, and assistant, Link Simmons, took refuge
on "Danger Island." Pursued ashore, they were befriended by Morgan, a castaway, who helped them elude Chongo and his gang.

Packaged for Kellogg's and NBC, The Banana Splits was an
experiment to hold down production costs and yet give the semblance
of a sixty-minute cartoon show. Officially titled Kellogg's of Battle
Creek Presents the Banana Splits Adventure Hour, a prime time
preview was telecast September 6, 1968 and the cereal commercials
were integrated throughout the program featuring the animal characters. In part, the series was planned in response to growing
clamor over hard-action superhero cartoons, which had dominated
early Saturday programming since the mid-sixties. In a major
change in its philosophy, NBC switched to non-violent comedy and
fantasy formats in 1968-1969.

The introduction of life-like animal characters was a novel
approach, whose success encouraged NBC and its rivals to present
such costumed concepts as H. R. Pufnstuf* (q. v. ). During the
first season, the format helped to make The Banana Splits the top-
rated attraction in its timeslot.


BANG-SHANG LALAPALOOZA SHOW, THE  See  ARCHIES, THE


BARKER BILL'S CARTOON SHOW

Component Series
    FARMER AL FALFA, KIKO THE KANGAROO, PUDDY THE
    PUP, other TERRY TOONS

Network History
    Premiere: November 18, 1953
    CBS/Nov 1953-Nov 1956/Wednesday, Friday 5:00-5:15 PM
    Last Program: November 25, 1956
Sponsor: Post Sugar Jets


Syndicated History

FARMER AL FALFA

Distributor: CBS Films/1956-1971; Viacom International/1971-
Producer: Paul Terry
Company: Terrytoons/200 B&W films, 6-8 minutes (1930-1938)

Host
    "Barker Bill"

    Barker Bill's Cartoon Show hawked the vintage black-and-white films from the Terrytoons library in this first network weekday cartoon series. Leased from producer Paul Terry (1888-1971), whose most auspicious character was Mighty Mouse (q. v. ), the program featured forty-two "Farmer Al Falfa" shorts and one hundred fifty-eight other theatrical cartoons, including Puddy the Pup, Kiko the Kangaroo and classic adaptations like "Cinderella" and "The Three Bears." Seen twice a week from WCBS, New York, with a picture of an actor called "Barker Bill" as host, the films were simply dropped into the fifteen-minute show, with an off-camera announcer handling the introductions and commercials.

Animated by Terry, a staff artist at J. R. Bray Studios, the coverall-clad white-bearded rube was introduced as a spry and mischievous character in Farmer Al Falfa (Bray 1916). The silent films were included once a month in the Bray Pictograph, a weekly screen magazine with a cartoon at the end, released by Paramount Pictures. After he founded Terrytoons, and into the early sound era, Terry continued to produce the "Farmer Al Falfa" series, particularly featuring cats and mice, for Twentieth Century-Fox Films. Unlike his contemporary, Felix the Cat (q. v. ), the bespectacled old coot lacked a distinct personality, and before the advent of storymen the films were often incongruent. In one "Terry Fable, " a gang of mice raided the farmer's ice box and built themselves a giant sandwich. But before they could take a bite, the scene switched to Farmer Al riding in his car, and the mice were not seen again in the same film.

In 1955, Terry sold his 1, 400 "Terry Toons" in a $3. 5 million package to CBS. After Barker Bill ended, the films were syndicated, debuting October 22, 1956 on the Terry Toons Club, later retitled Terry Toons Circus, hosted by Claude Kirchner, 7:00-7:30 PM weekdays on WOR, New York. Meantime, under producer Bill Weiss, the Terrytoons studio continued as a division of CBS Films with releases for theaters and programs for the network. Terrytoons ended formally when CBS Films was divested in 1971, under an FCC order requiring the networks to rid themselves of their program syndication and cable-TV subsidiaries.


BARKLEYS, THE

Network History
    Premiere: September 9, 1972
    NBC/Sep 1972-Sep 1973/Saturday 10:30-11:00 AM
    Last Program: September 1, 1973
Executive Producers: David DePatie, Friz Freleng
Directors: Bob McKimson, Sid Marcus, Spencer Peel
Company: DePatie-Freleng Enterprises/13 films

Principal Characters and Voices

| | |
|---|---|
| Arnie Barkley | Henry Corden |
| Agnes Barkley | Joan Gerber |
| Terri Barkley | Julie McWhirter |
| Chester Barkley | Steve Lewis |
| Roger Barkley | Gene Andrusco |

The Barkleys were an "All in the Litter" pack of canines, dominated by the intransigent head of the middle class doggie household. Modeled after the outspoken Archie Bunker, the loud-mouth Arnie Barkley was the vulnerable parent in this parody of the prime time hit comedy All in the Family (CBS, 1971-1979), based on the British series Till Death Do Us Part. Agnes was his harried wife who frequently sided with their children, a girl Terri and the boys, Chester and Roger. A bus driver, Arnie spent a good deal of time arguing with his free-spirited pups in a demonstration of the generation gap that existed between them. He spent time at golf and ping pong with his oldest son, Chester, but he could see no reason to give similar attention to his daughter, who could only do "girl things" such as sewing and going to taffy-pull parties. Of course, it was the youngest son, Roger, also feeling neglect, who once ran away and joined a circus. Each episode involved the clash of one of Arnie's dogged opinions with the views of someone who did not share it, in such stories as "Lib and Let Lib," "Law and Miss-order" and "For the Love of Money."

BARNEY BEAR  See  MGM CARTOONS

BARNEY GOOGLE AND SNUFFY SMITH  See  KING FEATURES TRILOGY

BATFINK

Syndicated History
    Premiere: Fall 1967
Distributor: Screen Gems-Columbia Pictures Television/1967-
Executive Producer: Hal Seeger
Company: Hal Seeger Productions with Screen Gems (CPT)/100 films, 5 minutes

Principal Characters and Voices

Batfink                          Frank Buxton
Karate                           Len Maxwell

Batfink was an invincible cartoon crime-fighter with "wings of steel," protected in time of peril by his large batwings which acted as an impregnable shield. The mousey-looking, pointy-eared character used his Super Sonic Sonar to track down crackpots and criminals. Created by Hal Seeger, a veteran Fleischer Studios animator and originator of Milton the Monster (q.v.), the series was another anthropomorphic parody of the famed caped crusader, Batman* (q.v.). With no pretense at an alter identity, the brave bat was called into action on the hotline from the Chief of Police. Batfink and his trusted companion, the life-like husky Karate, chased about in pursuit of their foes in the "Batillac," a Volkswagen-like car with wings on the rear fenders.

Intended for flexible local programming, the episodic stories pitted the pair against Robber Hood, the hoodlum horseman, Daniel Boom, the notorious booby trapper, Old King Cruel, the charity swindler, Mr. Flick, the Monstrous Master Movie Maker, and Beanstalk Jack, the fiendish farmer. Brother Goose left clues to his crimes in rhyme, the Chameleon was a quick-change artist, and Ebeneezer a freezer. Lacking the originality of Batman's colorful antagonists, most of the episodes were devoted to Hugo A Go Go, a deranged scientist. Batfink's arch-nemesis, Hugo, whose son was named Goo Goo, invented brain-washing fluid he squirted from his buttonhole flower, tickle sticks and a laser-shooting mono-cle, among other items, to perpetrate his crimes. Generally rather silly, at best Batfink was an authentic flying hero, the sole mammal capable of true flight.

## BATMAN AND ROBIN

### Network History

THE BATMAN/SUPERMAN HOUR
    Premiere: September 14, 1968
    CBS/Sep 1968-Sep 1969/Saturday 10:30-11:30 AM

THE ADVENTURES OF BATMAN
    CBS/Sep 1969-Sep 1970/Sunday 7:30-8:00 AM
    Last Program: September 6, 1970

THE NEW ADVENTURES OF BATMAN
    Premiere: February 12, 1977
    CBS/Feb 1977-Sep 1977/Saturday 10:30-11:00 AM

THE BATMAN/TARZAN ADVENTURE HOUR
    CBS/Sep 1977-Jan 1978/Saturday 11:00-12:00 AM
    CBS/Jan 1978-Sep 1978/Saturday 10:30-11:30 AM

TARZAN AND THE SUPER 7
    CBS/Sep 1978-Sep 1979/Saturday 10:30-12:00 AM
    CBS/Sep 1979-Sep 1980/Saturday 12:30-1:30 PM

BATMAN AND THE SUPER 7
    NBC/Sep 1980-May 1981/Saturday 11:00-12:00 AM
    NBC/May 1981-Sep 1981/Saturday 9:30-10:30 AM
    Last Program: September 5, 1981

### Syndicated History

SUPERMAN/AQUAMAN/BATMAN (1968-1969)

Distributor: Warner Brothers Television/1970-
Executive Producers: Allen Ducovny (1968-1969), Norman Prescott,
    Louis Scheimer (1977)
Producers: Norman Prescott, Louis Scheimer (1968-1969), Don

Christensen (1977)
Directors: Hal Sutherland (1968-1969), Don Towsley (1977)
Company: Filmation Studios for Ducovny Productions/17 films
    (1968-1969); Filmation Productions with National Periodicals/16
    films (1977)

Narrator
    Jackson Beck (1968-1969)

Principal Characters and Voices

Bruce Wayne/Batman      (1968-1969) Bud Collyer
                             (1977) Adam West
Dick Grayson/Robin      (1968-1969) Casey Kasem
                             (1977) Burt Ward
Barbara Gordon/Batgirl  (1968-1969) Jane Webb
                             (1977) Melendy Britt
Alfred Pennyworth       (1968-1969) Olan Soulé
Bat-Mite                     (1977) Lennie Weinrib

    Batman and Robin joined the TV cartoon crime-fighters in
1968-1969, tangling with some famous strangers who disturbed the
peace in Gotham City. Secretly known only to their loyal butler
Alfred as the town's caped-and-cowled peacekeepers, clean-cut
millionaire-philanthropist Bruce Wayne and Dick Grayson, his
teenage ward, occupied their time in stately Wayne manor with
French and judo lessons until a Bat-signal from the police chief
summoned them to derring-do. Two straight action stories were
seen in each episode of The Adventures of Batman, with the cul-
tured and orphaned pair sometimes joined by Batgirl, police commissioner Gordon's daughter, Barbara. Creating problems for the
trio with their infernal skullduggery were such bizarre Batfoes as
The Riddler, Catwoman, Mad Hatter, Simon the Pieman, the frigid,
fiendish Mr. Freeze, the clown prince of crime, The Joker, and
The Penguin, that pudgy purveyor of perfidy.
    Following a seven-year network hiatus, Bat-Mite, a simian-
like supermascot, replaced Alfred and provided prankish monkey-
shines in The New Adventures of Batman. It was voiced by the
stars from the prime time fantasy adventure, Batman* (q.v.);
Adam West continued to speak as the caped crusader in his camp-
counselor baritone and Burt Ward as the Boy Wonder in his standard boy voice, punctuated by such expressive exclamations as
"Gleeps!" Seemingly unjailable, still at large and causing chaos
were The Penguin, The Joker, Mr. Freeze, The Riddler and Catwoman, but the half-hour episodic stories also featured the foul
schemes of Zarbo, Clay Face, The Chameleon, Electro, the sugar-
happy crook, Sweet Tooth, and Moon Man, an astronaut who became
a criminal every full moon.
    Incorporated were all the familiar Batparaphernalia and Bat-
vehicles, including "Batscooters" and the single-seater "Whirly-
Bats" introduced by artists Carmine Infantino and Murphy Anderson, who continued the National Periodicals' comic after 1964. The
creation of artist Bob Kane and writer Bill Finger for Detective

Comics Number 27 (May 1939), the animated Batman and Robin captured the moral essence of their work with the gaudy characters roaring out of their secret Batcave in the "Batmobile" to protect life, limb and property and scourge crime and corruption.

First coupled with Superman (q. v. ), The Adventures of Batman continued in repeats in 1969-1970 before on-going syndication. Between September 10, 1977 and September 2, 1978 The New Adventures were rerun with Tarzan, Lord of the Jungle (q. v. ) as The Batman/Tarzan Adventure Hour and afterwards as a segment of Tarzan and the Super 7 (q. v. ). Starting September 27, 1980 on NBC, they were repeated as Batman and the Super 7 with the prior Tarzan components, "Webwoman," "Manta and Moray, " "The Freedom Force" and "Super Stretch and Micro Woman. " On ABC, Batman and Robin starred in "The Caped Crusader Caper" (Dec 16, 1972) on The New Scooby-Doo Movies (q. v. ) and as members of the "Justice League of America" on Superfriends (q. v. ).


BATMAN AND THE SUPER 7  See  BATMAN AND ROBIN and
     TARZAN AND THE SUPER 7


BATMAN/SUPERMAN HOUR, THE  See  BATMAN AND ROBIN and
     SUPERMAN


BATMAN/TARZAN ADVENTURE HOUR, THE  See  BATMAN AND
     ROBIN and TARZAN, LORD OF THE JUNGLE


BATTLE OF THE PLANETS

Syndicated History
     Premiere:  October 1978
Distributor:  Sandy Frank Film Syndication/1978-
Executive Producer:  Jameson Brewer
Producer/Director:  David Hanson
Company:  Gallerie International Films; Tatsunoko Productions,
     Japan/85 films

Principal Characters and Voices

| | |
|---|---|
| 7-Zark-7/Keyop | Alan Young |
| Zoltar | Keye Luke |
| Mark Venture | Casey Kasem |
| Princess | Janet Waldo |
| Jason | Ronnie Schell |
| Tiny/Dr. Anderson | Alan Dinehart |

Battle of the Planets was an ongoing war between the forces of Earth and Spectra, a catastrophic world whose resources had declined. Defending Earth's galaxy from the desperate designs of Zoltar, the ruler of the dying plant, was G-Force, a superhuman watchdog squad commanded by Mark Venture, a daring leader. The other members were the headstrong Jason, whose impetuosity often had to be restrained; Tiny, the oversized pilot of the group's spaceship, "The Phoenix"; the bright and witty Princess, who had a crush on Mark; and an impish little humanoid named Keyop, that had a malfunction which caused the peculiar manner in which he spoke. The G-Force members had many extraordinary powers, and when banded together could cause a devastating whirlwind.

The missions were directed by 7-Zark-7, a guardian robot in Center Neptune, the unit's computerized headquarters. For a pet, he had a loyal robot dog, 1-Rover-1, and as an assistant, Susan, a never-seen secretary. Her romantic off-screen voice frequently made his antennae quiver. Assisting at the nerve center was Doctor Anderson, the security officer who advised G-Force and 7-Zark-7. The defender's spacecraft was also a phenomenal asset. To escape great peril, it was capable of transformation from conventional rocket vehicle into ghostly fiery bird, resembling the legendary Arabian Phoenix.

Zoltar was the principal antagonist who coveted Earth's ecological abundance. The Emperor Ming-like ruler received his orders from a more powerful galactic being, The Spirit, called "Oh, Luminous One" because only his two evil eyes were seen on a monitor. Hatching plots and invading Earth by surrogate means, Zoltar launched robot armies and an armada of strange spacecraft in his attacks. G-Force fought his endless spaceships in the shape of turtle, wasp, shark, scorpion, sea dragon, praying mantis and other monstrous forms. Lending a lighter touch, the youthful heroes once prevented the capture of Earth's sugar supply, which would have deprived the world of sweets.

Seen in forty-four markets in its first year of syndication, the action-filled fantasy was one of several Japanese cartoons achieving popularity again following the smash success of the movie, Star Wars (TCF, 1977). The first imported Japanese hit since the late sixties, it was produced by the same studio that filmed Speed Racer (q. v.). Originally televised in Japan as a daily serial between October 1, 1972 and September 29, 1974 under the title Gatchaman, eighty-five of the one hundred one half-hours were re-dubbed in English. A new series, Gatchaman-F, premiered October 1, 1978 in Japan as a sequel. The title was derived from "Gooseman" or "Ganderman" in Japanese, based on the Oriental view of the Goose as a strong and brave bird.


BEAGLES, THE

<u>Network History</u>
Premiere: September 10, 1966
CBS/Sep 1966-Sep 1967/Saturday 12:30-1:00 PM
Last Program: September 2, 1967
Executive Producer: Treadwell Covington
Company: Total TV Productions with Lancelot Productions/26 films

Principal Characters

    Stringer
    Tubby

    The Beagles were a pair of rock-and-roll canines whose misadventures frequently landed them in the doghouse. An obvious attempt to cash in on the sound-alike name of The Beatles (q. v.), the Liverpool mop-headed musicians whose cartoons debuted on ABC in 1965, the ludicrous and undistinguished series starred two floppy-eared dogs named Stringer and Tubby.

BEANY AND CECIL

Network History

MATTY'S FUNNIES WITH BEANY AND CECIL
    Premiere: January 6, 1962
    ABC/Jan 1962-Dec 1962/Saturday 7:00-7:30 PM

THE BEANY AND CECIL SHOW
    ABC/Jan 1963-Sep 1965/Saturday 11:30-12:00 AM
    ABC/Sep 1965-Dec 1965/Sunday 10:30-11:00 AM
    ABC/Jan 1966-Jan 1967/Sunday 10:00-10:30 AM
    ABC/Jan 1967-Sep 1967/Sunday 9:30-10:00 AM
    Last Program: September 3, 1967
Sponsor: Mattel Toys (1962-1963)

Syndicated History

Distributor: ABC Films/1968-1972; Worldvision Enterprises/1972-
    1977; Intercontinental Communications/1977-
Producer/Director: Bob Clampett
Company: Snowball Studios for Bob Clampett Productions/78 films

Principal Characters

    Cecil, the Seasick Sea Serpent
    Beany Boy
    Captain Horatio K. Huffenpuff
    Dishonest John
    Crowy the Crow

Voices

    Bob Clampett
    Jim McGeorge
    Erv Shoemaker
    Eddie Brandt
    Freddie Morgan
    Sody Clampett
    Bobby Clampett

Beany and Cecil, an adventurous little boy and his pal, a
seasick sea serpent, made the only successful transition from a
children's puppet program to a network cartoon show.  The storyline adhered closely to that of Time for Beany* (q. v. ), the pioneering syndicated puppet fantasy, also created by Bob Clampett.
Beany Boy, as his friend Cecil called him, was the nephew of
Captain Horatio K. Huffenpuff, a braggart noted for his whoppers,
and the commander of the good ship "Leakin' Lena. "  A cheery
bright-eyed lad, Beany was dressed in blue coveralls and a cap
with a propeller on top, which created a national merchandising
fad in the early fifties.  His buddy Cecil was a large green sea
creature, an affectionate and protective soul who became sick when
it stormed but was always Johnny-on-the-spot to rescue his pal
when danger threatened.

Sailing the seven seas with Crowy the Crow, in their quest
for adventure the trio explored the universe from the undersea
world to outer space, meeting characters with whimsical names.
There were Hare-cules and Ben Hare, Beepin' Tom, Little Ace
from Outer Space and The Guided Muscle, Jack the Knife and Go
Man Van Gogh, and the muscular numskull, Tearalong the Dotted
Lion.  Nothing was sacrosanct.  Baseball was lampooned by Baby
Ruthy and Little Homer, westerns by Buffalo Billy, Pop Gunn,
Tommy Hawk, Slopalong Catskill and Davy Crickett, the classics
by William Shakespeare Wolf, and stereotypes of all kinds, like
Careless the Mexican Hairless and Peking Tom.  Among the no-
table guests who relished voicing the parts were John Carradine,
Scatman Crothers, Arlene Harris, Robert Clary, Mickey Katz,
Gonzalez-Gonzales, and Sammee Tong.

The familiar arch foe was that rascal of the rotter's school,
Dishonest John, whose sneering-laugh "Nya ha ha!" was imitated
by fans everywhere.  D. J. was still up to his old dirty tricks,
which always backfired.  For the seasick Cecil, who on occasion
was afflicted also by a romantic heart malady, Cecelia McCoy, a
beguiling she-serpent, made her initial appearance.  The films
continued the corny puns and witty satire of the original presentation, and ended with a catchy song that nearly every viewer could
recite by heart,

> So come kids, wind up your lids,
> We'll flip again real soon
> With Beany Boy
> And Your Obedient Serpent in
> A Bob Clampett CartooOOoon!

The characters were first animated in 1958 for a TV pilot,
"Beany and Cecil Meet Billy the Squid, " featuring original music
by Bob and his wife Sody, and released theatrically as A Bob
Clampett Cartoon with "Beany and Cecil" (UA, 1960).  Optioned by
the Mattel Toy Company, the series debuted in prime time in January 1962 as Matty's Funnies with Beany and Cecil, replacing
Casper, The Friendly Ghost (q. v. ) and other vintage Famous Studios' shorts on Matty's Funday Funnies (q. v. ).  Three months later
the title was shortened to simply Beany and Cecil and beginning
January 5, 1963, moved to Saturday mornings as The Beany and
Cecil Show.  Three episodic segments were seen in each half-hour;

the premiere included "The Spots Off a Leopard," "Invasion of
Earth by Robots," and "Cecil Meets the Singing Dinosaur." In the
last cartoon the gang sailed to No Bikini Atoll to capture a vocalizing Brontosaurus.

A veteran Hollywood artist, Clampett made the first Mickey
Mouse dolls for Walt Disney in 1930 when in his teens, and a
year later went to work as a successful cartoonist. He worked on
the first "Merrie Melodies" sound cartoon released by Warner Brothers Pictures at the Harman-Ising "Looney Tunes" Studio. As a
member of the "little creative group" at the Leon Schlesinger Studio,
and at the "Termite Terrace" bungalow on the Warner's Sunset lot,
Clampett helped originate some of the most popular animated characters on the screen, such as Porky Pig (q. v.) and Bugs Bunny
(q. v.). Made a director in 1936, Bob created Tweety Pie and contributed to the development of Sylvester the Cat and Daffy Duck
(q. v.).

Beany and Cecil ran for six years on the network before
entering syndication all over the world. In 1979-1980 in Canada,
it became a top-rated weekend show on French language television.


BEATLES, THE

Network History
    Premiere: September 25, 1965
    ABC/Sep 1965-Sep 1967/Saturday 10:30-11:00 AM
    ABC/Sep 1967-Sep 1968/Saturday 12:00-12:30 PM
    ABC/Sep 1968-Apr 1969/Sunday 9:30-10:00 AM
    Last Program: April 20, 1969
Sponsors: A. C. Gilbert Toys, Quaker Oats, Mars Candy

Syndicated History

Distributor: Firestone Program Syndication/1969-1979; Gold Key
    Entertainment/1979-
Executive Producer: Al Brodax
Company: King Features Syndicate Television/39 films

Principal Characters and Voices

John Lennon/George Harrison        Paul Frees
Paul McCartney/Ringo Starr         Lance Percibal

The Beatles, whose rock songs revolutionized the musical
arts, helped refashion the look of Saturday morning television as
well with this hit series. Apart from the syndicated animated
slapstick of The Three Stooges (q. v.), the show was unusual in
that it caricatured "popular performers," the first of the treatment
to appear regularly on the networks. Figure animation was not new,
and was used in the earliest silent theatrical cartoons, such as J. R.
Bray Studios' Colonel Heezaliar (1915-1925). But the idea of ani-
mating personalities for their own TV series became a mini-trend,
pioneered and followed on ABC, notably with The Brady Kids (q. v.),

The Osmonds (q. v. ), and The Jackson 5ive (q. v. ).  And the rock music and comedic format would be emulated for the next ten years by animated teenage groups of every description, including anthropomorphic adaptations.

Following their fantasy adventures around the globe, each show contained two stories involving the world famous quartet, set in exotic locales from the jungles of Africa to the North Pole.  Creating the pattern for their hit animated movie, The Yellow Submarine (UA, 1968), seen as a CBS Special October 29, 1972, each segment was built around one of their tunes.  In the premiere, to their song "I Want to Hold Your Hand, " the mop-headed quartet explored the ocean floor in a diving bell and encountered a lovesick octopus.  Similarly, in "A Hard Day's Night" the rock group was depicted rehearsing in a haunted house.  Although the singing was dubbed from recordings made by the musicians themselves, the dialogue portions were imitations voiced by professionals.  This consideration was imposed by the network because it was believed too difficult for American children to understand the entertainers speaking in their native Liverpoolese.  Also included was a sing-a-long segment, resurrected from the Max Fleischer "Screen Songs" (PAR, 1929-1938), but without the bouncing ball.

The series was packaged by King Features Syndicate, which owned exclusive rights to the Beatles' cartoon characters, and animated by studios in London and Sydney, Australia.  In a quest for authenticity, the artists repeatedly screened the Beatles' movies to study their physical characteristics and mannerisms.  In this fashion, they were able to capture the fast, jerky-moving John Lennon, the group's leader, the loose-limbed and frequently frowning George Harrison, the poised and stylish Paul McCartney and the easy-going Ringo Starr.  A consistent high rater, even in syndication, The Beatles was ABC's second major success following Bugs Bunny (q. v. ), and elevated its entire Saturday lineup into a viable competitor and provided $3 million gross revenue the first year.


BEETLE BAILEY  See  KING FEATURES TRILOGY


BETTY BOOP

Syndicated History

CARTOON CARNIVAL
    Premiere:  March 26, 1956
    WABD, New York/Monday-Friday 6:00-6:30 PM

THE BETTY BOOP SHOW
    Return:  Fall 1971
    Distributor:  UM&M-TV/1956-1966; National Telefilm Associates/ 1971-
    Producer:  Max Fleischer
    Director:  David Fleischer
    Company:  Fleischer Studios for Paramount Pictures/100 films, 6-8 minutes (1930-1939)

Principal Character and Voices

| Betty Boop | (1930-1931) Margie Heintz |
| | (1931) Kate Wright |
| | (1931) Bonnie Poe |
| | (1931-1933) Little Ann Little |
| | (1933-1939) Mae Questel |

Betty Boop, the happy-go-lucky wide-eyed cartoon star of the thirties, was resurrected twice on television in her theatrical shorts, the second time around tinted in color.   Artist Grim Natwick, who later animated Walt Disney's Snow White, originated the unnamed female character that first appeared in Dizzy Dishes (Aug 9, 1930), the sixth "Talkartoon" produced by Fleischer Studios. Natwick caricatured Helen Kane (1903-1966), the Paramount Pictures star and popular singer, as a little French poodle with spit curls, long ears, and feminine legs.   The canine prototype was a café entertainer who parodied the "Boop-boop-a-doop" songstress in the film which starred Bimbo, a floppy-eared pooch lifted from the studio's silent series Out of the Inkwell (q. v. ).   The poodle appeared intermittently in the series until Bimbo's Initiation (Jul 24, 1931), when the little singing dog became a regular.   Any Rags (Jan 2, 1932) marked the debut of the humanized Betty Boop, although another prototype had appeared with Rudy Vallee in the bouncing-ball "Screen Song" version of Betty Coed (Aug 1, 1931), from which she derived her first name.   Producer Max Fleischer hired two songwriters, Sammy Timberg and Sam Lerner, to create songs especially for the Boop films, which became Paramount's number one cartoon attraction in the early thirties.   In her scanty black dress, lone garter, and high-pitched sweet voice, Betty was featured in musicals, gag comedies, light-hearted adventure tales, classic fairy tales, and surrealistic mystery dramas.   On July 14, 1933, she introduced to theater audiences Popeye the Sailor (q. v. ), who endured as Fleischer's major star.

Betty Boop was voiced by five actresses, but the last two were the most memorable.  Born Ann Rothschild, Little Ann Little had been a musical comedy star in the "Greenwich Village Follies" before she won the part for two years.  Both Ann and Mae Questel bore a striking resemblance to Betty Boop, and came to the studio via a Paramount talent contest.   After six years, Questel became identified with the role and went on to voice other Fleischer-Famous Studios characters such as Olive Oyl, Little Audrey, and Casper, The Friendly Ghost (q. v. ).   She is remembered also as Aunt Bluebelle in the TV commercials for Scott Towels.   Along with the three previous actresses, Ann and Mae were called as witnesses in April 1934, in Helen Kane's unsuccessful quarter-million-dollar lawsuit over unauthorized use of her "Boop-boop-a-doop" vocal characterization.

Extensively merchandised, Boop paraphernalia of all kinds, including watches, tea sets, and dolls, have become valued collectibles.   A children's radio show, Betty Boop Fables, lasted one year with Questel voicing the role.   And Betty Boop (KFS, 1935-1938) was a Sunday newspaper comic drawn by Bud Counihan and always signed by Max Fleischer.   The animated cartoons ended with Yip,

Yip, Yippey (Aug 11, 1939). Readers interested in more Betty Boop history should see The Fleischer Story (Nostalgia Press, 1976) by Leslie Carbaga.

After the pre-1948 Paramount films were sold for television in late 1955, the Betty Boop cartoons were syndicated as part of the "Cartoon Carnival" package and seen weekdays on Captain Video's Cartoons over WABD, New York, beginning in March 1956. Later acquired by National Telefilm Associates, duplicate negatives were hand color-painted in Korea and re-released in 1971 as The Betty Boop Show with four cartoons in each half-hour program. Containing vintage subject matter and music, the time-worn films failed to rekindle much enthusiasm except from the most fervent fans of "Ain't she cute, boop-boop-a-doop, sweet Betty," who celebrated her fiftieth birthday in 1980.


## BIRDMAN AND THE GALAXY TRIO

### Network History
Premiere:  September 9, 1967
NBC/Sep 1967-Sep 1968/Saturday 11:00-11:30 AM
NBC/Sep 1968-Dec 1968/Saturday 12:00-12:30 PM
Last Program:  December 28, 1968

### Syndicated History

### CAPTAIN INVENTORY

Distributor:  Taft H-B Program Sales/1973-1979; Worldvision Enterprises/1979-
Executive Producers:  William Hanna, Joseph Barbera
Company:  Hanna-Barbera Productions/20 films

### Principal Characters and Voices

| | |
|---|---|
| Ray Randall/Birdman | Keith Andes |
| Birdboy | Dick Beals |
| Falcon 7/Vapor Man | Don Messick |
| Meteor Man | Ted Cassidy |
| Galaxy Girl | Virginia Eiler |
| Avenger (Birdman's eagle) | |

Birdman and the Galaxy Trio flew to bizarre adventures on earth and far distant worlds in three alternated flights of fantasy in each show. A premise derived from the legendary Athenian Icarus, whose father Daedalus made him wings of wax and feathers, Birdman was conceived by comic book artist Alexander Toth, a National Comics (NP) artist who began directing TV art on Space Angel (q. v.). His new aerohero somewhat resembled, and the Egyptian genesis closely paralleled, the prior feathered crime-fighter from the comics, Hawkman, who made his television debut on The Superman/Aquaman Hour of Adventure (q. v.) and was seen on Superfriends (q. v.).

Saved from a fiery death by Ra, the Sun god and Hawk deity, Ray Randall was bestowed with wings, lightning-fast flight, and a powerful weapon. Charged by exposure to the sun's rays, as Birdman he lasered "Solar Ray Beams" from his knuckles, which could melt anything on contact. A blue-winged, yellow-costumed super-hero, he wore a black domino mask and yellow helmet with a red-winged bird crest, and was protected by a Solar Shield to deflect his enemy's deadly beams and projectiles. Alerted to insidious plots by his chief, Falcon 7, on a TV screen, the super-patriot soared into action through the mouth of his hollow volcano headquarters to the echoing scream, "Bird Man-n-n-n!" A huge blue American eagle called Avenger was his faithful companion and frequently his savior, and in some episodes he was teamed with Birdboy.

Birdman was a champion of freedom against the enemies of mankind, and generally his opponents were deranged scientists, bent on conquest and wealth through terror and blackmail. "Cumulus, The Storm King," threatened to paralyze the whole nation with his blanketing-fog machine, and Professor Kailoff to destroy it with his manufactured earthquakes and the metal robot Morga. Equally adept at soaring beneath the sea, in the "Pirate Ploy" Birdman battled Dr. Shark, who stole a navy bathyscaphe to mine gold from the ocean's floor. Other foes included Reducto, X the Eliminator, Magnatroid, Vulturo, Chameleon, Birdgirl, the Ruthless Ringmaster, Nitron, the Human Bomb and Dr. Millenium, his archenemy. In This Man Dawson (SYN, 1959-   ), Keith Andes, who among other roles later starred as Jeff Morgan on Paradise Bay (NBC, 1965-1966), was heard as the virile voice of the hero.

More commonplace in ancestry, The Galaxy Trio were just weird transformed humans with peculiar skills, organized as a watchdog Galaxy Patrol roving the universe in their spaceship "Condor I." Vapor Man could assume any gaseous or mist form, Galaxy Girl defied all nature's known laws, and the brutish rock-hard Meteor Man had large pointed ears like Dr. Spock and enormous strength like The Thing. Commanded by Intergalactic Security, the trouble-shooters were dispatched to solve desperate predicaments on alien planets. They had a run-in with space pirate Cragg on planet K-7, blanketed in sleeping gas while his robot machines plundered the national treasuries. On Meterous they subdued an uprising headed by Molten I, emperor of the lava men. And on Orbus 4, they put down a revolution by robots under the cunning Computron, who had imprisoned its benevolent ruler Calex. Influenced by the superhero-combo trend, like The Fantastic Four (q. v.), the Toth-designed cartoons also borrowed techniques from the popular space adventure, Star Trek (NBC, 1966-1969). For example, the trio displaced themselves from their orbiting auto-piloted spacecraft to planetary sites via "Blazon Tubes."

Reacting to the second great wave of clamor over children's programming that began to swell in the mid-sixties, because of hard-action fantasy cartoons, NBC began a major programming change in 1968-1969. Reportedly at a loss of $750,000, Birdman and the Galaxy Trio, Samson and Goliath (q. v.), and Super President and Spy Shadow (q. v.) were dropped in mid-season in favor of tamer comedy programs. Several additional episodes of Birdman, one of their higher rated programs, were in production at the time. The superhero banishment on NBC would last until November 1976 when the repackaged Space Ghost (q. v. ) and Frankenstein, Jr. (q. v. ), originally promoted by Fred Silverman for CBS, returned to bolster the network's flagging ratings. With the exception of Space Ghost, ironically most of the early created-for-TV superbeings were far outclassed by Birdman, which was packaged in a successful syndicated show.


BOZO THE CLOWN

Syndicated History
    Premiere: December 8, 1958
    WGN, Chicago/Monday-Friday 6:00-6:30 PM CST
Distributor: Larry Harmon Pictures/1958-1978; Allworld Telefilm
    Sales/1978-
Producer: Larry Harmon
Company: Larry Harmon Pictures/156 films, 6 minutes

Principal Characters and Voices

Bozo the Clown/Butch                    Larry Harmon

    Bozo the Clown, the pippity-poppity pop-up children's record star, began a new television career in 1958, appearing in animated cartoons. During the forties, Capitol Records netted $20 million from the storyteller's successful recordings, voiced by Pinto Colvig (1892-1967), a former Walt Disney story man. Colvig, who left the studio in 1937, periodically returned until his death to record for Disney his familiar voice characterization as Goofy. Along with Stan Freberg, Daws Butler and June Foray, Colvig was placed under a five-year contract to Capitol to record all their children's records. With the advent of television, the Bozo fad had run its course, and the profits began to dwindle.
    In 1956, Larry Harmon, formerly seen as Commander Comet* (q. v. ), bought the television rights to the character and produced a series of cartoons between 1958 and 1962 for the children's market. Featuring the vaudeville-like misadventures of the wisecracking red-headed clown and Butch, his little pal, the episodes were liberally sprinkled with Bozo's familiar idiom, such as "Gosh all polliwogs" and "Skubbe dubee do. " Late in 1958, the short films began appearing on local stations, often in existing hosted cartoon shows. In this manner, Bozo debuted in December 1958 on Bugs Bunny and Friends on WGN, Chicago. But the producer's concept soon gelled for a half-hour daily show with a live Bozo as the host for the cartoons, and in 1959 this format began to appear on local stations. It was the beginning of the highly successful packaged variety series, Bozo the Clown* (q. v. ), and its sequels.

BRADY KIDS, THE

Network History
   Premiere: September 16, 1972
   ABC/Sep 1972-Sep 1973/Saturday 10:30-11:00 AM
   ABC/Sep 1973-Aug 1974/Saturday 11:00-11:30 AM
   Last Program: August 31, 1974

Syndicated History

Distributor: Paramount TV Sales/1974-
Executive Producer: Sherwood Schwartz
Producers: Louis Scheimer, Norman Prescott
Director: Hal Sutherland
Company: Filmation Productions with Paramount Television/22
   films

Principal Characters and Voices

Greg Brady                          Barry Williams
Peter Brady                         Christopher Knight
Bobby Brady                         Michael Lookinland
Marcia Brady                        Maureen McCormick
Janice Brady                        Eve Plumb
Cindy Brady                         Susan Olsen
Marlon                              Larry Storch
Ping and Pong (Brady's twin pandas)
Mop Top (Brady's dog)

     The Brady Kids were transferred to Saturday morning car-
toons while their middle-class conglomerate family was still a hit
in prime time.   The three boys and three girls, aged seven to fourteen, seen on The Brady Bunch (ABC, 1969-1974), were recreated
in self-likeness and voiced their own parts.   Typically model
youngsters, wholesome and well-scrubbed, the stereotyped suburban-
dwelling brood were the first children to appear simultaneously in a
live action and animated series, on the same network.
     Under their nominal leader Greg, the oldest boy, the epi-
sodes found the Brady Kids gathered in their backyard tree-top
clubhouse, where the action began.   Deciding to pursue interest in
some current event or perform a special deed, they merrily set
forth to adventure, accompanied by their pets.   Mop Top was their
playful shaggy dog, Ping and Pong their twin Chinese-jibberish-
speaking Pandas, and Marlon, a magical black myna bird that used
his mystical powers to transport them to different locations and
historic past events.   As a bubblegum rock group called "The
Bradys," the children performed as musicians and singers.
     The scenarios centered on their school activities and fantasy
junkets with the aid of Marlon, once foiling the plans of two poachers in Africa out of concern for endangered species in the two-
part episode "Jungle Bungle."   Several adventures included comic
book "guest" characters.   Superman and Lois turned up when two
crooks used invisible paint to help rob a bank in "Cindy's Super

Friend. " Diana Prince appeared as their science teacher, and later as Wonder Woman when she joined the gang at ancient Olympic Games in "It's All Greek to Me. " Even the Lone Ranger and Tonto showed up in "Long Gone Silver, " like the others, to enhance viewer attraction.   Each episode incorporated educational observations and such pro-social themes as fair play, good sportsmanship, and the consequences of cheating.

Barry Williams became something of a teenage idol as Greg in the evening series, receiving sixty-five thousand fan letters per week in 1971.   Without particular success, Barry and several of the other children tried to turn their TV popularity into recording careers.   The youngsters appeared later with their series parents, Florence Henderson and Robert Reed, on The Brady Bunch Hour (ABC, 1977), a TV variety show-within-a-show, in which Eve Plumb was replaced as Jan by Geri Reischl.

The cartoon series was preceded by two ABC promotional programs.   The Brady Kids Preview (Sep 15, 1972) introduced excerpts from their program, and "The Brady Kids on Mysterious Island" (Sep 9, 1972) was the initial hour-long presentation on The ABC Saturday Superstar Movie (q. v. ).   Interestingly, the prime time and cartoon series ended a day apart, August 30 and 31, 1974.

## BUFORD AND THE GALLOPING GHOST

### Network History

YOGI'S SPACE RACE/THE BUFORD FILES, THE GALLOPING GHOST
   Premiere:  September 9, 1978
   NBC/Sep 1978-Oct 1978/Saturday 8:00-9:30 AM
   NBC/Nov 1978-Jan 1979/Saturday 11:00-12:00 AM

BUFORD AND THE GALLOPING GHOST
   NBC/Feb 1979-Sep 1979/Saturday 12:00-12:30 PM
   Last Program:  September 1, 1979
Executive Producers:  William Hanna, Joseph Barbera
Producer:  Art Scott
Director:  Ray Patterson
Company:  Hanna-Barbera Productions/13 films

### Principal Characters and Voices

| | |
|---|---|
| Buford Bloodhound/Nugget Nose | Frank Welker |
| Cindy Mae/Rita | Pat Parris |
| Woody | Dave Landsburg |
| Sheriff Duprés | Henry Corden |
| Deputy Goofer | Roger Peltz |
| Wendy | Marilyn Schreffler |
| Mr. Fuddy | Hal Peary |

Buford and The Galloping Ghost was a repackaged show, combining two prior series about a southern bloodhound and an ectoplasmic horse. Set in Pendike County way down south, The Buford Files starred a lavender dog that bayed at full moon and helped solve mysteries with an "Aw Shucks t'warn't nothing" embarrassed demeanor. His voice was not unlike that of Goofy, Walt Disney's famous canine, and his nose turned red when he detected a clue. The southern-accented, droopy-looking tracker was partnered in the adventures with the teenagers Cindy Mae and Woody, whose voice and "Gol-lee!" were straight from Jim Nabors' rural rube, Gomer Pyle. While searching for their friend Jeffrey Crowley in the premiere, the unwanted helpers aided a recalcitrant Sheriff Duprés and his deputy, Goofer, by recapturing the convicts, Billy and Luke Scroggins, a pair of thieving swamp rats. Plotted in spooky bayou settings, the stories featured fake supernatural goings-on, as a device to shroud criminals engaged in hijackings and kidnappings in such nefarious schemes as "The Vanishing Stallion," "The Missing Gator" and "The Swamp Saucer." Buford was the key to the unmasking and their demise.

The Galloping Ghost was a sway-backed, decrepit equine named Murgitroyd, an apparition with Walter Brennan's voice and a nose for gold. One sniff drove him wild. Nicknamed "Nugget Nose," the cantankerous horse's companions were Rita and Wendy, the LaVerne and Shirley (ABC, 1976- ) of the Golden West. The teenagers were the Dude Ranch employees of Mr. Fuddy, voiced like Hal Peary's Great Gildersleeve, who did not believe in ghosts, four-footed or otherwise. But when in need of the phantom horse's help, which was at least once each episode, the girls chanted "Galloping Ghost don't be late, come and help us right away!" And quick as the bugled sound of "Charge!," the ancient white steed galloped to the rescue in such stories as "Klondike's Kate," "Pests in the West" and "Mr. Sunshine's Eclipse."

The mystery-adventure and comedy-fantasy were introduced as components of the ninety-minute series, Yogi's Space Race (q. v.), and were coupled in their own time slot after the show was shortened on February 3, 1979.


## BUGS BUNNY

Component Series
  DAFFY DUCK, FOGHORN LEGHORN, PEPE LE PEW, SPEEDY
  GONZALES, SYLVESTER, TWEETY PIE, others

Syndicated History

BUGS BUNNY THEATER/BUGS BUNNY AND HIS FRIENDS
  Premiere: September 14, 1956
  WABD, New York/Friday 7:30-8:00 PM
Distributor: Associated Artists Productions (pre-1948)/1956-1959;
  United Artists Television (pre-1948)/1959- ; Warner Brothers
  Television (post-1948)/1964-

Network History

THE BUGS BUNNY SHOW

Premiere: October 11, 1960
ABC/Oct 1960-Sep 1962/Tuesday 7:30-8:00 PM
ABC/Apr 1962-Sep 1967/Saturday 12:00-12:30 PM
ABC/Dec 1967-Sep 1968/Sunday 10:30-11:00 AM
CBS/Sep 1971-Sep 1973/Saturday 8:00-8:30 AM
ABC/Sep 1973-Sep 1974/Saturday 8:00-8:30 AM
ABC/Sep 1974-Aug 1975/Saturday 8:30-9:00 AM
Last Program: August 30, 1975

THE BUGS BUNNY/ROAD RUNNER HOUR
Premiere: September 14, 1968
CBS/Sep 1968-Sep 1970/Saturday 8:30-9:30 AM
CBS/Sep 1970-Sep 1971/Saturday 8:00-9:00 AM
CBS/Sep 1975-Nov 1976/Saturday 8:30-9:30 AM
CBS/Nov 1976-Sep 1977/Saturday 9:00-10:00 AM
CBS/Sep 1977-Oct 1977/Saturday 8:00-9:00 AM
CBS/Oct 1977-Nov 1977/Saturday 8:30-9:30 AM

THE BUGS BUNNY/ROAD RUNNER SHOW
CBS/Apr 1976-Jun 1976/Tuesday 8:00-8:30 PM
CBS/Nov 1977-Feb 1981/Saturday 9:00-10:30 AM
CBS/Mar 1981-Sep 1981/Saturday 8:30-10:00 AM

Producer: Hal Geer
Directors: Friz Freleng, Ben Hardaway, Bob Clampett, Frank Tashlin, Chuck Jones, Abe Levitow, Dave Detiege, Tex Avery, Gerry
Chiniquy, Cal Dalton, Art Davis, Ken Harris, Maurice Noble
(1938-1964)
Company: Warner Brothers Cartoons (UA-TV)/327 films, 6-8
minutes (1930-1948); Warner Brothers Pictures (WB-TV)/520
films, 6-8 minutes (1948-1964); Warner Brothers Television/35
films, 90 minutes, 24 films, 60 minutes, 78 films, 30 minutes
(1960-   )

Host
Dick Coughlan (1960-1962)

Principal Characters and Voices

Bugs Bunny/Yosemite Sam/
   Tasmanian Devil          Mel Blanc
Elmer Fudd         (1940-1958) Arthur Q. Bryan

Bugs Bunny turned forty in 1979 and is probably the best
known rabbit in the world. The economic lures of recycling have
contributed greatly to his fame. The cartoon star's vintage films
have been in continuous syndication for a quarter century on local
stations since their premiere, September 14, 1956, a record-
shattering feat surpassed only by Popeye the Sailor (q.v.), who
made his TV bow four days earlier. Seen on network schedules
for twenty-one consecutive years, Bugs Bunny appeared for ten
years on ABC and in 1980-1981 had starred for eleven years on
CBS. On network television, the carrot-munching gray rabbit has

far out-distanced the spinach-eating sailor and is the longest running cartoon character seen in a regular series.

Originally produced between 1939 and 1963 by Leon Schlesinger Studios and the Warner Brothers Cartoon Division, with a few made by DePatie-Freleng Enterprises in 1964, the Bugs Bunny films were not made especially for children. But since the mid-fifties they have been telecast on children's shows of one kind or another, at first with a local host. The pre-1948 cartoons premiered on WABD, New York, introduced by Sandy Becker on Bugs Bunny Theater, and nine days later, September 23, 1956, on the Bugs Bunny Cartoon Show, KTLA, Los Angeles, emceed at 6:00-6:30 PM PST, Sunday, by Skipper Frank Herman. Optioned by ABC, the post-1948 films were scheduled in prime time between 1960 and 1962 as The Bugs Bunny Show, also with a host. In between the cartoons, which included Daffy Duck, Sylvester the Cat, Tweety Pie, Foghorn Leghorn, Speedy Gonzales, Pepe Le Pew and others, Dick Coughlan exchanged chatter with his puppet-animals in a hollow tree. Before the program ended, on September 25, 1962, a non-hosted daytime version began on April 7, 1962. Since then, Bugs Bunny has cavorted mainly for the delight of youngsters on Saturday mornings and in specials.

A great deal of inventive tomfoolery went into the Bugs Bunny films, which were developed by the artists at Schlesinger Studios, Warner's cartoon arm between 1935 and 1944. When Schlesinger died, he was credited with having created Bugs, but it seems certain he had little to do with it. Although the genesis has been hotly disputed by several former directors, the fact emerges that, like many cartoon characters, he was not the creation of one individual. An unnamed goofy-looking prototype was the target of Porky's Hare Hunt (Apr 30, 1938), directed by Ben Hardaway and based on a story by Bob Clampett. Two films featured early versions of the long-eared buck-toothed hare, Presto Change-o (Mar 25, 1939) and Hare-um Scare-um (Aug 12, 1939). The gradual emergence of the character was due to the freewheeling artists who worked on the following films, story men Tedd Pierce and Mike Maltese, and animators Friz Freleng, Robert McKimson, Tex Avery, and Chuck Jones. Jones maintains that the name was coined when Hardaway, who was nicknamed "Bugs," asked cartoonist Charles Thorson to draw him up a model rabbit. The sketch complete, Thorson noted "Bugs' bunny" in one corner and passed it on. The name was first used when director Tex Avery made A Wild Hare (Jul 27, 1940), and it has hung on ever since. Avery initially made Bugs a Brooklynese smart-aleck and gave him his famous line "What's up, Doc?," while coolly brandishing his half-eaten carrot.

The film also introduced Elmer Fudd, a classic foil, the first of a succession of characters who would be partnered with Bugs. Equipped with his shotgun, ready for another fruitless pursuit of the unperturbed "Wascally Wabbit," the tubby befuddled hunter would do battle with Bugs for the next twenty years. The droopy red-mustached Yosemite Sam, with his uncontrollable temper, was added as a new nemesis in Hare Trigger (May 5, 1945). Then Robert McKimson's wonderfully silly Tasmanian Devil swirled onto the screen like a tornado in Devil May Hare (Jun 19, 1954), as a delightful zany adversary for the blasé rabbit. Yet, the greatest pairing of all was with the lunatic Daffy Duck, the craziest of the Warner's cartoon characters, with whom Bugs made his funniest films, beginning with Rabbit Fire (May 9, 1951).

Through the years, certain traits and disciplines were developed for the comic hare. For example, usually Bugs Bunny first made his appearance in a natural rabbit habitat, and unlike Woody Woodpecker, Bugs was never mischievous without reason. His pranksterish roles were tempered, and he evolved into a venerable upstart hero, an impish-like champion of the underdog. In a sense he was a counter-revolutionary. Only when he was threatened or disturbed did he decide it was time to fight back. But in moments of personal peril he could be resourceful, cunning, and maniacally ruthless. The animators gave Bugs his indefatigable, nonchalant self-assurance, and few cartoon characters have been endowed with such a strong film personality.

When the second wave of criticism over children's television descended in the early seventies, Bugs Bunny was singled out as Mr. Violence. Some of the films were re-edited by ABC to eliminate the distasteful scenes, much to the dismay of their creators. "Conflict is the source of the comedy," Jones remarked. "If you take out the action, what do you have left?" To a point, Squire Rushnell, vice president of ABC children's entertainment, agreed. "There's a vast difference between the Three Stooges kind of mayhem, with cracks on the head, pokes in the eyes, and punches in the belly, and the fantasy of Bugs Bunny being knocked through a wall and coming out on the other side in good shape." But when Warner Brothers told ABC that in order to keep the show they would have to take an additional half-hour of Road Runner cartoons, Rushnell refused. "The Road Runner epitomizes the old-style cartoons that play heavily on aggressiveness and action," he said.

CBS thought differently, however, and re-edited the cuckoo-like bird cartoons and has telecast The Bugs Bunny/Road Runner Show since September 14, 1968. A consistent ratings leader, on November 26, 1977 it was expanded to ninety-minutes. Faith Heckman, director of CBS children's programming, spliced together some films for five prime time half-hour programs in April-June 1976, including director Friz Freleng's 1958 Oscar winner, Knighty Knight Bugs (Aug 23, 1958), the series' only Motion Picture Academy Award. The first show received a whopping thirty-two per cent audience share and the series encouraged a string of prime time specials. With Michael Tilson Thomas conducting, Bugs played piano in "Carnival of Animals" (Nov 22, 1976); this was followed by the Bugs Bunny "Easter Special" (Apr 7, 1977), "... in Space" (Sep 6, 1977), "Howloween Special" (Oct 26, 1977), "A Connecticut Yankee in King Arthur's Court" (Feb 23, 1978), "How Bugs Bunny Won the West" (Nov 15, 1978), "Valentine Special" (Feb 14, 1979), "A Hare-Brained Thanksgiving" (Nov 15, 1979), "Looney Christmas Tales" (Nov 27, 1979), "... Busting Out All Over" (Apr 21, 1980), "Mystery Special" (Oct 15, 1980), and "All-American Hero" (May 4, 1981), all cut together from the vintage cartoons. Capitalizing on the exposure, the studio released its second compilation of films in 1979, retitled The Bugs Bunny/Road Runner Movie (WB, 1980), with five complete shorts and scenes from others re-edited and directed by Jones.

The pre-1948 package acquired from AAP by United Artists Television included 53 Bugs Bunny and 22 Daffy Duck cartoons among the 327 films, enhancing their syndicated demand. Impressed by UA-TV's financial success, Warner's retained its post-1948 library. In addition to the Bugs Bunny series, the 520 films were re-packaged for the networks under the titles, The Porky Pig Show (q. v. ), The Road Runner Show (q. v. ), Sylvester and Tweety (q. v. ) and The Daffy Duck Show (q. v. ), and syndicated also as Bugs Bunny and His Friends.

For both the packagers and networks the financial returns have been phenomenal. In its ninety-minute form, Bugs Bunny brought CBS about $4. 5 million in net revenues in 1978-1979, contributing about $2 million in direct profit. The most successful show in the Warner Television library, Bugs Bunny has been its most consistent money maker. Extensively licensed, the prolifer-ating rabbit has had his own comic books since they were first distributed by Western Publishing in 1941, Sunday newspaper comic for NEA since 1942 and daily strip since 1948. As a costumed actor, he has danced and sung in "Bugs Bunny Meets the Super-heros" (1979) and "Bugs Bunny in Space" (1980) and in arena stage revues, and has made animated TV commercials for Dr. Pepper and others. Supplying the voice of Bugs, as well as most of the Warner's cartoon characters, was the uniquely versatile Mel Blanc who, oddly enough, says he is allergic to carrots.


BULLWINKLE SHOW, THE

Component Series
    AESOP AND SON, DUDLEY DO-RIGHT OF THE MOUNTIES,
    FRACTURED FAIRY TALES, PEABODY'S IMPROBABLE HISTORY

Network History
    Premiere: September 24, 1961
    NBC/Sep 1961-Sep 1962/Sunday 7:00-7:30 PM
    NBC/Sep 1962-Sep 1963/Sunday 5:30-6:00 PM
    NBC/Sep 1963-Sep 1964/Saturday 12:30-1:00 PM
    ABC/Sep 1964-Sep 1973/Sunday 11:00-11:30 AM
    Last Program: September 2, 1973

Syndicated History

Distributor: Filmtel International/1964-1979; DFS Program Ex-
    change/1979-
Producers: Jay Ward, Bill Scott
Directors: Bill Hurtz, Pete Burness, Ted Parmelee
Company: Jay Ward Productions with Producers Associates for
    Television/78 films

Narrators

    William Conrad/"Bullwinkle"

Edward Everett Horton/"Fractured Fairy Tales"
Charles Ruggles/"Aesop and Son"

Principal Characters and Voices

| | |
|---|---|
| Bullwinkle B. Moose/Dudley Do-<br>Right/Mr. Peabody | Bill Scott |
| Rocket J. Squirrel/Natasha<br>Fatale/Nell | June Foray |
| Snidely Whiplash | Hans Conried |
| Boris Badenov/Inspector Fenwick | Paul Frees |
| Sherman | Walter Tetley |

The Bullwinkle Show starred a blanket-eared, wall-eyed, stupid-looking moose, and his smarter pal, Rocky, the flying squirrel. With some additional episodes and new components, it was lifted from the earlier Rocky and His Friends (q. v.). In that series, the oafish moose captured both critical acclaim and audience fancy and, capitalizing on his popularity, was promoted to host his own show. The serials were the wraparound segments, drenched in funny satire, witty puns, and laced with comical action. The amusingly different heroes were themselves a put-down of the traditional cute animal characters in fairyland tales.

As earlier aficionados were aware, Bullwinkle B. Moose and Rocket J. Squirrel were up-home boys from Frostbite Falls, Koochiching County, Minnesota. For most of their continued adventures, they were engaged in a recurring struggle with a pair of sinister agents employed by Mr. Big, a midget headquartered at the Krumlin, and his immediate inferior, Fearless Leader, a scarfaced Nazi type. They matched what wits they had with the ineptomaniac Boris Badenov, who sounded like Bert Gordon's Mad Russian, and his deadly companion, Natasha Fatale, who looked like Garbo and talked like Gabor. These good old-fashioned spies from Pottsylvania spoke in thick Slavic accents. Narrated by William Conrad, later known as Frank Cannon (CBS, 1971-1976), the intrigue abounded in personage and place parody. For example, François Villain was not a French symbolist poet, but a bad guy, Gorgeous Gorge was not a wrestler but a gap in the Canadian Rockies, "violence" were flowers, and a crime wave was a hairstyle adopted by lawbreakers in the 1890s.

At first, the programs were introduced by a Bullwinkle puppet who once, in a light-hearted admonition, asked all tots in the audience to pull the knobs off their sets. "In that way," the Moose assured them, "we'll be sure to be with you next week." After about twenty thousand small-fry complied, NBC was furious. So a week later they were asked to put them back on with glue, "and make it stick!" Soon thereafter, the puppet Moose, voiced by Bill Scott, the chief writer, was dropped.

The components included several holdovers from Rocky, also created by Scott and Jay Ward. On "Fractured Fairy Tales," Edward Everett Horton narrated classic children's stories such as "Red Riding Hood," in which the sole goal of a mature and sincere wolf was to kick the Ridinghood habit. "Peabody's Improbable History" presented the historic trips of the knowledgeable dog and his young friend Sherman, via the Wayback Machine. Also, Charles Ruggles told ludicrous up-dated animal fables credited to the Greek philosopher in "Aesop and Son." In short segments, Bullwinkle reappeared as the nonsensical "Mr. Know-it-all," fielding queries read by Rocky, and in "Bullwinkle's Corner" read a minute-and-a-half of inane poetry like "I Shot an Arrow Into the Air."

In a new segment, a member of the Royal Canadian Mounted Police was continually humiliated by his enemies in the Northwest Territory, "over-run by Canadians and smugglers." An impeccably correct but unknowing failure, the blond, square-jawed, thick-headed lawman was "Dudley Do-Right of the Mounties," repackaged later as The Dudley Do-Right Show (q. v.). Dudley's girlfriend, Nell, the daughter of his boss, Inspector Fenwick, was usually in the clutches of his arch enemy, Snidely K. Whiplash. In one episode of this hissing-good melodramatic spoof, Do-Right, beside himself with rage, picked up the nearest object and hurled it at Whiplash. Unfortunately it happened to be Nell. As Whiplash caught her, he snarled, "I have her, and you shall never have her back--nor any other part of her!"

With clean fun for children and sparkling wit for adults, Bullwinkle was one of the most sophisticated, imaginative and humorous of the made-for-TV cartoons. Vigorously promoted, the moose was honored with a helium balloon likeness in Macy's 1961 Thanksgiving Day Parade and merchandised in novelties and toys. The NBC series was switched to Saturday beginning September 23, 1963 and ending September 5, 1964. Popular for over a decade, while coincidentally in syndication, it returned for nine years on ABC beginning September 20, 1964.


## BUTCH CASSIDY AND THE SUN DANCE KIDS

Network History
    Premiere:  September 8, 1973
    NBC/Sep 1973-Dec 1973/Saturday 10:00-10:30 AM
    NBC/Jan 1974-Aug 1974/Saturday 11:30-12:00 AM
    Last Program:  August 31, 1974
Executive Producers/Directors:  William Hanna, Joseph Barbera
Producer:  Alex Lovy
Company:  Hanna-Barbera Productions/13 films

Principal Characters and Voices

| | |
|---|---|
| Butch Cassidy | Chip Hand |
| Merilee | Judy Strangis |
| Harvey | Mickey Dolenz |
| Steffy | Tina Holland |
| Elvis (the gang dog) | |

Butch Cassidy and the Sun Dance Kids were a teenage musical foursome and no relation to the infamous pair of western desperados. Butch was the lead singer of a smash bubblegum rock group, and the kids were backup music-makers, Merilee, Harvey and Steffy. Together with their dog Elvis, the group traveled the globe over, to concerts arranged by the World Wide Talent Agency, a front for an international spy ring. Actually a young team of undercover agents working for the United States government, Butch and the gang foiled espionage plots and exposed unsavory spies in such stories as "The Scientist," "The Counterfeiters," "Orient Express" and "Operation G-Minus," each containing a rock tune by the quartet.

 The cartoons were a contrived attempt to ride the popularity of the smash hit movie, <u>Butch Cassidy and the Sundance Kid</u> (TCF, 1969), starring Paul Newman and Robert Redford. The feature was based on an authentic pair of early train and bank robbers. Robert LeRoy Parker (1866-1937) worked for a time as a butcher and later used, among others, the alias "Butch Cassidy," the name adopted from the outlaw Mike Cassidy with whom he first rode. And Harry Longabaugh (1863-1908), once jailed in Sundance, Wyoming, was thereafter known as the "Sundance Kid."

## C. B. BEARS

Component Series
 BLAST OFF BUZZARD, HEYYYYY, IT'S THE KING, POSSE
 IMPOSSIBLE, SHAKE, RATTLE AND ROLL, UNDERCOVER
 ELEPHANT

Network History
 Premiere: September 10, 1977
 NBC/Sep 1977-Jan 1978/Saturday 8:00-9:00 AM

GO GO GLOBETROTTERS
 NBC/Feb 1978-Sep 1978/Saturday 8:30-10:30 AM
 Last Program: September 2, 1978
Executive Producers: William Hanna, Joseph Barbera
Producer: Alex Lovy
Company: Hanna-Barbera Productions/13 films, 60 minutes

Principal Characters and Voices

| | |
|---|---|
| Hustle | Daws Butler |
| Bump | Henry Corden |
| Boogie | Chuck McCann |
| Charlie (voice only) | Susan Davis |

BLAST OFF BUZZARD

Blast Off Buzzard (non-speaking)
Crazy Legs (non-speaking)

HEYYYYY, IT'S THE KING

| | |
|---|---|
| The King/Yukayuka | Lennie Weinrib |

| | |
|---|---|
| Big H | Sheldon Allman |
| Skids | Marvin Kaplan |
| Clyde | Don Messick |
| Zelda | Susan Silo |
| Sheena | Ginny McSwain |

## POSSE IMPOSSIBLE

| | |
|---|---|
| Big Duke/Stick | Daws Butler |
| Blubber | Chuck McCann |
| Sheriff | Bill Woodson |

## SHAKE, RATTLE AND ROLL

| | |
|---|---|
| Shake | Paul Winchell |
| Rattle | Lennie Weinrib |
| Roll | Joe E. Ross |
| Sidney Merciless | Alan Oppenheimer |

## UNDERCOVER ELEPHANT

| | |
|---|---|
| Undercover Elephant | Daws Butler |
| Loud Mouse | Bob Hastings |
| Chief | Mike Bell |

C. B. Bears was the lead-off comedy for this hour-long package with six cartoon components. In an anthropomorphic turnabout on the prime time hit, Charlie's Angels (ABC, 1976-1981), the bruin trio were all-purpose investigators, of sorts, who received their assignments from the heard-but-not-seen Charlie, a sultry-toned distaff dispatcher. The persevering leader of the three bears was Hustle, voiced like Phil Silvers, and his cohorts were Bump the buffoon and the small cub Boogie, the rambunctious sparkplug. Traveling to their assignments in a disguised headquarters-on-wheels, a garbage truck equipped with C. B. radio and closed-circuit TV, the trouble-prone trouble-shooters excelled at getting in and out of fantastic predicaments in such episodes as "The Doomsday Mine," "The Fright Farm" and "Island of Terror."

An animalized parody on the worldly-wise adolescent, Arthur Fonzerelli, portrayed by Henry Winkler on the fifties situation comedy Happy Days (ABC, 1974- ), "Fonzie" was a leader of beasts in "Heyyyyy, It's the King." Hip, slick and cool, the pompadour-maned lion headed a neighborhood gang of distinctive animals, including Big H the hippo, Clyde the ape, Skids the alligator, Yuka-yuka the mole, Zelda the ostrich and Sheena the lioness, in and out of sticky situations like "The Carnival Caper" and "Hot Gold Fever."

A bird on the wing after a hot-footed desert snake called Crazy Legs, "Blast Off Buzzard" was a silent chase and self-destruct comedy with effects and music in the tradition of The Road Runner (q.v.).

Among others, John Wayne was caricatured in "Posse Impossible," a sagebrusher that could have been titled "The Three Misfitters." A trio of clumsy cowpokes, Big Duke, Blubber and

Stick were the deputies of the Matt Dillon self-styled Sheriff of a western town called Saddle Sore. They rescued a kidnapped saloon proprietress in "Big Duke and Li'l Lil," the latter a sound-alike and spitting image of Mae West.

Another spritely trio, "Shake, Rattle and Roll" operated the Haunted Inn--three ghosts with the voice characterizations of comedians Hugh Herbert (1887-1952), Lou Costello (1906-1959) and Marty Allen. They were beset by their own kind, vacationing spooks with problems who needed a rest from their scary jobs, particularly Sidney Merciless.

And in a throw-back to Mission: Impossible (CBS, 1966-1973), a bumbling international agent named "Undercover Elephant" spoiled the plots of sinister masterminds in such assignments as "The Moaning Lisa," a fake apparition voiced like Paul Lynde, continually handicapped by his partner, Loud Mouse.

On February 4, 1978, the cartoons were combined in a two-hour series under the umbrella title Go Go Globetrotters, featuring repeats of The Harlem Globetrotters (q.v.). With the exception of the impossible posse's Blubber, a dead-ringer for Dan Blocker's Hoss Cartwright on Bonanza (NBC, 1959-1973), about the only thing not satirized or carbon-copied on the NBC show was something from an NBC show.


CBS CARTOON THEATER

Component Series
    DINKY DUCK, GANDY GOOSE, HECKLE AND JECKLE, LITTLE
    ROQUEFORT

Network History
    Premiere: June 13, 1956
    CBS/Jun 1956-Sep 1956/Wednesday 7:30-8:00 PM
    Last Program: September 5, 1956
Producer: Mike Grilikes
Company: CBS Terrytoons/52 films, 5-6 minutes

Host
    Dick Van Dyke

Principal Characters and Voices

| | | |
|---|---|---|
| Dinky Duck | (1939-1953) | |
| Gandy Goose | (1938-1955) | Arthur Kay |
| Heckle | (1946-1955) | Dayton Allen/Roy Halee |
| Jeckle | (1946-1955) | Dayton Allen/Roy Halee |
| Little Roquefort/Percy | | |
|   the Cat | (1950-1955) | Tom Morrison |

    CBS Cartoon Theater was the first network prime time animated series and presented the theatrical films of producer Paul Terry which were sold to the network in 1955. Originating from

WCBS, New York, the setting was Dick Van Dyke's living room, where he traded small talk with the "Terry Toons" characters, who responded on film clips. In the premiere, Heckle and Jeckle maneuvered Van Dyke into a trap and the host carried on a conversation with Little Roquefort. Featuring four cartoons in each program, the first show screened the black magpies in Flying South (Aug 15, 1947), Dinky Duck in Welcome Home Stranger (Oct 3, 1941), Gandy Goose and Sour Puss the Cat in Wide Open Spaces (Nov 1, 1950), and Cat Happy (Aug 18, 1950) with Little Roquefort, the pixie-like mouse's first cartoon with Percy the Cat.

The summer program was the initial network regular appearance for Van Dyke, who rose to stardom as Rob Petrie on The Dick Van Dyke Show (CBS, 1961-1966). The "Terry Toons" were rotated also as segments on Mighty Mouse Playhouse (q. v. ) and beginning in October 1956 on the network's series starring Heckle and Jeckle (q. v. ).


## CALVIN AND THE COLONEL

Network History
    Premiere: October 3, 1961
    ABC/Oct 1961-Nov 1961/Tuesday 8:30-9:00 PM
    ABC/Jan 1962-Sep 1962/Saturday 7:30-8:00 PM
    Last Program: September 22, 1962

Syndicated History

Distributor: MCA-TV/1964-
Producers: Joe Connelly, Bob Mosher
Company: Kayro Productions/26 films

Principal Characters and Voices

| | |
|---|---|
| Colonel Montgomery J. Klaxon | Freeman Gosden |
| Calvin Burnside | Charles Correll |
| Maggie Belle Klaxon | Virginia Gregg |
| Sister Sue | Beatrice Kay |
| Gladys | Gloria Blondell |
| Oliver Wendell Clutch | Paul Frees |

Calvin and the Colonel was a thinly disguised Amos 'n' Andy in a situation comedy about a family of southern animals living in a big city up north. The prime time series was created by that old-time blackface pair, Freeman F. Gosden (1896- ) and Charles J. Correll (1890-1972), regarded as originators of the first great radio show, possibly the most popular ever broadcast. The principal voice characterizations were similar to the black dialect first used by the team, January 12, 1926 on WGN, Chicago and later on The Amos and Andy Show (NBC, 1929-1948/CBS, 1948-1954). When the program was transferred to television on CBS between 1951 and 1953, actual black actors were hired to play the parts and Gosden and Correll produced the series. Blacks charged that the cast were stereotypes and a disgrace to their race, and after the films were syndicated continuing protests by the NAACP eventually forced them off television in 1966. Following the nighttime lead of The Flintstones (q. v. ), the pair created an animated situation comedy with a similar format, using animals to avoid a sensitive racial issue.

Colonel Montgomery J. Klaxon was a crafty fox and Calvin Burnside, a cigar-smoking bear whose brains were in hibernation the year around. Thick of voice and head, Calvin was a shiftless but lovable rogue, Klaxon's best friend. In "The Television Job," Maggie Belle, the Colonel's wife, and Sister Sue, his foxy sister-in-law, forced the lazy no-account to take a job delivering TV sets. Abhorring all forms of work, particularly physical, the Colonel fast-talked the dim-witted Calvin into helping him without pay. Other episodes included "The Colonel's Old Flame," "Sister Sue and the Police Captain" and "Colonel Out-Foxes Himself." Calvin's girlfriend was Gladys, a French Poodle, and Oliver Wendell Clutch, a weasel, was a conniving lawyer.

Not a particularly engaging or comical adaptation of the pair's radio and TV shows, after one year on ABC it was syndicated for children's programming. Produced by Van Beuren for RKO, Amos and Andy were voiced by Gosden and Correll for a pair of early theatrical cartoons, The Rasslin' Match (Jan 5, 1934) and The Lion Tamer (Feb 2, 1934).


CAPTAIN AMERICA  See  MARVEL SUPERHEROES, THE


CAPTAIN AND THE KIDS, THE  See  FABULOUS FUNNIES, THE
    and MGM CARTOONS


CAPTAIN CAVEMAN AND THE TEEN ANGELS

Network History

SCOOBY'S ALL-STAR LAFF-A-LYMPICS
    Premire:  September 10, 1977
    ABC/Sep 1977-Jan 1978/Saturday 9:00-10:00 AM
    ABC/Jan 1978-Sep 1978/Saturday 9:30-11:00 AM

SCOOBY'S ALL-STARS
    ABC/Sep 1978-Nov 1978/Saturday 10:00-11:30 AM
    ABC/Nov 1978-Sep 1979/Saturday 9:00-9:30 AM

CAPTAIN CAVEMAN AND THE TEEN ANGELS
    ABC/Mar 1980-Jun 1980/Saturday 10:30-11:00 AM
    Last Program:  June 14, 1980
Executive Producers:  William Hanna, Joseph Barbera
Producer:  Alex Lovy
Director:  Charles A. Nichols
Company:  Hanna-Barbera Productions/8 films, 30 minutes, 16
    films, 11 minutes

Principal Characters and Voices

| | |
|---|---|
| Captain Caveman | Mel Blanc |
| Dee Dee Sykes | Verneé Watson |
| Brenda Chance | Marilyn Schreffler |
| Taffy Dare | Laurel Page |

Captain Caveman and the Teen Angels comprised an investigative team, seeking the solution to perplexing mysteries. A blustery superhero with unpredictable powers, whose action cry was a frenetic scream "Captain Cave-man-n-n-n-n!," the midget-sized, stone-age character clobbered his sneaky foes with a magical club. Not only was it a weapon, but in the hinged-end had a small bird that could accomplish nearly any feat imaginable to achieve his purpose. Set free from a prehistoric block of glacier ice, "Cavey" was the formidable protector of the Teen Angels, unleashed to subdue the conniving crooks they encountered during their dangerous missions. An adolescent version of the deceptively able and sexy crime-fighters on the prime time hit, Charlie's Angels (ABC, 1976-1981), the trio included Brenda, an intellectual and brainy black girl who always carefully explained the meaning of the clues, Dee Dee, an excitable strawberry blond whose ingenious schemes helped expose the culprits, and the mild-mannered brunette Taffy, who seemed to do little but react to the scary situations.

Confronted with a nagging puzzle in each episode, in "Kentucky Cavey" they unravelled the disappearance of the racehorse, Kentucky Rose. Hoping to buy dirt-cheap the oil-rich farm of Dee Dee's Uncle Jefferson Sykes, Brent Butler kidnapped the thoroughbred before a big race to prevent the nag from winning a large stake, which was needed to pay off the mortgage. And in "The Scarifying Seaweed Secret," the Teen Angels exposed a thieving first mate, who electronically controlled a robot shark that frightened divers away from the underwater treasure sought by Captain Jacques La Farge, off the coast of Florida. An important aspect of each mystery was the incorporation of simple clues, encouraging deductive reasoning on the part of young viewers.

Captain Caveman premiered in 1977-1978 as a segment of the two-hour series, Scooby's All-Star Laff-A-Lympics (q. v.) and continued as a component of the shortened Scooby's All-Stars, which ended September 7, 1979. Frequently seen as two episodes of the latter program, the show was repeated in this half-hour format, replacing Spider-Woman (q. v.), beginning March 8, 1980. With Wilma Flintstone and Betty Rubble, Captain Caveman returned in 1980-1981 in new comedies on The Flintstones Comedy Show, a continuation of The Flintstones (q. v.).


CAPTAIN FATHOM

Syndicated History
    Premiere: 1966
Distributor: Entertainment Corporation/1966-1970; Video-Media/
            1970-1975
Producer: Dick Brown

Director: Clark Haas
Company: TV III, Cambria Studios/39 films

Principal Character and Voice

Captain Fathom                              Warren Tufts

     Captain Fathom commanded the submarine "Argonaut" and scourged undersea villainy with his crew. Using illustrative art style, and live action type direction, staging and cutting techniques, the adventures were the underwater counterpart of Cambria Studios' Clutch Cargo (q. v.) and Space Angel (q. v.), the "TV Comic Strips."


CARTOON FUN

Network History
    Premiere: September 26, 1965
    ABC/Sep 1965-Dec 1965/Sunday 4:30-5:00 PM
    Last Program: December 19, 1965
Executive Producer: Peter Piech
Company: Producers Associates for Television/13 films

     Cartoon Fun was an interim program featuring repeats of The Adventures of Hoppity Hooper (q. v.), a jumping frog, "Dudley Do-Right of the Mounties," a dedicated lawman and unknowing failure introduced on The Bullwinkle Show (q. v.), "The World of Commander McBragg," a boastful adventurer seen on Tennessee Tuxedo (q. v.), and "Aesop and Son," a modern version of the fables narrated by Charles Ruggles, initially on Rocky and His Friends (q. v.). An hour-long Yuletide show, December 12, 1965, featured the "Christmas" mishaps of Hoppity Hooper and additional episodes of the other series.


CARTOONIES

Component Series
    THE CAT, GOODIE THE GREMLIN, JEEPERS AND CREEPERS, others

Network History
    Premiere: April 6, 1963
    ABC/Apr 1963-Sep 1963/Saturday 11:00-11:30 AM
    Last Program: September 28, 1963
Producer: Seymour Kneitel
Directors: Seymour Kneitel, Dave Tendlar, James Culhane
Company: Paramount Cartoon Studios/39 films, 6-8 minutes

Hosts
    Paul Winchell
    Jerry Mahoney
    Knucklehead Smiff

Principal Characters and Voices

The Cat                    (1960-1962) Dayton Allen
Goodie the Gremlin         (1961-1963)
Jeepers/Creepers              (1960)

  <u>Cartoonies</u> was typical of the early hosted network shows
with ventriloquist Paul Winchell and his wooden sidekicks, Jerry
Mahoney and Knucklehead Smith, filling the gaps between three
theatrical shorts with jokes, nonsense and commercials.  The program featured films from the "Modern Madcaps" and "Noveltoons"
series produced between 1958 and 1963 at Paramount Cartoon
Studios in New York under Seymour Kneitel.  Several stories that
were planned for <u>Casper, The Friendly Ghost</u> (q. v.), which was
sold by Paramount in the Famous Studios backlog in 1958 to Harvey Publishing, were reworked by the animators for a new character, <u>Goodie the Gremlin</u> (Apr 1961), that was seen in the premiere.  Overly eager to right human frailties, both real and
imagined, Goodie had a knack of turning the simplest problem into
a mushrooming catastrophe.  Subsequent programs presented the
two mutts, "Jeepers and Creepers" (1960), the forerunner of
"Swifty and Shorty" (1964-1966), and the adventures of a supersleuth, "The Cat," (1960-1962), whose voice sounded like Cary
Grant's.
  For the first few weeks, the series was titled <u>Cartoons-
ville</u> and was the summer replacement for the junior version of
<u>ABC</u>'s quiz game, <u>Make a Face</u>* (q. v.).


CASPER AND THE ANGELS  <u>See</u> CASPER, THE FRIENDLY
 GHOST


CASPER, THE FRIENDLY GHOST

Network History

MATTY'S FUNDAY FUNNIES/HARVEYTOONS
 Premiere:  October 11, 1959
 ABC/Oct 1959-Sep 1960/Sunday 5:00-5:30 PM
 ABC/Sep 1960-Sep 1961/Friday 7:30-8:00 PM
 ABC/Oct 1961-Dec 1961/Saturday 7:00-7:30 PM
 Last Program:  December 30, 1961

THE NEW CASPER CARTOON SHOW
 Premiere:  October 5, 1963
 ABC/Oct 1963-Sep 1967/Saturday 11:00-11:30 AM
 ABC/Sep 1967-Sep 1969/Saturday 9:00-9:30 AM

THE NEW ADVENTURES OF CASPER
 ABC/Sep 1969-Dec 1969/Saturday 8:00-8:30 AM
 Last Program:  December 27, 1969

## CASPER AND THE ANGELS
Premiere: September 22, 1979
NBC/Sep 1979-Nov 1979/Saturday 8:30-9:00 AM
NBC/Nov 1979-Apr 1980/Saturday 11:00-11:30 AM
NBC/Apr 1980-May 1980/Saturday 9:00-9:30 AM
Last Program: May 3, 1980

Syndicated History

HARVEY CARTOONS (1963-1973)

THE NEW CASPER CARTOON SHOW (1970-1973)

CASPER, THE FRIENDLY GHOST AND COMPANY (1974- )

Distributor: ABC Films/1963-1972; Worldvision Enterprises/1972-
Executive Producers: Sam Buchwald (1946-1951), Seymour Kneitel,
 Isadore Sparber (1951-1959); William Hanna, Joseph Barbera
 (1979-1980)
Producer: Art Scott (1979-1980)
Directors: Bill Tytla, Dave Tendlar, Ralph Bakshi, Dan Gordon,
 Shamus Culhane (1946-1959); Ray Patterson, George Gordon,
 Carl Urbano (1979-1980)
Company: Famous Studios (1942-1959)/244 films, 6-8 minutes
 (1959-1961); Paramount Cartoon Studios for Harvey Films/26
 films (1963-1969); Hanna-Barbera Productions/13 films (1979-
 1980)

Principal Characters and Voices

| Casper | (1946-1959) Mae Questel/Norma McMillan/ |
| | Gwen Davies/Cecil Roy |
| | (1979-1980) Julie McWhirter |
| Herman | (1947-1959) Arnold Stang |
| Katnip/Baby Huey | (1947-1959) Syd Raymond |
| Little Audrey | (1948-1958) Mae Questel |
| Minnie | (1979-1980) Laurel Page |
| Maxi | (1979-1980) Diane McCannon |
| Hairy Scary/ | |
| Commander | (1979-1980) John Stephenson |

    Casper, the Friendly Ghost, who haunted theaters from the
mid-forties, first materialized on television in 1959. The meek
little apparition, who struggled to befriend humans and animals
alike, only to have his transparent appearance frighten them away,
made his debut onscreen in The Friendly Ghost (May 5, 1946).
The 1944 brainchild of animator Joe Oriolo, Casper was created
for an unsold children's book with writer Sy Reitt; the story was
submitted to Famous Studios and mushroomed into a theatrical
series between 1946 and 1959. To provide additional grist for the
naive little do-gooder stories, several supporting characters were
developed, including Nightmare the Ghost Horse, Spooky, Wendy,
The Good Little Witch, and, as antagonists, the evil Ghostly Trio.

Always cute and giggly, but seldom funny, Casper appeared for over eight years in two ABC series. The events leading to the four-fingered sprite's TV stardom began with his comic books, licensed with other studio creations to Jubilee (1949), St. John's (1950) and Harvey Publishing (1953), where he became the keystone feature of their line. In 1958, Harvey bought all rights to the characters and the cartoons from Famous, the successor to Fleischer Studios established by Paramount Pictures in 1942. Retitled "Harveytoons," they subsequently enjoyed great TV exposure, which in turn bolstered the sales of Harvey comics. Excluding Popeye the Sailor (q.v.), the package contained such notable series as "Baby Huey" (1951-1959), "Herman and Katnip" (1947-1959) and "Little Audrey" (1948-1958). With others, these films and Casper debuted on Matty's Funday Funnies (q.v.) and were syndicated in January 1963 as Harvey Cartoons and repackaged in the mid-seventies as Casper, The Friendly Ghost and Company.

The New Casper Cartoon Show in 1963-1969 presented some post-1963 films produced by Paramount Cartoon Studios, the 1956 successor to Famous. Mixed with the old films, two Casper episodes and one other comedy made up the half-hour show. Briefly retitled The New Adventures of Casper, off-network the series was syndicated until amalgamated in the seventies into one package. In special promotions, Casper was an official recruiter for the Boy Scouts of America and an honorary astronaut who flew to the moon, painted on the outside of "Apollo 16."

Given a new locale and vocabulary, Casper was revived on NBC in 1979-1980. Uttering such cosmic age expressions as "Leapin' Lasers!," the polite poltergeist was a guardian ghost in the year 2179 for a celestial pair of female cops in Casper and The Angels. Maintaining law and order in Space City in their "Space Coupes," the Space Patrol Officers were the scatter-brain redhead Minnie, and Maxie, a black girl with all the smarts. For contrast, a pair of klutzy patrolmen was added in some episodes; Nerdly and Fungo proved to be the weaker sex in stories laced with overtones of women's rights. With a voice and face not unlike comedian Ed Wynn, and sporting a yellow bow tie beneath a red nose, a new apparition named Hairy Scary stole the show. The befuddled spectre was a clumsy buffoon who supplied most of the fun in the routine comedy-crime stories which burlesqued some well-known personalities like Marion Lorne. The cast succeeded in foiling "The Ice Heist," "The Cat Burglar," "The Space Pirate," "The Ghost Busters" and had a hilarious time on "Casper's Camp Out" with some space youngsters, in the two episodes seen in each program. Still four-fingered, the cute sprite also starred in NBC Specials, Casper's Halloween (Oct 30, 1979) and Casper's First Christmas (Dec 18, 1979).


CATTANOOGA CATS, THE

Component Series
AUTOCAT AND MOTORMOUSE, IT'S THE WOLF, AROUND THE WORLD IN 79 DAYS

Network History
   Premiere: September 6, 1969
   ABC/Sep 1969-Sep 1970/Saturday 9:00-10:00 AM
   ABC/Sep 1970-Sep 1971/Sunday 10:30-11:00 AM
   Last Program: September 5, 1971
Executive Producers/Directors: William Hanna, Joseph Barbera
Company: Hanna-Barbera Productions/17 films

Principal Characters and Voices

| | |
|---|---|
| Country | Bill Callaway |
| Groovey | Casey Kasem |
| Scoots | Jim Begg |
| Kitty-Jo/Chessie | Julie Bennett |

AROUND THE WORLD IN 79 DAYS

| | |
|---|---|
| Phileas Fogg | Bruce Watson |
| Jenny Trent | Janet Waldo |
| Happy/Smirky | Don Messick |
| Crumden | Daws Butler |
| Bumbler | Allan Melvin |

AUTOCAT AND MOTORMOUSE (1969-1970)  See  MOTORMOUSE
   AND AUTOCAT

IT'S THE WOLF (1969-1970)  See  MOTORMOUSE AND AUTOCAT

   The Cattanooga Cats were the cartoon hosts for this hour-
long package, bridging four components in short filmed sketches.
The quintet of rakish felines included singers Kitty-Jo and Chessie
and musicians Scoots, Groovey and Country, their leader, who provided a big-beat tune as a bubblegum rock group.   A free adaption
of Jules Verne's 1873 classic novel, "Around the World in 79 Days"
chronicled the globe-circling adventures of Phileas Fogg, his pet
cat Smirky, and able companions Jenny Trent and her pet dog,
Happy.   Attempting to shave one day off the remarkable feat accomplished by his relative, "Finny's" timetable was upset continually by the nasty schemes of his arch enemy Crumden and his
lackey, Bumbler, in such exotic episodes as "India or Bust,"
"Swiss Mis-Adventure," "Arabian Daze" and "Hawaiian Hang-up."
The comedy-adventures were coupled with the humorous skits and
music of The Cattanooga Cats when reduced to a half-hour, September 13, 1970 and repeated on Sunday.
   The other segments were "It's a Wolf," which depicted the
hapless attempts of Mildew to make a meal of Lambsy under the
protective eye of Bristol Hound, and two episodes of "Autocat and
Motormouse," sort of a Tom and Jerry (q. v. ) on wheels, engaged
in cutthroat racing contests.   Under the reversed title, Motormouse
and Autocat (q. v. ) the freewheeling series was rerun with "It's a
Wolf" on ABC in 1970-1971.


CHALLENGE OF THE SUPERFRIENDS  See  SUPERFRIENDS

CHARLIE BROWN  See  PEANUTS


CLUE CLUB

Network History
    Premiere:  August 14, 1976
    CBS/Aug 1976-Sep 1976/Saturday 9:30-10:00 AM
    CBS/Sep 1976-Nov 1976/Saturday 11:30-12:00 AM
    CBS/Nov 1976-Sep 1977/Saturday 8:30-9:00 AM

THE SKATEBIRDS/WOOFER AND WIMPER, DOG DETECTIVES
    CBS/Sep 1977-Nov 1977/Saturday 9:30-10:30 AM
    CBS/Nov 1977-Jan 1978/Saturday 8:00-9:00 AM

CLUE CLUB
    CBS/Sep 1978-Sep 1979/Sunday 9:30-10:00 AM
    Last Program:  September 9, 1979
Executive Producers:  Joseph Barbera, William Hanna
Producer:  Iwao Takamoto
Director:  Charles A. Nichols
Company:  Hanna-Barbera Productions/16 films

Principal Characters and Voices

Larry                          David Joliffe
D. D.                          Bob Hastings
Pepper                         Patricia Stich
Dotty                          Tara Talboy
Woofer                         Paul Winchell
Wimper                         Jim McGeorge
Sheriff Bagley                 John Stephenson

    Clue Club featured a group of bright teenagers and their
dogs, who shared a common love of mysteries.  Ever alert to
puzzling misfortune, and always on the scene, Larry was the
black-headed leader of the crime-solving club, which included
D. D., a redheaded lad, and the blond-haired girl, Pepper.  While
checking out clues or trailing a suspect, the members kept in
touch via C. B. radio with their research genius, thirteen-year-old
Dotty, sometimes through coded messages.  Located at their clubhouse in a garage, "Dynamite Dotty" could quickly supply the low-
down on their friends or foes at a touch of her computer keys.
Sharing in the adventures were the club's southern bloodhounds,
Woofer and Wimper, decked out in Sherlockian hats.  The lethar-
gic Woofer slept and grumbled a lot, annoyed by his more energetic
pal.  The comic canine sleuths provided sub-plot humor and occasionally sniffed out key clues.
    In "The Real Gone Gondola Caper," the Clue Club solved the
disappearance of Clara Caldwell, owner of the Blizzard Mountain
Lodge, who was kidnapped by her scheming nephew, Tom, who
wanted to sell the resort for a tidy sum to a rival.  Of course,
Sheriff Bagwell was around investigating the disappearance too and
was nearby to take custody of the greedy guy.  Other mysteries

included "The Disappearing Airport Caper," "The Weird Seaweed Creature Caper" and "The Vanishing Train Caper." An adaptation of the "who-done-it?" formula, each episode built to a suspenseful last commercial break, allowing young viewers to participate with their own solutions to the crime before the final explanation based on the clues and the dénouement of the culprit.

Ending September 3, 1977, the cartoons returned on September 10, 1977, retitled Woofer and Wimper, Dog Detectives as a segment of The Skatebirds (q.v.), and ran until January 28, 1978. Again as Clue Club, the series was repeated beginning September 10, 1978.


CLUTCH CARGO

Syndicated History
    Premiere:  March 9, 1959
    WNTA, New York/Monday-Friday 5:25-5:30 PM
Distributor:  George Bagnell/1959-1970; Video-Media/1970-1975
Producer/Director:  Dick Brown
Company:  Cambria Studios/260 or 52 films, 5 or 30 minutes

Principal Characters and Voices

| | |
|---|---|
| Clutch Cargo | Richard Cotting |
| Swampy | Hal Smith |
| Spinner/Paddlefoot | Margaret Kerry |

    Clutch Cargo, a serialized comic strip adventure, starred a muscular square-jawed, flaxen-haired hero. Filmed in five installments, each story was planned for five-minute weekday programming, with a reprise in a half-hour format on Saturdays. A onetime cartoonist for the newspaper strip Buz Sawyer (KFS, 1943- ), Clark Haas created the series in partnership with producer Dick Brown and film technician Ed Gillette. Animated largely by camera movement, the films were combined with live action Syncro-Vox, invented by Gillette, which superimposed actual moving lips reading the dialogue over the mouth of the characters. Clutch Cargo and his sidekicks, Swampy, a little boy Spinner and his flop-eared pup Paddlefoot, were threatened by a variety of crackpots and surly villains, including the tyrannical Colonel Bascom B. Bamshot. Seen on over one hundred stations, the low-budget adventures were popular through the early sixties. Produced between 1957-1960, the illustrative art style and live action type direction were somewhat similar to The NBC Comics syndicated as Telecomics (q.v.), and called "TV Comic Strips" by Brown.


COLONEL BLEEP

Syndicated History
    Premiere:  Fall 1957
Distributor:  Richard H. Ullman/1957-

Executive Producer: Richard H. Ullman
Producer: Robert Buchanan
Company: Soundac Color Productions/100 films, 5 minutes

Principal Characters
    Colonel Bleep
    Squeak the Puppet
    Scratch the Caveman

Colonel Bleep was a dedicated peacekeeper maintaining law
and order in a universe a million light years in the future.   An
angular little guy with his head enclosed in a round space helmet
with antennae on top, Bleep was head of the Police Department on
the planet Pheutora.   His space deputies were Squeak the Puppet, a
little boy with hinged limbs, not unlike Pinocchio, and Scratch the
Caveman, wearing skins and all brawn and no brain.   The principal
antagonist was the evil scientist Dr. Destructo, an escaped convict
from the Pheutora jail pursued by Bleep and his pals in his spaceship "The Wonder Rocket."   Known as "the master criminal of the
universe," Dr. Destructo established a base on Pluto and from there
plotted to conquer the galaxy with his gang of outlaws.   Using very
limited animation, the series was presented in five-minute serialized
adventures, with five segments comprising a complete story described by a narrator.


## COMMONWEALTH CARTOON PACKAGE

Component Series
    FLIP THE FROG, TALES OF THE GENIE, TERRYLAND,
    WILLIE WHOPPER, others

Syndicated History
    Premiere:  c1951
Distributor/Owner:  Commonwealth Films/c1951-1972; Black Hawk
    Films/1972-
Producers:  Paul Terry (1921-1929), Ub Iwerks (1930-1936)
Company:  Fables Studio-Pathé/304 B&W films, 5-6 minutes (1921-
    1929); Celebrity Productions/112 B&W, 25 color films, 5-6
    minutes (1930-1936); Van Beuren Studios/15 films, 5-6 minutes

Commonwealth Cartoon Package contained several vintage
theatrical series used for local programming in the fifties including
the sugar coated pills of wisdom produced by Paul Terry (1887-
1971).   Over three hundred silent "Aesop's Fables" (1921-1929),
animated by Fables Studio and released by Pathé Film Exchange,
were retitled "Terryland" by Commonwealth, which added sound
effects and music.   Many of the films featured the spry rural rube
Farmer Al Falfa, created by Terry, and appeared between 1950-
1952 on TV Tots Time (q. v. ), seen locally on WENR, Chicago and
the ABC Eastern Network.   The package also included three series
produced by Ubbe Ert "Ub" Iwerks (1901-1971), Walt Disney's fellow Kansas City artist, who created Mickey Mouse and animated

Plane Crazy (May 15, 1928), Steamboat Willie (Jul 29, 1928) and
The Skeleton Dance (May 10, 1929), the last two Disney's landmark
films. Financed by Pat Powers, Disney's distributor, Iwerks produced his films through Celebrity Productions (1930-1936). Debuting
in Fiddlesticks (Aug 16, 1930), "Flip the Frog" (1930-1933) was his
first character and evolved into a happy-go-lucky humanized amphibian walking upright in thirty-eight routine films, often involving his
girlfriend and a bully. Flip was produced in black-and-white and
released by MGM as was his successor, "Willie Whopper" (1933-
1934), a chubby, freckled-faced little boy who told tall tales in
fourteen undistinguished cartoons, the first Play Ball (Sep 16, 1933).
Launched with Jack and the Beanstalk (Nov 30, 1933), Iwerks also
produced a series of twenty-five color films based on fairy tales,
folklore and literature titled "Comicolor Cartoons" (1933-1936),
which had some inspired scenes and included such stories as The
Headless Horseman (Oct 1, 1934), Don Quixote (Nov 26, 1934) and
Tom Thumb (Mar 30, 1936). Commonwealth serialized this series
in two-parts along with fifteen "Rainbow Parades" (1934-1936) produced by Van Beuren Studios, to provide eighty color cartoons under the new title "Tales of the Genie." Other Van Beuren films
were distributed by Official Films Cartoons (q. v. ) and included in
the Unity Pictures Theatrical Cartoon Package (q. v. ).


COOL McCOOL

Component Series
    HARRY McCOOL

Network History
    Premiere:  September 10, 1966
    NBC/Sep 1966-Dec 1966/Saturday 11:00-11:30 AM
    NBC/Jan 1967-Sep 1967/Saturday 12:00-12:30 PM
    NBC/Sep 1967-Aug 1968/Saturday 12:30-1:00 PM
    NBC/May 1969-Aug 1969/Saturday 9:30-10:00 AM
    Last Program:  August 30, 1969

Syndicated History

Distributor:  Firestone Program Syndication/1969-1979; Gold Key
    Entertainment/1979-
Producer:  Al Brodax
Company:  King Features Syndicate Television/20 films

Principal Characters and Voices

Cool McCool/Harry McCool          Bob McFadden
Number One/Riggs                  Chuck McCann
Friday                            Carol Corbett


    Cool McCool was a gadget-brandishing supersleuth whose
business was "danger." The second series, following Courageous
Cat (q. v. ), conceived by comic book artist Bob Kane, the co-

creator of Batman* (q. v. ), its lead character spoofed Chester
Gould's hawk-nosed detective Dick Tracy (q. v. ) with a liberal mix
of Ian Fleming's intrepid secret agent James Bond (Macmillan,
1953). Taking orders from his boss, Number One, Cool had a
secretary named Friday and was aided by Riggs, a scientific genius
who created all manner of devices, including his transistorized radio
mustache. He also provided the gadgets for the agent's "Coolmo-
bile, " in which he chased a half-dozen recurring master criminals.
The Rattler stole Professor B. Fuddled's shrinking formula and a
Truth Telling Machine. The Owl and his henchwoman, The Pussycat, organized the nation's birds into a crime syndicate, which a
TV network peacock joined. Dr. Madcap used his living hats to
steal the priceless Pearl of Punjab, and with Greta Ghoul, his accomplice, robbed the Potts Gold Company. "The greatest windbag
on earth, " Hurricane Harry threatened to blow down the cities of
the world unless he received a million-dollar ransom. And the
Jack-in-the-Box used a magnet to capture rockets launched at Cape
Carnivorous. These dastardly deeds were ultimately righted,
naturally, by the daring action of the coolest detective of them all.
        Also featured was one mis-adventure of "Harry McCool, "
the father of Cool. Harry and his companions, Tom and Dick,
were klutzy policemen commanded by the hard-nosed Sergeant, in
comedies reminiscent of Matt Sennett's Keystone Kops flickers.
They chased about a lot in slapstick antics, pursuing such thieves
and hijackers as the Green Dragon, the Wood-Chopper, Mighty
Morris and Big Benny. Each half-hour show combined four six-
minute episodic segments of the two series.


COURAGEOUS CAT AND MINUTE MOUSE

Syndicated History
    Premiere: September 1960
Distributor: Prime TV Films/1960-
Executive Producer: Sam Singer
Producers: Marvin Woodward, Reuben Timmins
Director: Sid Marcus
Company: Trans Artists Productions/130 films, 5 minutes

Principal Characters and Voices

Courageous Cat/Minute Mouse          Bob McFadden

        Courageous Cat and Minute Mouse, unlike most similar
animal pairs, worked together as a team of masked superheroes.
Lacking subtlety, the series was conceived by comic book artist
Bob Kane, as an anthropomorphic parody on Batman* (q. v. ), his
famous caped crusader. Based in the Cat Cave, Courageous took
his orders from a dog, the Police Chief of Empire City. The
crime-fighters pursued their cunning animal adversaries in the
"Catmobile" and were equipped with the thousand-purpose Catgun,
a Catgimmick variant on Batman's utility belt. The weapon apparently fired everything except bullets, often squirting their

enemies with sticky glue or enmeshing them in a net. Numbered among their descriptive antagonists were Shoo Shoo Fly, Professor Shaggy Dog, Rodney Rodent, Black Cat, Iron Shark, Harry the Gorilla and the insane genius, Professor Noodle Stroodle. One of the more humorous villains was a cigar-chomping amphibian that spat out dialogue in Edward G. Robinson's gangster style in "The Case of the Frogmen." The half-hour programs presented four or five episodes, among them "The Case of the Professor's Machine," "The Case of the Blinking Planet," "The Case of the Mad Cowboys," "The Case of the Minced Spies" and "The Case of the Saggin' Dragon."

## CRUSADER RABBIT

Syndicated History
    Premiere: Fall 1949

(NEW) CRUSADER RABBIT
    Premiere: Fall 1957
Distributor: Jerry Fairbanks (NBC)/1949-1951; Creston (Regis Films)
    /1957-1965; Wolper TV Series (Metromedia)/1965-1969
Executive Producers: Jerry Fairbanks (1949-1951); Shull Bonsall
    (1957-1958)
Producers: Jay Ward, Alexander Anderson (1949-1951)
Company: Television Arts Productions/195 B&W films, 4 minutes
    (1948-1951); Creston Studios/260 films, 4 minutes (1957-1958)

Narrator
    Roy Whaley (1949-1951)

Principal Characters and Voices

| | | |
|---|---|---|
| Crusader Rabbit | (1949-1951) | Lucille Bliss |
| | (1957-1958) | Ge Ge Pearson |
| Ragland T. Tiger | | Vern Louden |
| Dudley Nightshade | (1949-1951) | Russ Coughlan |

Crusader Rabbit holds the dual distinction of being the first cartoon serial and the first limited animation series made for television. A small, long-eared rabbit, Crusader was partnered with a larger companion, Ragland T. Tiger, both of whom walked upright in their adventures. The mock-Arthurian characters were conceived in 1948 by Jay Ward and Alexander Anderson, the nephew of cartoon producer Paul Terry, and appeared in a presentation film, "The Comic Strips of Television" with two other features, "Hamhock Jones," a detective, and Dudley Do-Right (q.v.). Through Jerry Fairbanks, a contract film supplier for the network, NBC financed several films starring the pair. They were designed as four-minute cliffhangers with five installments comprising a complete story, and could be stripped separately on weekdays or strung together for a weekly program. "We wanted to get the effect of an animated comic strip," Ward said. "The commercials would go in between the short segments." A landmark TV concept, the format was used for over a decade by subsequent cartoon producers.

Produced in San Francisco and Hollywood between 1948 and 1951, the initial films were turned down by the network in February 1949, but the series was continued under Fairbanks for syndication. The NBC O&O stations picked up the cartoons for such local programs as Children's Theater (WNBT/WRCA/WNBC, 1949-1961), hosted by Ray Forrest in New York. In 1951, Crusader Rabbit led the list of the five most popular programs among Chicago smallfry over such formidable competition as Hopalong Cassidy* (q. v.), Wild Bill Hickok* (q. v.), Howdy Doody* (q. v.) and Uncle Mistletoe* (q. v.).

Seemingly determined to please themselves as well as their audience, the producers created their stories around punned titles like "West We Forget" and "Gullible's Travels." Crusader, whose hometown was Galahad Glen, was the quick-witted leader of the courtly team, while Rags possessed the strength and propensity for getting both of them in trouble. The chivalrous pair once were confronted by Arson and Sterno, a two-headed, fire-breathing dragon that constantly bickered with itself and had a bad case of heartburn. The redressing heroes told the monster he was serving evil. "We know," replied the heads in unison, "but a job's a job, and think of the residuals we'll get." Later the heroes were seen in the deadly clutches of a python. Understanding music could perhaps save them, for the snake had a cobra fondness for tunes and longed to sway in a basket, "Quick Rags," said Crusader, "whistle a chorus of Dixie!" But Rags hesitated, afraid that it had not been cleared. "Is it in the public domain?" Other nasty villains they encountered were the brutish and diabolical Brimstone Brothers, Bigot and Blackheart, Archilles the Heel, Babyface Barracuda, Belfry Q. Bat, Wetstone Whiplash and their arch nemesis, the dastardly Dudley Nightshade. A departure from the mayhem associated with physical action, the series relied heavily on situation comedy, deriving humor from the satiric knight-errantry, comical antagonists and contemporary dialogue.

Production ceased in 1951 when a lawsuit arose over the rights to the black-and-white series. Commercial producer Shull Bonsall, owner of TV Spots, bought the rights from NBC after a long, involved legal battle involving T. A. P. and Fairbanks against the network. The matter was concluded when Bonsall bought Television Arts, granting Ward and Anderson all rights to their other characters, including a moose and flying squirrel which Ward later starred in Rocky and His Friends (q. v.). Through his Creston Studios, Bonsall produced a new color series in 1957-1958, maintaining the format and flavor of the original cartoons with such themes as "Claude Beauty on African Safari" and "The Search for the Missing Link." Thirteen hour-long stories in ten four-minute installments were produced, allowing for commercial breaks. The new Crusader Rabbit was syndicated also, appearing on NBC O&O stations, serialized in New York on Hi Mom (WRCA, 1957-1959) and later on WNBC between 1961 and 1963 and 1964-1966, and beginning April 11, 1959 on KNBH, Los Angeles, hosted by Ken Peters.

CYBORG BIG "X"

Syndicated History
    Premiere:  Fall 1967
Distributor:  Transglobal Company/1967-
Company:  Tokyo Movie Studios, Japan, Global Production Company/
    59 B&W films

Principal Character
    Akira/Cyborg Big "X"

    Cyborg Big "X, " alias Akira, had the brain of a human and
the body of a robot.  Armed with a special magnetic pen, his sole
weapon, Big "X" (ten) battled his contemporary enemies in the
criminal world.  The half-hour science fiction series was adapted
from the Japanese comic strip Big X, created in 1963 by Osamu
Tezuka, the originator of Astro Boy (q. v. ).  The program debuted
on Japanese television August 3, 1964 and ended October 4, 1965.
In Japan it was known simply as Big X.


DAFFY DUCK SHOW, THE

Component Series
    FOGHORN LEGHORN, PEPE LE PEW, SPEEDY GONZALES,
    others

Network History
    Premiere:  November 4, 1978
    NBC/Nov 1978-Sep 1979/Saturday 10:30-11:00 AM
    NBC/Sep 1979-Dec 1979/Saturday 8:00-8:30 AM
    NBC/Dec 1979-Sep 1981/Saturday 10:30-11:00 AM

Executive Producer:  Hal Geer
Directors:  Friz Freleng, Art Davis, Chuck Jones, Robert McKim-
    son, Rudy Larriva, Phil Monroe, Ted Bonniker, Alex Lovy
    (1948-1967)
Company:  Warner Brothers Television/16 films

Principal Characters and Voices

Daffy Duck/Speedy Gonzales/
    Pepe Le Pew                          Mel Blanc

    The Daffy Duck Show debuted inauspiciously as a mid-season
replacement in a repackaged program from the Warner Brothers
post-1948 cartoon library.  For over twenty years the lisping black
drake was a supporting character on the various TV shows of Bugs
Bunny (q. v. ) and its spin-offs.  Created by director Fred "Tex"
Avery for his fledgling fling in the theatrical film Porky's Duck
Hunt (Apr 17, 1937), perhaps the looniest of all the "Looney Tunes"
produced by Leon Schlesinger Studios, the character was informally
called "The Crazy-Darnfool Duck. "  Bob Clampett animated the

now-famous scene in which Porky admonished everyone, "Be v-v-very q-q-quiet," as he lurked in the reeds near a pond.   Then, at the sight of the lone mallard, an army of hunters sprang up from the grass to fill the sky with buckshot.   When the smoke cleared, the energetic duck hopped spastically on the water, turned hand-springs, bounced on his head, and splashed on the surface, crying "Hoo-hoo, Hoo-hoo," in the fashion of comedian Hugh Herbert (1887-1952), and finally danced away to infinity.   The film owed its hilarious moments to the superb direction of Avery, who made Daffy the top banana and Porky, its star, more of a straight man.   Subsequently developed as a thoroughly selfish, avaricious, and somewhat cowardly character, the web-footed loony was officially christened in his second film, Daffy Duck and Egghead (Jan 1, 1938), and was firmly established as a foul feathered friend through his black coloring.

Among the rotated supporting films were those featuring Bob McKimson's Foghorn Leghorn, the cigar-smoking rooster voiced like Kenny Delmar's Senator Claghorn, that debuted in Walky Talky Hawky (Aug 31, 1946), and his feisty antagonist Henry Hawk, that bowed in The Squawkin' Hawk (Aug 1, 1942), and McKimson's fastest mouse in all Mexico--first seen in Cat-Tails for Two (Aug 29, 1953) and later in Speedy Gonzales (Sep 17, 1955), an Oscar-winner as the Best Short Subject.   Also, there was the amorous French skunk Pepe Le Pew, originated by story man Tedd Pierce in the Charles Boyer style of sophisticated braggadocio, directed by Chuck Jones in his premiere, The Odor-able Kitty (Jan 5, 1945). Daffy appeared with several other Warner's characters, including Sylvester the Cat, that had his own TV series, Sylvester and Tweetie (q.v.).   Often teamed with other cartoon stars, he was matched effectively with Porky Pig, for example in Jones' sublimely silly Robin Hood Daffy (Mar 8, 1958), in which he was a hapless hero of Sherwood Forest, encumbered by his buck-and-a-quarter staff.   But of all his partners, Daffy was at his best when paired with Bugs Bunny, since his aggressive approach contrasted well with Bugs' laid-back personality.

Including many with Speedy, twenty-one films starring Daffy were produced between 1964 and 1967 by DePatie-Freleng Enterprises for Warner's.   Also, graphically, he first appeared with other studio characters in Looney Tunes and Merry Melodies comic books for Dell and in 1953 in his own Daffy comics, the title expanded to Daffy Duck in 1959 and continued in 1963 by Gold Key. His TV bow came in 1955 in the syndicated Looney Tunes (q.v.), a black-and-white pre-1948 cartoon package withdrawn in 1969. Between 1970 and 1971, Daffy and Pepe Le Pew comedies were seen on The Lancelot Link, Secret Chimp Show* (q.v.).   Using some new bridges and wraparounds, Daffy's films were re-edited for some NBC half-hour specials, Daffy Duck's Easter Show (Apr 1, 1980), supported by Speedy and Sylvester, and Daffy Duck's Thanks-for-giving Special (Nov 20, 1980).

DASTARDLY AND MUTTLEY IN THEIR FLYING MACHINES

Network History
    Premiere:  September 13, 1969
    CBS/Sep 1969-Sep 1970/Saturday 9:30-10:00 AM
    CBS/Sep 1970-Sep 1971/Saturday 1:00-1:30 PM
    Last Program:  September 3, 1971
Theme:  "Stop That Pigeon" by Bill Hanna, Hoyt Curtin

Syndicated History

THE FUN WORLD OF HANNA-BARBERA

Distributor:  Taft H-B Program Sales/1977-1979; Worldvision Enterprises/1979-
Executive Producers/Directors:  William Hanna, Joseph Barbera
Producer:  Iwao Takamoto

Principal Characters and Voices

Dick Dastardly/The General                Paul Winchell
Muttley/Yankee Doodle/Klunk/
    Zilly                                 Don Messick

    Dastardly and Muttley in Their Flying Machines featured a
pair of goof-ups in endless pursuit of a carrier pigeon, bearing a
message for the good guys.  Drawing its inspiration from the film
Those Magnificent Men in Their Flying Machines (TCF, 1965), it
made Dick Dastardly a near caricature of British comedian Terry-
Thomas, the archetypal villain in the movie.  And the self-minded
canine Muttley, as well as the concept, owed something to the success of "Snoopy and the Red Baron." It might have been better
titled "Those Malevolent Men in Their Flying Machines," since
Dastardly was a despicable scoundrel partnered with the less than
staunch hound as First World War aviators.  The rakish airmen
were members of the Vulture Squadron, under orders from The
General, who commanded them by phone to repeatedly intercept
the vital messages of the elusive American courier, Yankee Doodle
Pigeon.  But the ninnies continually fell victim to their own me-
chanically flawed aircraft, Rube Goldberg-like machines invented by
two hopelessly misfit mechanics, the Dopey-like Klunk and the cowardly Zilly, who interpreted Klunk's blubbering jibberish.  In their
mission to "Stop That Pigeon," the original title of the series, the
accident-prone aces chased their quarry in all manner of bizarre
planes, intricately designed by Iwao Takamoto.  But the plucky
pigeon defiantly tootled "Charge!" on his bugle and flew on his way,
unperturbed by their silly schemes.
    Dastardly, whose favorite expletive was "Drat!," and in ex-
treme emphasis "Double or Triple Drat!," and Muttley, noted for
mumbles like "snackle-razzle-futzal-crazz," appeared in the two
wraparound segments.  Between were "Wing Dings," a short segment featuring the characters in three slapstick sight-gags.  In
"The Magnificent Muttley," a day-dream sequence, the dog por-

trayed classic heroes, as in "The Masked Muttley," a zany take-off on The Lone Ranger* (q. v. ).   In his regular role, the canine was an anti-hero, frequently a bumbler, called upon to "Do something Muttley!" when one of Dastardly's devices misfired.   Often he held out for a coveted medal as a reward for his selfish acts of heroism.

Dastardly and Muttley was part of a new Saturday cartoon comedy line-up initiated in 1969-1970 by Fred Silverman, CBS vice president for daytime programs.   At his suggestion, the pair were lifted as nasty tricks competitors from The Wacky Races (q. v. ), and replaced two other characters originally designed for the series, becoming spin-off animated pioneers with The Perils of Penelope Pitstop (q. v. ).


## DEPUTY DAWG

Syndicated History
   Premiere:  October 1, 1960
   WGN, Chicago/Saturday 10:00-10:30 AM CST
Distributor:  CBS Films/1960-1971; Viacom International/1971-

Network History

THE DEPUTY DAWG SHOW
   Premiere:  September 11, 1971
   NBC/Sep 1971-Jan 1972/Saturday 9:00-9:30 AM
   NBC/Jan 1972-Sep 1972/Saturday 8:30-9:00 AM
   Last Program:  September 2, 1972
Executive Producer:  Bill Weiss
Directors:  Arthur Barsch, Robert Kuwahara, Connie Rasinski,
   Dave Tendlar
Company:  CBS Terrytoons/104 films, 5-6 minutes (1960-1970),
   52 films (1971-1972)

Principal Characters and Voices

Deputy Dawg/Vincent Van Gopher/
   Ty Coon/The Sheriff          Dayton Allen


Deputy Dawg was an amiable but not too bright lawman trying to uphold law and order in Mississippi, and hounded by a posse of pranksters.   In scenarios with more dialogue jokes than sight gags, the films followed the established formula of a central character surrounded by a supporting cast of funny animals.   Among the pot-bellied southern deputy's friends and foes were the buck-tooth, nearsighted Vincent "Vince" Van Gopher, Ty Coon, a bow-tie-wearing Raccoon, Muskie the Muskrat and Pig Newton, a no-account that tried to rob the local corn fields.   The other episodic characters ranged from a Fox and a Tennessee Walkin' Horse to a Beaver and a catfish-poaching Pelican.   Deputy Dawg's immediate superior, The Sheriff, appeared as the only human caricature in the stories. Created and written principally by Larz Bourne, aided by storymen

Jack Mercer, Chris Jenkyns and others, the comedies were generally based on the bumbling peacekeeper's staggering ineptitude, resolved by his often accidental and astonishing good luck in such stories as "The Fragrant Vagrant," "Peanut Pilferer," "Dagnabit, Rabbit" and "Mama Magnolia's Pecan Pies."

First syndicated in 1960, Deputy Dawg was featured in some one hundred fifty local children's shows, sponsored by W. H. Lay Potato Chips in forty-seven markets. Mainly seen on Saturdays or late afternoons, the cartoons were often coupled with several other syndicated series and appeared on WGN, Chicago, in this format. NBC contracted for a half-hour version in 1971-1972 and CBS Terrytoons repackaged the series with new bridges, thirty-three "Gandy Goose" and eighty-eight other "Terry Toons," combining two color cartoons with two featuring Deputy Dawg in each show. After the program premiered in 1960, executive producer Bill Weiss received a number of requests from Twentieth Century-Fox Films' exchange managers, particularly in Texas, to release the TV cartoons to theaters. Consequently, the studio produced four theatrical cartoons featuring the character, beginning with Where There's Smoke (Feb 1962), directed by Bob Kuwahara.


## DEVLIN

Network History
    Premiere: September 7, 1974
    ABC/Sep 1974-Aug 1975/Saturday 10:00-10:30 AM
    ABC/Sep 1975-Feb 1976/Sunday 10:30-11:00 AM
    Last Program: February 15, 1976

Syndicated History

Distributor: DFS Program Exchange/1979-
Executive Producers: William Hanna, Joseph Barbera
Producer: Iwao Takamoto
Director: Charles A. Nichols
Company: Hanna-Barbera Productions/16 films

Principal Characters and Voices

Ernie Devlin            Mike Bell
Tod Devlin              Mickey Dolenz
Sandy Devlin            Michele Robinson
Hank                    Norman Alden

Devlin was the family name of three orphaned youngsters, aged eleven to twenty, who supported themselves as a daredevil motorcycle stunt team. Catapulting through a ring of fire and performing other hazardous feats, Ernie was the eldest and a star attraction with a small traveling circus. His teenage brother, Tod, was a behind-the-scenes skilled mechanic, who was also skilled at various stunts and helped work out the complicated routines for their act. Their younger sister, Sandy, another accomplished rider, rounded out the troupe. Substituting a healthy family relationship for overt violence, the series emphasized the teamwork of the youngsters and their ability to solve problems on their own, as encouraged by Hank, the circus owner and a paternal figure. Operating out of their motor home, the Devlins used their skills in pleasant if perfunctory adventure stories, involved in a motor cross-like roundup of escaped menagerie animals in "Save That Lion," and overcoming sabotage to their motorbikes by an invidious co-performer during a tricky routine in "The Challenge." Other episodes included "Victory over Fear," "Tod's Triumph" and "Sandy's Turn."

Safety tips pertaining to motorcycle riding were presented in each show, such as the use of protective helmets and obeying speed laws and driving standards.


DICK TRACY SHOW, THE

Syndicated History
    Premiere: September 7, 1961
    WPIX, New York/Monday-Friday 5:00-5:30 PM
Distributor: UPA Productions of America/1961-

Network History

ARCHIE'S TV FUNNIES
    Return: September 11, 1971
    CBS/Sep 1971-Sep 1972/Saturday 10:30-11:00 AM
    CBS/Sep 1972-Sep 1973/Saturday 12:00-12:30 PM
    Last Program: September 1, 1973
Executive Producer: Henry G. Saperstein
Director: Abe Levitow
Company: UPA Pictures/130 films, 5 minutes (1960-1961)

Principal Character and Voice

Dick Tracy                          Everett Sloane


    The Dick Tracy Show added some partners for Chester Gould's scrupulously honest detective, to help the black-haired, eagle-nosed sleuth battle some master criminals from his comics. In different episodic adventures, Tracy was teamed with Heap O'Calorie, The Retouchables Squad, Hemlock Holmes, Jo Jitsu, a master of karate and ju jitsu, and Go Go Gomez, a Mexican gumshoe voiced by Mel Blanc, somewhat like his characterization for Speedy Gonzales. In the original stories, the law enforcers tangled with five sets of partners-in-crime, whose grotesque appearance or mannerisms were suggested by their names: Sketch Paree and The Mole, Pruneface and Itchy, Flattop and B B Eyes, Stooge Villa and Mumbles, and The Brow and Noodles. Voices for the characters were supplied by Blanc, June Foray, Paul Frees, Joan Gardner and Benny Rubin.
    Steely of eye and square of jaw, Dick Tracy was the first realistic police-adventure comic strip, showing death in detail. It

can claim an important niche in American comics' history, and it inspired a morgue full of imitators.  Born as a Sunday newspaper feature, October 4, 1931, for The Chicago Tribune-New York News Syndicate, it appeared as a daily strip a week later.  An anthology of the plainclothes detective's adventures was published as The Celebrated Cases of Dick Tracy (Chelsea House, 1970 & 1980), with an introduction by Ellery Queen.  Included was a memorable set of bad guys, whose names often spelled their worst traits backwards and nearly always matched their appearance:  villains such as The Blank, a faceless man whose name was Frank Redrum, Jerome Trohs, a midget who was scalded to death in a shower, Big Boy, Haf-and-Haf, Angeltop and Torcher.  Gould also created such endearing characters as Gravel Gertie, B. O. Plenty, Junior Tracy, Diet Smith and Vitamin Smith.  Tracy and Tess Trueheart were married on Christmas Day in 1949, daughter Bonnie Braids was born two years later and son Joseph Flintheart Tracy, twenty-four years after that.  Gould retired in 1977 and the strip was continued by writer Max Collins and artist Rick Fletcher.  A radio show, films and TV series in 1950-1951 were adapted as Dick Tracy* (q. v. ) and the strip generated a parody, Fearless Fosdick* (q. v. ), a detective so inept that he once killed forty-two people while trying to arrest a balloon vendor.

Originally titled "The Adventures of Dick Tracy," the TV cartoons were designed in a flexible format for use with an on-camera, local station host, known as the "Chief."  On WPIX, New York, the episodes were stripped on weekdays and introduced by a costumed "Chief," Joe Bolton.  Between 1971 and 1973, several films were reprised on CBS as segments of Archie's TV Funnies, one of the sequels of The Archies (q. v. ).


## DO DO--THE KID FROM OUTER SPACE

Syndicated History
    Premiere:  August 23, 1965
    KHJ, Los Angeles/Monday-Friday 4:00-4:30 PM PST
Distributor:  Fremantle International/1965-1970
Producers:  John Halas, Joy Batchelor
Company:  Halas and Batchelor, London/78 films, 5 minutes

Principal Characters
    Do Do
    Compy
    Professor Fingers


Do Do--The Kid from Outer Space and his pet Compy were aliens from the atomic planet Hena Hydro.  The normal looking youngster and his strange looking companion were dispatched to Earth to assist Professor Fingers, who was engaged in research delving into unresolved scientific mysteries.  One of the earliest English TV cartoon series distributed in the United States, during its first run syndication the episodes were stripped weekdays on KHJ, Los Angeles, supported by two other animated series.

DR. SEUSS

Network History
Premiere: December 18, 1966
CBS/Dec 1966-Dec 1978/Periodic/Various PM
ABC/Oct 1979- /Periodic/Various PM

Executive Producer: Theodor Seuss Geisel
Producers: Chuck Jones, David DePatie, Friz Freleng
Directors: Chuck Jones, Hawley Pratt, Alan Zaslove
Company: Chuck Jones Enterprises, Geisel Productions/5 films
(1966-1978); DePatie-Freleng Enterprises, Geisel Productions/3
films (1975-1980)

Narrators
Boris Karloff (1966)
Hans Conried (1970-1973)
Eddie Albert (1972)

Principal Characters and Voices

| | | |
|---|---|---|
| The Grinch | (1966 & 1979) | Thurl Ravenscroft |
| Cat in The Hat | (1972 & 1973) | Allan Sherman |
| Zax/Sylvester/McBean | (1973) | Bob Holt |
| Joe/Sam | (1973) | Paul Winchell |
| Pontoffel Pock | (1980) | Wayne Morton |

Dr. Seuss, the pseudonym of writer-illustrator Theodor
Seuss Geisel for over forty juvenile books, brought his fantasy
stories to television in a sprightly series of periodic specials.
With The Cat in The Hat (1957) Dr. Seuss began a revolution in
young children's readers; his "Beginner Books" became renowned
for their brilliance in interesting the very young in actual reading.
Through the origination of absurd nonsense creatures, given such
names as Yuzz-a-ma-Tuzz, and the invention of new words, Geisel
created what he termed "logical insanity" in the Dr. Seuss books.
He graduated from Dartmouth College, was a humorist and cartoonist for Judge, Vanity Fair, Liberty and other national magazines,
an advertising illustrator for the "Quick Henry, the Flit!" cartoons
for Standard Oil of New Jersey, and a filmmaker with the U.S.
Army Signal Corps during the Second World War. Two of his doc-
umentary films won Academy Awards, as did his UPA cartoon
Gerald McBoing-Boing (q. v.), which became a TV series. Known
for his absurd and floppy animals, which he says are "real people,
sort of," Geisel's books were first adapted by Chuck Jones.
The most famous Dr. Seuss character was the nasty, anti-
Christmas Grinch. First published in 1957, "How the Grinch Stole
Christmas" became the most expensive half-hour animated cartoon
created for television when it premiered on December 18, 1966.
CBS paid $315,000 for two showings. Narrated by Frankenstein's
immortal monster, Boris Karloff (1888-1969), the fantasy was set
in Whoville, the home of the Whos, whimsical animal-like creatures
that lived in pumpkin-shaped houses and liked to celebrate Christmas.

North of Whoville lived The Grinch, with green skin, red eyes and a heart two sizes too small, a creation that grew out of Geisel's disdain for Yuletide commercialism.   The Grinch hated Christmas-- the noise of the toys, the singing, the feast of roast beast--even more than Scrooge did, and in a grim plan decided to steal the holiday.   Three original songs by Geisel and Albert Hague were featured, with the original soundtrack released on King Leo records.

A 1970 Peabody award honored the CBS Dr. Seuss series, then comprised of "The Grinch" and "Horton Hears a Who" (Mar 19, 1970), also based on a 1957 book and narrated by Hans Conried. Horton was a good-hearted elephant that saved Whoville from the menacing Wickersham Brothers and Vlad Vlad-i-koff, the bother- some black-bottomed eagle.   In a deliciously chilling original story, "Halloween is Grinch Night" (Oct 28, 1979), the foul-tempered meanie was revived on ABC, when a small boy was blown away from Whoville in a howling night wind, to find himself face-to-face with the dreaded Grinch atop Mt. Crumpit.

"The Cat in The Hat" (Mar 10, 1971) also narrated by Con- ried, and "The Lorax" (Feb 7, 1972), introduced by Eddie Albert, each contained three or four original songs, like the first specials. The audacious Cat captivated children with all sorts of wild and wonderful fun and games, while looking for his helpmates, Thing One and Thing Two, a goldfish named Karlos K. Krinklebein and a three-handled family "gradunza. "   Dr. Seuss struck a blow for ecology in verse, detailing the gnome-like Lorax's crusade to save the Trufulla Tree, which became an endangered species because its silken tufts could be knitted into practically anything, destroying the habitat of the humming fish, barbaloots and swomee swans.

"Dr. Seuss on the Loose" (Oct 15, 1973) presented a trio of stories in rhyme narrated by Conried.   A tale of snobbery began the fun in "The Sneetches, " about the star-bellied beach birds who put down their plain-bellied cousins.   "The Zax" concerned a couple of stubborn travelers and "Green Eggs and Ham" told about a fellow who would not eat strange-looking food.   The first Dr. Seuss film written for television, "The Hoober-Bloob Highway" (Feb 19, 1975) was about a special thoroughfare by which all creatures arrived on Earth--but not before they were treated to a vision of their future on the planet, described in tongue-twisting verse containing towns' names like Bodja-Nodja-Stan and North Nizza-Skrinza-Bo.

The musical-comedy travels of a likeable pickle factory bungler on a flying piano was the premise of "Pontoffel Pock, Where Are You?" (May 2, 1980).   The magical instrument whisked Pock off to comical mishaps in a Ruritanian Kingdom and a romantic es- capade with an Arabian Princess in fanciful fairy Godmother fashion.


DRAK PACK

Network History
    Premiere:  September 6, 1980
    CBS/Sep 1980-Feb 1981/Saturday 11:30-12:00 AM
    CBS/Mar 1981-Sep 1981/Saturday 12:30-1:00 PM

Executive Producers:  William Hanna, Joseph Barbera
Producer:  Doug Patterson
Director:  Chris Cuddington
Company:  Hanna-Barbera Productions, Australia/13 films

Principal Characters and Voices

| | |
|---|---|
| Drak, Jr. | Jerry Dexter |
| Frankie/Howler | Bill Callaway |
| Big D | Alan Oppenheimer |
| Dr. Dred | Hans Conried |
| Vampira | Julie McWhirter |
| Mummy Man | Chuck McCann |
| Toad/Fly | Don Messick |

    Drak Pack featured three teenage boys fighting on the side of justice, in an attempt to atone for their ancestors' unsavory exploits. Drak, Jr., Frankie and Howler comprised the do-gooder group, which possessed the "Drak Wack" power to transform themselves into the super mighty monsters, Dracula, Frankenstein and the Werewolf.  By simply clasping their right hands together and uttering the magic word, "Wacko," they could use their extraordinary skills against all evildoers.  In their secret laboratory, they answered to communications on a TV screen from Big D, great-grandfather Dracula, and were out to thwart the plots of O. G. R. E., the Organization of Generally Rotten Enterprises.  The nefarious leader of this organization was the brilliant and egotistical Dr. Dred, headquartered on Skull Island, who roamed the earth to perpetrate his evil intrigues in the "Dredgible," a huge airship.  His henchpersons were Toad, Fly, Mummy Man and Vampira, who could turn herself into a venomous viper or spider.  With the aid of his renegade rascals, the dastardly doctor unleashed his diabolical inventions upon an unwitting world.  In various episodes Dr. Dred used a camera which turned people into fold-away snapshots; a machine which shrank the Eiffel Tower, Big Ben, the Statue of Liberty and Fort Knox and its gold, so that he could steal them; instigated a plot to scare guests out of a swank hotel in order to turn it into a posh hideout for supercriminals; and, the ultimate horror, converted the monuments of the world, including Easter Island, Egypt's Pyramids and Mount Rushmore, into his own likeness.  In the end, naturally, it was good over greed, right that conquered wrong, and niceness triumphant against naughtiness, due to the dedication of the super-powered alter-egos of the terrific trio.
    Despite its "Incredible Hulkian" overtones and similarity to the earlier live-action crimefighters on Monster Squad* (q. v.), the series was one of the better Saturday morning entries, with fine scripting and characterizations, in particular the voice of Hans Conried as Dr. Dred.


DRAWING POWER

Component Series
    THE BOOK REPORT, BUS STOP, PET PEEVES, PROFESSOR

RUTABAGA, SUPERPERSON U. , WHAT DO YOU DO DAD, (MOM)?

Network History
   Premiere: October 11, 1980
   NBC/Oct 1980-May 1981/Saturday 12:30-1:00 PM
   Last Program: May 16, 1981
Executive Producers: George Newall, Tom Yohe
Director: George Newall
Company: Newall and Yohe Productions/13 tapes--films

Cast

Pop                                    Bob Kaliban
Lenny                                  Lenny Schultz
Kari                                   Kari Page

   Drawing Power interposed actors portraying animators with
the product of their art, cartoons with a conscious emphasizing of pro-
social messages and educational features.   The setting was a small
studio where Pop, a white-haired old pro, and his assistants, Lenny
and Kari, spent their workday.   Pegged on a central theme like
tolerance, the show began with the cast exchanging banter on their
different faddish garb and trading aphorisms such as "it's what's inside
that counts. "   The chatter segued into the principal cartoon, an
episode of "Superperson U" with a costumed superhero enacting a
moral on the subject, showing what it's like to be in the other fellow's shoes and to respect differences in dress, language and race.
Various animated segments were incorporated in different shows,
including "Bus Stop, " highlighting indigenous people such as the
Amish and their customs and history; "What Do You Do, Dad
(Mom)?, " explaining various jobs and careers; and "The Book Re-
port, " featuring Dewey Decimal, a cartoon character who inter-
viewed and interacted with the characters from a juvenile novel.
Shorter features included a fast-spieling TV pitchman, "Professor
Rutabaga, " who presented bits on health and nutrition--once all
about carrots; "It's a Wacky World, " about oddly behaving animals
and curious events; "Pet Peeves, " a chance for pets to tell humans
what's on their minds, and "Turkey of the Week, " which presented
a Golden Gobbler award to one of the really rotten tots, such as
messy Harry.
   Overindulgent in maxims and messages and not particularly
entertaining, the hodgepodge series was produced in New York by
Newall-Yohe Productions, who were responsible for ABC's award-
winning Schoolhouse Rock (q. v. ).


DUDLEY DO-RIGHT SHOW, THE

Component Series
   AESOP AND SON, FRACTURED FAIRY TALES, PEABODY'S
   IMPROBABLE HISTORY

Network History
Premiere: April 27, 1969
ABC/Apr 1969-Sep 1970/Sunday 9:30-10:00 AM
Last Program: September 6, 1970

Syndicated History

DUDLEY DO-RIGHT AND HIS FRIENDS

Distributor: Filmtel International/1970-1979; DFS Program Exchange/1979-
Producers: Jay Ward, Bill Scott
Directors: Bill Hurtz, Pete Burness, Ted Parmelee
Company: Jay Ward Productions with Producers Associates for Television/38 films

Narrator
Paul Frees

Principal Characters and Voices

| | |
|---|---|
| Dudley Do-Right | Bill Scott |
| Nell Fenwick | June Foray |
| Snidely Whiplash | Hans Conried |
| Inspector Fenwick | Paul Frees |

The Dudley Do-Right Show toplined an artless Royal Canadian Mountie, chivalrous to a fault but a preposterous, unknowing failure. As prior fans had learned, Dudley resembled dimpled-jaw, blond movie actor Kirk Douglas in profile, but not in I.Q. After accidentally spending three miserable hours in a sewer, while enroute to become a movie star, Dudley, believing himself guilty of trespassing, turned himself in to the nearest North Alberta Mountie camp, five hundred miles from his home. Shocked at his foul deed, Inspector Fenwick recruited him as a member of the Mounted Police to follow his proud family tradition, for "A Do-Right must always do right!"
The epitome of Victorian morality, while his intentions were honorable and his posture upright and martial, Do-Right was a boneheaded klutz. With pedantic obedience to orders, Dudley regularly galloped across the countryside facing backward, pursuing Snidely K. Whiplash, the most diabolical of fiends. One morning he was oblivious to his girl friend Nell, who was tied across some railroad tracks. Fortunately, his mount, named Horse, rescued the Inspector's daughter. Horse was in every way the better man, a fact realized by Nell, who continually refused Dudley's proposals because she preferred the steed. At every opportunity, Dudley was outwitted by the villainous Whiplash, and regularly roughed up his boss by mistake. When danger threatened, he rarely responded. "Come quickly," a terrified townsman once implored. "Someone is engaged in sabotage!" "Is that so?" replied Dudley. "I know a couple engaged in Montreal, or is it Toronto?"
Introduced in 1961 as a new component on The Bullwinkle

Show (q. v. ), the mountie was conceived in 1948 and the character used by Jay Ward and Alexander Anderson in a pilot film titled "The Comic Strips of Television," which included Crusader Rabbit (q. v. ). One of the more humorous non-animal cartoons created for TV, the melodramatic spoof was laced with verbal humor and rib-tickling fun, written mainly by Bill Scott. In the repackaged series, the supporting features were drawn from Ward and Scott's earlier programs, Bullwinkle and Rocky and His Friends (qq. v. ), and included "Fractured Fairy Tales" narrated by Edward Everett Horton, "Aesop and Son" narrated by Charles Ruggles, and "Peabody's Improbable History." In syndication these elements were replaced by comedies from other series, particularly those seen on King Leonardo and His Short Subjects (q. v. ) and Tennessee Tuxedo (q. v. ).

## DYNOMUTT, DOG WONDER

Network History

THE SCOOBY-DOO/DYNOMUTT HOUR
    Premiere:  September 11, 1976
    ABC/Sep 1976-Nov 1976/Saturday 9:30-10:30 AM

THE SCOOBY-DOO/DYNOMUTT SHOW
    ABC/Dec 1976-Sep 1977/Saturday 9:00-10:30 AM
    Last Program:  September 3, 1977

SCOOBY'S ALL-STAR LAFF-A-LYMPICS/THE BLUE FALCON AND DYNOMUTT
    Return:  September 10, 1977
    ABC/Sep 1977-Mar 1978/Saturday 9:00-11:00 AM
    Last Program:  March 11, 1978

DYNOMUTT, DOG WONDER
    Return:  June 3, 1978
    ABC/Jun 1978-Jul 1978/Saturday 12:00-12:30 PM
    ABC/Jul 1978-Sep 1978/Saturday 8:00-8:30 AM
    Last Program:  September 2, 1978

THE GODZILLA/DYNOMUTT HOUR WITH THE FUNKY PHANTOM
    Return:  September 27, 1980
    NBC/Sep 1980-Nov 1980/Saturday 8:00-9:00 AM
    Last Program:  November 15, 1980
Executive Producers:  William Hanna, Joseph Barbera
Producers:  Alex Lovy, Don Jurwich
Company:  Hanna-Barbera Productions/16 films (1976-1977), 8
    films, 11 minutes (1977-1978)

Narrator
    Ron Feinberg

Principal Characters and Voices
    Dynomutt                              Frank Welker

Blue Falcon               Gary Owens
Mayor                  Larry McCormick
Focus 1              Ron Feinberg

Dynomutt, Dog Wonder, was the faithful robot companion of the Blue Falcon, a red-caped and blue-cowled champion of justice. The metallic hound had a system of miniaturized transistors which allowed him to extend his limbs or neck and use them to perform extraordinary feats. Although he was supposed to be the ultimate canine colossal, the blue-caped crusader turned out to be the pen-ultimate canine screwup. Dynomutt called his partner "B. F. , " a superhero in the tradition of Batman* (q. v. ), who was frequently his savior and often his victim. The Blue Falcon was continually hamstrung by the various deficiencies of his electronic sidekick, whose voice was reminiscent of Red Skelton's befuddled rustic, Clem Kadiddlehopper. The crimefighters worked for the Mayor of Big City and were aligned against an array of master criminals with descriptive names like The Blob, Tin Kong, Queen Hornet and the Red Vulture.

The creation of Joe Ruby and Ken Spears, Dynomutt was introduced in tandem with Scooby Doo (q. v. ) in 1976-1977. The following year four new two-part episodes were retitled The Blue Falcon and Dynomutt as part of Scooby's All-Star Laff-A-Lympics, the first two-hour Saturday morning cartoon show in network history. The cartoons were replaced in March 1978 by additional segments of Captain Caveman and the Teen Angels (q. v. ), and in Summer 1978 the films were repeated as Dynomutt, Dog Wonder in a separate half-hour program. After the ABC run, the klutzy canine moved to NBC at the beginning of the strike-delayed 1980-1981 season and was paired with Godzilla (q. v. ), featuring also reruns of The Funky Phantom (q. v. ).


8TH MAN

Syndicated History
    Premiere: September 7, 1965
    WPIX, New York/Tuesday 4:00-4:30 PM
Distributor: ABC Films/1965-1972
Producer: Mitsuteru Yokoyama
Company: TCJ Animation Center, Japan/52 B&W films

Principal Characters

    Peter Brady/8th Man
    Police Chief Fumblethumbs

8th Man, a super android, was endowed with the likeness, memory and courage of a police detective killed while pursuing a notorious criminal. Remade into "Tobor the 8th Man" by Professor Genius ("Dr. Tani" in the Japanese version), he resumed the chase for his own killer, Saucer Lip ("Mukade"), under his own name, Peter Brady ("Rachiro Azuma"), operating out of the Metropolitan International Police Headquarters. Only Chief Fumblethumbs knew his secret identity. From the same mold as the Marvel Comics' superheroes, 8th Man was involved with a host of arch-criminals, among them Dr. Demon, the Satan brothers, the knife-wielding Apache and an international spy organization known as Intercrime ("The Black Butterfly"), headed by Dr. Yurei. A ma-chine with human feelings, 8th Man (Shōnen, 1963-1966) was cre-ated by artist Jirō Kuwata and scriptwriter Kazumasa Hirai as a Japanese comic strip in April 1963 and adapted for a TV cartoon show. The series was redubbed in English by Joe Oriolo Studios.


EMERGENCY + 4

Network History
        Premiere: September 8, 1973
        NBC/Sep 1973-Dec 1973/Saturday 9:30-10:00 AM
        NBC/Jan 1974-Aug 1975/Saturday 9:00-9:30 AM
        NBC/Sep 1975-Sep 1976/Saturday 8:00-8:30 AM
        Last Program: September 4, 1976

Syndicated History

Distributor: MCA-TV/1977-
Executive Producer: Janis Diamond
Producers: Fred Calvert, Michael Caffey
Director: Fred Calvert
Company: Mark VII Ltd., Fred Calvert Productions with Universal
        Television/23 films

Principal Characters and Voices

Paramedic Roy DeSoto                 Kevin Tighe
Paramedic John Gage                  Randolph Mantooth
Carol Harper                         Sarah Kennedy
Matthew Harper                       David Joliffe
Jason Phillips                       Donald Fullilove
Randy Aldrich                        Peter Haas
Flash (a dog)
Charlemayne (a myna bird)
Bananas (a monkey)


        Emergency + 4 was built around the fictional exploits of the Paramedical Rescue Service of the Los Angeles County Fire Depart-ment. In this animated spin-off from the prime time siren-drama Emergency (NBC, 1972-1977), Kevin Tighe and Randolph Mantooth voiced their self-likenesses as Squad 51 paramedics. The plus four were Carol and Matt, a sister and brother, and the boys Jason and Randy, a group of youngsters trained in life-saving techniques. To-gether with their pets, the dog Flash, myna bird Charlemayne, and Bananas the monkey, they were always ready to assist the firemen. In the premiere, "Desert Storm," DeSoto and Gage were testing a dune buggy rescue vehicle and encountered two reckless bikers, who refused to heed their warnings, and Dr. Bonner, looking for histori-

cal evidence of a U. S. Army Camel Corps experiment. The para-
medics rescued his daughter when she was trapped by an angry
mountain goat. After accidentally starting a fire in a Ghost Town,
the bikers escaped a rock slide and stole the vehicle which contained anti-snake venom needed to save the scientist's life after he
had been bitten by a rattlesnake. The youngsters recovered the
buggy, surviving a flash flood and desert sandstorm, and the plot
was resolved when the humbled bikers agreed to help Dr. Bonner
in his search, spurred on by the discovery of a camel jawbone by
Flash. In such other episodes as "Danger at Fantasy Park," "Fire
at Sea," "Oil's Well" and "S. O. S. Help Us," they dealt with natural
calamities, fires on land and sea, persons suffering from medical
ailments and "danglers," individuals suspended or trapped in life-
and-death situations.

   Although the series was criticized because the episodes frequently depicted the children as participants in some deadly peril,
the heroic rescue theme was enhanced by several educational features. Instructional safety tips with do's-and-don'ts were interwoven into the stories, along with practical demonstrations of
mouth-to-mouth resuscitation and simple medical first aid. Fire
Departments throughout the country requested prints of the episodes to show at fire prevention and safety seminars for children.

   Tighe and Mantooth became children's favorites on the nighttime series created by producer Jack Webb's Mark VII Productions,
responsible for such TV hits as Dragnet (NBC, 1952-1970) and
Adam 12 (NBC, 1968-1975). More children watched the evening
program than the cartoon show and made Emergency the only program to compete successfully against the Saturday blockbuster hit,
All in the Family (CBS, 1971-1979). Like the transformation of
The Brady Kids (q. v.), Tighe and Mantooth were the first adults
caricatured for an animated series, coincidentally, while their program was a hit in prime time. In a nighttime preview of the network's 1973-1974 children's line-up, the pair hosted NBC Starship
Rescue (Sep 7, 1973), featuring excerpts of the show along with
other Saturday morning programs.


FABULOUS FUNNIES, THE

Component Series
   ALLEY OOP, BROOM HILDA, EMMY LOU, THE CAPTAIN AND
   THE KIDS, NANCY AND SLUGGO

Network History
   Premiere: September 9, 1978
   NBC/Sep 1978-Jan 1979/Saturday 12:00-12:30 PM
   NBC/Feb 1979-Sep 1979/Saturday 12:30-1:00 PM
   Last Program: September 1, 1979
Executive Producers: Louis Scheimer, Norman Prescott
Producer: Don Christensen
Directors: Ed Friedman, Marsh Lamore, Gwen Wetzler, K.
   Wright, Lou Zukor
Company: Filmation Productions/13 films

Principal Characters and Voices

| | |
|---|---|
| Broom Hilda/Sluggo/Oola/Hans and Fritz Katzenjammer | June Foray |
| Nancy | Jayne Hamil |
| Captain Katzenjammer/King Guzzle | Alan Oppenheimer |
| Alley Oop | Bob Holt |

The Fabulous Funnies were promoted by the network as "The World's Greatest Comics," but the hyperbole was hardly justified. Of the animated comics, only Vincent T. Hamlin's chisel-chested Alley Oop (Aug 7, 1933) and Rudolph Dirks' long-running classic The Captain and the Kids (Jun 14, 1914) had any real distinction. Moreover, these funnies were hardly funny. Four features were seen each week, tied together by a common pro-social theme and narration in rhyme. Introduced with the admonition, "We're here to make one thing clear, a lot of woe comes from undue fear," the premiere dealt with trepidation. Frightened by the portentous arrival of creatures from another planet, "Broom Hilda" conquered her timidity when the landing became fact, finding the aliens not so strange after all. Muscular caveman "Alley Oop" taught his Stone Age friends a lesson in tolerance, overcoming their dread of a strange tribe with whom they later shared the same hunting grounds. Young jowly "Nancy" helped Sluggo, her slum pal, subdue his braggadocio and fear of flying. And Fritz, of "The Captain's Kids," calmed Hans' jittery apprehension over an absolutely painless vaccination.

Invincible in the truest tradition of Popeye the Sailor (q. v.), Alley Oop possessed Herculean strength and over-sized forearms which resembled those of the salty seaman. The prehistoric muscleman rode a pet dinosaur named Dinny, and brought order to the Kingdom of Moo, ruled by King Guzzle, his treacherous Grand Vizier Foozy, and Queen Umpateedle in his NEA strips. Tamed down from an axe-swinging, bullheaded rough-neck, who spent a great deal of time fighting over his sweetheart Oola in the comics, Alley became an animated sage who taught his pals social lessons such as the need for teamwork and understanding. A popular song in 1960, "Alley Oop" was recorded by the Hollywood Argyles.

With an innate instinct for mischief, Hans and Fritz continued their pranks at the expense of their long-suffering Mama and the irascible Captain Katzenjammer. Modeled on German cartoonist Wilhelm Busch's nineteenth-century destructive brats, Max and Moritz, the pair of young miscreants were born December 12, 1897 for the "American Humorist," the Sunday supplement of The New York Journal. Venerable screen troupers, The Katzenjammer Kids appeared in silent animated films produced by Charles Bowers in 1915 for the Chicago Tribune-News Syndicate. Another series was supervised by Gregory LaCava in 1916-1918 for International Film Service, financed by William Randolph Hearst to publicize his syndicated comic strips. The impossible and uncontrollable boys were revived in 1914 as The Captain and the Kids in Pulitzer's New York World, after a landmark lawsuit between Dirks and

Hearst in which the artist won the rights to the characters but not the title.  Under new artists, The Katzenjammer Kids continued for King Features, and Dirks' strip for United Features Syndicate.  Afterwards, The Captain and The Kids appeared in MGM sound cartoons; fifteen films beginning with Cleaning House (Feb 19, 1938) and ending with Mamma's New Hat (Feb 11, 1939).

A rather ineffectual fifteen-hundred-year-old witch whose black magic often misfired, Broom Hilda (CNS, 1970) was the creation of Russell Myers, and was inspired by the Publishers-Hall comic strip The Wizard of Id (Nov 9, 1964).  Despite her abrasive nature and voice, which resembled that of the hoarse-throated Marjorie Main, the spellmaker was an endearing character who used her powers to satisfy whims and peeves more than to terrorize. The films included her comics' coterie:  Gaylord, the intellectual buzzard that seldom heeded her commands; Irwin, the shy and shaggy troll; and the insolent Grebler, the master of insult, with a voice imitation of Charles Nelson Reilly.

The straightforward bright-eyed Nancy (UFS, 1940) interjected trivial facts in her thematic films, such as "Humming bird wings flutter seventy times a second and are the only birds that can fly backwards. "  Conceived by Ernie Bushmiller, the precocious youngster made her debut in the twenties as the niece of Fritzi Ritz.  Paired with the pseudo-tough Sluggo in the late forties, the strip finally achieved popularity in the fifties and was adapted between 1949 and 1963 for the comic books, Nancy and Sluggo by UFS, St. John Publishing and lastly Gold Key.

A tried-and-true comics concept that sacrificed humor and fun for preaching, The Fabulous Funnies lost the ratings race after one year to its more entertaining competition.  Several of the component cartoons were repeats, previously televised as segments of Archies TV Funnies, one of the programs featuring The Archies (q. v. ).


## FAMILY CLASSICS THEATER

Syndicated History
        Premiere:  November 14, 1971
        WCBS, New York/Sunday 5:00-6:00 PM
Sponsors:  Fun Group, General Mills (1971-1973); Kraft Division, General Foods (1973-1974)
Distributor:  Leonard M. Sive and Associates/1971-1975
Executive Producers:  Walter J. Hucker, William Hanna, Joseph Barbera
Company:  Air Programs International, Australia/8 films, 60 minutes; Hanna-Barbera Productions/3 films, 60 minutes

Family Classics Theater presented some old favorites and adult masterpieces that became the universal property of children through simplification in juvenile novels.  Nationally sponsored in the Fall, eleven hour-long animated specials, based on literary classics, were telecast and repeated between 1971 and 1975.  The loyal Merry Men in Lincoln Green appeared in the first season premiere, "The Legend of Robin Hood" (Nov 14, 1971), followed

by Robert Louis Stevenson's all-time favorite, "Treasure Island"
(Nov 28, 1971), and a reprise of Charles Dickens' perennial "A
Christmas Carol" (Dec 12, 1971), which debuted earlier as a CBS
Special, December 13, 1970. In 1972, repeats of these films were
complemented by Daniel Defoe's practical account of the castaway
"Robinson Crusoe" (Nov 23, 1972) and Mark Twain's tale of two
boys in Tudor, England, "The Prince and the Pauper" (Nov 26,
1972). Along with encores, six new features made their debut in
1973. A pair of swashbuckling adaptations from the fertile pen of
Alexandre Dumas included "The Count of Monte Cristo" (Sep 23,
1973) and "The Three Musketeers" (Nov 23, 1973). Two exciting
adventures from the prolific Stevenson detailed the experiences of
David Balfour in "Kidnapped" (Oct 23, 1973) and Dick Shelton and
his companion Matcham, in the historical romance "The Black Arrow" (Dec 1, 1973). Completing the schedule were the amazing
exploits of "The Swiss Family Robinson" (Oct 28, 1973) by Johann
R. Wyss, and Jules Verne's nautical speculation, "Twenty Thousand
Leagues Under the Sea" (Nov 22, 1973). Reruns were seen in 1974
and 1975 and the films were later separately reprised, several of
them on Famous Classic Tales (q. v. ).


FAMOUS ADVENTURES OF MR. MAGOO, THE  See  MR. MAGOO


FAMOUS CLASSIC TALES

Network History
    Premiere: November 15, 1975
    CBS/Nov 1975-  /Periodic/Various AM & PM

Sponsor: Fun Group, General Mills
Executive Producers: William Hanna, Joseph Barbera, Walter J.
    Hucker
Company: Hanna-Barbera Pty, Ltd. , Australia/5 films, 60 minutes;
    Air Programs International, Australia/6 films, 60 minutes

    Famous Classic Tales was a series of hour-long animated
features for children. Basically, the specials were a network continuation of the syndicated films seen on Family Classics Theater
(q. v. ) and occasionally included repeats like "The Three Musketeers" (Nov 22, 1979). The programs were scheduled around the
Fall holidays each year to promote Kenner Toys, part of the Fun
Group division of General Mills. The new cartoons began with
Jules Verne's tale about five refugees from a Confederate prison
on "The Mysterious Island" (Nov 15, 1975), which featured the re-
appearance of the undersea wizard, Captain Nemo. Others included
Sir Walter Scott's 1819 romantic tale of chivalry, "Ivanhoe" (Nov
27, 1975), and the mishaps of Natty Bumppo in "The Last of the
Mohicans" (Nov 29, 1975), by James Fenimore Cooper. Wearing
his coonskin cap for the first time in a cartoon adventure was
"Davy Crockett on the Mississippi" (Nov 20, 1976). Verne's story
about the fantastic airship of Robur, a power-hungry megalomaniac

who wanted to be "Master of the World" (Nov 23, 1976), was followed by adaptations of the author's first two novels, "Five Weeks
in a Balloon" (Nov 24, 1977) and "Journey to the Center of the
Earth" (Nov 13, 1977). Voiced by Alan Young, Anna Sewell's frisky
ebony stallion was animated for "Black Beauty" (Oct 28, 1978), and
Jonathan Swift's Lilliputians and Brobdignagians for "Gulliver's
Travels" (Nov 18, 1979). The Thanksgiving debut of a half-hour
Russian version of E. T. A. Hoffmann's "The Nutcracker" (Nov 22,
1979) featured Tchaikovsky's enchanting music and the tall tales of
a Baghdad merchant retold in "The Adventures of Sinbad" (Nov 23,
1979). Together with encores of the films, Charles Dickens' "A
Christmas Carol" (Dec 13, 1970) was repeated periodically between
1975 and 1980.


FANGFACE

Network History
    Premiere: September 9, 1978
    ABC/Sep 1978-Nov 1978/Saturday 8:30-9:00 AM
    ABC/Nov 1978-May 1979/Saturday 11:00-11:30 AM
    ABC/Jun 1979-Sep 1979/Saturday 8:00-8:30 AM
    Last Program: September 8, 1979

THE PLASTIC MAN COMEDY-ADVENTURE SHOW/FANGFACE AND
    FANGPUSS
    Premiere: September 22, 1979
    ABC/Sep 1979-Dec 1979/Saturday 9:00-11:00 AM
    ABC/Dec 1979-Sep 1980/Saturday 9:00-10:30 AM
    Last Program: September 27, 1980
Executive Producers: Joe Ruby, Ken Spears
Producer: Jerry Eisenberg
Director: Rudy Larriva
Company: Ruby-Spears Enterprises/12 films (1978-1979), 16 films
    (1979-1980)

Principal Characters and Voices

Sherman Fangsworth/Fangface
    Baby Fangs/Fangpuss          Frank Welker
Kim                              Susan Blu
Biff                             Jerry Dexter
Puggsy                           Bart Braverman

    Fangface was a shaggy one-fanged werewolf, the imperceived
alter-identity of Sherman Fangsworth. An insipid-looking blond-
haired teenager, "Fangs" became a jocular lycanthrope whenever he
glanced at or even saw a picture of a full moon. Only the sun or
its image could bring him back to normal. His friends were Kim,
a Eurasian-looking girl, a stereotypical boy, Biff, and the pork-pie-
hatted Puggsy. They drove around together in his "Wolf Buggy" to
encounter danger and excitement. "Fangs" and "Pugs" were modeled on long-faced actor Huntz Hall and pint-sized Brooklynese-

talking Leo Gorcey (1915-1969), two of the movies' original Dead End Kids and later of The Bowery Boys. Reminiscent of their vocal characterizations, Fangface repeated everything, "I did good, eh Pugs, I did good?" while Puggsy murdered the English language with such expressions as "Leapin' Ignipotamuses!" and "I'll be transmorgified!"

In the comedy-mysteries, Fangface was endowed with super strength and senses and used his nose to sniff out the location of Chang Ling, a missing explorer on Misty Island, where the youngsters encountered the monstrous Ape Men. On Pelegrosso Telegrosso Island they aided Dr. Melendez, seeking to recover the ancient tablet which contained a clue to Montezuma's treasure, stolen by Mr. Gruver, a notorious antiquities thief. In "Don't Abra When You Cadabra," the gang located a boxcar of electronics hijacked by the power-hungry Mysto the Magician. And in "A Heap of Trouble," the premiere, "Fangs" helped his buddies outwit an evil scientist who created a monster called The Heap, that strongly resembled the Incredible Hulk (q. v. ), but was blue instead of green.

Created by Joe Ruby and Ken Spears, the premise of a man who turns into a ravaging beast at full moon had been filmed since 1934, but was not popularized until The Wolf Man (UP, 1941) with Lon Chaney, Jr. as the hirsute horror. Resurrected from ancient Teutonic mythology, the basic story dates from The Were-Wolf (1890) by Clemence Housman, hailed as the greatest tale of lycanthropy ever written. The graphic humorous treatment of Fangface was the first project of Ruby and Spears under their own production banner, following their work as a creative writing team for Hanna-Barbera Productions, DePatie-Freleng Enterprises and Krofft Productions, and a stint as consultants to ABC network children's programs.

In the second season, a sequel titled Fangface and Fangpuss was incorporated in their two-hour package, The Plasticman Comedy-Adventure Show (q. v. ). The series featured the same cast and introduced Baby Fangs, Fangsworth's baby brother who became the pre-adolescent werewolf Fangpuss with a look at a round moon, in such comedy-mysteries as "The Creepy Goon from the Spooky Lagoon," "The Film Fiasco of Director Diastro" and "The Evil Design of the Vulture Man's Mind."


FANTASTIC FOUR, THE

Network History
Premiere: September 9, 1967
ABC/Sep 1967-Sep 1968/Saturday 9:30-10:00 AM
ABC/Sep 1968-Aug 1969/Saturday 11:30-12:00 AM
ABC/Sep 1969-Mar 1970/Sunday 10:30-11:00 AM
Last Program: March 15, 1970

THE NEW FANTASTIC FOUR
Premiere: September 9, 1978
NBC/Sep 1978-Oct 1978/Saturday 10:30-11:00 AM
NBC/Nov 1978-Sep 1978/Saturday 8:30-9:00 AM
Last Program: September 1, 1979

Syndicated History

CAPTAIN INVENTORY

Distributor (1967-1970 films): Taft H-B Program Sales/1973-1979;
  Worldvision Enterprises/1979-
Executive Producers: William Hanna, Joseph Barbera (1967-1970);
  David DePatie, Friz Freleng (1978-1979)
Director: Brad Case (1978-1979)
Company: Hanna-Barbera Productions/20 films (1967-1970); DePatie-
  Freleng Enterprises/12 films (1978-1979)

Principal Characters and Voices

| | |
|---|---|
| Reed Richards/Mr. Fantastic | (1967-1970) Gerald Mohr |
| | (1978-1979) Mike Road |
| Sue Richards/Invisible Girl | (1967-1970) Jo An Pflug |
| | (1978-1979) Ginny Tyler |
| Bengamin Grimm/The Thing | (1967-1970) Paul Frees |
| | (1978-1979) Ted Cassidy |
| Johnny Storm/The Human Torch | (1967-1970) Jack Flounders |
| H E R--B | (1978-1979) Frank Welker |

    The Fantastic Four had extraordinary individual powers, the
result of mysterious cosmic rays which bombarded the rocketship
they were testing. After they crash-landed safely, scientist Reed
Richards found his skin turned to plastic, became as tensile as a
rubber band and adopted the name Mr. Fantastic. His blond wife
Sue became the now-you-see-her, now-you-don't Invisible Girl, and
her teenage brother Johnny Storm could burst into flames at will as
The Human Torch. The family friend, Ben Grimm, was turned
into a monstrous rock-like being, a muscled powerhouse called The
Thing. With the exception of the orange-colored monster, the superhumans were outfitted in blue jumpsuits with a "4" in a white
circle on their chests, and together sped to their adventures in
their "U-Car." All-purpose trouble-shooters, the four used their
new powers to battle such heinous villains as the iron-masked Dr.
Doom, Galactus, Klaws, the Red Ghost and the Mole Man, a sub-
terranean ruler bent on world conquest. Adapted from the comic
book quartet created for Fantastic Four Number One (Marvel, Nov
1961), by writer-editor-publisher Stan Lee with artist Jack Kirby,
the ABC cartoon series between 1967 and 1970 relied heavily upon
the original published stories and design supervised by art director
John Romita.
    In The New Fantastic Four created by Lee for NBC in 1978-
1979 a wise-cracking computer, the Humanoid Electronic Robot "B"
model, called H. E. R. --B, and programmed not to make mistakes,
was substituted for the firebug Johnny Storm. Known as "The Fan-
tasticar," their new vehicle was an amazing flying automobile that
resembled an oversized bathtub. With their robot, the three transformable humans met another group of weird machines and monsters, including The Giant Vacuum Cleaner in New York, the evil
master of magnetism, The Magneto, the green pointy-eared aliens

from Andromeda Galaxy named Scrulls, the Phantom of Film City, Medusa and the durable Dr. Doom, and the Mole Man.

The second series was more faithful to the foibles of the characters, who were given human hang-ups in the comics. Often overreacting, Sue in retrospect would apologize, "Well, perhaps I was a little over eager." The Thing, who suffered tremendous insecurity because of his hideous appearance, was frequently depicted as tense and uptight. The scenarios featured sassy verbal by-play between the monster and HER--B, which could not understand his lack of self-control. The brute was a spin-off in 1979-1980, headlining his own adventures in Fred and Barney Meet The Thing (q. v.), which presented a new cartoon personality, Benjamin Grimm as a teenage boy, Benjy.


FANTASTIC VOYAGE

Network History
    Premiere: September 14, 1968
    ABC/Sep 1968-Aug 1969/Saturday 10:30-11:00 AM
    ABC/Sep 1969-Dec 1969/Saturday 12:00-12:30 PM
    ABC/Jan 1970-Sep 1970/Sunday 10:00-10:30 AM
    Last Program: September 6, 1970

Syndicated History

Distributor: Twentieth Century-Fox Television/1970-
Executive Producers: Louis Scheimer, Norman Prescott
Director: Hal Sutherland
Company: Filmation Productions/17 films

Principal Characters and Voices

| | |
|---|---|
| Commander Jonathan Kidd | Marvin Miller |
| Erica Stone | Jane Webb |
| Cosby Birdwell | Ted Knight |
| The Guru (non-speaking) | |

Fantastic Voyage detailed the hazardous expedition by a bacteria-sized quartet of medical experts through a famous professor's bloodstream. The ticklish premise was based on a story by Otto Clement and J. Lewis Bixby, produced by Saul Davis as the movie, Fantastic Voyage (TCF, 1966), and novelized by Isaac Asimov. In the feature, the team was shrunk to the size of a mere speck and traveled in a miniaturized nuclear-powered submarine, "Proteus" (U-91035). But in the cartoons, the race-against-death took place aboard "The Voyager," a minuscule spaceship that entered the carotid artery. The patient was a noted scientist who was smuggled from behind the Iron Curtain and incurred a serious brain injury during his escape. His close friend, Commander Jonathan Kidd, decided to take a team of specialists inside the defector's brain and repair the damage.

Voiced by Marvin Miller, remembered as the gratuity-doling

Michael Anthony on The Millionaire (CBS, 1945-1960), Kidd headed
the Combined Miniature Defense Force (C. M. D. F. ), a secret United
States government agency that possessed the technical ability to
shrink humans to germ size with a special ruby laser.   His assistants were the brainy biologist Erica Stone, a physician named
Cosby Birdwell and a servant called The Guru, a silent master of
mysterious powers.   During the trip, the task force was challenged
by the biological forces of evil and disease within the professor's
body, episodic hurdles they had to overcome in their urgent mission.    Particular functions of the anatomy were pointed out, like
the heart and lungs, in an educational reminder for young viewers,
and the series imparted health wisdom during the journey, such as
the effects of prolonged smoking.   The series was marked by hokey
suspense and some very fine visual qualities.


FARMER AL FALFA  See  BARKER BILL'S CARTOON SHOW and
   COMMONWEALTH CARTOON PACKAGE


FAT ALBERT

Network History

FAT ALBERT AND THE COSBY KIDS
   Premiere:  September 9, 1972
   CBS/Sep 1972-Sep 1976/Saturday 12:30-1:00 PM
   CBS/Sep 1976-Sep 1977/Saturday 12:00-12:30 PM
   CBS/Sep 1977-Jan 1978/Saturday 12:30-1:00 PM
   CBS/Jan 1978-Sep 1978/Saturday 12:00-12:30 PM
   CBS/Sep 1978-Sep 1979/Saturday 12:30-1:00 PM

THE NEW FAT ALBERT SHOW
   CBS/Sep 1979-Aug 1980/Saturday 11:30-12:00 AM
   CBS/Sep 1980-Sep 1981/Saturday 12:00-12:30 PM

Executive Producer:  William H. Cosby, Jr.
Producers:  Louis Scheimer, Norman Prescott
Directors:  Don Christensen, Hal Sutherland, Don Towsley, Lou
   Zukor
Company:  Bill Cosby Productions with Filmation Studios/52 films

Host
   Bill Cosby

Principal Characters and Voices

Fat Albert/Mushmouth/Mudfoot/
   Dumb Donald/Brown Hornet       Bill Cosby
Russell/Bucky                     Jan Crawford
Weird Harold                      Gerald Edwards
Rudy/Devery                       Eric Sutter

Fat Albert and The Cosby Kids were a band of north Phila-
delphia young black chums, derived from the wry memory and comic
imagination of the comedian's childhood years in a Depression-era
neighborhood. The unlikely hero was Fat Albert, a sloppy, rotund
peacemaker whose favorite expression was "Hey, hey, hey," who
provided the example for working out the group's difficulties and
problems. Among his pals were the tall and gangly Old Weird
Harold, the oafish Dumb Donald, Rudy the Rich Kid, the conniver,
Weasel, the unintelligible Mushmouth and smaller Russell, modeled
after Bill Cosby's younger brother. Members who occasionally
gathered at the clubhouse in the city junkyard were Bucky, Mudfoot,
Devery and others. Acting as host for the cartoons, through his
narration Cosby underscored each program's theme and reinforced
the lesson that the gang experienced.

Responding to mounting criticism over exploitive children's
programming, Cosby pioneered the use of humor and entertainment
in this animated format to instruct young people in social and ethical behavior. Designed for affective learning, the series dealt with
such intangibles as influencing feelings, behavior and value judgment.
The stories emphasized such peer-group problems as the show-off
and braggart, the child who lied to impress others and the larger
child who exploited little tots. The plots also dealt with such daily
challenges as frustration, getting attention, understanding and ac-
cepting differences between persons, playing hookey, creativity, and
personal courage or the lack of it. In 1979-1980, The New Fat Albert Show took the friends from their salvage yard setting and bused
them to school in another part of town where they encountered different life styles, new experiences and problems to solve. Introduced in a cartoon show within the premise, "The Brown Hornet,"
a masked do-gooder with the tenacity of Superman and the finesse of
Inspector Clouseau, appeared in brief adventures to help the gang
solve some of their problems. The films were created under the
supervision of a panel of scholars and educators including Dr. Gordon L. Berry of U.C.L.A.

The series was spurred by the reception to a half-hour prime
time NBC Special, Hey, Hey, Hey, It's Fat Albert (Nov 12, 1969),
in which the Tackle Football Championship of the World was at stake.
Subsequently, the Cosby characters appeared in a go-cart race on
NBC in Weird Harold (May 4, 1973) and a pair of CBS thirty-minute
programs, featuring the do's and don'ts of trick-or-treating on The
Fat Albert Halloween Special (Oct 24, 1977) and The Fat Albert
Christmas Special (Dec 18, 1977).

Lauded for its attitude and content, Fat Albert demonstrated
that an educational-message show could be commercially competitive.
Acclaimed also as a landmark series in minority programming, Fat
Albert was actually the third animated program featuring principally
a black cast. Predecessors were The Harlem Globetrotters (q.v.)
and ABC's The Jackson 5ive (q.v.). The second longest-running
cartoon show on the CBS Saturday schedule, behind Bugs Bunny
(q.v.), in its ninth season in 1980-1981, Fat Albert was a grand
high point, encompassing proven educational and social value among
the network children's programs.

FELIX THE CAT

Syndicated History
Premiere: June 1953
WATV, New York/Monday-Saturday 5:00-5:30 PM

(NEW) FELIX THE CAT
Premiere: January 4, 1960
WNEW, New York/Monday-Friday 6:00-6:30 PM
Distributor: Pathé Films/1953-1959; Alan Enterprises/1960-
Producers: Pat Sullivan (1919-1933); Joe Oriolo (1958-1960)
Company: Pat Sullivan Studios/150 B&W silent films, 5-7 minutes
(1919-1933); Felix the Cat Productions for Trans-Lux Productions
/260 films, 4 minutes (1958-1960)

Principal Characters and Voices

Felix the Cat/Poindexter/
The Professor/Rock
Bottom                           (1960) Jack Mercer

Felix The Cat, the first cartoon superstar, made his initial
transition to the small screen a bit more gracefully than his more
sophisticated successors. In spite of the rudimentary storylines
and the absence of dialogue, the visual humor and simplified black-
on-white drawings reproduced well on low-definition colorless television. Resurrected from the storage vaults, one hundred fifty of
the silent films released by M. J. Winkler, largely through Pathé,
were syndicated in 1953. Fred Sayles first acquired and screened
them locally in New York on his Junior Frolics (WATV, 1949-1956)
and the famous feline that walked like a human captivated a new
generation of young admirers.
     A former lightweight boxer, movie exhibitor, and newspaper
cartoonist for Pulitzer's New York World, Australian-born Pat Sullivan (1888-1933) opened his own animation studio in 1916 and later
copyrighted Felix and claimed credit for his creation. But the true
genius behind his development was a shy artist named Otto Messmer,
who joined Sullivan's studio after the First World War. Messmer
was the unsung originator, designer, director, and animator of
Felix, one of the world's important characters in the history of
personality animation. At the height of his phenomenal fame in the
mid-twenties, Felix was as popular as Charles Chaplin, Buster
Keaton, and Harold Lloyd in theaters around the world, and has
always been better known and appreciated in Europe, particularly
in Great Britain. As French academician Marcel Brian put it in a
famous 1954 essay, "Felix is not a cat, he is the Cat. Or better
to say yet, he is a supercat."
     His film debut came in 1919 in the Paramount Screen Maga-
zine after John R. Bray left the studio to release his films through
Goldwyn. Producer John King asked Sullivan for contributions to
the weekly feature, which included an animated cartoon. "The
studio being busy, Sullivan asked me to do one in my spare time,

at home," Messner said. He quickly animated a cartoon featuring a black cat being outwitted by a mouse. Paramount liked it and contracted for more. Originally nameless, the cat was a continuing character in Feline Follies. In the early twenties he appeared in Musical Mews as Felix, a contraction of feline félicité, meaning "good luck cat," as suggested by King. Messmer continued to produce two films per month, and these were distributed worldwide by Margaret Winkler beginning in 1921. Felix did not survive the transition to sound, except for a brief revival by Van Beuren Studios in color with music in 1936, and was relegated to comic strips for the next twenty-five years.

The Felix cartoons were the first to express an individual personality in drawings that moved. The character was able to think, to reason, to solve problems and to communicate his ideas and desires. Messmer made ingenious use of exclamations and question marks which would appear above his head, and of his tail, which the cat would sometimes grasp and change into whatever useful shape suited his purpose, like a fish hook or baseball bat. A British song was written by Ed Bryant and Hubert David about his most famous trait, "Felix Kept On Walking" (Lawrence Wright, 1923). When puzzled, he would pace about, head down, shoulders hunched, hands clasped behind his back, scowling intensely, and this became known as "The Felix Walk." The format generally concentrated on these brief visual gags until Felix in Fairyland (1920), when the plot was thickened by a surprise visit from the good fairy. Granted one wish, Felix decided to visit Fairyland. During his magical journey, he met several Mother Goose characters and solved their nursery rhyme problems with his usual rascality. Widely licensed for toys, novelties, and even a pet food, Felix anticipated by a half-dozen years Walt Disney's remarkable merchandising success. In the late twenties, Felix became America's pioneer TV co-star with Mickey Mouse, when RCA engineers sent a picture of his likeness, a papier-mâché doll, all the way to Kansas, where it was test-analyzed for quality on primitive sixty-line receivers.

In 1954, Joe Oriolo Studios took over the production of the comic strip and between 1958 and 1960 produced new color episodes of "Pat Sullivan's" Felix the Cat. Fred Scott was among the first to introduce the series as host of Felix and His Friends weekdays on WNEW, New York, a program which included other cartoons. Rather than using his tail in humorous twists, Felix acquired a magic black bag, and, as the theme song foretold, "Whenever he gets into a fix, he reaches in his bag of tricks." Devised as a cliff-hanger, five episodes comprised a complete story, which could be strung together for a half-hour show. Many of the segments concerned the ill-fated attempts of The Professor and his bulldog accomplice Rock Bottom to snitch the bag for their own perfidious purpose. In some adventures, Felix was involved with the Professor's nephew, Poindexter, a brainy junior scientist, a dog, Sniffer, and Walter, a walrus. In a voice that was annoyingly strident, Felix moved through the slow-paced adventures with uninspired dialogue, a forced laugh that sounded like a villain, and ended each episode in stilted if not archaic slang, signing off with "Right-E-O!"

FESTIVAL OF FAMILY CLASSICS

Syndicated History
    Premiere:  September 17, 1972
    WABC, New York/Sunday 7:00-7:30 PM
Distributor:  Taft H-B Program Sales/1972-1979
Executive Producers:  Arthur Rankin, Jr., Jules Bass, William
    Hanna, Joseph Barbera
Company:  Rankin-Bass Productions, Hanna-Barbera Productions/18
    films

      Festival of Family Classics was the umbrella title for a mix-
ture of animated fairy tales, folk stories and literary adaptations for
children.  Largely redubbed Japanese cartoons, plus a few made in
Australia, the syndicated package provided local stations with attractive graphic programming during the ascendancy of the network TV
cartoon vogue.  WABC, New York began its programs with the timeless story of the rags to riches rise of "Cinderella" (Sep 17, 1972),
famed for its pumpkin chariot.  Grimm's bewitched princess in
"Sleeping Beauty" (Jan 21, 1973) and bewitched prince in "Snow-
White and Rose-Red" (Mar 4, 1973) were included, along with such
fantasy adventures as "Alice in Wonderland" (Feb 11, 1973), "Puss-
in-Boots" (Dec 9, 1972) and "The Arabian Nights" (Feb 4, 1973).
Such familiar fare as Mark Twain's "Tom Sawyer" (Feb 25, 1973)
and the ship-wrecked exploits of "Swiss Family Robinson" (Jan 13,
1973) and "Robinson Crusoe" (Feb 18, 1973) were presented, along
with a version of Henry Wadsworth Longfellow's epic Indian poem,
"Hiawatha" (Sep 24, 1972).  Viewers could contrast the English
feats of "Robin Hood" (Nov 26, 1973) with those of the American
folk heroes "Paul Bunyan" (Jan 7, 1973) and "Johnny Apple Seed"
(Nov 5, 1972).  A pair of Jules Verne classics were seen, each in
two parts: "20,000 Leagues Under the Sea" (Oct 1 & 8, 1972) and
"Around the World in 80 Days" (Nov 12 & 19, 1972).


FLINTSTONES, THE

Component Series
    PEBBLES AND BAMM BAMM (1972-1973), THE SHMOO, THE
    THING (1979-1980), THE FRANKENSTONES (1980- )

Network History
    Premiere:  September 30, 1960
    ABC/Sep 1960-Sep 1963/Friday 8:30-9:00 PM
    ABC/Sep 1963-Dec 1964/Thursday 7:30-8:00 PM
    ABC/Dec 1964-Sep 1966/Friday 7:30-8:00 PM
    NBC/Jan 1967-Aug 1969/Saturday 10:00-10:30 AM
    NBC/Sep 1969-Dec 1969/Saturday 12:00-12:30 PM
    NBC/Dec 1969-Sep 1970/Saturday 11:30-12:00 AM
    Last Program:  September 5, 1970

THE FLINTSTONES COMEDY HOUR
    Premiere:  September 9, 1972

CBS/Sep 1972-Sep 1973/Saturday 11:00-12:00 AM
Last Program:   September 1, 1973

THE FLINTSTONES SHOW
Return:   September 8, 1973
CBS/Sep 1973-Jan 1974/Saturday 8:00-8:30 AM
Last Program:   January 26, 1974

THE NEW FRED AND BARNEY SHOW
Return:   February 3, 1979
NBC/Feb 1979-Sep 1979/Saturday 11:00-11:30 AM
Last Program:   September 15, 1979

FRED AND BARNEY MEET THE THING
Premiere:   September 22, 1979
NBC/Sep 1979-Nov 1979/Saturday 9:00-10:00 AM

FRED AND BARNEY MEET THE SHMOO
NBC/Nov 1979-Nov 1980/Saturday 9:00-10:30 AM
Last Program:   November 15, 1980

THE FLINTSTONES COMEDY SHOW
Premiere:   November 22, 1980
NBC/Nov 1980-Sep 1981/Saturday 9:00-10:30 AM

Sponsors:   Winston, Alka-Seltzer, One-A-Day Vitamins (1960-1966),
Post Cereals (1967-1974), others

Syndicated History

THE FLINTSTONES (1960-1966 films)

FRED FLINTSTONE AND FRIENDS (1972-1974 films)

Distributor:   Screen Gems-Columbia Pictures Television/1966-   ;
Claster Television Productions/1977-1979
Executive Producers:   William Hanna, Joseph Barbera
Producers:   Art Scott (1979-1980); Don Jurwich, Alex Lovy, Oscar
Dufau, Carl Urbano (1980-1981)
Directors:   William Hanna, Joseph Barbera (1960-1966); Charles A.
Nichols (1972-1974); Ray Patterson, George Gordon, Don Jurwich
(1979-1980)
Company:   Hanna-Barbera Productions/166 films (1960-1966), 16
films (1972-1974), 13 films, 30, 60 & 90 minutes (1979-1980),
13 films, 60 & 90 minutes (1980-1981)

Principal Characters and Voices

| Fred Flintstone | (1960-1977) Alan Reed |
| | (1977-    ) Henry Corden |
| Wilma Flintstone | (1960-    ) Jean VanderPyl |
| Barney Rubble/Dino | (1960-    ) Mel Blanc |
| Betty Rubble | (1960-1964) Bea Benaderet |

|  |  |
|---|---|
|  | (1964-1966) Gerry Johnson |
|  | (1972-1974) Gay Hartwick |
|  | (1979-    ) Gay Autterson |
| Hoppy/Baby Puss/ Woolly/Snoots | (1960-1966) Don Messick |
| Pebbles Flintstone | (1963-1966/ 1979-1980) Jean Vander Pyl |
|  | (1971-1972) Sally Struthers |
|  | (1972-1974) Mickey Stevens |
|  | (1980-    ) Russi Taylor |
| Bamm Bamm Rubble | (1963-1966/ 1979-1980) Don Messick |
|  | (1971-1974) Jay North |
|  | (1980-    ) Michael Sheehan |
| George Slate | (1960-1966/ 1979-1980) John Stephenson |
| Moonrock | (1971-1974/ 1980-    ) Lennie Weinrib |
| Penny | (1971-1974/ 1980-    ) Mitzi McCall |
| Wiggy | (1971-1974) Gay Hartwig |
|  | (1980-    ) Gay Autterson |
| Cindy | (1971-1972) Gay Hartwig |
| Fabian | (1971-1972) Carl Esser |
| Schleprock | (1971-1974/ 1980-    ) Don Messick |
| Bronto | (1972-1973) Lennie Weinrib |
| Zonk/Stub | (1972-1973) Mel Blanc |
| Noodles | (1972-1973) John Stephenson |
| Shmoo | (1980-    ) Frank Welker |
| Chester/Captain Caveman | (1980-    ) Mel Blanc |
| Cavemouse | (1980-    ) Russi Taylor |
| Lou Granite/Narrator | (1980-    ) Ken Mars |
| Sergeant Boulder | (1980-    ) Lennie Weinrib |

THE THING (1979-1980)

| | |
|---|---|
| The Thing | Joe Baker |
| Benjy Grimm | Wayne Norton |
| Kelly | Noelle North |
| Betty/Miss Twilly | Marilyn Schreffler |
| Ronald Radford | John Erwin |
| Dr. Harkness/Stretch | John Stephenson |
| Spike | Art Metrano |
| Turkey | Michael Sheehan |

THE SHMOO (1979-1980)  See  NEW SHMOO, THE

THE FRANKENSTONES (1980-    )

| | |
|---|---|
| Frank Frankenstone | Charles Nelson Reilly |
| Hidea Frankenstone | Ruta Lee |
| Atrocia Frankenstone | Zelda Rubinstein |

Frank "Freaky" Frankenstone, Jr.   Paul Reubens
Rockjaw                             Frank Welker

    The Flintstones invaded adult viewing hours for six years
between 1960 and 1966, the first and longest running animated situation comedy seen on nighttime television.   Thereafter on the networks, the fanciful Stone Age stories about blue-collar domesticity
were relegated totally to the province of children in repeats and
spin-offs with new characters and formats on Saturday mornings.
Deriving humor chiefly from the anachronism of prehistoric settings in which the concerns were those of contemporary middle-
class suburban life, the stars were Fred and Wilma Flintstone and
their best friends, Barney and Betty Rubble, the typical couple
next door.   Everyone wore skins and lived in the city of Bedrock,
population 2,500, the seat of Cobblestone County, 250 miles below
sea level.   The muscular Fred contributed his exuberant yell
"Yabba-dabba-do" to everyone's vocabulary and was boastful, am-
bitious and not too bright.   But he was little Barney's hero, no
matter how many boners he pulled, whether they were at work as
dinosaur-powered crane operators for the Rock Heap and Quarry
Construction Company or in their losing fights with their wives,
when they wanted a night out with their lodge members, The Royal
Order of Water Buffalos.
    In their split-level caves, the two families enjoyed all the
conveniences of the twentieth-century.   When they gathered for an
evening of song, Fred picked out the tunes on a Stoneway.   They
danced to the latest rock music supplied by Fred's hi-fi, a long-
beaked bird applying his bill to a stone record.   Fred's shaver
was a clamshell with a bee in it, the kitchen garbage-disposal unit
contained a famished buzzard caged beneath the sink, and Betty
much admired Wilma's vacuum cleaner, a baby mastodon with a
long trunk on rock rollers.   A necessity and a status symbol wor-
shipped by suburbanites, the Flintstone's "Cavemobile" predated
the use of fossil fuel.   It came equipped with tail fins fashioned
out of tree trunks, a palm-thatched roof, steam-roller wheels to
smooth out the rock roads, and was propelled by simply having the
passengers run it along with their feet.
    The characterizations of the cave-dwelling neighbors owed a
great debt to the Kramden and Norton couples in The Honeymooners
(CBS, 1955-1959/1966-1970), the situation comedy starring comedian
Jackie Gleason and his foil, Art Carney.   Where Ralph and Ed pursued bowling one night a week, so did Fred and Barney, with stone
bowling balls.   Like Ralph, Fred had a big mouth and small brain,
was the fall-guy for the most blatant con-artist and was endlessly
involved in get-rich-quick schemes that backfired.   Capitalizing on
cultural contrasts and inventive modern artifacts in the first two
seasons, the episodes followed the easier forms of slapstick.   Yawn-
ing and stretching on his patio one morning, Fred was kayoed by the
delivery of the 90-lb Bedrock Daily Slate, a newspaper chiseled in
a stone slab.   Also involved in the gags were comical animals like
Dino, the Flintstone's dog-like baby dinosaur, called a "Runtasau-
rus."   Gradually introduced were a prehistoric menagerie, including the Rubbles' "Kitty," Baby Puss, a saber-toothed tiger, Woolly,

the woolly mammoth, Hoppy, the kangaroo, and a sort of paleolithic panting Pekingese, Snoots, a big-nosed "Snorkasaurus."

In the 1962-1963 season, the comedies became even more domesticated with the pregnancy of Wilma and a whole new set of pre-and-post maternity jokes. After much fanfare, the auspicious occasion occurred at the Bedrock Rockapedic Hospital at approximately 8:00 PM, February 22, 10,000 B.C. (but on television in 1963). The date heralded the arrival of a baby daughter, whom the Flintstones named Pebbles. For an added surprise in the Fall, the Rubbles adopted a baby boy, Bamm Bamm, and the scenarios focused on the growing pains of the children and proud parents.

During the final prime time season, Ann-Margret was heard as Ann-Margrock and Tony Curtis as movie star, Stony Curtis. Other satiric characters were Ed Sullystone, a TV host, Eddy Brianstone, a teenage impressionist, attorney Perry Masonry, who never lost a case, and Lollobrickida, a pretty cook. In a parody on The Addams Family (ABC, 1964-1966), a macabre pair named Weirdly and Creepella Gruesome moved into a cave nearby, believing everyone else in Bedrock a bit odd, and the alien creature Gazoo, voiced by Harvey Korman, arrived from the planet Zetox to perform good deeds for Fred and Barney in their primitive land. The recurring supporting characters included Wilma's mother, Mrs. Flaghoople, Fred's boss, George Slate, the newspaper boy, Arnold, and Rollo, the Flintstone's overly efficient robot servant.

Teenagers saved The Flintstones, which was panned by such critics as The New York Times' Jack Gould, who called it an "inked disaster." The series was the number one favorite program of the adolescent age group and millions of younger children used the show as an excuse to stay up until nine o'clock on Friday night. The youngsters gave The Flintstones high ratings and made it a Friday night leader; and after two seasons ABC moved it to earlier hours to accommodate a younger audience. It ended on September 2, 1966. In 1963, the Ideal Toy Company brought out its Pebbles doll and line of accessories, which added $20 million to the Hanna-Barbera coffers, and Post Cereals introduced its Pebbles breakfast foods. Nearly three thousand items were licensed for merchandise tie-ins and by 1964 Hanna-Barbera was receiving royalties on comic strips and fifty-five million copies of The Flintstone Comics through Charlton publishers. Recognizing its potential, NBC repeated the series on Saturdays beginning January 17, 1967.

CBS cemented the juvenile orientation in 1971-1972 when they revived as teenagers, Pebbles and Bamm Bamm (q.v.). Focusing on their activities and problems at Bedrock High School with their friends, Moonrock, Penny, Wiggy, Fabian and Cindy, the cartoons were repeated in 1972-1973 on The Flintstones Comedy Hour. In some new episodes featuring their parents and pals, Schleprock was a long-haired, gloomy-gus guy whose presence was an ill omen for whatever project was at hand. Also hampering their plans and providing racing competition for Bamm Bamm and Moonrock in their "Cave Buggy" was The Bronto Bunch, a rowdy rock-cycle gang led by its namesake and comprised of Zonk, Noodles and Stub. Pebbles was often the dupe of some con-artist like Faginstone, who

hoodwinked the gang into stealing merchandise from a department
store in an adaptation of the Charles Dickens story. And after
Pebbles enrolled in their phoney art school, Slipstone and Rocko
received their comeuppance when they turned art thieves. A
rancher with Walter Brennan's voice, Pebble's uncle, Hot Rock
Flintstone, appeared during a trip out west on a long-horned
Brontosaurus roundup. The segments were bridged with short
vignettes, two-liner gags and a dance-of-the-week, like "The
Pterodactyl Flap." The cartoons were repeated on The Flintstones Show in 1973-1974 and rotated in a continuation of Pebbles
and Bamm Bamm until Fall 1976, thereafter syndicated as segments on Fred Flintstone and Friends.

In February 1979, NBC re-dubbed thirteen original episodes
featuring Fred's dumbest schemes, resurrected under the title The
New Fred and Barney Show. That fall Fred and Barney Meet The
Thing sandwiched two segments of a teenage version of the incredible rock-like superhuman created by Stan Lee for The Fantastic
Four (q. v.). The format was tied together with jokes and sketches
and incorporated pro-social messages derived from the experiences
of four Centerville High School students: Benjy, the level-headed
core of the plots, the danger-prone and snobbish Betty, her young
freckle-faced sister Kelly, and Ronald Radford, a wealthy spoilsport. Dr. Harkness was an understanding neighbor and Miss
Twilly one of their teachers, reminiscent of Marion Lorne. The
antagonists were the Yancy Street Gang, a trio of motorcycle row-
dies, Turkey, Stretch and the leader, Spike. Whenever trouble
threatened, Benjy would place two halves of his ring together and
with the incantation, "Thing Ring do your thing!," transform himself into the blue-trunked, orange Goliath, who spoke like Jimmy
Durante and used his brute strength to resolve the crisis. In
December the show was expanded to ninety-minutes as Fred and
Barney Meet The Shmoo by adding the mystery-comedies introduced
separately in Fall 1979 as The New Shmoo (q. v.).

A ninety-minute package with six major elements, The Flintstone Comedy Show was NBC's premiere Saturday morning entry in
the 1980-1981 season. Apart from "The Flintstone Family Adventures," in separate comedies Fred wanted nothing to do with some
new neighbors, a gruesome family of monsters called "The Frankenstones," not unlike The Munsters (CBS, 1964-1966), headed by
Frank and his wife, Hidea, their teenage offspring, Atrocia and
Freaky, and their weird household pet, Rockjaw. Featuring the
exploits of the zany superhero "Captain Caveman," Wilma and
Betty were paired as reporters for Lou Granite, editor of the
Bedrock Daily News, involved with such master criminals as the
Masquerader and Tigra, who were vanquished by "Cavey," the
alter-identity of Chester, the paper's bespectacled copyboy. Ad-
ditionally, Fred and Barney turned up as "The Bedrock Cops" with
The Shmoo, working for Sergeant Boulder, and "Pebbles, Dino and
Bamm Bamm" found mysterious goings-on in such locales as Scarey
Valley. "Dino and Cavemouse" appeared in short, chase comedies
based on the formula of Tom and Jerry (q. v.). The cartoons were
tied together by educational segments, riddles, how to make various
simple toys, scrambled mixed-up celebrity faces, exercise and

health tips and a dance-of-the-week like "The Captain Caveman Hop." An NBC Special half-hour, prime time program introduced the new Bedrock citizens on The Flintstones New Neighbors (Sep 26, 1980), and this was followed by The Flintstones Meet Rockula and Frankenstone (Oct 3, 1980).

Before the first five episodes were telecast in 1960, the original voices of Fred and Barney were replaced by Alan Reed and Mel Blanc. One of radio comedy's great straight men, Reed was the original Daddy to Miss Fanny Brice's Baby Snooks (NBC, 1937-1951), the poet Falstaff Openshaw on The Fred Allen Show (CBS, 1940-1944/NBC, 1945-1949) and a movie and stage star. Born Ted Bergman, Reed died at age 69 in 1977 and was replaced in the series and TV commercials by Henry Corden. Fred and Barney were the spokesmen for Flintstone's Chewable Vitamins, which caused a flap among children's advertising critics and in 1972 resulted in Chock's and other companies withdrawing all their tot-oriented TV ads. The Flintstone's characters have appeared in costumed-likeness at amusement parks, in ice shows, parades, personal appearances and a CBS Special The Flintstones on Ice (Feb 11, 1973) and The Flintstone Arena Show (Jun 25, 1981), an NBC Special hosted by Michael Landon. A feature-length animated film, A Man Called Flintstone (COL, 1966), was eventually televised, followed by a pair of NBC Specials, A Flintstone Christmas (Dec 7, 1977) and The Flintstone's Little Big League (Apr 6, 1978).

Bill Hanna and Joe Barbera created The Flintstones, their fourth animated TV series, after they discovered that adults comprised sixty per cent of the nighttime audience watching The Huckleberry Hound Show (q. v.). Together with Yogi Bear (q. v.), these three programs firmly established Hanna-Barbera Productions as a major Hollywood cartoonery and by the late sixties as the world's largest producer of animated entertainment films.


## FONZ AND THE HAPPY DAYS GANG

Network History
      Premiere: November 8, 1980
      ABC/Nov 1980-Sep 1981/Saturday 9:00-9:30 AM

Executive Producers: William Hanna, Joseph Barbera
Producers: Tom Swale, Duane Poole
Company: Hanna-Barbera Productions/13 films

Principal Characters and Voices

| | |
|---|---|
| Arthur "Fonz" Fonzarelli | Henry Winkler |
| Richie Cunningham | Ron Howard |
| Ralph Malph | Donny Most |
| Cupcake | DiDi Conn |
| Mr. Cool | Frank Welker |

Fonz and the Happy Days Gang turned up as cartoon characters in this animated fantasy series based on a Wellsian premise.

Lifted from the nostalgic prime time situation comedy hit, Happy Days (ABC, 1974-  ), network television's number one program in the 1976-1977 season, the "Fonz," his dog, Mr. Cool, plus Richie and Ralph became involved with a flaky time machine piloted by a cosmic calamity, a futuristic teenage girl nicknamed Cupcake.  Accidentally trapped onboard the saucer-like spaceship and activating its controls, the gang traveled through time to different years and locales in their ill-fated attempts to return to 1957 Milwaukee. Time and again, the take-charge, poised Arthur Fonzarelli extricated his pals from threatening danger in strange lands, while complications were supplied by the comic capers of his canine and the magical "zaps" of the zealous Cupcake, whose best intentions always backfired.  During the episodic adventures, the worldly and hip hero thwarted two thieves out to steal a lost city's jewels, freed Richie and Ralph, who were held captive by Amazon women in "It's a Jungle Out There," and unmasked a devious ship owner posing as the Witch of Salem in "You'll Never Get Witch." In other stories ranging from ancient Greek civilization to fantastic worlds in distant galaxies, Fonz and the Happy Days Gang sustained their characterization and idiom, like Richie's "Wait one minute, Bucko," popularized in the nighttime series.

Originally the story of two students at Jefferson High School, Milwaukee, the prototype of Happy Days, centered on the Cunningham family in the mid-fifties, was a segment titled "Love and the Happy Day," starring Ron Howard and Anson Williams, which appeared in February 1972 on Love, American Style (ABC, 1969-1974). For a more extreme contrast, Arthur Fonzarelli was added as a street-wise, motorcycle-riding pal, an addition that made the prime time series a hit and a major TV star out of supporting actor, Henry Winkler.  In adapting the characters for a Saturday morning cartoon, ABC implemented a practice the network pioneered in 1972 with The Brady Kids (q. v. ).


## FRANKENSTEIN JR. AND THE IMPOSSIBLES

Network History
    Premiere:  September 10, 1966
    CBS/Sep 1966-Sep 1967/Saturday 10:00-10:30 AM
    CBS/Sep 1967-Sep 1968/Saturday 9:00-9:30 AM
    Last Program:  September 7, 1968

THE SPACE GHOST/FRANKENSTEIN JR.
    Return:  November 27, 1976
    NBC/Nov 1976-Sep 1977/Saturday 11:00-11:30 AM
    Last Program:  September 3, 1977

Syndicated History

CAPTAIN INVENTORY

Distributor:  Taft H-B Program Sales/1973-1979; Worldvision Enterprises/1979-

Executive Producers:  William Hanna, Joseph Barbera
Director:  Charles A. Nichols
Company:  Hanna-Barbera Productions/18 films

Principal Characters and Voices

| | | |
|---|---|---|
| Frankenstein Jr. | | Ted Cassidy |
| Buzz Conroy | | Dick Beals |
| Professor Conroy | | John Stephenson |
| Multi Man | (1966-1968) | Don Messick |
| Fluid Man | (1966-1968) | Paul Frees |
| Coil Man | (1966-1968) | Hal Smith |

Frankenstein Jr. and The Impossibles plied their superhero
trade separately, one as a space-flying fighter of fiendish schemes
and the others as a trio of undercover agents posing as a rock
group.  Unlike his progenitor, conceived by novelist Mary Shelley
for Frankenstein or a Modern Prometheus (1818), Junior was a
fifty-foot-tall computerized, rocket-powered robot in a domino
mask, and could think and talk clearly.  The creation of Buzz
Conroy, a Tom Swiftian-like boy scientist and the heroic offspring
of Professor Conroy, the caped super titan was activated with a
radar ring worn by the young red-headed lad.  Once aboard his
back, Buzz would give the command "Allakazoom!" and the pair
would blast off from his father's mountain top laboratory to eradi-
cate evil.  In Buck Rogers fashion, Buzz could fly as well, using
his Maneuvering Rocket Belt.  Armed with Junior's magnetic ray,
a frost mist which froze their foes stiff, and other inventive weapons, they were Johnny-on-the-spot to triumph over the Spyder Man,
Colossal Junk Monster, Gigantic Ghastly Genie, Birdman, the Alien
Brain from outer space, the wicked wizard of electronics, Dr.
Shock, and the master of the supernatural from far off Pennsyl-
trania, Dr. Spectro and his Ghoulish Ghost Maker Machine.
        A bubblegum rock group called The Impossibles was trans-
formed into comic book-style crusaders against crime, with the
catch-cry "Rally-Ho!"  The trio was summoned to do "the impossible" by their chief, Big D, via a small TV set in the crook of a
guitar.  Each of the musicians could transform himself in some
unique way.  Coil Man had limbs that could extend like a huge
spring, Multi Man could become unlimited facsimiles of himself,
and Fluid Man was able to ooze into any form of liquid.  Traveling about in their "Impossicar," in the cause of justice they outwitted such grotesque criminals as the Satanic Surfer, Insidious
Inflator, Diabolical Dauber, Fiendish Fiddler, Terrible Twister and
the Spinner, a spider-like cyborg who stole a million dollar tiara.
They also captured The Burrower, an earth worm bank-robber and
his henchman Muddy, and freed the Shah of Shis-Ka-Bob, who was
being held for ransom by The Bubble Man.  Two episodes of The
Impossibles were seen among the three eight-minute films in each
show.
        Repackaged as The Space Ghost/Frankenstein, Jr., the
episodes of the masked robot were repeated on NBC as a replacement for ratings failures in 1976-1977.  It marked the return to

the network of the cartoon superhero, a genre which had been banned since 1970 in a programming policy change.

FRED AND BARNEY MEET THE SHMOO  See  FLINTSTONES, THE

FRED AND BARNEY MEET THE THING  See  FLINTSTONES, THE

FUNKY PHANTOM, THE

Network History
   Premiere:  September 11, 1971
   ABC/Sep 1971-Sep 1972/Saturday 9:00-9:30 AM
   ABC/Sep 1972-Sep 1973/Saturday 12:00-12:30 PM
   Last Program:  September 1, 1973

THE GODZILLA/DYNOMUTT SHOW WITH THE FUNKY PHANTOM
   Return:  September 27, 1980
   NBC/Sep 1980-Nov 1980/Saturday 8:00-9:00 AM
   Last Program:  November 15, 1980

Syndicated History

THE FUN WORLD OF HANNA-BARBERA

Distributor:  Taft H-B Program Sales/1977-1979; Worldvision
   Enterprises/1979-
Executive Producers:  William Hanna, Joseph Barbera
Producer:  Iwao Takamoto
Company:  Hanna-Barbera Productions/17 films

Principal Characters and Voices

| | |
|---|---|
| Jonathan Muddlemore | Daws Butler |
| Skip | Mickey Dolenz |
| Augie | Tommy Cook |
| April | Tina Holland |
| Boo (Muddlemore's cat) | |
| Elmo (Skip's bulldog) | |

   The Funky Phantom, a spunky spectre from the American Revolutionary War, visited some of his old haunts in these comedy-mysteries.  After hiding from pursuing Redcoats in 1776, Jonathan Muddlemore became entrapped in a large grandfather clock at his mansion in East Muddlemore, somewhere in New England.  When three present-day teenagers took refuge there during a thunderstorm, and reset the clock-hands to twelve, the blithe "Spirit of '76" emerged as an incorrigible storyteller, name-dropper and helpmate, with a voice imitation of comedian Bert Lahr (1895-1967).  Piling in their jeepster vehicle, named the "Looney Duney," and with his cat Boo riding atop his tricorn, "Muddy" and his new

friends, Skip, April, Augie and their gruff Bulldog Elmo, toured to
adventures based largely on early American folktales and colonial
history.  In "The Headless Horseman, " the travelers visited Sleepy
Hollow, where they met a twentieth-century descendant of school-
master Ichabod Crane and cleverly solved an updated mystery based
on the legend written by Washington Irving (1783-1859).  Still jittery
over any unexpected noise, which caused his panicky outcry, "The
Redcoats are coming!  The Redcoats are coming!, " the skitterish
ghost and his cat became transparent when suddenly frightened.
More often than not, the transformation took place when their ectoplasmic appearance was needed most, to help expose malefactors in
such stories as "The Liberty Bell Caper, " "The Hairy Scarey
Houndman" and "Ghost Town Ghost. "

Several episodes were repeated on NBC at the beginning of
the strike-delayed 1980-1981 season, appearing with reruns of
Godzilla (q. v. ) and Dynomutt, Dog Wonder (q. v. ).


FUNNY COMPANY, THE

Syndicated History
Premiere:  September 9, 1963
KHJ, Los Angeles/Monday-Friday 5:30-6:00 PM PST
Theme:  "The Funny Company" by Bill Walker and Ken Snyder
Sponsor:  Mattel Toys (1963-1966)
Distributor:  Carson-Roberts Advertising/1963-1966; CBS Films/
1968-1971; Bloom Film Group/1971-
Executive Producer:  Ken Snyder
Associate Producer:  Leo Salkin
Animation Producer:  Sam Nicholson
Company:  The Funny Company/260 films, 5 minutes

Principal Characters and Voices

| | |
|---|---|
| Buzzer Bell/Shrinkin' Violette | Dick Beals |
| Polly Plum | Robie Lester |
| Merry Twitter/Jasper N. Park | Nancy Wible |
| Terry Dactyl | Ken Snyder |
| Dr. Todd Goodheart/Belly | |
|     Laguna/Dr. Von Upp | Hal Smith |
| The Wisenheimer | Bud Hiestand |
| Broken Feather | Tom Thomas |
| Superchief (an air horn) | |

The Funny Company, an enterprising club of neighborhood
children, used their collective wits and energy to wholesome purpose.  Like a mix of the Little Rascals (q. v. ), whose hijinks influenced the animated concept, and a Junior Achievement Club,
the youngsters made money at odd jobs cleaning out attics, print-
ing hand bills, and selling items and services.  Buzzer Bell was
the president, Polly Plum, secretary, Merry Twitter, the genial
and giggly treasurer, and Jasper N. (National) Park a boy genius
and inventor who was aided by Dr. Todd Goodheart, an elderly and

most knowledgeable gentleman. Their buddies were Terry Dactyl, a wisecracking Pterodactyl that did not know he was extinct, Shrinkin' Violet, a shy little girl who shrank when embarrassed, and Broken Feather and Superchief, a pair of Indians. Working out of their ramshackle clubhouse, the children also operated The Funny Company Detective Agency. In pursuit of their commissions, they encountered unscrupulous foreign agents trying to filch secret plans and sundry citizens on the shady side of the law. Two of the principal villains were Belly Laguna, a Balkan bad man, and Dr. Von Upp, who wanted to be "von up" on everyone. Always triumphant over its ill-intentioned foes, the company owed its success to the unbridled youthful enthusiasm and diligent work of its members.

Cleverly sandwiched between the wraparound cartoon segments were two-minute educational elements on the natural and physical sciences, other lands and peoples, business and industry, sports, hobbies, folklore, "how to" subjects and others. Appropriate to each episode's storyline, the clips were from industrial and public service films or shot on contract assignment, and introduced through the Wisenheimer, an electronic brain invented by Jasper. It was the forerunner of the computer on Marlo and the Magic Movie Machine* (q.v.), that would arrive fifteen years later. "Wisenheimer, Wisenheimer, clickety clacks ... crank it up and get the facts," was the command. And then the squiggly-lined oscilloscopic voice described the informative live action films, like the dramatic role played by the Ladybird Beetle in the plant-insect world, or life on the canals of Bangkok. In 1966, a six-year-old boy pulled a drowning two-year-old girl from the Ohio river and revived her by using a method he had learned through watching an episode entitled "Resuscitation."

Several later producers borrowed elements from The Funny Company, which was superbly innovative. It was conceived and written by Ken Snyder as a response to FCC Chairman Newton Minow's 1961 speech urging more cultural and educational children's programming. For the first three years, the series was licensed to Mattel, the California toy maker whose year-around use of network television revolutionized toy advertising. As a result, the series became a pioneer in barter programming. To encourage stations to buy The Funny Company, Mattel agreed to purchase one-minute participations or adjacencies on a two-year non-cancellable contract, at the same price the station paid for an unlimited run for each five-minute episode, during the license period. In effect, the stations set their own price for the series and the commercials. By the end of 1963, the program had been sold in ninety markets; it later expanded to one hundred and ten cities, and local station Funny Company clubs were in operation coast-to-coast.

TV stations adapted the films for their own format. On KHJ, Los Angeles, they appeared as a half-hour weekday strip show hosted by Johnny Coons, known to millions of young fans in the fifties from the Uncle Johnny Coons Show* (q.v.). To promote the program locally, the station and Mattel held a sneak preview at twenty Fox West Coast Theaters, Saturday morning, September 6, 1963. In New York, The Funny Company was seen on WOR at

3:30-5:00 PM weekdays, beginning September 23, 1963, as a ninety-minute show emceed by Morty Gunty and featuring guests and star performers. Each film opened with the theme:

> We have a company that you can join for free,
> and kids in every neighborhood belong ...
> It's The Funny Company.

Like any other club, the company had a password, "Keep Smiling," which ended each episode. The simple smiling face that appeared on round yellow stick-ons and stationery in the late sixties was the trademark of The Funny Company, used on giveaway buttons by many stations to promote the program.


FURTHER ADVENTURES OF DR. DOLITTLE, THE

Network History
    Premiere: September 12, 1970
    NBC/Sep 1970-Sep 1971/Saturday 10:00-10:30 AM
    NBC/Sep 1971-Sep 1972/Saturday 8:00-8:30 AM
    Last Program: September 2, 1972

Syndicated History

DR. DOLITTLE

Distributor: Twentieth Century-Fox Television/1972-
Executive Producers: David DePatie, Friz Freleng
Company: DePatie-Freleng Enterprises with TCF-TV/17 films

Principal Characters and Voices

| | |
|---|---|
| Dr. John Dolittle | Bob Holt |
| Tommy Stubbins | Hal Smith |
| Sam Scurvy | Lennie Weinrib |
| Mooncat/other animals | Don Messick/Barbara Towers |
| The Grasshoppers | Ronnie Fallon/Colin Julian/ |
| | Annabell |

The Further Adventures of Dr. Dolittle animated the world-wide travels of the eccentric country physician from Puddleby-on-the-Marsh, who could talk with animals. The invention of English-American author and illustrator Hugh Lofting (1886-1947), Doctor Dolittle was developed in letters he wrote to his small son from the Front during the First World War. The cartoons were pegged loosely on Lofting's nine acclaimed juvenile novels published between 1920 and 1952, beginning with The Story of Dr. Dolittle. Possessing a bent for natural history and a love of pets, he abandoned his practice "among the best people" to serve the animals he greatly preferred. Among Dolittle's permanent household animals were Polynesia, the parrot that taught him animal talk, beginning with the ABC's of the birds, Chee Chee the monkey, and his housekeeper, Dab Dab the duck. The reliable and conscientious Tommy Stubbins, son of Jacoby Stubbins, the Puddleby cobbler, eventually

persuaded the Doctor to teach him animal languages and in return
became his devoted young assistant.

To satisfy his scientific curiosity and ambition to travel, Dr.
Dolittle, his pets and fourteen-year-old Tommy embarked on an expedition to Africa, South America and the far corners of the globe,
on his ship "Flounder," with a new pet, Mooncat, a lunar kitten.
During their adventures they were constantly beset by the villainous
Sam Scurvy, a pirate obsessed with a power-mad scheme to dominate nature's creatures and determined to learn the animal conversation secret.   Aided by Tommy, the Doctor rescued animals from
the designs of Scurvy and frustrated his fiendish plans in such stories as "The Tomb of the Phoenix Bird," "The Silver Seals at the
Circus," "The Land of the Tiger Moo" and "The Baffled Buffalo."
When things became overly humdrum, a rock group called The
Grasshoppers provided a big-beat tune.

The program was produced in association with Twentieth
Century-Fox Films, which owned the property rights and produced
the musical version of Dr. Dolittle (1967), starring Rex Harrison,
which was telecast as a three-hour ABC children's special on November 21, 1973.   Anthony Newley was seen also as the Doctor,
hosting a show on animals for a CBS Library Special* (q.v.).


GALAXY GOOF-UPS, THE

Network History

YOGI'S SPACE RACE/THE GALAXY GOOF-UPS
    Premiere:   September 9, 1978
    NBC/Sep 1978-Oct 1978/Saturday 8:00-9:30 AM

THE GALAXY GOOF-UPS
    NBC/Nov 1978-Jan 1979/Saturday 8:00-8:30 AM
    Last Program:   January 27, 1979
Executive Producers:   William Hanna, Joseph Barbera
Producer:   Art Scott
Director:   Ray Patterson
Company:   Hanna-Barbera Productions/13 films

Principal Characters and Voices

| | |
|---|---|
| Officers Yogi Bear/Huckleberry Hound | Daws Butler |
| Officer Scarebear | Joe Besser |
| Officer Quack-Up | Mel Blanc |
| Captain Snerdly/General Blaster Blowhard | John Stephenson |

The Galaxy Goof-Ups teamed those enduring stars, Yogi
Bear and Huckleberry Hound, with a new cast of supporting characters in space adventures.   Initially a component comedy in the
ninety-minute series, Yogi's Space Race (q.v.), the dopey bruin
and blue dog were paired as Officers of the Galaxy Guardians.   A

group of misfits, they patrolled distant star systems from Command Central, located in the outer reaches of space.   Receiving orders from Captain Snerdly, a caricature and sound-alike of comedian Joe Flynn (1924-1974), Yogi and Huck were joined by newcomers Scarebear, reminiscent of Curly Howard of The Three Stooges (q. v. ) and Quack-Up, a modish version of the looney Daffy Duck (q. v. ).   Rocketing off in their ''Space Wagon'' to defend the universe, the fumbling four were assigned superhuman tasks through which they stumbled to a successful conclusion.   Directed to capture the sinister Space Spider by Commanding General Blaster Blowhard, the Goof-Ups used their secret weapon, the MR-12 mini-rocket, and Huck's official Galaxy Guardian mini-computer to untangle his sticky web and defeat the power-hungry villain.   In other episodes they recovered the original Space Station U. S. A. for the Galaxonian Museum, after it had been stolen by the richest man in the Galaxy, and tangled with Tacky Cat and the Vampire of Space.   On some feeble excuse, sandwiched in the middle of each adventure was a disco scene, featuring the gyrations of the goofy quartet to such up-beat tunes as ''Space Happy. ''

On November 4, 1978, Yogi's Space Race was reduced to one-hour and The Galaxy Goof-Ups was lifted from the package to appear in the Saturday lead-off timeslot for three months on the revised schedule.


GEORGE OF THE JUNGLE

Component Series
    SUPER CHICKEN; TOM SLICK, RACER

Network History
    Premiere:   September 9, 1967
    ABC/Sep 1967-Sep 1968/Saturday 11:30-12:00 AM
    ABC/Sep 1968-Aug 1969/Saturday 12:00-12:30 PM
    ABC/Sep 1969-Dec 1969/Sunday 10:00-10:30 AM
    ABC/Jan 1970-Sep 1970/Saturday 11:30-12:00 AM
    Last Program:   September 5, 1970


Syndicated History

Distributor:   Worldvision Enterprises/1972-
Producers:   Jay Ward, Bill Scott
Directors:   Bill Hurtz, Pete Burness, Ted Parmelee
Company:   Jay Ward Productions/16 films


Principal Characters and Voices

George/Tom Slick/Gertie
    Growler/Super Chicken          Bill Scott
Ursula/Bella/Marigold             June Foray
Ape/Fred                          Paul Frees
District Commissioner             Daws Butler

George of the Jungle was a klutzy apeman, as dumb as he was strong, who was unmindful of his hazardous surroundings in the Imgwee Gwee Valley in Africa.  In each episode a new calamity befell the tiger skin-clad hero, who forgetfully plunged to the ground from his tree-house with some regularity.  A rib-tickling spoof of the vine-swinging Tarzan of the Apes (All-Story, Oct 1912), created by novelist Edgar Rice Burroughs (1875-1950), the films toplined a comedy trilogy, the best of the TV cartoons conceived by writer Bill Scott in partnership with Jay Ward.  Drenched in puns and double entendre, the stories reached a new zenith in zany impersonations of movie actors--a device for which the studio was noted since Rocky and His Friends (q. v. ).  An oversized purplish gorilla that talked like mellow-toned Ronald Colman (1891-1958), Ape served as George's counselor and confidant while Bella and Ursula played Jane to his Tarzan-like role.  Using his jungle man scream, he summoned his friendly elephant Shep, which the moron thought was his big grey peanut-loving puppy.  One day a herd of termites appeared instead.  "You sure you had the right call?, " asked Ape.  "Right call, " answered George, flipping through his red rescue book, "but wrong area code. "  Often called to deliverance by jungle phone, the Tooki Tooki bird, the apeman protected the territory from the threatening poachers, animal tamer Claude Badly and his first aide Ernest Conflab, and the conniving con-artists Tiger and Weavel, look-and-sound-alikes of scraggly actor Robert Newton and Henry Daniell, the foxy-looking villain.  "A friend to you and me, " and apparently to everyone, George assisted the District Commissioner, a voice imitation of unctuous British actor Eric Blore; Dr. Killer Mandaro, Africa's greatest witch doctor, with the voice of Tony Curtis; and helped find the missing Dr. Alfred Sprizer, who sounded like George Jessel.  Undaunted, except for crashing into an occasional tree, George always triumphed with the help of Ape, Shep or the local natives who loved him because, as the Chief put it, "George swings, man!"

"Tom Slick, Racer, " with his sparkling smile and all-American blondish good looks, was an all-time good sport and simple-minded dupe.  Overcoming unorthodox and crafty competitors in events on land, in the air and on and under water, Tom raced endlessly in machines of every description from Skate Boards and Swamp Buggies to Submarines and Hot Air Balloons.  Most often behind the wheel of his "Thunderbolt Grease Slapper, " the resolute and immaculate Slick once entered the $50, 000 Bigg Race, sponsored by millionaire Tiny Bigg.  Pitted against such opponents as the wily oriental Foo On You in his "Dragonster" and Sir Philip Prince in his "One Wheel Curb Hugger, " Tom's arch rival was the habitual nail-biter and evil cheater, Baron Otto Matic, driving his "Four Pipe Blow Master" and accompanied by Clutcher, his obsequious henchman and mechanic.  Beset at every turn by their foul schemes, the racing sport politely swore, "I'm hurt to the quick! That Otto Matic is no gentleman!"  Usually manipulating his last-minute wins was the clever Gertie Growler, his crusty grandmother, aided by his faithful, gushing girlfriend Marigold, whose favorite exclamation was "Splendafabulous!"  A perfect-mannered sportsman to a fault, Tom's only love was racing, much to amorous

Marigold's frustration, and he had a maniacal allegience to the rules of the game, much to hot-tempered Gertie's exasperation.

"Super Chicken," the best of the nouveau cartoon superanimals, was heralded by his famous "cry in the sky," a cackled-call "charge!" The alter-identity of Henry Cabot Henhouse III, a mild-mannered wealthy scientist, the chicken became a heroic crime-fighter after a slug of Super Sauce. His miraculous discovery was doled out in time of need by his butler, Fred the Lion, and trans-formed Henry into a masked, caped and rapier-armed superbird with extraordinary strength and ability. But unlike <u>Superman</u> (q. v. ), which the films satirized, the pair usually soared to the scene of crimes in the "Supercoop," an all-purpose plane. In a contest be-tween the most popular wizards in the world on the Isle of Lucy, they battled the Warlock Merlin Brando, who sounded like Phil Silvers and whose magic mirror spoke like Boris Karloff. They jailed Wild Ralph Hiccup, who spoofed John Wayne as a plane rob-ber; and a cunning fiend too slippery for the police, The Oyster, who stole the world's biggest pearl; and ended the cavalcade of crime wrought by the bandit of Sherwood Park, in downtown Pitts-burgh, Rotten Hood and his band of merry men, Fried Tucker. Also, Super Chicken foiled the plans of a classmate from Tick Tock Tech, the Harvard School of Watch Repair, the renegade rich man, Appian Way, who stole Rhode Island; ended the money-mad scheme of the green-back launderer, Shrimp Chop Fooey, who re-marked "All Superheroes look alike to me"; and the career of an eccentric bank-robber called The Noodle, who stole the bird's mind and made him just another dumb cluck. Fred always answered Henry's commands with "Roger Wilcox" and was the fall-guy in nearly every episode. Battered and grumbling, he was continually admonished by his boss, "You knew the job was dangerous when you took it, Fred."

Filled with insider gags to please the funny-bone of the pro-ducers, <u>George of the Jungle</u> overcame its limited animation handi-caps through imaginative characters and clever, genuinely witty dialogue, simple enough for children and perceptive enough for adults. In syndication it has become a revered classic among a growing cult of aficionados.


GERALD McBOING-BOING SHOW, THE

Network History
    Premiere: December 16, 1956
    CBS/Dec 1956-Mar 1957/Sunday 5:30-6:00 PM
    CBS/May 1958-Oct 1958/Friday 7:30-8:00 PM
    Last Program: October 3, 1958

Syndicated History

UPA CARTOON PARADE

Distributor: UPA Productions of America/1959-
Executive Producer: Stephen Bosustow

Producer:   Robert Cannon
Directors:  George Dunning, Ernest Pintoff
Company:    UPA Pictures/13 films

Narrator
  Bill Goodwin

Principal Character
  Gerald McBoing-Boing (non-speaking)

        The Gerald McBoing-Boing Show was hosted by a beany-
wearing little boy who spoke with sounds rather than words.   A
creation of the fertile mind of Theodor Geisel, better known as
popular author and humorist Dr. Seuss, the character appeared
between 1951 and 1956 in four UPA theatrical cartoons directed
by Robert "Bobe" Cannon.   Adapted from Geisel's morality tale
about tolerance by writers Bill Scott and Phil Eastman, Gerald
McBoing-Boing (Jan 25, 1951) was the 1950 animated Oscar-winner
and featured in the TV premiere.   Constantly rejected from the age
of two, when he first tried to speak but could only come up with
the disturbing sound, "Boing-Boing," Gerald was a cheery, round-
faced, tow-headed lad whose expanded repertoire of strange noises
brought only ridicule.   After running away from home, he was discovered by a radio executive and his talent to produce sound effects
for his station finally brought Gerald fame, esteem and understanding from his parents and peers.   Eloquent in its form and content,
the cartoon was a splendid example of stylized graphics that were
derived from the many traditions of contemporary art, and offered
a welcome change from cute animal fantasies.
        Commissioned by CBS, the program was the first cartoon
show made in part for television and including educational elements.
Among the component features were "Mr. Charmeley Meets a Lady,"
which demonstrated basic etiquette, "Legends of America and the
World," "Meet the Artist" and "Meet the Inventor," which documented discoveries such as Samuel Morse's invention of the tele-
graph.   In an amusing but impressionable manner, different maxims
were underscored in films like "The Little Boy Who Ran Away."
And there were fun and fantasy in "The Twerlinger Twins," about
two little girls who attended music and dancing school and could not
remember their lines; and in the adventures of "Dusty of the Circus," who could talk to animals.   Some of the episodes contained
such notable UPA films as Madeline (Nov 27, 1952), based on
the Ludwig Bemelmans story, and James Thurber's The Unicorn in
the Garden (Sep 24, 1953), Christopher Crumpet (Jun 25, 1953),
and a day in the life of some musical instruments, The Oompahs
(Jan 24, 1952).   Bill Goodwin supplied off-camera narration inter-
preting Gerald's sounds in the wraparound segments
        The limitations of the character and the pedagogical content
mitigated against the series, as did the production costs, and CBS
ordered only thirteen shows.   The series ended March 24, 1957,
but was repeated in Summer 1958, marking the second network cartoon series seen in prime time following the CBS Cartoon Theater
(q.v.).   A token of good taste, fresh in concept as well as execution, the parts were better than the whole.   After their network run

the films were relegated to foreign distribution and, without Gerald McBoing-Boing and other theatrical cartoons, the components were placed in syndication during the seventies as the UPA Cartoon Parade.


GIGANTOR

Syndicated History
    Premiere: January 5, 1966
    WPIX, New York/Wednesday 7:00-7:30 PM
    Distributor: Alan Enterprises/1966-1974
    Producer: Mitsuteru Yokoyama
    Company: TCJ Animation Center, Japan/52 films

Principal Characters

    Gigantor
    Jimmy Sparks

    Gigantor was a jet-propelled flying robot controlled by twelve-year-old Jimmy Sparks. Originally a newspaper comic by Mitsuteru Yokoyama titled Tetsujin 28gō (Shōnen, 1958-1966), which began in April 1958, the features and films were the progenitors of the giant robot theme in Japan, which surfaced in the United States with such imitations as Frankenstein, Jr. (q. v.). According to the background legend, a pair of scientists had begun work on Gigantor before the Second World War at a secret Japanese Weapons Institute, and the robot was finally completed in 1955 to assist Inspector Blooper and the Japanese police in their war against crime. The son of scientist Dr. Sparks ("Dr. Kaneda" in the Japanese version), young Jimmy ("Shōtarō") manned the simple control box of the metallic leviathan, which had a small helmet-covered head and a rocket engine on its back, and together they fought an array of villains.
    In the first episode, Gigantor was captured for a time by Dr. Katzmeow, who wanted to make a duplicate for a competitor. In other stories, Professor Brainy tried to replace Jimmy with his creation, a robot superlad, and the pair had run-ins with Dr. Bugaboo, The Scalawag and Mr. Ugablob, who had a plan to conquer the world through a freeze ray. Many of the plots dealt with arch criminals who tried to steal Gigantor's control mechanism, jam the radio guidance signals or steal Professor Sparks' plans in order to build an army of Gigantors for their own sinister purpose. The arch enemy was Dr. Franken, a jealous inventor of mechanical monsters and robots bent on destroying Gigantor, Earth's mighty superhero, known in Japan as "Iron Man no. 28."
    Produced and shown on Japanese TV between 1963 and 1967, Gigantor rocketed the premise into prominence in the seventies, when over two dozen Nippon cartoon series debuted, each presenting giant robots that defended humanity against alien invaders and lunatic scientists. The films were acquired and edited for English audiences by Al Singer and Fred Ladd.

GODZILLA

Component Series
JANA OF THE JUNGLE, THE ADVENTURES OF JONNY QUEST

Network History

GODZILLA POWER HOUR
Premiere: September 9, 1978
NBC/Sep 1978-Oct 1978/Saturday 9:30-10:30 AM

GODZILLA SUPER 90
NBC/Nov 1978-Sep 1979/Saturday 9:00-10:30 AM
Last Program: September 1, 1979

THE GODZILLA SHOW
Return: September 8, 1979
NBC/Sep 1979-Nov 1979/Saturday 11:30-12:00 AM
NBC/Apr 1980-Sep 1980/Saturday 12:00-12:30 PM
NBC/May 1981-Sep 1981/Saturday 9:00-9:30 AM
Last Program: September 5, 1981

THE GODZILLA/GLOBETROTTERS ADVENTURE HOUR
Return: November 10, 1979
NBC/Nov 1979-Apr 1980/Saturday 8:00-9:00 AM
NBC/May 1980-Sep 1980/Saturday 8:00-9:00 AM
Last Program: September 20, 1980

THE GODZILLA/DYNOMUTT HOUR WITH THE FUNKY PHANTOM
Return: September 27, 1980
NBC/Sep 1980-Nov 1980/Saturday 8:00-9:00 AM
Last Program: November 15, 1980

THE GODZILLA/HONG KONG PHOOEY HOUR
Return: November 22, 1980
NBC/Nov 1980-May 1981/Saturday 8:00-9:00 AM
Last Program: May 16, 1981
Executive Producers: William Hanna, Joseph Barbera
Associate Producer: Doug Wildey
Director: Ray Patterson
Company: Hanna-Barbera Productions and Toho Productions with
UPA Pictures/26 films

Principal Characters and Voices

| | |
|---|---|
| Godzilla | Ted Cassidy |
| Godzooky | Don Messick |
| Captain Carl Majors | Jeff David |
| Dr. Quinn Darien | Brenda Thomson |
| Pete | Al Eiseman |
| Brock | Hilly Hicks |

JANA OF THE JUNGLE (1978-1979)

| Jana | B. J. Ward |
| Montaro | Ted Cassidy |
| Dr. Ben Cooper | Mike Bell |
| Tiko (Jana's kutamundi) | |
| Ghost (Jana's jaguar) | |

JONNY QUEST (1978-1979)   See   ADVENTURES OF JONNY QUEST, THE

Godzilla, a four-hundred-foot-tall prehistoric amphibian, rose anew from the sea as a cartoon superhero.  A beast that walked upright and exhaled smoke and flame, the Iguanodon-like creature became the friend of a research ship's crew after they rescued the trapped Godzooky, a pint-sized relative.  Their faithful playmate for life, "Zookie" was a jolly green dragon with a broad smile, always trying to imitate the gigantic Godzilla but unable to scare anyone very much; at best he could only blow smoke rings.  Commanded by Captain Carl Majors, the "Calico" was equipped with the latest scientific paraphernalia, like Jacques Cousteau's "Calypso."  Dr. Quinn Darien was the chief acientist, the bespectacled Brock was her black teenage assistant, and Pete, her tow-headed young nephew.  Traveling around the world, the crew tried to straighten things out environmentally and lend a hand in emergencies.  Often investigating some unexplained phenomenon, they were faced constantly with deadly peril, but as Pete frequently explained, "Godzilla will save us."  By simply pushing a button on his hand-sized electronic signaller, Captain Majors could summon the creature, who would rise uncannily near their ship from the depths, ready for action.

The stories pitted monster against monster, and apart from his fiery breath Godzilla emitted powerful laser beams from his eyes.  Facing all manner of King Kong-like adversaries, while searching for the source of geothermal energy in Dew Line Village, the huge dragon saved the crew from "The Sub-Zero Terror," Huachucha, an ice monster, and from a creepy looking blob that fed on nuclear energy in "The Breeder Beast."  The reptile matched his muscle with the Lava Monster, and with the Gold Temple Guardians at the ruins of Kayak Nor, and doggedly battled the Firebird, a pterodactyl-like predator enroute to the Arctic to lay its eggs.  "You mean like when a salmon swims upstream?," Pete asked.  "Exactly," said Dr. Darien, "and that would mean the earth would be invaded by millions of Firebirds."  Fortunately, Godzilla won.

The property was suggested to NBC as a straight adaptation by Henry Saperstein, president of UPA Pictures which owned the American rights, but it was Joe Barbera who dreamed up Godzilla as a cartoon hero.  Doug Wildey, the artist who created The Adventures of Jonny Quest (q.v.), which in part the series resembled, developed the idea and contributed Godzooky as comic relief.  Based on a story by Shigeru Kayama, released in Japan as Gojira (Toho, 1954), the first movie featuring the character, Godzilla, King of the

Monsters (AIP, 1956), became a worldwide hit. The story told of the revival of the reptile through nuclear radiation and its rampaging devastation of Tokyo. Although a string of sequels became increasingly esoteric, the Godzilla pictures always made money and developed a cult following.

Introduced on the Godzilla Power Hour in 1978-1979, the adventures were sandwiched between two eleven-minute segments of "Jana of the Jungle." A blond girl, who wore a tiger skin like Sheena and summoned animals like Tarzan, Jana was the heroine of the Amazon bush, where she met no end of bad guys. With her pet kutamundi Tiko and albino jaguar Ghost, her never-ending quest was to locate her father, lost when he was swept away by the raging river. Her friend and companion was Montaro, an Aztec-looking chief in a blue headdress and loincloth, who carried a magical "staff of power." Fleet of foot and tough as an Amazon, Jana wore a magical power necklace with a disc she detached and used as a Frisbee-like weapon and tool. In various episodes, the jungle girl located and returned the Azumi's stolen Black Pearl to Shandur, their Chief; escaped from the ape-like warrior men called Hatuckis; and rescued Lieutenant Steve Lee from sacrifice to the Fire Demon by the witch doctor Shaman, after his plane crashed while carrying an Implosion bomb. One morning Jana was captured by wild savages and asked Montaro, "What was it you said the Gorgas do with their captives?" "You do not want to know," he answered. Fortuitously, since she escaped, youngsters never learned.

On November 4, 1978 the series was retitled Godzilla Super 90 and expanded by the repeats of The Adventures of Jonny Quest. After a solo stint as The Godzilla Show in Fall 1979, the episodes were repeated beginning in December, successively repackaged with The Harlem Globetrotters (q.v.), Dynomutt, Dog Wonder (q.v.), The Funky Phantom (q.v.), and Hong Kong Phooey (q.v.). The Godzilla Show was again accorded its own thirty-minute timeslot on April 12, 1980, with two programs featuring the monster running simultaneously until Fall, and returned May 23, 1981 until the end of the season.


GO GO GLOBETROTTERS  See  HARLEM GLOBETROTTERS, THE


GO GO GOPHERS

Network History
      Premiere: September 14, 1968
      CBS/Sep 1968-Sep 1969/Saturday 8:00-8:30 AM
      Last Program: September 6, 1969

Syndicated History

UNDERDOG

Distributor: Filmtel International/1969-1979; DFS Program Exchange/1979-

Producers: Treadwell Covington, Peter Peich
Company: Total TV Productions with Leonardo TV Productions/24
films

Principal Characters and Voices

| | |
|---|---|
| Ruffled Feather/Sergeant Okey Homa | Sandy Becker |
| Running Board | George S. Irving |
| Colonel Kit Coyote | Kenny Delmar |

Go Go Gophers, a pair of cunning rodents that were really Indians, made life miserable for some coyotes that were really the United States Cavalry. The double-talking, scheming Ruffled Feather and his interpreter Running Board, who spoke in explosively incomprehensible gibberish, were the native residents of Gopher Gulch. Their mortal enemy was Colonel Kit Coyote, the spitting image of Teddy Roosevelt, a blustery Army officer who spent most of his time planning new ways to drive the stubborn redmen from their lands. He was buttressed by a Sergeant and aide, who looked and talked like John Wayne in the early episodes; in later segments the voice impersonation was dropped. Pitted against the conniving Colonel, who was a stickler for military regulations, the buck-toothed braves devised a string of ingenious and successful plots to protect their territorial rights and freedom in such stories as "Don't Fence Me In," "Tanks to the Gophers," "Gatling Gophers" and the "Tricky Tepee Caper."

Introduced in 1966-1967 on Underdog (q. v.), the series was repackaged with some new episodes at the instigation of Fred Silverman, the network daytime programming chief. Between the wrap-arounds, also repeated from Underdog was "Klondike Kat," an inept northwest territory Mountie that took his orders from Major Minor. Operating out of frigid Fort Frazzle, the red coated tabby was engaged in a hapless effort to catch the elusive Savoir Faire, a French mouse and notorious filcher of pastry, pies and goodies, whose catch-phrase was "Savoir Faire is everywaire!" Klondike's favorite reply was, "One of these days I'm gonna make mincemeat of that mouse!"

## GOOBER AND THE GHOST CHASERS

Network History
   Premiere: September 8, 1973
   ABC/Sep 1973-Aug 1974/Saturday 10:30-11:00 AM
   ABC/Sep 1974-Aug 1975/Sunday 11:00-11:30 AM
   Last Program: August 31, 1975

Syndicated History

FRED FLINTSTONE AND FRIENDS

Distributor: Claster TV Productions/1977-1979

Executive Producers: William Hanna, Joseph Barbera
Producer: Iwao Takamoto
Director: Charles A. Nichols
Company: Hanna-Barbera Productions/16 films

Principal Characters and Voices

| | |
|---|---|
| Goober | Paul Winchell |
| Gilly | Ronnie Schell |
| Ted | Jerry Dexter |
| Tina | Jo Anne Harris |
| Laurie Partridge | Susan Dey |
| Chris Partridge | Brian Forster |
| Tracy Partridge | Suzanne Crough |
| Danny Partridge | Danny Bonaduce |

Goober and the Ghost Chasers closely adhered to the successful comedy-mystery formula built around a lovable but fainthearted
dog and a group of plucky teenagers. Basically the same mix as
developed for Scooby-Doo (q. v. ), the youngsters were Gilly, Tina
and Ted, staff members of Ghost Chasers magazine, and their comical mascot, Goober. The difference was that, while the Great
Dane was scared of his own shadow and would run and hide, in
times of stress or high emotion Goober became ectoplasmic. Unlike The Funky Phantom (q. v. ), however, the canine's red-and-
yellow stocking cap remained visible to demark his presence. Usually partnered with the blond-haired Gilly, the brainy, bespectacled staff photographer, Goober and the gang traveled about the
country to investigate such reported manifestations as "The Haunted
Wax Museum, " a headless ghost at Wilt Chamberlain's Dude Ranch,
and Captain Ahab's etheric double in a New England fisherman's
mansion. Armed with electronic and scientific gear, the teenagers
tried to document genuine spirits and exposed the phoney perpetra-
tors of revenant happenings. Several caricatured guest stars were
incorporated in the episodes, with frequent appearances by Laurie,
Chris, Tracy and Danny Partridge, voiced by the original cast members from the prime time situation comedy, The Partridge Family (ABC
(1970-1974), also animated for Partridge Family: 2200 A. D. (q. v. ).


GREAT GRAPE APE, THE

Network History

THE NEW TOM AND JERRY/GRAPE APE SHOW
    Premiere: September 6, 1975
    ABC/Sep 1975-Sep 1976/Saturday 8:30-9:30 AM
    Last Program: September 4, 1976

THE TOM AND JERRY/GRAPE APE/MUMBLY SHOW
    Return: September 11, 1976
    ABC/Sep 1976-Nov 1976/Saturday 8:00-9:00 AM
    Last Program: November 27, 1976

THE GREAT GRAPE APE
    Premiere:  September 11, 1977
    ABC/Sep 1977-Sep 1978/Sunday 11:00-11:30 AM
    Last Program:  September 3, 1978
Executive Producers:  William Hanna, Joseph Barbera
Producer:  Iwao Takamoto
Director:  Charles A. Nichols
Company:  Hanna-Barbera Productions/16 films

Principal Characters and Voices

Grape Ape                          Bob Holt
Beegle Beagle                      Marty Ingels


    The Great Grape Ape motored about with his canine buddy,
Beegle Beagle, a hustler from the carney tent who was out to make
a buck with his new discovery.  A thirty-foot-tall purple primate,
he rode atop the straw-hatted dog's small car because he was too
large to fit inside.  Possessed of incredible stupidity, the gorilla
croaked and grunted his way through ridiculous situations, using his
tremendous strength to help his pal.  Searching for the perfect
specimens in "Flying Saucery," an alien scouting party of little
green men captured the Earthlings and submitted the pair to a
series of scientific tests on their distant planet.  Encouraged by
their sub-mental intellect, they decided to invade the inferior
Earth, only to be thwarted by the feisty, fast-talking Beagle and
the King Kong-like ape, who became a powerful gladiator when
aroused.  The stories included titles like "The Grape Race,"
"Grape Marks the Spot," "Grapefinger," "The Indian Grape Call"
and "Ali Beagle and the Forty Grapes."  Also infatuated with his
name, the gorilla constantly muttered "Grape Ape, Grape Ape" in
his resonant bass voice and cheerfully addressed his good buddy as
"Beeg-ily, Beeg-ily," which became the catch-words of the series.
    Two episodes of The Grape Ape initially alternated in 1975-
1976 with three of Hanna-Barbera's Tom and Jerry (q.v.) and were
repeated in Fall 1976 on The Tom and Jerry/Grape Ape/Mumbly
Show.  In 1977-1978, two episodes were rerun as The Great Grape
Ape, whose colorful titles aped those on the Pink Panther (q.v.).


GROOVIE GOOLIES, THE

Network History

SABRINA AND THE GROOVIE GOOLIES
    Premiere:  September 12, 1970
    CBS/Sep 1970-Sep 1971/Saturday 9:00-10:00 AM

THE GROOVIE GOOLIES
    CBS/Sep 1971-Sep 1972/Sunday 7:30-8:00 AM
    ABC/Oct 1975-Feb 1976/Saturday 10:30-11:00 AM
    ABC/Feb 1976-Sep 1976/Sunday 10:30-11:00 AM
    Last Program:  September 5, 1976

Syndicated History

THE GROOVIE GOOLIES AND FRIENDS

Distributor:  Metromedia Producers Corporation/1978-
Executive Producers:  Louis Scheimer, Norman Prescott
Producer:  Hal Sutherland
Company:  Filmation Productions/16 films

Principal Characters

> Count Dracula
> Hagatha
> Frankie
> Bella La Ghostly
> Sabrina
> Wolfie
> Bonapart
> Mummy
> Dr. Jekyll-Hyde
> Ghoulihand
> Hauntleroy
> Ratso and Batso

Voices

> Jane Webb
> Howard Morris
> Larry Storch
> Larry Mann

The Groovie Goolies, an eclectic collection of merry monsters, joked, sang and·frolicked in eerie Horrible Hall.  The owner was none other than that master sorcerer, Count Dracula, known as "Drak," who talked like MGM chortler Frank Morgan (1890-1949), napped in a comfy casket and flapped about as a transformed vampire bat.  It was convenient at times, particularly when he was being pursued by Lovesick Loveseat, an amorous sofa that continually tried to embrace him.  Hagatha, Dracula's plump wife, gave lessons in low cuisine on "From the Witch's Kitchen."  Most of the time she slaved over a hot cauldron, aided by Salem, her capricious cat, and Broom Hilda, her mischievous bristly broom.  With the voice and likeness of bulky British comedy star, Dame Margaret Rutherford (1892-1972), in her spare time the three-hundred-year-old crone listened to her advisor, Magic Mirror, and gossiped on the Tel-Bone with her sister Nagatha.
A large lovable lug, Frankie (Frankenstein), the son of Dracula and Hagatha, was fond of dimwitted pranks and bizarre bedtime stories.  Rover was his affectionate pet dinosaur and Orville, The Thing-Eating Plant, his pet gluttonous gardenia, a voracious consumer of anything animal, vegetable or mineral.  Providing advice for the lovelorn and the daily Horror-scope via the Tel-Bone, Bella La Ghostly was Horrible Hall's morbidly glamorous

switchboard operator. Hip and hairy, Wolfie (Wolfman) was the athletic type. Always on the move, he whizzed about via surf-board, skateboard and his custom-built "Wolfwagon." His pet was Fido, a flying piranha fish. An accident-prone skeleton who lisped like punch-drunk comedian "Slapsie" Maxie Rosenbloom (1903-1976), Bonapart literally fell into pieces in a heap of disconnected bones whenever he was involved in a collision. Bonapart's buddy, the Mummy, was a TV news announcer and a first-aid expert, who sounded like Ed Wynn (1886-1966) and became unwound a bit too easily.

Among the other macabre characters, Dr. Jekyll-Hyde was a schizophrenic two-headed doctor who made haunted house calls; Ratso and Batso, pint-sized meanies modeled on Eddie Wolfgang, scion of The Munsters (CBS, 1964-1966), who constantly brewed up trouble in their "Invent-ory" lab; Hauntleroy, a spirited, practical-joking ghost; Ghoulihand, seemingly all thumbs, a giant hand like "The Thing" on The Addams Family (q. v.), that served as Drak's handyman and occasionally played the piano; Tiny Tomb and Miss Icky, a long-haired ukulele player and his girlfriend; and Askit Casket, a lid-flapping source of wit and wisdom.

The only normal-looking visitor to the cobwebbed castle was the winsome Sabrina, The Teenage Witch (q. v.), who never-theless managed to connive and cavort with the worst of them. Originally packaged as the hour-long series Sabrina and The Groovie Goolies, under the fatherly eye of Fred Silverman, head of CBS daytime programming, the ghoulish group was created to support the young sorceress when Sabrina was separated in 1970 from The Archies (q. v.). One of the most humorous animated comedies produced by Filmation, although overly cluttered with characters and "things," its variety-comedy-music format was borrowed largely from the prime time ratings hit, Rowan and Martin's Laugh-In (NBC, 1968-1973). A "Weird Windows" seg-ment featured two-liner gags, Hagatha told her bedtime stories with off-beat casting, the bandaged banterer reported the ghoulish news in the Mummy Wrap-Up and Frankie appeared in sketches as Sooper Gool, "able to leap haunted houses in a single bound." Also musically inclined, The Groovie Goolies gathered for a rock tune in each show, in such originals as "C'mon, C'mon to the Goolie Picnic" and "The Goolie Garden," where the strangest things vegetate.

The series completed its CBS run on September 17, 1972 and returned October 25, 1975 on ABC, replacing the first half-hour of the network's worst show ever, Uncle Croc's Block (q. v.).


HANNA-BARBERA NEW CARTOON SERIES, THE

Component Series
 LIPPY THE LION, TOUCHÉ TURTLE, WALLY GATOR

Syndicated History
 Premiere: September 3, 1962
 WPIX, New York/Monday-Friday 5:00-5:30 PM

Distributor: Screen Gems--Columbia Pictures Television/1962-
Executive Producers/Directors: William Hanna, Joseph Barbera
Company: Hanna-Barbera Productions with Screen Gems (CPT)/
   156 films, 5 minutes

Principal Characters and Voices

| | |
|---|---|
| Lippy the Lion/Wally Gator | Daws Butler |
| Hardy Har Har | Mel Blanc |
| Touché Turtle | Bill Thompson |
| Dum Dum | Alan Reed |
| Mr. Twiddles | Don Messick |

The Hanna-Barbera New Cartoon Series packaged three different animal comedies for the syndicated children's market.   Produced for flexible programming, each series included fifty-two episodic films which could be used on existing shows, slotted individu-
ally under their own titles or strung together for longer time peri-
ods.   A half-hour format was adopted by WPIX, New York, under
the umbrella title Cartoon Zoo, with Milt Ross hosting the show as
the Zoo Keeper.   The trilogy of well-defined anthropomorphic characters relied heavily on the mannerisms of well-known performers
and their voice impersonations.   A bouncy musical theme introduced
the star of each series, establishing the background through the
lyrics.
   Dashing into action brandishing his trusty saber, "Touché
Turtle" lived the life of an Alexandre Dumas hero with Dum Dum,
a simple-minded sheep dog.   "Hero work done cheap, all credit
cards accepted" was his motto, and his catch-phrase, "Touché and
away!, " was answered by his laggard companion with "Wait for me,
Touché. "   Occupied with aiding those in distress, the pair plied
their trade in such fantasies as "High Goon, " "Red Riding Hoodlum, " "Black Is the Knight" and "Satellite Flight. "   The mushmouth voice of the chivalrous terrapin, supplied by Bill Thompson,
was a near sound-alike of his MGM basset hound, Droopy, which
was based on Wallace Wimple, his creampuff character introduced
on radio's Fibber McGee and Molly (NBC, 1931-1957).
   A bon vivant man-about-town, "Wally Gator" was the special
frustration of Mr. Twiddles, the zoo curator.   "A swinging gator
from the swamp" that mimicked "the perfect fool, " Ed Wynn (1886-
1966), he offered the comic's wry comment, "Just my luck, don't
you know, " after stumbling into such misfortunes as the "Phantom
Alligator, " "Gosh Zilla, " "The Forest Prime Evil" and "Which Is
Which Witch?"
   In a cocky interpretation of slapstick comedian Joe E. Brown
(1892-1973), "Lippy the Lion" was partnered with the sorrowful
Hardy Har Har, a pessimistic hyena.   A con-artist of the old
school, Lippy, together with his pal, was involved in such misadventures as "Flim Flam, " "Phoney Pony, " "Witch Crafty" and
"Double Trouble. "

HARDY BOYS, THE

Network History
    Premiere: September 6, 1969
    ABC/Sep 1969-Sep 1970/Saturday 10:30-11:00 AM
    ABC/Sep 1970-Dec 1970/Saturday 12:00-12:30 PM
    ABC/Jan 1971-Sep 1971/Saturday 12:30-1:00 PM
    Last Program: September 4, 1971

Syndicated History

Distributor: Twentieth Century-Fox Television/1971-
Executive Producers: Louis Scheimer, Norman Prescott
Company: Filmation Productions with TCF-TV/17 films

Principal Characters and Voices

| | |
|---|---|
| Frank Hardy | Byron Kane |
| Joe Hardy | Dal McKennon |
| Wanda Kay Breckenridge | Jane Webb |
| Pete | |
| Chubby | |

The Hardy Boys became a bubblegum rock group in their
animated adventures, taking time out to solve some local mysteries
while on a world-wide concert tour. A timeworn formula popularized by the enormous success of The Beatles (q.v.), the touring
concept was copied by over one dozen children's series after 1965,
and presented in every graphic form including the anthropomorphic.
In their exploits, teenage sleuths Frank and Joe Hardy were augmented by three friends, Pete, Chubby and Wanda Kay Brecken-
ridge. Known as the musical group, The Hardy Boys Plus Three,
they presented a contemporary rock tune in a live action segment
accomplished by the real life group, The Hardy Boys, who achieved
brief minor fame as recording artists. Oriented toward straight
adventure in exotic locales, the cartoons were realistically drawn
and took their cue from The Monkees* (q.v.), a contemporary ratings hit incorporating zany slapstick comedy.
    The original characters were created by Edward L. Strate-
meyer, whose juvenile mysteries were ghosted by writers under the
pseudonym F. W. Dixon, a best-selling series published by Grosset
and Dunlap since 1927. Two live-action TV adaptations were based
on the novels, a pair of serials titled The Hardy Boys* (q.v.),
seen on The Mickey Mouse Club* (q.v.) and the hour-long 1977-
1979 ABC entry, The Hardy Boys Mysteries* (q.v.).


HARLEM GLOBETROTTERS, THE

Network History
    Premiere: September 12, 1970
    CBS/Sep 1970-Sep 1971/Saturday 10:30-11:00 AM

CBS/Sep 1971-Sep 1972/Saturday 9:00-9:30 AM
CBS/Sep 1972-May 1973/Sunday 7:30-8:00 AM

GO GO GLOBETROTTERS
NBC/Feb 1978-Sep 1978/Saturday 8:30-10:30 AM
Last Program: September 2, 1978

THE SUPER GLOBETROTTERS
Premiere: September 22, 1979
NBC/Sep 1979-Nov 1979/Saturday 10:00-10:30 AM
NBC/Apr 1980-May 1980/Saturday 8:00-8:30 AM

THE GODZILLA/GLOBETROTTERS ADVENTURE HOUR
NBC/Nov 1979-Apr 1980/Saturday 8:00-9:00 AM
NBC/May 1980-Sep 1980/Saturday 8:00-9:00 AM
Last Program: September 20, 1980

Syndicated History

Distributor (1970-1973 films): Worldvision Enterprises/1979-
Executive Producers: William Hanna, Joseph Barbera
Producers: Iwao Takamoto (1970-1973), Art Scott (1979-1980)
Directors: Ray Patterson, Carl Urbano, George Gordon (1979-1980)
Company: Hanna-Barbera Productions/22 films (1970-1973), 13 films (1979-1980)

Principal Characters and Voices

| | | |
|---|---|---|
| Freddy "Curly" Neal/Sphere Man | | Stu Gilliam |
| Geese Ausbie/Multi-Man | | John Williams |
| Meadowlark Lemon | (1970-1973) | Scatman Crothers |
| Gip | (1970-1973) | Richard Elkins |
| Bobby Joe Mason | (1970-1973) | Eddie Anderson |
| Pablo | (1970-1973) | Robert DoQui |
| Granny | (1970-1973) | Nancy Wible |
| Nate Branch/Fluid Man | (1979-1980) | Scatman Crothers |
| Sweet Lou Dunbar/ Gismo Man | (1979-1980) | Adam Wade |
| Twiggy Sanders/ Spaghetti Man | (1979-1980) | Buster Jones |
| Crime Globe | (1979-1980) | Frank Welker |
| Announcer | (1979-1980) | Michael Rye |
| Dribbles (Globetrotter's dog 1970-1973) | | |

The Harlem Globetrotters, a team of highly skilled exhibition basketball players, first arrived in two-dimensional form in 1970-1971. A landmark series, the Globetrotters shared with Josie and the Pussycats (q.v.) the distinction as the first Saturday morning network cartoon show to star minority characters. Both programs were the godchildren of Fred Silverman, CBS vice president of program planning and development. Organized by Abe Saperstein,

January 27, 1927, the original team was known as the Savoy Big Five, because they played at Chicago's Savoy Ballroom. A sports-show phenomenon, acclaimed as the "Wizards of the Court," various Globetrotter squads have appeared professionally on all seven continents. For the initial animated series with black stars it was a remarkable success, pulling a 38 rating share of the audience in the first year.

Featuring their comic misadventures on-and-off the court while on an exhibition tour, Meadowlark Lemon, Curly, Gip, Bobby Joe and Geese were the principal athletes caricatured and given new voices. Under the nominal leadership of Lemon, the Globetrotters were always on the side of the underdog, happenstance black heroes who remedied wrongs and outwitted unprincipled crooks, the climax always coming in the game. Dribbles was their mascot, a humorous ball-handling pooch in basketball shoes. A white-haired, bespectacled, young-at-heart, Granny drove their red-white-and-blue team bus and was their head cheer leader. Involved with such unlikely characters as robots and monsters, on one occasion the Globetrotters played a mix of the two, the Creeply Transylvania Giants. Out west they foiled the villainous mortgage-forecloser Silas Craig, and in a race to Hawaii outsmarted the evil cheater Captain Wretchly. "The Great Geese Goof-Up" concerned a pair of jewel thieves, Lefty and Louie Callahan, who rented a trained boxing kangaroo named Hoppy as an accomplice. Believing Geese had been transformed into the animal through sorcery by Zippo the Great, his magician-owner, the Globetrotters included the bouncing marsupial as a teammate in the big game. As disguised members of the All-Stars, the culprits tried to retrieve their stolen goods from the kangaroo's pouch. But during the contest they were unmasked and jailed when Granny turned up with the real Geese, who had been hospitalized temporarily.

The Globetrotters first run on CBS ended May 20, 1973. After Silverman became President of NBC the series was repeated, beginning February 4, 1978 under the umbrella title Go Go Globetrotters, a two-hour package of reruns including the C. B. Bears (q. v.). And plans were launched almost immediately to update the series.

Reborn as the superheroes of sport in 1979-1980, the new squad was drawn from the contemporary Globetrotters and endowed with individual powers as bizarre, costumed crime-fighters. Summoned into action by the Crime Globe, an orbiting satellite, The Super Globetrotters assumed their alter-egos in their own lockers; the lockers conjured up by an amulet worn by Nate Branch. Curly became Sphere Man, with a large basketball-like head that transformed into any round ball. As Multi-Man, Geese was able to duplicate himself any number of times. Nate flowed or oozed anywhere as Fluid Man, Sweet Lou Dunbar carried an assortment of practical gadgets in his large Afro as Gismo Man, and Twiggy Sanders extended his tensile limbs to near infinity as Spaghetti Man. On the side of the law, the super athletes battled more unearthly antagonists, such as the Phantom Cowboy, Merlo the Magician, Tattoo Man, the fire-breathing Attila and his Horrible Huns, and Museum Man and his Fearless Fossils. The action always culminated in a wacky basketball game.

Beginning November 10, 1979, wraparound segments of The Super Globetrotters sandwiched a repeat of Godzilla (q. v. ) in a coupled adventure hour.


## HEATHCLIFF AND DINGBAT

Network History
Premiere: October 4, 1980
ABC/Oct 1980-Sep 1981/Saturday 11:00-11:30 AM
Last Program: September 5, 1981
Executive Producers: Joe Ruby, Ken Spears
Producer: Jerry Eisenberg
Director: Charles A. Nichols
Company: Ruby-Spears Enterprises/13 films

Principal Characters and Voices

Heathcliff/Spike                Mel Blanc
Dingbat                         Frank Welker
Sparerib/Nobody                 Don Messick

Heathcliff and Dingbat, an urbane cat, a crazy canine and his creepy pals, cavorted in separate comedies. Walking upright on two paws instead of four, Heathcliff was a crafty filcher of fish from garbage cans and anywhere else he could find them. The orange feline's special haunt was a local meat market where he was deft at purloining a finny dish from under the nose of the exasperated Mr. Schulz, who complained, "He did it again, but wait 'til next time!" A street-wise alley cat with savoir-faire, Heathcliff was involved also in fantasies with a periodic nemesis, Spike, a stubborn and not-too-smart bulldog. Adapted from the McNaught Syndicate comic strip by artist George Gately, Heathcliff (Sep 3, 1973) was the typical fat cat, self-assured and underhanded and a worthy successor to Sylvester and Felix the Cat (q. v. ). Two episodes starring Heathcliff alternated with a pair introducing Dingbat and the Creeps. Among the klutzy trio of new weirdos created by Joe Ruby and Ken Spears, Dingbat was a caped-and-fanged vampire canine partnered with a Jack o' Lantern wearing a baseball cap and sneakers and named Nobody, and a skeleton with a plumber's helper as a cap who was named Sparerib; their voices sounded like Bela Lugosi (1882-1956), Jimmy Durante (1893-1980) and Curly Howard (1906-1952). Sort of a mock-dreadful version of The Three Stooges* (q. v. ), with unique transformable abilities, the numskulls managed to turn every task into shambles as Odd Jobs, Inc. hired out as "Bungling Baby Sitters, " "Window Washouts" and restaurant waiters in "French Fried Creeps. "


## HECKLE AND JECKLE

Component Series
DINKY DUCK, GANDY GOOSE, LITTLE ROQUEFORT, TERRY

BEARS, other TERRY TOONS (1956-1971)

## Network History

THE HECKLE AND JECKLE CARTOON SHOW
  Premiere: October 14, 1956
  CBS/Oct 1956-Sep 1957/Sunday 1:00-1:30 PM
  CBS/Jan 1958-Oct 1959/Saturday 11:00-11:30 AM
  CBS/Oct 1959-Sep 1960/Saturday 10:00-10:30 AM
  CBS/Sep 1965-Sep 1966/Saturday 9:00-9:30 AM
  NBC/Sep 1969-Sep 1970/Saturday 8:00-9:00 AM
  NBC/Sep 1970-Jan 1971/Saturday 8:00-8:30 AM
  NBC/Jan 1971-Sep 1971/Saturday 8:30-9:00 AM
  Last Program: September 4, 1971

THE NEW ADVENTURES OF MIGHTY MOUSE AND
  HECKLE AND JECKLE
  Premiere: September 8, 1979
  CBS/Sep 1979-Sep 1980/Saturday 8:00-9:00 AM
  CBS/Sep 1980-Feb 1981/Saturday 8:00-8:30 AM
  CBS/Mar 1981-  /Sunday 8:00-8:30 AM

## Syndicated History

Distributor (1956-1966 films):  CBS Films/1960-1971; Viacom International/1971-
Executive Producers:  Bill Weiss (1956-1966); Louis Scheimer, Norman Prescott (1979-  )
Producer:  Don Christensen (1979-  )
Directors:  Art Bartsch, Bob Kuwahara, Connie Rasinski, Dave Tendlar (1956-1966)
Company:  CBS Terrytoons/26 films (1956-1966); Filmation Productions/13 films, 11 minutes (1979-  )

## Principal Characters and Voices

| | | |
|---|---|---|
| Heckle | (1946-1966) | Dayton Allen/Roy Halee |
| | (1979-  ) | Frank Welker |
| Jeckle | (1946-1966) | Dayton Allen/Roy Halee |
| | (1979-  ) | Frank Welker |
| Gandy Goose/Sourpuss | (1938-1955) | Arthur Kay |
| Dinky Duck | (1939-1957) | |
| Terry Bears | (1951-1955) | Roy Halee/Philip A. Scheib/ Doug Moye |
| Little Roquefort/Percy the Cat | (1950-1955) | Tom Morrison |

Heckle and Jeckle, the merry magpies that were born again on CBS in 1979-1980, made their television bow in the mid-fifties. The two identical black birds debuted in their theatrical cartoon The Uninvited Pests (Nov 29, 1946), a supporting comedy on the December 10, 1955 premiere of Mighty Mouse Playhouse (q. v. ). Their origins stemmed from an idea by producer Paul Terry to

feature animated look-alikes, and came to life in The Talking Magpies (Jan 4, 1946), directed by Mannie Davis and written chiefly by
Tom Morrison. No other studio had tried the concept before and
the use of magpies was unusual. One of the most successful of
the "Terry Toons" series, Heckle and Jeckle appeared in fifty-two
films produced for theaters and released by Twentieth Century-Fox
Films, seven made between 1960 and 1966. Completely unrestrained,
Heckle spoke in New York jive-talk and Jeckle in stilted British fal-
setto--"I say, old Chum, shall we partake?" Depicted as happy-go-
lucky adventurers, and often brash intruders in some innocent's af-
fairs, they were basically antagonistic and displayed a somewhat
warped sense of humor. As outlandish practical jokesters, the
peripatetic pair played strange and sometimes cruel tricks on their
opponents, particularly Dimwit Dog, their favorite foil. In several
films they employed a guise, turning up as doctors, bellhops,
mounties or newspaper reporters to torment their subjects. Like
Bugs Bunny (q. v. ), they were nonchalant under fire, and nothing
seemed to faze them.

After Terry sold his animated films to CBS in 1955, the
comedies were repackaged for the network's various children's programs. In Summer 1956, Heckle and Jeckle were featured in the
premiere of CBS Cartoon Theater (q. v. ), appearing in Flying South
(Aug 15, 1947), in which they knew the wolf that knew Red Riding
Hood's grandmother. Starring that fall in The Heckle and Jeckle
Cartoon Show, the birdbrains were seen for six-and-one-half years
on the networks, either heading or sandwiching other "Terry Toons"
featuring Little Roquefort and his antagonist Percy the Cat, the Ed
Wynn-inspired Gandy Goose and Jimmy Durante sound-alike Sourpuss, the vulnerable infant Dinky Duck with a falsetto voice and the
Terry Bears, the rascally twins with an irascible father. After the
first run ended September 24, 1960 on CBS, the cartoons were
placed in syndication, appearing simultaneously with the later repeats on the network from September 25, 1965 through September 3,
1966, and on NBC, beginning September 6, 1969.

Contrasted with their former abrasive personalities, the
pesky magpies were tranquilized and given intelligible voices for
their eleven-minute comedies on The New Adventures of Mighty
Mouse and Heckle and Jeckle. In stories depicting everything from
life in the Foreign Legion to a trip to Alice's Wonderland, the talking magpies continued their madcap mayhem, but without the previous malevolent and sometimes sadistic overtones. Moreover, their
better diction was stressed in demonstrations of good grammar,
exemplified in educational mini-segments on homonyms, appearing
between the cartoons on the program. Two episodes were seen on
the hour-long show in 1979-1980, reduced to one cartoon in 1980-
1981 when the series was cut to a half-hour.


HECTOR HEATHCOTE SHOW, THE

Component Series
    HASHIMOTO, SIDNEY, other TERRY TOONS

Network History
    Premiere: October 5, 1963
    NBC/Oct 1963-Sep 1964/Saturday 10:00-10:30 AM
    NBC/Oct 1964-Sep 1965/Saturday 9:30-10:00 AM
    Last Program: September 25, 1965

Syndicated History

Distributor: CBS Films/1965-1971; Viacom International/1971-
Executive Producer: Bill Weiss
Directors: Art Bartsch, Bob Kuwahara, Connie Rasinski, Dave
    Tendlar
Company: CBS Terrytoons/26 films

Principal Characters and Voices

Hector Heathcote/Hashimoto/
    Mrs. Hashimoto/Yuriko/
    Saburo                              John Myhers
Sidney                                  Lionel Wilson/Dayton Allen
Stanley/Cleo                            Dayton Allen
Winston (Heathcote's dog)

    The Hector Heathcote Show toplined a good-natured Colonial
era patriot, who was always present but never credited whenever
history was being made.  The creation of storyman Eli Bauer for
The Minute and 1/2 Man (Jul 1959), the first of fifteen theatrical
cartoons made by CBS Terrytoons between 1959 and 1963, Hector
was partnered in many of the historical fantasies with his hound
Winston.  In the tradition of the time-travel formula adapted from
H. G. Wells' The Time Machine (1895), the unsung hero in the tricorn hat answered the call to duty in many different epochs.  Among
his deeds, Hector readied the horse for Paul Revere's famous ride,
built the rowboat that carried George Washington and his troops
safely across the Delaware, aided his buddy Daniel Boone, Jr.,
and invented the harvester, although he was really working on the
first airplane.  In "The Big Clean-Up," the innocent little puritan
braved lawlessness in Untidy Gulch, a wild western town in the
1870s.  There he rescued the harassed town folk from the notorious bully Black Bart Bromide and his gang, accidentally, of course.
As in every episode, the narrator reminded viewers, "History has
recorded many great names, but only we know about Hector Heathcote!"
    When NBC bought The Hector Heathcote Show in 1963, new
cartoons were quickly produced in the "Heathcote" and "Hashimoto"
series to fill out the program.  Veteran staffer Bob Kuwahara created the Japanese mouse that debuted in the theatrical film Hashimoto San (Oct 1959).  Well versed in the art of judo, Hashimoto,
with his wife, Mrs. Hashimoto, and Yuriko and Saburo, his little
girl and boy, revealed the magical legends and romantic traditions
of his country to G. I. Joe, an inquisitive American newspaper

reporter.  Also added was the childish and neurotic "Sidney," created under the stewardship of Gene Deitch as a theatrical cartoon and debuting in Sick, Sick Sidney (Aug 1958), directed by Art Bartsch.  A lovable forty-two-year-old orphaned baby elephant with four left feet, Sidney spent most of his time looking for surrogate parents, and in Sidney's Family Tree (Dec 1958) managed to get himself adopted by a pair of jungle chimpanzees.  Incurably clumsy, the well-meaning pachyderm continually knocked down the jungle, to the despair of his friends, Stanley the Lion and Cleo the Giraffe. Several different theatrical Terry Toons, produced between 1955 and 1963, alternated with "Sidney" to round out the show.


H. E. L. P. ! !

Network History
     Premiere:  September 22, 1979
     ABC/Sep 1979-  /Periodic/Saturday, Sunday Various AM

Executive Producer:  Lynn Ahrens
Producer:  Phil Himmelman
Company:  Himmelman Associates for Dahlia Productions/8 films, 1 minute

     H. E. L. P. ! ! was a series of public service messages that spelled out "Dr. Henry's Emergency Lessons for People."  Scattered throughout the weekend children's schedule, the animated spots covered basic first aid for cuts, burns, drowning, choking, a bump on the head and other accidents, and were targeted for the youngster eight to fourteen years old.   The films were produced by Lynn Ahrens who penned the lyrics and music for ABC's teenage TV advisor, Dear Alex and Annie* (q. v. ).


HELP!  IT'S THE HAIR BEAR BUNCH!

Network History
     Premiere:  September 11, 1971
     CBS/Sep 1971-Sep 1972/Saturday 9:30-10:00 AM
     CBS/Sep 1973-Jan 1974/Sunday 7:00-7:30 AM
     CBS/Feb 1974-Aug 1974/Saturday 8:00-8:30 AM
     Last Program:  August 31, 1974

Syndicated History

THE YO YO BEARS

Distributor:  Taft H-B Program Sales/1974-1979
Executive Producers/Directors:  William Hanna, Joseph Barbera
Producer:  Charles A. Nichols
Company:  Hanna-Barbera Productions/16 films

Principal Characters and Voices

| | |
|---|---|
| Hair Bear | Daws Butler |
| Bubi Bear | Paul Winchell |
| Square Bear | Bill Callaway |
| Mr. Peevely | John Stephenson |
| Botch | Joe E. Ross |

Help! It's The Hair Bear Bunch followed the madcap adventures of three cagey bruins, unhappily quartered in Cave Block Number 9 at the Wonderland Zoo. Born in the aftermath of the late sixties' protest movement, the animated satire found the free-spirited trio asserting their rights to better living conditions. Hair Bear was the leader and instigator of the hairbrained schemes and had a voice like that of jovial buck-'n'-wing comedian Jack Oakie (1903-1978). Smaller Bubi Bear was his admiring and level-headed buddy and Square Bear, their simpleton pal. Complicating their plans was the ever-present symbol of authority, Mr. Peevely, the zoo keeper, and his bungling assistant, Botch. Together the three bears found one ingenious way after another to improve their lot in such plots as "Closed Circuit TV," "Raffle Ruckus," "No Space Like Home" and "The Bear Who Came to Dinner."

Off-network the inimical title was changed to The Yo Yo Bears.

HERCULOIDS, THE

Network History
Premiere: September 9, 1967
CBS/Sep 1967-Sep 1968/Saturday 9:30-10:00 AM
CBS/Sep 1968-Sep 1969/Saturday 11:30-12:00 AM
Last Program: September 6, 1969

GO GO GLOBETROTTERS/THE HERCULOIDS
Return: February 4, 1978
NBC/Feb 1978-Sep 1978/Saturday 8:30-10:30 AM
Last Program: September 2, 1978

Syndicated History

CAPTAIN INVENTORY

Distributor: Taft H-B Program Sales/1973-1979; Worldvision Enterprises/1979-
Executive Producers/Directors: William Hanna, Joseph Barbera
Company: Hanna-Barbera Productions/18 films

Principal Characters and Voices

| | |
|---|---|
| Zandor/Zok/Igoo/Tundro | Mike Road |
| Tara | Virginia Gregg |

Dorno                                      Teddy Eccles
Gloop/Gleep                                Don Messick

The Herculoids were an army of bizarre beasties, the invincible defenders of a jungle planet in a distant galaxy.  Resembling apocryphal prehistoric creatures, Zok was a flying dragon
that could emit powerful laser rays from his eyes and tail, Tundro
the Tremendous an armored, ten-legged rhinoceros with a horn that
served as a repeating cannon, and Igoo, a granite-like, King Kong-
size gorilla with formidable brute strength.  A pair of formless,
fearless wonders, Gloop and Gleep were protean and tensile, could
separate into parts or become blobs of any size.  The main pastime
of the grotesque group was to protect Zandor, their benevolent King,
his wife, Princess Tara and their blond-headed son, Dorno, from
an endless succession of invading robot machines and hyperthyroid
mutants from alien worlds.  Flying atop the dragon Zok, Zandor
was armed with a shield and a sling-shot that could hurl small but
powerful missiles.  With his quintet of weird animals, he defended
his peaceful Utopian land from such terrors as the Faceless People,
Destroyer Ants, Raider Apes, Mutoids, Arnoids, Zorbots, the Mek-
kano mechanical men and the Ogs, a strange form of vegetable life.
Two episodic eleven-minute fantasies comprised the science
fiction show, which was conceived and designed by comic book artist Alexander Toth and Joe Barbera.  Initially part of Fred Silverman's superhero derring-do line-up on CBS, the cartoons were rerun as a mid-season replacement on NBC in 1978, coupled with
The Harlem Globetrotters (q. v. ) under the umbrella title Go Go
Globetrotters.


HERE COMES THE GRUMP

Network History
    Premiere:  September 6, 1969
    NBC/Sep 1969-Sep 1970/Saturday 9:00-9:30 AM
    NBC/Sep 1970-Sep 1971/Saturday 11:30-12:00 AM
    Last Program:  September 4, 1971
Executive Producers:  David DePatie, Friz Freleng
Company:  DePatie-Freleng Enterprises/17 films

Principal Characters and Voices

Terry Dexter                               Jay North
Princess Dawn                              Stefanianna Christopher
The Grump                                  Rip Taylor
Bib (Terry's dog)
The Jolly Green Dragon (The
    Grump's steed)

Here Comes the Grump, the alarm cry of the villagers,
signaled the arrival of the ill-natured, gnome-like rascal riding on
the back of the Jolly Green Dragon.  Resentful of all the merry-
making going on in his land, the grouchy spoilsport laid a Curse

of Gloom on the realm.  Seeking redress from the hex, the inhabitants turned for help to a young boy, Terry, and his dog, Bib.
Magically transported to the spellbound kingdom, Terry met Princess Dawn, the only other person apart from himself who was unaffected by the Grump's curse.  The Princess told him about a
Crystal Key, hidden by the malevolent sprite in the Cave of the
Whispering Orchids, which could lift the dreaded spell.  Accompanied by the Princess, Terry and Bib set out in a balloon-car to
begin their search for the Land of a Thousand Caves.  To protect
the Key's hiding place, the Grump continually hindered the trio
along the way in "The Great Thorn Forest," "The Lemonade Sea,"
"Cherub Land," "Snow White City" and "Echo Island."  But each
story found the bumbling Jolly Green Dragon doing more to help
Terry and Bib than he did to aid his own master.

The fairyland premise was created by DePatie-Freleng Enterprises to fit the new children's programming philosophy NBC inaugurated in 1968-1969, encompassing shows with expanded elements
of fantasy, humor and style.


HONG KONG PHOOEY

Network History
Premiere:  September 7, 1974
ABC/Sep 1974-Aug 1975/Saturday 9:00-9:30 AM
ABC/Sep 1975-Sep 1976/Saturday 8:00-8:30 AM
NBC/Feb 1978-Sep 1978/Saturday 8:00-8:30 AM
Last Program:  September 2, 1978

THE GODZILLA/HONG KONG PHOOEY HOUR
Return:  November 22, 1980
NBC/Nov 1980-May 1981/Saturday 8:00-9:00 AM

HONG KONG PHOOEY
NBC/May 1981-Sep 1981/Saturday 11:30-12:00 AM
Last Program:  September 5, 1981

Executive Producers:  William Hanna, Joseph Barbera
Producer:  Iwao Takamoto
Director:  Charles A. Nichols
Company:  Hanna-Barbera Productions/16 films

Principal Characters and Voices

Penrod Pooch/Hong Kong Phooey     Scatman Crothers
Sergeant Flint                    Joe E. Ross
Rosemary                          Kathi Gori
Spot                              Don Messick


Hong Kong Phooey, a bungling canine, triumphed fortuitously
as a crime-fighter with the aid of Spot, his surly cat.  Known at
the police station as the mild-mannered Penrod Pooch, the clumsy
janitor was particularly vexing to hard-nosed Sergeant Flint.

Called "Penry" by Rosemary, the switchboard and CB radio operator, whenever he learned that a notorious crook was in town he
would disappear into a secret room behind a snack machine, jump
into a file cabinet and reappear in oriental costume as the "Mutt of
Steel." Skilled in the martial arts through a correspondence course,
Phooey used his "accomplishment technique," ineffectual as it often
was, as a champion of justice. In the "Phooeymobile," secretly
garaged in a trashbin behind the station, the klutzy canine and his
snickering feline assistant tracked down such law breakers as the
Gum Drop Kid, a candy bandit who had a sweet racket; Mr. Tornado, a windy thief who stole the Sedonia diamonds; and a mischievous magician, Professor Presto and his henchman Big Tooth, a
mumbling monster. Frequently consulting his "Hong Kong Kung Fu
Book of Tricks," Phooey managed somehow to kayo his opponent,
sometimes with his slow-motion Hong Kong Phooey Chop, but most
often through the intervention of Spot.

   Personified in the movies by Chinese-American actor Bruce
Lee (1941-1973), remembered as Kato on The Green Hornet* (q. v. ),
and by David Carradine as the Chinese-American orphan Kwai Chang
Caine on Kung Fu (ABC, 1972-1975), the voguish revival of China's
ancient science of personal combat provided the inspiration for the
Asian crime-fighter spoof. Two eleven-minute capers were seen in
each program, with such titles as "Penthouse Burglaries," "Grand-
ma Goody," "Goldfisher" and "Batty Bank Mob." After the ABC
run ended on September 4, 1976, NBC repeated the episodes beginning February 4, 1978 and resurrected the show again in 1980-
1981, initially coupled with Godzilla (q. v. ) through May 16, 1981.


HOT WHEELS

Network History
   Premiere: September 6, 1969
   ABC/Sep 1969-Sep 1970/Saturday 10:00-10:30 AM
   ABC/Sep 1970-Sep 1971/Saturday 11:00-11:30 AM
   Last Program: September 4, 1971
Theme: "Hot Wheels," by Mike Curb and the Curbstones.
Producers: Fred Crippen, Ed Smarden, Ken Snyder
Director: Irving Spector
Company: Pantomime Pictures, Ken Snyder Productions/17 films

Principal Characters and Voices

| | |
|---|---|
| Jack Wheeler/Doc Warren | Bob Arbogast |
| Janet Martin | Melinda Casey |
| Mickey Barnes/Kip Chogi | Albert Brooks |
| Ardeth Pratt | Susan Davis |
| Tank Mallory/Dexter Carter | Casey Kasem |
| Mother O'Hare | Nora Marlowe |
| Mike Wheeler | Michael Rye |

   Hot Wheels engendered respect for a timeless teenage passion, hot-rodding, through the responsible experiences of a souped-

up car club.  Dedicated to the advancement of law-abiding, safe
driving practices, the series involved a young group of dragster
enthusiasts from Metro City High School, organized as members of
the Hot Wheels Racing Club.  The dependable leader was straightforward Jack Wheeler, a seventeen-year-old senior and typical all-
American boy.  A skilled and cool driver behind the wheel of his
car, "The Jack Rabbit Special," he was affectionately nicknamed
"Rabbit" by his classmates and acknowledged as the best driver in
the club.  Inheriting his love of racing from his father, Jack ex-
hibited potential as a professional racer, which both pleased and
worried Mike Wheeler, a former racing car champ who had been
forced to retire after a crippling accident.  Pretty, vivacious and
smart Janet Martin was Jack's girlfriend and the daughter of the
Police Commissioner.  "Rabbit's" teenage buddies were an apprentice
mechanic, Mickey Barnes, and Kip Chogi, an African ambassador's
son.  Tomboy Ardeth Pratt had a crush on Mickey and an all-
consuming ambition to become a race car driver.

Ciudad The club was headquartered at Wheeler Motors, owned by
Jack's father, a garage and custom car firm that specialized in
racing cars and modified production models.  Tank Mallory was
Wheeler's absent-minded mechanic, a recent high school graduate
and a product of Doc Warren's Auto Shop course.  More than just
a teacher, Warren was a friend and advisor to the Hot Wheels and
an honorary member.  The club's local hangout was a cafe and
soda fountain operated by Mother O'Hara and aptly named "Mother's."

Jack and his safety-conscious friends were pitted against
Dexter's Demons, a rival car club and their continuing antagonists.
Dexter Carter, an arrogant and wealthy classmate who was banned
from the Hot Wheels for his heedless acts and disrespect for the
law, recruited his own gang of drop-out toughs, buying their loyalty
with leather jackets, crash helmets and car repairs.  The roaring
action depicted the pitfalls of speeding, irresponsible driving and
street racing in contests that contrasted the sane and superior
methods of the Hot Wheels with the foolhardy recklessness of the
Demons.  Jack and the cast delivered explicit messages on driving
safety and obedience of the laws of the road in twenty-second mini-
segments incorporated within the series, which was Anamorphic
computer-animated.

Mattel Toys, one of the participating sponsors, marketed a
very popular line of matchbox car models as the "Hot Wheels" collection.  The company was instrumental in placing the show on ABC
through Carson/Roberts Advertising, although the toy commercials
were not aired on the program.  Designed by Alexander Toth, Hot
Wheels became a comic book by National Periodicals.  The catchy
theme, "Hot Wheels, Hot Wheels, keep a turnin' now ...," was
written at the instigation of the advertising agency by Mike Curb.
Abandoning a lucrative music and recording business for a political
career, Curb was elected Lieutenant Governor of California in 1978.


HOUNDCATS, THE

Network History
    Premiere:  September 9, 1972

NBC/Sep 1972-Dec 1972/Saturday 9:30-10:00 AM
NBC/Dec 1972-Sep 1973/Saturday 8:00-8:30 AM
Last Program:  September 1, 1973
Executive Producers:  David DePatie, Friz Freleng
Directors:  Sid Marcus, Robert McKimson, Spencer Peel, Brad
Case
Company:  DePatie-Freleng Enterprises/13 films

Principal Characters and Voices

| | |
|---|---|
| Stutz | Daws Butler |
| Musclemutt | Aldo Ray |
| Rhubarb | Arte Johnson |
| Puttypuss | Joe Besser |
| Dingdog | Stu Gilliam |

The Houndcats, a secret intelligence organization, attempted
absurd and knotty assignments in comedy-adventures set in the
American west.  A quintet of highly specialized government operatives, all dogs and cats, the undercover trouble-solvers rode to
their missions in their flivver, "Sparkplug, " a Stutz Bearcat.
Their daring and resourceful feline leader, not coincidentally, was
named Stutz and was aided in the intricate schemes by Puttypuss,
the cat-of-a-thousand faces, Dingdog, the daredevil stuntman,
Musclemutt, the brawny ex-weightlifter and Rhubarb, the wacky
canine genius and inventor.  The stories ranged from "The Great
Gold Train Mission" and "The Over the Waves Mission" to "The
French Collection Mission" and "The Outta Sight Blight Mission. "
Each adventure detailed the crafty step-by-step planning and final
inept execution of their assignments, which always went awry but
somehow ended fortuitously.
    An animated mix of two prime time formats, the premise
spoofed the Impossible Missions Force with its astounding array of
sophisticated electronic gadgetry on Mission:  Impossible (CBS,
1966-1973) and the pair of adventurers tackling risky tasks in the
American southwest in 1914 on the Bearcats (CBS, 1971), played
by Rod Taylor and Dennis Cole.


HUCKLEBERRY HOUND SHOW, THE

Component Series
    PIXIE AND DIXIE, YOGI BEAR (1958-1960), HOKEY WOLF
    (1960-1962)

Syndicated History
    Premiere:  October 2, 1958
    WPIX, New York/Thursday 6:30-7:00 PM
Sponsor:  Kellogg's Cereals (1958-1962)

YOGI AND HIS FRIENDS (1967)

Distributor:  Screen Gems--Columbia Pictures Television/1958-

Executive Producers/Directors:  William Hanna, Joseph Barbera
Company:  Hanna-Barbera Productions with Screen Gems (CPT)/55
 films

Principal Characters and Voices

Huckleberry Hound/Yogi Bear/
 Dixie/Mr. Jinks/Hokey Wolf/
 Ziggy                              Daws Butler
Boo Boo/Pixie/Iggy                  Don Messick
Ding-a-Ling                         Doug Young

     Huckleberry Hound, a persevering pooch that perceived only
the good in life, never the bad, became television's first new cartoon superstar.  Blissfully singing a few bars of "Clementine," the
little blue canine was stoic to a fault, unruffled when trees fell on
him or drawbridges collapsed under him, or when he was blown up
in rockets.  Whatever happened, he picked himself up, shrugged off
his misfortune, and drawled, "Man, that was a right heavy tree" or
some such masterpiece of understatement.  Agonizingly slow in
thought, movement and speech, Huckleberry spoke with a twangy
rural accent supplied by Daws Butler, a gifted voice man from
South Carolina with a repertoire of over thirty distinct characterizations.  His imitation of an easy-going Tennessee home-spun guy,
who never got mad no matter how much he was outraged, inspired
producers Bill Hanna and Joe Barbera to create a series around
the character.  Butler's drawl had been used initially by Tex Avery
in the "Droopy" cartoons between 1943 and 1957 at MGM, where he
replaced Bill Thompson.  After the studio shut down its animation
department in Spring 1957, where Hanna and Barbera directed and
produced Tom and Jerry (q.v.), the partners began their own studio
and Huckleberry Hound was their second TV series and their first
big hit.  The program was syndicated in 1958 by Screen Gems and
sponsored by Kellogg's Cereals, and by Fall 1960 an estimated sixteen million Americans, as well as viewers in Canada, much of
Europe and most of Latin America and Japan, regularly watched the
amiable bloodhound with the droopy eyes on two hundred stations in
the first new all-cartoon show.  For outstanding achievement in
children's programming in 1959, Huckleberry Hound was the first
animated cartoon voted an Emmy by the Television Academy.
     The noblehearted Huck assumed a number of guises in his
exploits.  The tenacious mutt became a member of the French
Foreign Legion, an American fireman, an international veterinarian
trying to extract a lion's aching tooth, and the swashbuckling Purple
Pumpernickel, who hounded a tyrant who refused to permit his subjects to pay their taxes with credit cards.  In other light-hearted
fantasies, Huckleberry was a professor who saved the nation from
a destructive Idaho potato endowed with an evil brain, a Scotland
Yard Inspector who grappled with a monstrous Monster Schnitzel,
a Jekyll-and-Hyde character transformed from a docile scientist
Wiener Schnitzel, and the last surviving member of the Pennsyl-
Tucky Huckleberry Family, feuding with the last surviving member
of the Doodleberry family.  Not unlike those practical jokers

Heckle and Jeckle (q. v. ), Huck met a pair of crafty crows, Iggy and Ziggy, that dreamed up new methods of torment.  But all ended well, because to Huck nobody was really bad or dishonest. Barbera wrote the first twenty-six installments and the remainder of the seven-minute comedies were scripted by Warren Foster, a twenty-year veteran gag writer for Bugs Bunny (q. v. ).  While the films were loaded heavily with slapstick action, they were not frightening and never presented vicious, villainous antagonists.

The two companion cartoons were no less important to the success of the show.  A method-acting cat, Mr. Jinks spent his time trying to catch "Pixie and Dixie," a pair of devil-may-care mice, distinguished by Pixie's blue bow tie and Dixie's red vest. Despite repeated clobbering by the roguish rodents, Mr. Jinks was something of a masochist who sounded like the early Marlon Brando and in each episode yowled, "I love those meeces to peeces!"  Of course the southern-accented mice made allowances for the occasional attacks by Mr. Jinks, for he was not a malevolent feline but simply a tomcat doing what came naturally.

Yogi Bear (q. v. ), a cartoon star of major importance, debuted in supporting comedies on the series.  The incurable filcher of picnic baskets from visitors to Jellystone Park, Yogi was bright in a stupid way and was always being punished.  Along with his small bear-buddy Boo Boo, he enjoyed trying to cadge food in devious ways.  Bearing a startling resemblance to Art Carney's humorous sewer-engineer Ed Norton, the pork-pie hatted Yogi, who also spoke the comic, became an immediate success on the show and in 1961 was elevated to star in his own series.

In Fall 1960, "Hokey Wolf" was substituted as a component comedy.  With a voice and characterization lifted from Phil Silvers' fast-talking Sergeant Bilko, Hokey was a brash con-artist whose stooge was Ding-a-Ling, a cute little fox.  Operating with typical élan, he was the particular vexation of Douglas, the watchdog, and The Farmer, a Walter Brennan sound-alike.

Together with Yogi Bear and other Hanna-Barbera created characters, Huckleberry Hound launched a multi-million-dollar merchandising business, with hundreds of novelties and toys placed on the market.  By 1962, the studio was reaping an annual profit of over one million dollars from licensing contracts using their cartoon animals.  Huck's widespread popularity was immortalized when the crew of the United States Coast Guard icebreaker "Glacier" named a tiny island Huckleberry Hound in the Antarctic's Bellingshausen Sea, an honorarium that will probably mystify future naval historians.  In children's television, Huckleberry Hound made an even more historic contribution, accelerating an alliterative zoofull of descendants.  For the next ten years, almost every development in the TV cartoon genre could be traced back to the techniques and hints implicit in one or more of the series which made up this half-hour show.


I AM THE GREATEST: THE ADVENTURES OF MUHAMMAD ALI

Network History
     Premiere: September 10, 1977

NBC/Sep 1977-Jan 1978/Saturday 10:30-11:00 AM
Last Program: January 28, 1978
Executive Producer/Director: Fred Calvert
Producer: Janis Marissa Diamond
Company: Farmhouse Films/13 films

Principal Characters and Voices

| | |
|---|---|
| Muhammad Ali | Muhammad Ali |
| Frank Bannister | Frank Bannister |
| Nicky | Patrice Carmichael |
| Damon | Casey Carmichael |

I Am the Greatest: The Adventures of Muhammad Ali brought the world's boxing champ to Saturday mornings, vocally and in cartoon likeness, as a multi-talented demigod and poem-spouting good sport. Joining Ali in his adventures were his young niece and nephew, Nicky and Damon, and his public relations man, Frank Bannister. In stories displaying his worldly knowledge and remarkable athletic abilities, "the greatest" living boxer vanquished villains in "The Haunted Park" and "The Great Bluegrass Mountain Race" and triumphed over the "Terror in the Deep" and "The Werewolf of Devil's Creek." In his debut, "The Air Fair Affair," after the injured Damon was flown to a hospital from a Montana ranch, Ali demonstrated his super strength by hoisting the plane so that a damaged wheel could be repaired. Not only that, Ali repaid Dr. Wilbur Johnson by serving as his co-pilot in the Fair Air Race, in which he overcame the efforts of two envious competitors to sabotage the plane. Without any experience, he managed to fly the aircraft and help win the event. Typically, since each film contained a moral, Ali admonished in rhyme, "They played their pranks on the oldest guy, they didn't know they picked on the Champ of the Sky. So don't forget these important words, consequence jokes are for the birds."

Ali's heroics were unable to save the series, which ended after a brief five-month run, with the cartoons amortized locally as reruns until September 1978 on the NBC O&O stations and some affiliates. It was the fourth network animated series with essentially an all-black cast, following The Harlem Globetrotters (q.v.), The Jackson 5ive (q.v.) and The Fat Albert Show (q.v.). Sometimes the program was logged simply as The Adventures of Muhammad Ali.

INCH HIGH PRIVATE EYE

Network History
    Premiere: September 8, 1973
    NBC/Sep 1973-Dec 1973/Saturday 8:30-9:00 AM
    NBC/Jan 1974-Aug 1974/Saturday 9:30-10:00 AM
    Last Program: August 31, 1974

## Syndicated History

Distributor: Taft H-B Program Sales/1978-1979; DFS Program Exchange/1979-
Executive Producers: William Hanna, Joseph Barbera
Producer: Iwao Takamoto
Director: Charles A. Nichols
Company: Hanna-Barbera Productions/13 films

## Principal Characters and Voices

| | |
|---|---|
| Inch High | Lennie Weinrib |
| Lori | Kathi Gori |
| Gator | Bob Luttell |
| Mr. Finkerton | John Stephenson |
| Braveheart (Inch High's dog) | |

Inch High Private Eye had a penchant for doing things the hard way, which was no great surprise considering his size. "The World's Biggest Littlest Detective" was a thumbnail-sized Maxwell Smart, with suitable dialogue borrowed from Get Smart (NBC, 1964-1968/CBS, 1969-1970), the hit prime time take-off on the counterspy genre. The trench-coated gumshoe worked for Finkerton's Detective Agency, taking orders from its head man, who sounded like flustery comic-actor Joe Flynn (1924-1974). That Inch High accomplished anything at all was a tribute to his normal-sized niece Lori and her boyfriend, the muscular numskull Gator, whose Gomer Pyle backwoodsy rhetoric was sprinkled with "Golly Gee's." The tiny sleuth used the brandy cask on the collar of Braveheart, his St. Bernard, to store his weapons and disguises. When not riding about in the pendant earring of his cute blond kin, Inch High motored with his companions to the scene of the crime in the silent "Hushmobile," which was garaged in an underground freight elevator whose doors were camouflaged with trash cans. The stories were filled with Lilliputian gags and even when you could not see the tiny hero you knew he was there by his screaming action-cry, "Geronimo!" His specialty was solving bizarre thefts of furs, paintings, objets d'art and gems, by such contrived criminals as Spumoni, the great Doll Maker and his henchman, Pistachio, Super Flea, the Cat Burglars and the Music Maestro.

Off-network, the series was shown frequently with Wheelie and the Chopper Bunch (q.v.) and The Jetsons (q.v.) to provide fifty-two weekly half-hours for local programming.


INCREDIBLE HULK, THE  See  MARVEL SUPERHEROES


INTERNATIONAL ANIMATION FESTIVAL, THE

## Network History
Premiere: April 7, 1975
PBS/Apr 1975-Jun 1975/Weekly, Various AM and PM

Last Program: June 30, 1975
Executive Producer: Zev Putterman
Producer: Sheldon Renan
Company: KQED, San Francisco for PBS/13 films-tapes

Hostess
    Jean Marsh

        The International Animation Festival presented classic,
pioneer and experimental films along with acclaimed award honor-
ees, featuring a variety of techniques.   Actually more of a survey
than a pastiche, the films were introduced by Jean Marsh, remembered as Rosie, the maid in Upstairs, Downstairs (PBS, 1974-1977).
Among the primitive graphic forms were the Fantasmagorie (1908) and
the Automatic Moving Company (1911) by French pioneer Emil Cohl,
and the Magician by Oskar Fischinger.   Examples of technique
ranged from Canadian Norman McClaren's experimental drawing on
film to James Thurber's Many Moons, which was based on original
drawings.   Four or five cartoons from different countries were
featured in each program, including Inauguration, a Czech satire
about a ribbon cutting ceremony, and Edgar Allan Poe's The Masque
of the Red Death by Yugoslavia's Zagreb Studios, and such American
Oscar-winners as Chuck Jones' The Dot and The Line (MGM 1965)
and Faith and John Hubley's The Hole (1962), with the voice of jazz
trumpeter Dizzy Gillespie.   Although the program was not aimed at
juveniles, many PTV stations telecast the series on Sunday afternoons, affording interested youngsters a historical glimpse of international film animation.


IRON MAN  See  MARVEL SUPERHEROES


JABBERJAW

Network History
    Premiere:  September 11, 1976
    ABC/Sep 1976-Nov 1976/Saturday 9:00-9:30 AM
    ABC/Dec 1976-Sep 1977/Saturday 8:30-9:00 AM
    ABC/Sep 1977-Sep 1978/Sunday 10:30-11:00 AM
    Last Program:  September 3, 1978
Executive Producers:  William Hanna, Joseph Barbera
Producer:  Iwao Takamoto
Director:  Charles A. Nichols
Company:  Hanna-Barbera Productions/16 films

Principal Characters and Voices

Jabberjaw                      Frank Welker
Clam-Head                      Barry Gordon
Bubbles                        Julie McWhirter
Shelly                         Pat Parris
Biff                           Tommy Cook

Jabberjaw was a senseless shark that played the drums in a teenage rock group called The Neptunes, living in an oceanic world in 2076. The finny star acted like an anthropomorphic version of childish Curly Howard of The Three Stooges (q. v. ), and his favorite expression, "I don't get no respect!, " was borrowed from comedian Rodney Dangerfield. "Jabber" traveled to gigs in different undersea cities in the "Aquacar" with his four fellow musicians, the black-haired bandleader Biff, the giddybrained blond girl Bubbles, a haughty brunette prima donna Shelly, and his particular buddy, Clam-Head, a reddish chowderhead whose excited exclamation was "Wowee, wow, wow, wow!" Created by Joe Ruby and Ken Spears, the characters and their interaction followed the teenage-group-plus-cute-animal formula which the pair helped devise for the early adventures of Scooby-Doo (q. v. ). The stories came complete with briny James Bond villains, among them Sourpuss Octopuss, Phantom Kelp, El Eel and The Piranha. Once the Neptunes interceded in a plot to blackmail Aquahama City by the deranged scientist Dr. Lo, a Ming the Merciless type who threatened its destruction with his Gorgon Monster. Resembling a submerged tyrannosaurus, the reptile was enlarged to titanic proportions by Lo's ray machine. Unwittingly, Jabberjaw saved the metropolis by reducing the beast to goldfish size through reversing the beam. Using the "Let's get out of here" format, each episode incorporated a slapstick chase scene to a tune vocalized by the bubblegum rock group.


## JACKSON 5IVE, THE

### Network History
Premiere: September 11, 1971
ABC/Sep 1971-Sep 1972/Saturday 9:30-10:00 AM
ABC/Sep 1972-Sep 1973/Saturday 8:30-9:00 AM
Last Program: September 1, 1973

### Syndicated History

Distributor: Worldvision Enterprises/1974-
Executive Producers: Arthur Rankin, Jr. , Jules Bass
Producers: John Halas, Joy Batchelor
Director: Robert Balser
Company: Halas and Batchelor, London, for Rankin-Bass Productions and Motown/23 films

### Principal Characters and Voices

| | |
|---|---|
| Jackie | Sigmund Esco Jackson |
| Tito | Toriano Adarryl Jackson |
| Jermaine | Jermaine Lajaune Jackson |
| David | Marion David Jackson |
| Michael | Michael Joe Jackson |

The Jackson 5ive, makers of hit Motown records in the late sixties, were animated in self-likeness for this comedy-music series. Voicing their own roles were twenty-year-old Jackie, eighteen-year-old Tito, seventeen-year-old Jermaine, fourteen-year-old David and thirteen-year-old Michael, who were discovered in 1968 by vocalist Diana Ross.  The black singing stars from Gary, Indiana, presented two of their popular songs each week along with a make-believe off-stage adventure in such stories as "Cinderjackson," "The Wizard of Soul," "Rasho Jackson" and "Michael in Wonderland."  A separate segment spotlighted Michael and his various brothers in a short black-out sketch.  The Jacksons also appeared live in the filmed commercials to push Post Cereals, one of the show's participating sponsors.

Animated by Halas and Batchelor Studios, London, The Jackson 5ive was the second network series to headline an all-black cartoon cast, following The Harlem Globetrotters (q. v.).  Starred in numerous TV specials, the popular singing quintet, with their brothers Randy and La Toya and sisters, Maureen and Janet, premiered June 16, 1976 for four weeks on CBS in a half-hour summer variety show, The Jacksons, continued between January 26 and March 9, 1977 and produced by their father, Joe Jackson, with Richard Arons.

## JEANNIE

Network History
    Premiere:  September 8, 1973
    CBS/Sep 1973-Aug 1974/Saturday 10:30-11:00 AM
    CBS/Sep 1974-Aug 1975/Saturday 9:00-9:30 AM
    Last Program:  August 30, 1975

Syndicated History

## FRED FLINTSTONE AND FRIENDS

Distributor:  Claster TV Productions/1977-1979
Executive Producers:  William Hanna, Joseph Barbera
Producer:  Iwao Takamoto
Director:  Charles A. Nichols
Company:  Hanna-Barbera Productions with Screen Gems (CPT)/16
    films

Principal Characters and Voices

| | |
|---|---|
| Jeannie | Julie McWhirter |
| Babu | Joe Besser |
| Corry Anders | Mark Hamill |
| Henry Glopp | Bob Hastings |

Jeannie popped into the life of Corry Anders when, while he was surfing at a California beach, he removed the stopper from a bottle he found exposed in the sand.  Emerging from her glass prison, the two-thousand-year-old damsel and an inept apprentice named Babu became the grateful servants of the teenager because he had set them free.  An adaptation of the prime time situation comedy, I Dream of Jeannie (NBC, 1965-1970), the comedy-fantasy transformed the sexy blonde played by Barbara Eden into a cute young namesake.  Unlike her progenitor, however, who evoked her powers by crossing hands over her chest and blinking her eyes, the cartoon genie's magic was activated by a swish of her pony-tail. Attempting his best to lead a normal life in spite of the pair's bothersome obligation, Corry concealed them from his mother, Mrs. Anders, and his Center City High School friends.  His best buddy, Henry Glopp, was the only other person aware of their presence.  Complicating matters was the snobbish snoop S. Melvin Farthinggale, who suspected that something strange was going on at the Anders' home and was continually nosing around.  Exercising their supernatural powers to serve and protect their new master, Jeannie and Babu constantly aggravated Corry with their well-intentioned magic, due to their unfamiliarity with American customs and lifestyles.  But they were unerring in seeing through the thinly veiled schemes of his designing girl friends and classmates who were envious of his athletic prowess and popularity in such episodes as "The Blind Date" and "The Decathlon."  When confronted with a particularly knotty situation, the winsome Jeannie and bumbling Babu could count on the counsel of Hadji, the wise master of all the genies.

JETSONS, THE

Network History
    Premiere:  September 23, 1962
    ABC/Sep 1962-Sep 1963/Sunday 7:30-8:00 PM
    ABC/Sep 1963-Apr 1964/Saturday 10:30-11:00 AM
    CBS/Sep 1964-Sep 1965/Saturday 11:30-12:00 AM
    NBC/Oct 1965-Sep 1966/Saturday 9:00-9:30 AM
    NBC/Sep 1966-Sep 1967/Saturday 11:30-12:00 AM
    CBS/Sep 1969-Sep 1970/Saturday 8:00-8:30 AM
    CBS/Sep 1970-Sep 1971/Saturday 1:30-2:00 PM
    NBC/Sep 1971-Jan 1972/Saturday 12:30-1:00 PM
    NBC/Jan 1972-Sep 1972/Saturday 10:00-10:30 AM
    NBC/Sep 1972-Jan 1973/Saturday 8:30-9:00 AM
    NBC/Jan 1973-Sep 1973/Saturday 9:00-9:30 AM
    NBC/Sep 1973-Aug 1975/Saturday 12:00-12:30 PM
    NBC/Oct 1975-Sep 1976/Saturday 12:00-12:30 PM
    NBC/Feb 1979-Sep 1979/Saturday 11:30-12:00 AM
    NBC/Sep 1979-Nov 1979/Saturday 12:30-1:00 PM
    NBC/Jan 1980-Apr 1980/Saturday 11:30-12:00 AM
    NBC/Apr 1980-Sep 1980/Saturday 11:00-11:30 AM
    NBC/Sep 1980-Nov 1980/Saturday 12:30-1:00 PM
    NBC/May 1981-Sep 1981/Saturday 11:00-11:30 AM
    Last Program:  September 5, 1981

Syndicated History

Distributor:  Taft H-B Program Sales/1971-1979; DFS Program Exchange/1979
Executive Producers/Directors:  William Hanna, Joseph Barbera

Company:   Hanna-Barbera Productions with Screen Gems (CPT)/24
films

Principal Characters and Voices

| | |
|---|---|
| George Jetson | George O'Hanlon |
| Jane Jetson | Penny Singleton |
| Judy Jetson | Janet Waldo |
| Elroy Jetson | Daws Butler |
| Cosmo C. Spacely | Mel Blanc |
| Stella Spacely/Rosie | Jean VanderPyl |
| Astro | Don Messick |

The Jetsons, a space-age family living in the twenty-first-
century, were a prime time ratings failure in the 1962-1963 season.   Only twenty-four episodes were produced, but when the
series was repeated on Saturday mornings these futuristic domestic
comedies became a reborn children's favorite, appearing for fourteen and one-half years on all three networks.   An employee of
Spacely Space Sprockets, who commuted to work in a jet-powered
bubble-car, George Jetson was a computer "digital index operator"
and lived with his red-headed wife Jane in the Skypad Apartments,
which were raised and lowered hydraulically to take advantage of
the best weather.   The apartment was equipped with the latest
technology, including a kitchen with a Food-A-Rack-A-Cycle, a
push-button automat that delivered anything on order.   Their
daughter Judy was a typical teenybopper agog over the latest singing idol, Jet Screamer, and a devotee of the Solar Swivel, the
latest dance craze.   A mischievous lad, their young son Elroy was
occupied with his amateur intergalactic radio set and was packed
off to school each morning in a pneumatic tube.   As in such live-
action situation comedies of the period as The Donna Reed Show
(ABC, 1958-1966), the stories developed from the everyday concerns and frustrations of the family members.   Several episodes
focused on utility robots.   The premiere introduced Rosie, an old
demonstration model acquired by Jane from the U-Rent-A-Robot-
Maid Service.   And George purchased an electronic apartment-
approved robot dog, Lectronimo, as a more reliable substitute for
their inept pet Astro, that haplessly tried to prevent a robbery by
a cat burglar.   Appearing also were George's boss, Cosmo C.
Spacely, a penny-pinching crab, and his wife, Stella, a haughty
woman's club member and charity activist.
      The durable series was the third nighttime entry produced
by Bill Hanna and Joe Barbera after the success of The Flintstones (q. v. ), and starred the voices of movie actors George
O'Hanlon and Penny Singleton.   Alias Joe McDoakes, O'Hanlon
starred in the Warner Brothers comedy shorts, Behind the 8-Ball,
and Miss Singleton was best known as the screen's memorable
Blondie.   Veteran Warner cartoon storymen Warren Foster and
Mike Maltese scripted the stories with Harvey Bullock, Larry
Markes and Tony Benedict.
      After its first run ended April 18, 1964 on ABC, The Jet-
sons was repeated on CBS for one season starting September 26,

1964 and was reprised again from September 13, 1969 through September 4, 1971. The episodes were rerun on NBC between October 2, 1965 and September 2, 1967 and from September 11, 1971 to September 4, 1976, beginning the final repeats February 3, 1979.

## JOHNNY CYPHER IN DIMENSION ZERO

Syndicated History
    Premiere: February 1967
Distributor: Warner Brothers Television/1967-
Producer: Joe Oriolo
Company: Seven Arts Television with Joe Oriolo Films/130
    films, 6 minutes

Principal Characters and Voices

| | |
|---|---|
| Johnny Cypher | Paul Hecht |
| Zena | Corinne Orr |

    Johnny Cypher in Dimension Zero was a Tom Swiftian junior scientist, who used his discovery of a time-travel device to oppose villainy in many forms and places. Often accompanied by his young distaff companion, Zena, he was involved with an army of antagonists, including Captain Krool, Mr. Mist, Dr. Flood, The Torchmen, The Abominable Snowman, The Mothmen, Captain Nogo, the evil Mr. ESP and Rhom, a super criminal. In the episodic stories, Johnny visited strange new worlds ranging from Volcos and the Red Forest to the Planet of the Little Men and the frigid Arctic. In their fantasy trips, the pair found "Terror in the Toy Shop," "The World of Lost Men," "The Runaway Rocket" and "The Door to the Future," and also encountered such diabolical weapons as the "Invisible Beam," "Liquifier Gun," "Seeds of Chaos," "Barclay's Bullet," "Giganticus Serum" and the "Multiplier Gun."
    The series was produced for flexible local programming and four episodes could be strung together for a half-hour show. Many of the villains' voices were supplied by Gene Allen.

## JOSIE AND THE PUSSYCATS

Network History
    Premiere: September 12, 1970
    CBS/Sep 1970-Sep 1971/Saturday 10:00-10:30 AM
    CBS/Sep 1971-Sep 1972/Saturday 11:30-12:00 AM
    Last Program: September 2, 1972

## JOSIE AND THE PUSSYCATS IN OUTER SPACE
    Premiere: September 9, 1972
    CBS/Sep 1972-Sep 1973/Saturday 10:30-11:00 AM
    CBS/Sep 1973-Aug 1974/Saturday 11:30-12:00 AM

NBC/Sep 1975-Oct 1975/Saturday 12:00-12:30 PM
NBC/Oct 1975-Sep 1976/Saturday 8:30-9:00 AM
Last Program:   September 4, 1976

Syndicated History

JOSIE

Distributor:   Taft H-B Program Sales/1975-1979; Worldvision Enter-
   prises/1979-
Executive Producers:   William Hanna, Joseph Barbera
Producer:   Iwao Takamoto
Director:   Charles A. Nichols
Company:   Hanna-Barbera Productions with Radio Comics/16 films
   (1970-1972), 16 films (1972-1974)

Principal Characters and Voices

| | |
|---|---|
| Josie | Janet Waldo |
| Melody | Jackie Joseph |
| Valerie | Barbara Pariot |
| Alan | Jerry Dexter |
| Alexander Cabot III | Casey Kasem |
| Alexandra Cabot | Sherry Alberoni |
| Sebastian/Bleep | Don Messick |

Josie and the Pussycats, a distaff teenage rock group with
long tails and ears that flapped, performed in two comedy-adventure
versions.   Josie was the saccharine red-headed leader, Valerie a
level-headed and brainy black girl and Melody, a scatterbrained
blond whose intuitive ears wiggled when danger threatened.   Their
singing voices were dubbed by the real life musical trio, Cathy
Douglas, Patricia Holloway and Cherie Moore (aka Cheryl Ladd).
Others were Alexander Cabot III, the group's young manager;
Alexandra, his brash brunette sister; Alan, their muscular tow-
headed friend; and Sebastian, Alexandra's comical black-and-white
cat.   Together, the teenagers became accidental meddlers, spoil-
ing sinister schemes in exotic locations while on a global concert
tour.   In Peru they outwitted a diamond-coveting madman known as
The Laser; they prevented the power-mad plan of The Serpent, a
Chinese mechanical toy maker in Hong Kong; and in Hawaii grounded
The Hawk, a dirigible-based rotter after the secret of a force field
formula freakishly recorded in Melody's sub-conscious mind.   Always menaced and in jeopardy from their crafty comic book villains,
the teenagers were hindered constantly by the witless acts of the
know-it-all Alexandra, who was often blinded by jealousy over Alan's
attentions to Josie, and by the fiascos created by her cringing
brother Alex.   Triggered by the repeated catch-phrase, "Let's get
out of here!," a Hanna-Barbera trademark, each episode included a
rollicking Keystone Kops-style chase scene, with background rock
music by the group, culminating in Alan's heroic plan to save the
day or capture the culprit.
   Returning in 1972-1974 in a change of venue as Josie and

the Pussycats in Outer Space, the gang was posing for publicity pictures atop a NASA spacecraft when the impulsive-minded Alexandra accidentally shoved the others into an open capsule hatch, landed on top of them and activated the blast-off mechanism.  Unexpected passengers on a celestial rocket ride, the teenagers encountered alien worlds when their spacecraft descended upon strange planetoids.   On Zelcor, Melody befriended a new mascot named Bleep, a duck-like creature that used sound waves as a weapon, and the group aided the ruler Zorb in foiling a power-grabbing plot by the deposed tyrant Karnak.   In the land of the Kat people on Katoria, they assisted King Kator by rescuing Queen Felina, held captive by the robot Mentor in his glass city, Labore.   Landing on Arcobia, they helped the Arcobians by exposing their Prime Minister Ruleo as the reprobate who stole the kingdom's all-powerful Robotrone with the aid of the Canyonians, a squatting purple people led by Gorgod.

Despite the contrived antagonists and heroic nonsense, Josie and the Pussycats was a landmark series created by John and Richard Goldwater and fostered by Fred Silverman, CBS vice president for program planning and development, and was notable for introducing the first minority heroine, the teenager Valerie.  With The Harlem Globetrotters (q. v.), the program marked a return to half-hour episodic stories; cartoon shows previously were split into shorter segments.   Also, the series popularized the comedy-adventure format involving stereotypical teenagers and their mascots menaced by weird characters and incorporating a comical chase scene; this became a successful formula in subsequent animated shows like Scooby-Doo (q. v.), Goober and the Ghost Chasers (q. v.) and variations like Jabberjaw (q. v.).

After the CBS run ended August 31, 1974, NBC repeated Josie and the Pussycats in Outer Space, starting September 6, 1975.

## JOT

### Syndicated History
Premiere:  1965
WFAA, Dallas/Various AM & PM
Distributor:  Southern Baptist Radio-TV Commission/1965-1975
Producers:  Ruth Byers, Ted Perry
Company:  Southern Baptist Radio-TV Commission/18 films, 4 1/2 minutes

### Principal Character
Jot

Jot, a bouncing dot, appeared in a religious series of short cartoons teaching moral and ethical lessons for children aged five to ten.   The stories dealt with simple right and wrong, poverty, racial differences and life in the urban ghetto.   An imaginative abstract utilizing the round shape inspired by children's drawings, Jot reflected a child's personality.   Sensitive to the inner world of thought and feeling, somewhat like a thermostat it changed shape and color to depict the struggles represented by a youngster's conscience. When Jot realigned itself with its inner standards, the dot regained spirit, balance and its perfect round shape. The expressive animated face of the character and its playmates displayed emotion as well as moral turmoil, and also changed shape and color to show joy or sadness.

The unique non-denominational concept was created and written by Ruth Byers, former director of dramatic children's productions at Paul Baker's Dallas Theater Center, and Ted Perry, also a Baker disciple. The abstract messages captivated and inspired children far beyond anticipation, requiring a volunteer group from twenty-two churches to answer the 175,000 letters that the films prompted. The films were seen as inserts on children's programs between 1965 and 1975 on about fifty stations.

## JOURNEY TO THE CENTER OF THE EARTH

Network History
Premiere: September 9, 1967
ABC/Sep 1967-Sep 1968/Saturday 10:30-11:00 AM
ABC/Sep 1968-Aug 1969/Saturday 11:00-11:30 AM
Last Program: August 30, 1969

Syndicated History

Distributor: Twentieth Century-Fox Television/1970-
Executive Producers: Louis Scheimer, Norman Prescott
Director: Hal Sutherland
Company: Filmation Productions with TCF-TV/17 films

Principal Characters and Voices

Professor Lindenbrook/Count
  Saccnuson      Ted Knight
Cindy Lindenbrook      Jane Webb
Alec McEwen/Lars/Torg      Pat Harrington, Jr.
Gertrude (Cindy's pet duck)

Journey to the Center of the Earth followed the exploits of Professor Oliver Lindenbrook through a labyrinth of eerie caverns, where he was menaced by such hazards as prehistoric hyperthyroid reptiles. Loosely based on the 1865 classic science fiction novel by French author Jules Verne and the 1959 movie adaptation by Twentieth Century-Fox Films, the cartoon treatment incorporated a pair of teenagers and scoundrels to provide juvenile appeal and melodramatic purpose. Uncovering the long-lost route deep into the Earth discovered by explorer Arnie Saccnuson, who descended only to die with the secrets he found there, Dr. Lindenbrook mounted a mission to unravel its mysteries. In the party were his guide Lars, his young niece Cindy, her classmate Alec McEwen and Gertrude, a pet duck. Aware of the Professor's intentions, Count Saccnuson, the last living descendant of the once-noble family,

decided to speed up his power-mad plan to use the Earth's core.
Following the adventurers with his man-servant Torg to implement
his villainous scheme, Saccnuson caused an explosion which inad-
vertently sealed the entrance, entrapping them all. Hindered as
much by the Count and his bungling confederate as by the denizens
and phenomena they encountered, Dr. Lindenbrook's party struggled
to survive and find a way to return to the Earth's surface.


JUNGLE BOOK, THE

Network History
    Premiere: January 9, 1975
    CBS/Jan 1975-  /Periodic/Various PM
Executive Producer: Chuck Jones
Producer: Oscar Dufau (1976)
Directors: Chuck Jones, Hal Ambro
Company: Chuck Jones Enterprises/3 films (1975-1976)

Narrators
    Orson Welles (1975)
    Roddy McDowall (1975-1976)

Principal Characters and Voices

Nag/Chuchundra                      Orson Welles
Rikki-Tikki-Tavi                    Shepard Menken
Darzee                             Lennie Weinrib
Nagaina/Darzee's wife/Mother/
    Matkah/Mother Wolf             June Foray
Father                             Les Tremayne
Teddy                             Michael LeClaire
Kotick/Sea Catch/Sea Cow/
    Killer Whale/Walrus/Mowgli/
    Shere Khan/Tabaqui/Bagheera/
    Akela/Baloo                    Roddy McDowall

    The Jungle Book, the first of two volumes of animal stories
for children, supplied the scenarios for three specials set in nineteenth-century India during British rule. Penned by Nobel laureate
Rudyard Kipling (1865-1936), and published in 1894 during his so-
journ in Vermont, the Bombay-born, English author's priceless
gifts to childhood were adapted by Chuck Jones. The molder and
instigator of such characters as Bugs Bunny (q.v.) and The Road
Runner (q.v.), Jones produced the first TV programs starring
Tom and Jerry (q.v.) and the whimsical creatures of Dr. Seuss
(q.v.).
    Orson Welles narrated and voiced characters for "Rikki-
Tikki-Tavi" (Jan 9, 1975), a mongoose that protected Teddy and
his family in the Segowlee cantonment from Nag and Nagaina, two
deadly king-cobras. The house pet of the young boy, Rikki-Tikki
had as garden friends the tailor-bird family, Darzee, and Chu-
chundra, a muskrat.

The offspring of the huge, gray Sea Catch and Matkah, his sleek, gentle-eyed wife, Kotick was "The White Seal" (Mar 24, 1975), the only snow-white pup born on Novastoshnah or North East Point on the Island of St. Paul in the Bering Sea. He was also the only one to rebel against the seal hunters' annual ravages of his colony in the tale related by Roddy McDowall. Horrified by the slaughter, Kotick followed the Sea Cows in his search for a new home and found a safe island where his fellow seals could live in peace without fear of man.

McDowall also narrated and provided voices for "Mowgli's Brothers" (Feb 11, 1976), the last of the trilogy, about an abandoned human baby adopted by a pair of compassionate wolves. With the aid of Baloo, a sleepy brown bear that taught the wolf cubs the Law of the Jungle, and a Black Panther, Bagheera, the wolves prevailed on the great gray leader, Akela, and the Seeonee Pack to accept the child as one of their own. He was named Mowgli, for naked "little frog," by his animal friends, who protected him from the evil tiger Shere Khan and his cowardly cohort, the jackal Tabaqui, that wished to kill the "man cub." Growing up unaware that he was different from the others, Mowgli was eventually called upon to use his human wits and save his lupine mentors from the plots of the scheming and vengeful Shere Khan.

Capturing suggestions of Kipling's India through the artwork, the specials continued in repeats through Summer 1981. Featuring the voices of Phil Harris, Louis Prima, George Sanders, Sterling Holloway and Bruce Reitherman as Mowgli, The Jungle Book (BV, 1967) was the last animated feature produced personally by Walt Disney and included the hit song "The Bare Necessities" by Terry Gilkyson.


KELLOGG'S PRESENTS THE BANANA SPLITS ADVENTURE HOUR
See  BANANA SPLITS ADVENTURE HOUR, THE


## KID POWER

### Network History
Premiere:  September 16, 1972
ABC/Sep 1972-Sep 1973/Saturday 11:30-12:00 AM
ABC/Sep 1973-Sep 1974/Sunday 10:00-10:30 AM
Last Program:  September 1, 1974
Executive Producers:  Arthur Rankin, Jr., Jules Bass
Company:  Rankin-Bass Productions/17 films

### Principal Characters and Voices

| | |
|---|---|
| Nipper | John Gardiner |
| Wellington | Charles Kennedy, Jr. |
| Oliver | Jay Silverheels, Jr. |
| Jerry | Allan Melvin |
| Connie | Carey Wong |
| Ralph | Gary Shapiro |

Sybil                               Michele Johnson
Diz                                 Jeff Thomas
Albert                              Greg Thomas
Polly (Wellington's Parrot)
General Lee (Nipper's Dog)
Tom (Ralph's Cat)

Kid Power celebrated the ethnic diversity of nine suburban
youngsters with humor and gentle social comment built around their
everyday lives and pastime activities.   Through an examination of
their interpersonal relationships as neighborhood members of "The
Rainbow Power Club, " the stories touched on such subjects as teamwork, honesty, peer pressure, racial and sexist prejudice and han-
dling new responsibilities.   The series was adapted from the newspaper comic strip Wee Pals (Register/Tribune, 1965-  ), created
by black cartoonist Morrie Turner, the 1972 chairman of the Child
Development and Media Forum at the White House Conference on
Children.   Turner's idea for an integrated strip was encouraged by
comedian Dick Gregory and fellow cartoonist Charles Schulz.   It
was thus no surprise that the characters from the popular Peanuts
(q.v.) dramatically influenced some of the Wee Pals.   Not unlike the
baseball-capped Charlie Brown, Nipper was a black lad who wore a
Confederate hat which covered his eyes and also had a dog named
General Lee.   From the same mold as Lucy, Sybil was a highly
enterprising, no-nonsense black girl who told fortunes instead of
dispensing psychology.   Among the others were the mischievous
Wellington, a long-haired white boy whose Parrot named Polly was
culturally integrated; the chubby bespectacled Oliver; Jerry, the
Jewish intellectual, and Connie the Tomboy.

A special prime time preview was telecast August 24, 1972,
featuring the Wee Pals in their first day at school.   The Bank
Street College of Education served as advisor for the program,
which was the third network series to present minority characters
in the main cast, following Josie and the Pussycats (q.v.) and The
Archies (q.v.) on CBS.   A bit too pro-social and preachy for children interested in fantasy entertainment, the show failed to attract
decent ratings.


KID'S KAPERS

Network History
     Premiere:   October 26, 1952
     ABC/Oct 1952-Jan 1953/Sunday 12:00-12:15 PM
     Last Program:   January 30, 1953

Kid's Kapers was one of the first cartoon shows on network
weekend television.   Although the exact content is not known, the
program featured vintage black-and-white films, possibly the "Flip
the Frog" (1930-1933) and "Willie Whopper" (1933-1934) theatrical
cartoons produced by Ub Iwerks for Pat Powers' Celebrity Pictures,
or the silent "Aesop's Fables" (1921-1929).

# KIMBA, THE WHITE LION

## Syndicated History
Premiere: September 11, 1966
KHJ, Los Angeles/Sunday 6:00-6:30 PM PST
Distributor: NBC Enterprises/1966-1971; National Telefilm Associates/1971-1979; Air Time International/1979-
Producer: Osamu Tezuka
Company: Mushi Productions, Japan with NBC Enterprises/52 films (1965-1966)

## Principal Character and Voice

Kimba                                    Billie Lou Watt

Kimba, the White Lion struggled to protect his peaceful jungle kingdom against vicious enemies and the perils of nature in this pacificist-tinged series. Descended from an Egyptian pet, a rare white lion believed to be the Spirit of the Sphinx and given by the Pharaoh Tut Tut to the Kickapeels tribe as their king, Kimba's lineage was royal indeed. Caesar, his father, was killed by a hunter and his mother was captured for a zoo. Kimba was born on a boat bound for Europe and escaped when it sank in a storm. Passing through cities on the way back to his homeland, the cub observed the many aspects of civilization. Acknowledged by the animals as their new monarch, he decided to establish an animal land with schools and farms. But Kimba was often in conflict with the older denizens who did not believe in his new ways and laws, and with humans who would not respect his rights or authority. In stories with an underlying anti-war theme, Kimba battled poachers and trappers, the Monster of Petrified Valley and the Magic Serpent, and defended his domain against "The Insect Invasion," "The Red Menace," "The Pretenders," "Destroyers from the Desert" and "The Gigantic Grasshopper." Aiding his efforts were his animal friends, Dan'l Baboon, Pauley Cracker, Tadpole, Samson and Roger Ranger, a human who believed in his plans for a peaceful and secure environment for his civilized animal society.

The series was based on Osamu Tezuka's popular comic strip Jungle Tatei ("Jungle Emperor") in the Manga Shōnen (1950-1954) and first run on Japanese TV. It was the first Nipponese import in color and NBC Enterprises insisted on the use of tint before it agreed to distribute the cartoons, after their experience in 1963 with Tezuka's Astro Boy (q.v.), which was filmed in black-and-white, severely limiting its syndication potential. The company did not pick up Tezuka's twenty-six episode sequel, however, which portrayed Kimba as an adult, married to his childhood sweetheart Kitty and with two cubs, one of them Rune, his son.


KING AND ODIE, THE  See  KING LEONARDO AND HIS SHORT
    SUBJECTS

KING FEATURES TRILOGY

Component Series
  BARNEY GOOGLE AND SNUFFY SMITH, BEETLE BAILEY,
  KRAZY KAT

Syndicated History
  Premiere: August 26, 1963
  KTLA, Los Angeles/Monday-Friday 5:30-6:00 PM PST
Distributor: Firestone Program Syndication/1963-1978; Gold Key
  Entertainment/1978-
Producer: Al Brodax
Company: King Features Syndicate Television/150 films, 5 1/2
  minutes

Principal Characters and Voices

| | |
|---|---|
| Private Beetle Bailey/Snuffy Smith | Howard Morris |
| Sergeant Snorkel/Barney Google | Allan Melvin |
| Krazy Kat | Penny Phillips |
| Ignatz Mouse | Paul Frees |

King Features Trilogy was a syndicated package with film
adaptations of familiar newspaper comics, designed for flexible
local programming. Depicting the amusing side of Army life at
Camp Swampy, commanded by General Halftrack, an elderly symbol of blustery authority, Beetle Bailey was a satire on the trials
and travails of an average G.I., the lowest of the low in the military hierarchy. With his eyes always hidden by his hat or helmet, Private Beetle was the eternal foul-up, constantly being
chewed-out by Sergeant Orville Snorkel, his platoon leader. While
policing the grounds, Beetle and his pals, Zero and Cosmo, accidentally massacred the Sarge's beloved leechie nut tree and had to
hastily "borrow" a replacement from a Chinese restaurant. On KP,
Beetle ruined Cookie's prize chili and broke most of the dishes, and
during war games the General entrusted a vital message to Bailey
and Zero, with disastrous results. Snorkel, who relished food as
much as he did ordering men around, maintained a covert affection
for the hapless Private, about the same as he displayed toward
Otto, his pet bulldog. And Beetle tried every manner of guise to
obtain passes from him to visit his girlfriend, Bunny. A reluctant
draftee, Beetle was Mort Walker's "Everyman," created during the
Korean War and first appearing September 3, 1950. The last
comic personality approved by William Randolph Hearst, at one
time the feature was in 1,600 papers around the world and tied
with Peanuts as the second most popular comic strip after the
long-running Blondie.
    Among the best known residents of Kokonino Kounty, Krazy
Kat had escalating problems with the brick-throwing Ignatz Mouse,
her unruly neighbor, and his nemesis, the hard-nosed Offissa Pupp,
a dedicated lawman. Apoplectic with habitual disgust for Krazy's
unswerving love for him, Ignatz's hot-tempered response was to hit

her on the head with a brick, resulting in his arrest by the Pupp.
The cat, mouse and dog cavorted in both fantasyland and domestic
comedies. To keep his mind off brick tossing, Krazy once bought
a car for Ignatz, but prevented the mouse from using it with her
constant tinkering. Another time Pupp dreamt of the pilgrims,
when kops were tops, kats wore hats, and mice that opened their
mouths received a public dunking. And Ignatz, Krazy and Pupp
trotted off to the nearest gym for a workout one day, where Krazy
almost killed Ignatz with the barbells. The idol of the intelligentsia
and auteurs, acclaimed by some critics as the greatest pure comic
strip ever, Krazy Kat began as an inauspicious family pet in
George Herriman's The Dingbat Family (New York Journal 1910),
eventually appearing October 28, 1913 as a separate Krazy Kat
strip. For silent films, "Krazy Kat" and Ignatz were animated by
Leon Searl, William C. Nolan, Bert Green and Frank Moser for
the Hearst-Vitagraph News Pictorial (1916), seen once a week
within the film magazine's bi-weekly format, debuting in Ignatz
Believes in Signs (Feb 22, 1916). Subsequent series were produced by Nolan for distributor Margaret J. Winkler (1926-1927)
and by Manny Gould and Ben Harrison for Paramount-Famous-
Lasky (1927-1929), followed by Gould and Harrison's sound films
for Columbia Pictures (1930-1940), syndicated in the fifties in the
Screen Gems Theatrical Cartoon Package (q.v.). The made-for-TV
series toned down much of the brick throwing violence associated
with the comic strip, but ignored Ignatz's three sons, Moshie,
Milton and Irving. The films did introduce his cousin Ixnay Mouse,
however, and several of Krazy's new relatives, cousins Fifi, Frit-
zie, Krooked Kat, Pole Kat and Chief Rain-in-the-Puss.

Barney Google and Snuffy Smith, a suave, mustachioed hustler and his ace foil, a rambunctious, simple-minded hillbilly, appeared in domestic backwoods comedies. One time Barney decided
to turn Hootin' Holler into another Sun Valley, but things got out of
hand when he tried to teach Snuffy, his wife Loweezy, and his
nephew Jughaid, how to ski, skate and bobsled. With Barney
Google up, Sparkplug came through over the Jerky Jockey and once
fell in love with Dolores Del Horso, encountering equestrian competition from Rudolph Horse. And Snuffy found himself in another
fracas with Clem Cutplug, his feuding foe, over Loweezy's lusty
hog calling. Emerging as one of the harried spouses in Married
Life (Chicago Herald 1916) by Billy De Beck (1890-1942), Take
Barney Google, For Instance first appeared June 17, 1919 on the
Herald-Examiner sports page, for a time devoting all his interest
to Sparkplug, the racehorse. The subject of a hit song in the
twenties, "Barney Google with the Goo-Goo-Googly Eyes," by Billy
Rose and Con Conrad, the character made his film bow in Tetched
in the Head (Oct 24, 1935), the first of four animated cartoons
produced in 1935-1936 by Charles Mintz Studios for Columbia.

Hindered by very limited action and characters lifted from
the pages of bygone eras, the TV cartoons were artistic and commercial failures, not even enthusiastically received by nostalgic
adults. With fifty episodic films in each series, under the title
Beetle and His Buddies the trilogy premiered in 1963 on KTLA,
Los Angeles, stripped weekdays. As a weekly series, the comics'

trio debuted September 7, 1963 on WPIX, New York at 6:00-6:30 PM, Saturday, hosted by Jack McCarthy.


KING KONG SHOW, THE

Component Series
    TOM OF T. H. U. M. B.

Network History
    Premiere: September 10, 1966
    ABC/Sep 1966-Sep 1967/Saturday 10:00-10:30 AM
    ABC/Sep 1967-Sep 1968/Saturday 11:00-11:30 AM
    ABC/Sep 1968-Aug 1969/Sunday 10:30-11:00 AM
    Last Program: August 31, 1969

Syndicated History

Distributor: Worldvision Enterprises/1972-
Executive Producers: Arthur Rankin, Jr., Jules Bass
Company: Rankin-Bass Productions with Videocraft International/ 24 films

Principal Characters

    King Kong
    Professor Bond
    Bobby Bond
    Susan Bond
    Tom
    Swinging Jack


    The King Kong Show resurrected for its hero the giant ape who was machine-gunned by a squadron of bi-planes in his last defiant stand atop the Empire State Building. In his cartoon adventures, Kong was befriended by an American family headed by a scientist, Professor Bond, his young son Bobby, and daughter Susan, on the remote palm-dotted Mondo, a prehistoric island in the Java Sea. Premiering in an hour-long ABC Special, September 6, 1966 at 7:30-8:30 PM, the movie monster launched his TV career doing battle with a throw-back to the Mesozoic era, an enormous, slimy denizen called Kraken that emerged from the sea. In subsequent Saturday episodes, the fifty-foot tall primate exhibited tender indulgence for his friends and used his colossal strength and primeval cunning in partnership with Bobby, fighting injustice, prehistoric creatures and a succession of diabolical villains like Dr. Who, a deranged scientist who sought to control Kong for his own nefarious ends.
    A mix of the James Bond and Lilliputian themes, the companion feature, "Tom of T. H. U. M. B.," concerned the investigations of tiny Tom and Swinging Jack, his oriental assistant who was skilled in the martial arts. The pair were secret agents from the Tiny Humans Underground Military Bureau (T. H. U. M. B.), assigned

missions too small for taller operatives to tackle.

One of the great mythopoeic creations of the twentieth-century, the sensitive simian Kong was originated by Merian C. Cooper and lifted from the most famous monster film of all time, King Kong (RKO, 1933), novelized by Delos W. Lovelace, and re-filmed in 1976 by Dino De Laurentiis and Paramount Pictures. The TV series was the first animated in Japan expressly for an American network presentation.


## KING LEONARDO AND HIS SHORT SUBJECTS

Component Series
THE HUNTER, TOOTER TURTLE, TWINKLES

Network History
Premiere: October 15, 1960
NBC/Oct 1960-Sep 1963/Saturday 10:30-11:00 AM
Last Program: September 28, 1963

Syndicated History

THE KING AND ODIE

Sponsor: General Mills (1963-1965)
Distributor: Filmtel International/1963-1979
Producers: Treadwell Covington, Peter Piech
Company: Leonardo TV Productions with Total TV Productions/39 films

Principal Characters and Voices

| | |
|---|---|
| King Leonardo/Biggie Rat | Jackson Beck |
| Odie Cologne/Itchy Brother/ Tooter | Allen Swift |
| Mr. Wizard | Frank Milano |
| The Hunter | Kenny Delmar |
| The Fox | Ben Stone |

King Leonardo and His Short Subjects offered a package of untroubled mirth starring quaint animals. A gentle king of beasts that ruled the mythical African domain of Bongo Congo, Leonardo was bolstered by his faithful retainer, Odie Cologne, a skunk whose obsequiously loyal "Sire!" did not quite conceal the fact that he was the real power behind the throne. Leonardo's principal foes were Itchy Brother and Biggie Rat, his goading accomplice. Actually the King's own blood brother, Itchy was an invidious pretender to the throne and in the premiere, "Riches to Rags," tried to convince Leonardo he had reformed. But no matter what the scheme, Odie continually thwarted the plots by the designing usurpers in such stories as "Nose for the Noose," "Duel to the Dearth," "Trial of the Traitors" and "Bringing in Biggie." The naive potentate was also threatened by sundry other crackpots such as the diabolical

Professor Messer in "Double Trouble" and "Switcheroo Ruler," who manufactured a pair of androids that looked like the King and Odie. Also involved in some stories was the flirtatious Carlotta, Odie's sister. Initially two-part serials, with the concluding episode seen the following week, in 1961-1962 the installments became the wrap-around cartoons for the fillers, with several in four parts.

Like many of his viewers, Leonardo spent a good deal of time watching TV and was addicted to cartoons, which allowed the introduction of several alternated series in 1960-1961. In a cops-and-robbers caper, "The Hunter" was a southern Bloodhound with the drawl of Kenny Delmar's radio-famed Senator Beauregard Claghorn ("I say, that's a joke son!,") who debuted in 1946 on The Fred Allen Show (NBC/CBS, 1934-1949). Working for Police Officer Flim Flanagan, the canine detective carried a card that read, "Have Nose, Will Hunt," usually did not stand a chance against The Fox, an adroit con-man who in the premiere stole the Brooklyn Bridge, and was continually upstaged by his smart-aleck nephew, Horrors. The Hunter stumbled through such plots as "Rustler Hustler," "Florida Fraud," "Racquet Racket" and "The Frankfurter Fix," always unable to jail his wily adversary.

A whimsical terrapin, mild-mannered "Tooter Turtle" acted out his fantasies whenever he wished through the sorcery of Mr. Wizard the Lizard of The Great Forest. Tooter debuted as a western Sheriff in "Two Gun Turtle" and assumed such identities as a lawman in "Highway Petrol-Man," "Knight of the Square Table," "Railroad Engineer" and "Robin Hoodwink," invariably botching his jobs and imploring the Wizard to return him to the Forest. Also the erudite tot "Twinkles" appeared in ninety-second cartoons dealing with elementary subjects for the preschooler.

The second color cartoon series on NBC's Saturday morning schedule, replacing the first run of Ruff and Reddy (q. v.), the films were repeated on CBS between 1963 and 1966 as components of Tennessee Tuxedo and His Tales (q. v.). Some of the early episodes of King Leonardo were combined with other comedies and re-run between 1963 and 1965 over CBS outlets on a spot market basis for General Mills. In general syndication, the series was retitled The King and Odie until the films were amalgamated with other programs in the seventies.

KRAZY KAT See KING FEATURES TRILOGY and SCREEN GEMS THEATRICAL CARTOON PACKAGE

LASSIE'S RESCUE RANGERS

Network History
   Premiere: September 8, 1973
   ABC/Sep 1973-Sep 1974/Saturday 10:00-10:30 AM
   ABC/Sep 1974-Aug 1975/Sunday 10:30-11:00 AM
   Last Program: August 31, 1975

Syndicated History

THE GROOVIE GOOLIES AND FRIENDS

Distributor:  Metromedia Producers Corporation/1978-
Executive Producers:  Louis Scheimer, Norman Prescott
Director:  Hal Sutherland
Company:  Filmation Productions with Lassie Television/18 films

Principal Characters and Voices

| | |
|---|---|
| Lassie | |
| Ben Turner | Ted Knight |
| Laura Turner | Jane Webb |
| Susan Turner | Lane Scheimer |
| Jackie Turner | Keith Sutherland |
| Ben Turner, Jr. /Gene Fox | Hal Harvey |

Lassie's Rescue Rangers, a remarkable team of eight wild animals led by the brave and intelligent collie, triumphed as expected over adversity and evil in this fantasy adventure. Known as The Forest Force, the members included a mountain lion named Toothless, Robbie the raccoon, Musty the skunk, Groucho the owl, Babbit the rabbit, Edgar the raven, Fastback the turtle and Clyde, a porcupine. Together with Lassie's new masters, the Turner Family, including Forest Ranger Ben Turner, his wife, Laura, and their children, Susan, Jackie and Ben Jr., they waged a continuing crusade to protect the tranquility of Thunder Mountain National Park, utilizing such modern equipment as their helicopter, "Rescue One." Joining them on several missions was the youngster's friend, Gene Fox, an Indian boy from the nearby Thunder Mountain Indian village, home of Chief Red Arrow.

Not content merely to protect the environment and pluck hapless tenderfeet from deadly peril, the Turners and members of the Forest Force journeyed to Alaska to find a lost team of firefighters, provided life-saving service after a tidal wave in Florida and a power failure in the nearby town of Vicksburg, assisted the U. S. Navy in the rescue of a frogman and in an underwater living experiment in a bathyscaphe, snatched a crashed and stranded Russian Cosmonaut from the brink of death, and even unmasked a flighty phantom who was disrupting filming on a Hollywood movie set. Through it all the dauntless dog was up to all the old tricks her viewers loved in the live-action adventures of Lassie* (q. v.), plus a few more. One episode found the animals locked in a cage by drug smugglers and the resourceful tan-and-white collie managed an ingenious escape by using one of Clyde's quills to pick the lock.

As a cartoon star, Lassie was introduced in an hour-long feature, "Lassie and The Spirit of Thunder Mountain" (Nov 11, 1972), seen as a segment of The ABC Saturday Superstar Movie (q. v.) and later repeated as two episodes of Rescue Rangers. The pilot was one of many animated adaptations of non-cartoon evening series, a network mini-trend that followed the Saturday morning purification of 1968-1969.

LAUREL AND HARDY

Syndicated History

LAUREL AND HARDY CARTOONS

LAUREL AND HARDY COMEDY SHOWS

Premiere: 1966

Distributor: Larry Harmon Pictures, Allworld Telefilm Sales/1966-
Executive Producers: Larry Harmon, William Hanna, Joseph
   Barbera
Company: Hanna-Barbera Studios for Wolper Productions/32 films;
   Larry Harmon Pictures/39 films

Principal Characters and Voices

Stan Laurel                          Jim McGeorge
Oliver Hardy                         Larry Harmon

   Laurel and Hardy Cartoons recaptured the essential characterization and likeness of the screen's finest comedy team, in two
separate syndicated series.   Somewhat like their slapstick silent-
and-sound two-reelers, the films depicted the misadventures of the
sorrowful-dimwit, scalp-scratching Stan Laurel (1895-1965) and the
genteel-pompous, tie-twiddling Oliver Hardy (1892-1957).   In 1961
Stan and Ida Laurel and Lucille Hardy Price assigned exclusive
rights to merchandise the comedians' names and likenesses to Larry
Harmon, producer of the cartoon and variety series, Bozo the Clown
(q. v. ).   His Laurel and Hardy Comedy Shows were being animated
about the time producer David L. Wolper engaged Hanna-Barbera
Studios to produce another series after the death of Laurel.   Through
a modus vivendi they received Harmon's permission to use the characters in exchange for the distribution rights, later assigned to Allworld Telefilm Sales.   Produced in five-minute episodes with four
intended per half-hour, the Wolper cartoons were standard fantasy
and contemporary comedies like "Hot Rod Hardy, " "Beanstalk
Boobs, " "Ali Boo Boo, " "Sitting Roomers" and "Riverboat Detectives. "   Despite the limited style, the films adhered to the pair's
unique comedy motifs.   A typical story followed the mounting exasperation of the fat and skinny derby-wearing team as they prepared for a picnic, set off with frayed tempers in a balky old
flivver, and encountered frustrating delays along the way and misfortune at the end.
   The animated revivals were inspired by the television redis-
covery of their comedy shorts and features made between 1926 and
1952, which became favorites of children and were licensed by Hal
Roach Studios for television since 1948 as Laurel and Hardy* (q. v. ).
In the wake of their popularity, merchandise of every description
using the comedians' faces, from wrist watches to spray deodorants,
began appearing on the market, and clips of Laurel and Hardy were
used in TV commercials.   A five-year court battle between Harmon
and the widows and Hal Roach Studios and its licensees was finally
resolved in an August 1975 Federal Court injunction, permanently
enjoining the defendants from using or licensing the comedians'

likenesses for advertising, commercial, film or publicity purposes.

Distributed for flexible programming after the ripple effect of the Laurel and Hardy films had diminished, the series achieved only limited success, and were seen in about thirty-five markets. The Laurel and Hardy Cartoons and Comedy Show were not the first animated versions of the famous film clowns.    Several theatrical shorts featured their caricatures, for example Walt Disney's Mickey's Polo Team (Jan 4, 1936).

## LINUS THE LIONHEARTED

### Network History
Premiere:   September 26, 1964
CBS/Sep 1964-Sep 1965/Saturday 11:00-11:30 AM
CBS/Sep 1965-Sep 1966/Saturday 10:30-11:00 AM
ABC/Sep 1966-Jan 1967/Sunday 9:30-10:00 AM
ABC/Jan 1967-Aug 1969/Sunday 10:00-10:30 AM
Last Program:    August 31, 1969
Sponsor:   Post Cereals (1964-1966)
Producer:   Ed Graham
Company:   Ed Graham Productions/39 films

### Principal Characters and Voices

| | |
|---|---|
| Linus | Sheldon Leonard |
| Sascha Grouse/Dinny Kangaroo/ | |
| Rory Raccoon | Carl Reiner |
| So Hi/The Giant | Jonathan Winters |
| Loveable Truly/Sugar Bear | Sterling Holloway |
| Billie Bird | Ed Graham |

Linus the Lionhearted was a try-hard if not a valiant king of beasts, ruling a desert island paradise.   One of the few Saturday morning cartoons to feature such high-powered voice talent as comedians Jonathan Winters and Sterling Holloway, plus Carl Reiner and Sheldon Leonard, the producers of The Dick Van Dyke Show (CBS, 1961-1966) and I Spy (NBC, 1965-1968), the series was based on the characters appearing on Post Animal Crackers and Sugar Crisps cereals.   Deriving comedy through the interplay of the distinct and humorous characterizations, accomplished in the recording studio like partly ad-libbed radio comedy shows, the cast included both witty animals and human figures.   With the charmingly sinister voice of the screen's most ominous hood, Leonard talked for Linus, a lion that plied his monarch trade over a bewildering domain from a comfortable throne, a barber's chair.   Numbered among his sometimes not-so-staunch subjects were the masked custodian of the Royal corn fields, Rory Raccoon, a grumpy spoilsport, Sascha Grouse, a slap-happy marsupial, Dinny Kangaroo and Billie Bird, a wacky mockingbird.   A regular visitor was Loveable Truly, a genial postman who dropped by with the latest news.

In his first cartoon voice role, Winters supplied the words for a small Chinese boy, So Hi, his doting mother and The Giant,

a club-swinging antagonist.  In one of the more hilarious segments,
The Giant accidentally hit himself in the foot with his club and let
fly a string of Oriental epithets like "Jumping Buddha" and "Twisted
Sneaker," extemporaneously captured on tape at a recording session.
The mild-mannered Sugar Bear appeared as an ursine troubador
with the soothingly smooth voice of Holloway.  Later dubbed by
several actors, for a time an imitation of crooner Bing Crosby,
Sugar Bear became the regular animated TV commercial spokesman for Post Super Sugar Crisp.  And Linus, who ended each episode with a little song, was honored by a balloon-likeness in Macy's
1969 Thanksgiving Day Parade.
      After the CBS run ended September 3, 1966 the episodes
were rerun on ABC beginning September 11, 1966.


LIPPY THE LION  See  HANNA-BARBERA NEW CARTOON SERIES,
   THE


LITTLE LULU

Syndicated History
      Premiere:  March 26, 1956
      WABD, New York/Monday-Friday 6:00-6:30 PM
Distributor:  National Telefilm Associates/1956-
Producer:  Sam Buchwald
Directors:  Seymour Kneitel, Isadore Sparber, Bill Tytla
Company:  Famous Studios for Paramount Pictures/26 films, 6-8
   minutes (1943-1948)

Principal Character and Voices

Little Lulu                    (1943-1946) Mae Questel
                               (1946-1948) Cecil Roy


      Little Lulu was a typical little girl from a typical urban
neighborhood, cast in stories about childhood and childhood fantasies.  The rosy-cheeked, long-curly-haired tyke was transferred
to the screen in Technicolor by Famous Studios, New York, a
continuation of Max and Dave Fleischer's Miami cartoonery after
Paramount Pictures severed the producers in 1942.  Apart from
the on-going Popeye The Sailor (q.v.) and The Adventures of
Superman (q.v.), which it replaced, Little Lulu was perhaps the
studio's best series in the forties.  Beginning with Eggs Don't
Bounce (Dec 24, 1943), Lulu and her "boyfriend," Tubby Tompkins,
appeared in such products of overactive childish imaginations as
Beau Ties (Apr 20, 1945), Lulu at the Zoo (Nov 17, 1944), Magi-
calulu (Mar 2, 1945), Bored of Education (Mar 1, 1946) and her
last film, The Dog Show-Off (Jan 30, 1948).  In The Baby Sitter
(Nov 28, 1947), the busy moppet chaperoned little Alvin, a tot
introduced in her comics to whom she told fairy tales about the
evil Witch Hazel and a small apprentice witch, Little Itch.  Seldom really funny, the amusing stories occasionally elicited a

chuckle and featured a fine title song by Fred Wise, Sidney Lipp-
man and Buddy Kaye. When the series was dropped in 1948, it
was replaced by "Little Audrey" (1948-1958), a new cartoon star
owned by the studio who exacted no royalty payments.

A popular favorite before her film debut, Little Lulu first
appeared as a single-panel cartoon in The Saturday Evening Post
(Jun 1935) by Marge, the pen name of Marjorie Henderson Buell.
Published irregularly since 1945 by Dell Comics (Western Publishing) and written by John Stanley for fourteen years, Little Lulu became a successful line of comic books in January 1948, with special
editions appearing through the fifties. In 1972 Western dropped
Marge's byline, assuming full control. Tubby had his own comic
book between 1952-1962. Also a newspaper comic, Little Lulu
(CNS, 1955-1967) was produced by writers Del Kimbrell and Del
Connell with several artists including Roger Armstrong.

The films, with others, were sold by Paramount in 1955 and
syndicated to stations, premiering the week of March 26, 1956 on
Captain Video's Cartoons, hosted by Al Hodge on WABD, New York
with Superman and Betty Boop (q. v. ). The characters were revived
in 1978-1979 for a pair of live-action adventures on the ABC Weekend Specials* (q. v. ). Distributed by ZIV International, a new series
of twenty-six half-hours starring Little Lulu was produced in Japan
in 1976-1977, but has not been programmed widely.


LONE RANGER, THE


Network History
    Premiere: September 10, 1966
    CBS/Sep 1966-Sep 1967/Saturday 11:30-12:00 AM
    CBS/Sep 1967-Sep 1968/Saturday 1:00-1:30 PM
    CBS/Sep 1968-Sep 1969/Saturday 1:30-2:00 PM
    Last Program: September 6, 1969

THE TARZAN/LONE RANGER ADVENTURE HOUR
    Premiere: September 6, 1980
    CBS/Sep 1980-Feb 1981/Saturday 12:30-1:30 PM
    CBS/Mar 1981-Sep 1981/Saturday 10:00-11:00 AM
    Last Program: September 5, 1981
Theme: "William Tell Overture" by Gioacchino Rossini
Executive Producers: Herb Klynn (1966-1969), Louis Scheimer,
    Norman Prescott (1980-    )
Company: Format Films with Lone Ranger Television/26 films
    (1966-1969); Filmation Productions with Lone Ranger Television/
    16 films (1980-    )

Principal Characters and Voices

Lone Ranger            (1966-1969) Michael Rye
                       (1980-    ) William Conrad
Tonto                  (1966-1969) Shepard Menken
                       (1980-    ) Ivan Naranjo

The Lone Ranger, the daring and resourceful masked rider of the plains, experienced his first brush with animation between 1966 and 1969. Arriving during the ascendancy of the hard-action superhero cartoons, the champions of law and order were transformed into near superhumans, the masked man as the world's greatest trick shot and his faithful Indian companion, Tonto, as a miraculous marksman with bow and arrow. In a mix of the science fiction and western genres, the pair took on a platoon of fantastic comic book-like foes, descriptive maniacs such as the Fly, Frogman, Black Widow, Prairie Pirate, Mephisto, Iron Giant, Black Knight, Terrible Tiny Tom, Mr. Happy and the Puppetmaster. Three episodic adventures were seen in each program, with titles like "Wrath of the Sun God," "Revenge of the Mole" and "The Day the West Stood Still." Far from the morality tales of the first filmed children's series, The Lone Ranger* (q. v.), sample stories involved the Monster of Scavenger Crossing, an encounter in the Valley of the Dead and a struggle with the Rainmaker, a deranged scientist able to destroy mankind through control of the weather.

The only thing on the plus side was the inventive graphics approach of Herb Klynn, who used impressionistic techniques with colored paper-collages for backgrounds and a mixture of artistic styles. The basic concept was encouraged by Fred Silverman, CBS daytime programming chief, who ordered and slotted six animated fantasy adventures back-to-back on the 1966-1967 Saturday morning schedule, which launched the superhero glut of the late sixties.

In a blend of people and events from late nineteenth-century American history, The New Adventures of the Lone Ranger in 1980-1981 returned to a more standard western format. Mounted on Silver, with his Indian saddle partner on Scout, the masked man again rode through the Old West defending justice and incorporating an educational lesson or two for young viewers. The episodic stories ranged from a plot against President Ulysses S. Grant at the ceremony joining the rail lines at Promontory Point, Utah, to the early development of oil fields in Texas. Reporter Nellie Bly and the Lone Ranger's young nephew Dan Reid, were up in the air in "The Great Balloon Race," and land stripping was detailed in a conservation show titled "Tall Timber," set on the Columbia River in the Northwest Territory. In "The Great Land Rush" of 1899, opening the Oklahoma Territory near Guthrie, the pair battled some Sooners and Tonto recapped the importance of the historical event in closing comments. True to the legend, the Lone Ranger occasionally left his silver bullet as a calling card and as in his last live-action films was a master of disguise. One of the more nostalgic episodes recounted how the masked man found the wounded Silver in Wild Horse Valley and the strange mystical bond that was forged between them.

In 1980-1981, the New Adventures were coupled with Tarzan, Lord of the Jungle (q. v.).

# LOONEY TUNES

Component Series
  BOSKO, BUDDY, DAFFY DUCK, PORKY PIG, others

Syndicated History
  Premiere: April 11, 1955
  WABD, New York/Monday-Thursday 6:30-7:00 PM, Friday 6:45-
  7:15 PM
  KTLA, Los Angeles/Monday-Friday 4:00-5:30 PM PST
Distributors: Guild Films/1955-1960; Warner Brothers Television/
  1960-1969; United Artists Television/1956-
Producers: Hugh Harman, Rudolph Ising, Leon Schlesinger,
  Edward Selzer
Company: Warner Brothers Cartoons (WB-TV)/190 B&W films,
  5-6 minutes (1930-1947); Warner Brothers Cartoons (UA-TV)/
  327 films, B&W & Color, 5-6 minutes (1930-1948)

Principal Characters and Voices

| | |
|---|---|
| Bosko | (1930-1933) Rudolph Ising/Carmen Maxwell |
| Honey | (1930-1933) Rochelle Hudson |
| Buddy | (1933-1935) Jack Carr |
| Porky Pig | (1935-1937) Joe Dougherty |
| | (1937-1948) Mel Blanc |
| Daffy Duck/others | (1937-1948) Mel Blanc |

Looney Tunes was the umbrella title for selected pre-1948
Warner Brothers theatrical cartoons, a coast-to-coast staple for
children's local hosted programming between 1955 and 1965. The
largest library of its kind, it consisted of over five hundred animated films distributed in two packages, at first 190 cartoons by
the studio under their film series name, "Looney Tunes." The
comedies premiered April 11, 1955 in both New York and Los
Angeles, seen weekday evenings on WABD hosted by Sandy Becker
and on Cartoon Carousel over KTLA, hosted by Skipper Frank
Herman. Entirely black-and-white films, the vintage group included mainly Bosko, Buddy and very early Daffy Duck and Porky
Pig cartoons, withdrawn from syndication in 1969 when the demand
for color made them obsolete. In 1956, Elliot Hyman's Associated
Artists Productions (later UA-TV) bought the pre-1948 Warner feature film library and remaining shorts. Syndicated as U.A.'s
Warner Brothers Cartoons, among the 327 films were 53 featuring
Bugs Bunny (q.v.), which were programmed for separate TV shows
beginning on September 14, 1956. Among the remainder were the
early "Merrie Melodies," twenty-two Daffy Duck cartoons and others
which were used on various local programs, including Bugs Bunny
and the existing Looney Tunes shows, starting in 1956-1957. Warner Brothers retained all rights to the characters, however, and
after they placed their post-1948 color cartoons in distribution in
1960, only their repackaged series were permitted to use the names
for such network programs as The Bugs Bunny Show (q.v.), The
Porky Pig Show (q.v.), The Road Runner Show (q.v.), Sylvester and

<u>Tweety</u> (q. v. ) and <u>The Daffy Duck Show</u> (q. v. ).
    The genesis of the title "Looney Tunes" and the Warner Brothers cartoon stable, which generated more lasting star characters than any rival studio, was a pilot, <u>Bosko the Talk-Ink Kid</u> (1929), made by former Disney animators <u>Hugh Harman and Rudolph Ising</u>. Impressed with their work, entrepreneur Leon Schlesinger, who helped back Warner's in the risky sound adventure <u>The Jazz Singer</u> (WB, 1930), sold the idea of a cartoon series to the brothers in 1930. The only stipulation was that each cartoon include a song from one of their feature films and published by their music company. Paraphrasing Disney's "Silly Symphonies," Harmon and Ising invented "Looney Tunes" for the initial Warner's series. The first film was <u>Sinkin' in the Bathtub</u> (WB, 1930), starring Bosko, a play on a song title introduced in the <u>Show of Shows</u> (WB, 1929). A round little black-faced fellow, who spoke with a Southern Black dialect, Bosko's later character and voice were altered markedly. For support he had a girlfriend named Honey and a dog called Bruno. The similarities to Mickey Mouse, Minnie and Pluto were obvious from the start. The thirty-eight Bosko films became the early mainstay of the studio, which was so pleased that a second monthly series was commissioned in 1931-1932 titled "Merrie Melodies." When Harmon and Ising left in 1933, they took Bosko with them and revived the character for <u>MGM Cartoons</u> (q. v. ). The Warner's replacement was Buddy, sort of a white-faced Bosko with a dog, Towser, who was forever saving his girlfriend Cookie from some terrible fate in two dozen cartoons between 1933 and 1935 until the introduction of <u>Porky Pig</u> (q. v. ).

MAGILLA GORILLA SHOW, THE

Component Series
    BREEZLY AND SNEEZLY (1964), PUNKIN' PUSS, RICOCHET
    RABBIT

<u>Syndicated History</u>
    Premiere: January 14, 1964
    WPIX, New York/Tuesday 7:00-7:30 PM
Sponsor: Ideal Toys (1964-1965)
Distributor: Screen Gems--Columbia Pictures Television/1964-

<u>Network History</u>
    Return: January 1, 1966
    ABC/Jan 1966-Sep 1967/Saturday 11:30-12:00 AM
    Last Program: September 2, 1967
Executive Producers/Directors: William Hanna, Joseph Barbera
Company: Hanna-Barbera Productions with Screen Gems (CPT)/
    26 films

<u>Principal Characters and Voices</u>

| | |
|---|---|
| Magilla Gorilla/Punkin' Puss | Allan Melvin |
| Mr. Peebles/Mush Mouse/Breezly | Howard Morris |

| | |
|---|---|
| Ogee | Jean VanderPyl |
| Ricochet Rabbit | Don Messick |
| Droop-a-Long/Sneezly | Mel Blanc |
| Colonel Fusby | John Stephenson |

The Magilla Gorilla Show was comprised of three eight-minute comedies, starring simple but well designed comical animals. The series took its title from a huge, sociable ape seen in the lead-off films. Banana-eating his patron out of business, Magilla was for sale in Mr. Peeble's Pet Shop window, where he did his best to attract a new owner from among the passers-by, mugging it up and demonstrating his various skills. He was the particular favorite of Ogee, a moneyless little girl who longed to have the gorilla for her own. The comedies followed the amiable ape's dilemmas with a succession of temporary masters, in such episodes as "Gridiron Gorilla," "Mad Scientist" and "Makin' with the Magilla." Among these masters were scoundrels who tried to exploit the gullible simian for some unlawful scheme. Repeatedly, the stories ended with his return to the exasperated shop keeper and his admiring little Ogee, of whom he was very fond.

A goofy polar bear and a more sensible arctic seal, "Breezly and Sneezly" were the on-going frustration of Camp Frostbite and its commander, Colonel Fusby, a sound-alike of comic actor Paul Ford (1901-1976). Constantly trying to join the service or filch a sumptuous meal, the pair adopted all manner of guises to infiltrate the Alaskan Army Base in such plots as "Armored Amour," "Birthday Bonanza" and "Furry Furlough." A mismatched rodent and a coyote that spoofed Matt Dillon and Festus Hagen on Gunsmoke (CBS, 1955-1975), "Ricochet Rabbit" was a western sheriff and his sluggish deputy was named Droop-a-long. Much faster than his snail-paced partner, the Rabbit's schtick was to chant "ping, ping, ping" and in a lightning flash and thunder boom he ricocheted with near invisible speed to catch many a desperado in "Annie Hoaxley," "Slick Quick Gun," "West Pest" and other episodes.

Thirty-two episodes of Magilla Gorilla were combined with twenty-three films of each of the supporting comedies to make up the twenty-six half-hour programs. In Fall 1964, "Punkin' Puss" and his foil Mush Mouse, a pair of feuding hillbillies in such backwoods comedies as "Courtin' Disaster," "Feudal Feud" and "Callin' All Kin," replaced "Breezly and Sneezly," which became a supporting segment on Peter Potamus and His Magic Flying Balloon (q.v.).

The fifth syndicated package produced by Hanna-Barbera for the juvenile market, The Magilla Gorilla Show was telecast initially in about fifty cities, including KCOP, Los Angeles at 6:30-7:00 PM PST Friday and on WGN, Chicago at 6:30-7:00 PM CST Monday for Ideal Toys. The company adapted the successful marketing approach pioneered by Mattel, the California toy maker whose year-around use of such network and syndicated series as Matty's Funday Funnies (q.v.) and The Funny Company (q.v.) revolutionized toy advertising. The program was repeated on the ABC Saturday schedule in 1966-1967 before returning to syndication as The Magilla Gorilla/Peter Potamus Show with new titles and bridges for fifty half-hour programs featuring the segments from both series.

MARINE BOY

Syndicated History
      Premiere:  October 1, 1966
      WTIC, Hartford/Saturday 10:00-10:30 AM
Theme:  "Marine Boy" by Kenjiro Niroshi and Norman Gimble
Distributor:  Warner Brothers Television/1966-
Producer:  Hinoru Adachi
Director:  Hirio Osania
Company:  Japan Telecartoons, Seven Arts Television (WB-TV)/78
      films

Principal Characters and Voices

| | |
|---|---|
| Marine Boy/Neptina/Cli Cli | Corinne Orr |
| Dr. Mariner | Jack Curtis |
| Bulton | Peter Fernandez |
| Piper | Jack Grimes |
| Splasher (Marine Boy's dolphin) | |

     Marine Boy was a daring aquatic hero, able to breathe underwater through the use of Oxygum, life-sustaining oxygen in tablet form.  A key member of the Ocean Patrol, he belonged to an international defense organization headed by his father, Dr. Mariner, and dedicated to preserving a safe world for all mankind, particularly beneath the seas.  Joining two regular crew mates, Bulton and Piper, the lad often helped man the "P-1," a rocket-flying submarine for use in outer space or in the briny deep. Most helpful in their cause were Marine Boy's loyal white dolphin, Splasher, his finny female heartthrob, Cli Cli and Neptina, an enticing mermaid.  Dr. Fumble, an oceanographer, invented the boy's special gear--jet flying boots, a bullet-proof wet-suit, an electric boomerang and the air-giving pills.  He used the inventions to battle the Patrol's foes, including Captain Kidd, Count Shark and a green gooey glob, Dr. Slime, who once captured Dr. Mariner.  The arch fiend held him for ransom, one million dollars in gold that was to be placed on the ocean floor near Plum Pudding Island.  Attempting instead to rescue his father, Marine Boy and his comrades were trapped in an undersea crevice. Through the use of her magical pearl, Neptina extricated her friends and together they eventually saved the Doctor.  The episodes featured special theme music for the patrol boat, Splasher and Neptina in addition to a multi-stanza theme song that began,
            It's Marine Boy,
            brave and free,
            fighting evil,
            beneath the sea.
     Less ominous and inscrutable than most animated Japanese series, Marine Boy began as a twenty-six-episode serial adventure, gained popularity and was expanded to seventy-eight half-hours. Produced between 1965 and 1968 and dubbed in English by Zavala-Riss Productions, the cartoons were among the first Japanese imports in color, which contributed to their marketability through the early seventies.

MARVEL SUPERHEROES

Component Series
CAPTAIN AMERICA, INCREDIBLE HULK, IRON MAN, MIGHTY
THOR, SUB-MARINER

Syndicated History
Premiere: September 2, 1966
KHJ, Los Angeles/Saturday 6:30-7:00 PM PST
Distributor: ARP Films/1966-
Executive Producer: Steve Krantz
Company: Paramount Cartoon Studios, Grantray-Lawrence Anima-
tion for ARP Films/65 films

Principal Characters

Steve Rogers/Captain America
Dr. Bruce Banner/Incredible Hulk
Tony Stark/Iron Man
Dr. Donald Blake/Mighty Thor
Prince Namor/Sub-Mariner

Marvel Superheroes was produced at the start of the network
superhero vogue to cash in on the demand for similar cartoons for
the syndicated market.   Conceived as a half-hour strip-show, with
a different super champion rotated each weekday, the characters and
stories were drawn from the publications of the Marvel Comics
Group and its predecessor, Timely Comics.   Utilizing very limited
techniques, sometimes film of the original art panels, the programs
were manufactured cheaply and quickly, with thirteen devoted to each
of five comic book stars, who battled a parade of crackpots and
crazed hyperthyroid creatures in this world and others.   The flexible
format allowed different local station options and a weekly schedule
was used by KHJ, Los Angeles, where the series debuted September
2, 1966 before the first daily run began September 12 on WGN,
Chicago at 6:30-7:00 PM CST and September 19 on WOR, New
York at 7:00-7:30 PM, hosted by an actor costumed as Captain
Universe.   Successively seen Monday through Friday were the
classic super-patriot Captain America (Timely, Mar 1941), the
brilliant scientist turned muddled monster, The Incredible Hulk
(Marvel, May 1962), the steel-encased gladiator Iron Man, first
published in Tales of Suspense (Marvel, Mar 1962), the surgeon
turned Norse god Thor, who debuted in Journey Into Mystery (Marvel, Aug 1962) and Sub-Mariner, the underwater crusader created
for Marvel Comics (Timely, Nov 1939).
Outfitted in a flag-inspired red, white and blue costume, with
a star on his chest and round shield, "Captain America" was the
alter ego of Steve Rogers.   The powerfully built all-American was
the result of a secret adrenalin serum, imbibed in an experiment
which turned him from a scrawny Army enlistee into a muscled
superman of extraordinary strength.   The character, the brainchild of Jack Kirby and Joe Simon, was assisted in the cartoons
by The Falcon, a black ghetto-dweller, and was pitted against such
bizarre antagonists as The Red Skull, his arch enemy.   In a prior

fifteen-chapter movie serial, Captain America (REP, 1944), starring
Dick Purcell, the actor had a different alter-identity as District
Attorney Grant Gardner.    And in a CBS pilot and TV movie, Captain
America (Nov 23 & 24, 1979), Reb Brown portrayed a blond-headed
drifter and neurotic introvert, a Vietnam veteran who considered
himself something of an anachronism, battling agents who sought
the secret of his serum powers.

    Not unlike the dual personality in Robert Louis Stevenson's
The Strange Case of Dr. Jekyll and Mr. Hyde (1886), Dr. Bruce
Banner was changed into a raging, green-skinned colossus through
accidental exposure to his own gamma-ray bomb developed for the
U. S. government.    Created by writer-editor Stan Lee and artist
Kirby, "The Incredible Hulk" was never understood by those he
encountered; he was feared as a hideous monstrosity and was usually mistaken for evil, even when he was simply frightened.
Given a certain tragic appeal, the super powerful Hulk's first foe
was General Thunderbolt Ross, the father of his girlfriend, Betty.
Later he tangled with the Gargoyle, a crazed foreign despot.   In
the CBS TV movie (Nov 4, 1977) and series, The Incredible Hulk
(CBS, 1978-  ), starring Bill Bixby as Banner and Lou Ferrigno
as the chisel-muscled, snarling titan, the transformation took place
when a lightning bolt struck him, and a more compassionate Hulk
could be triggered by similar bursts of electrical energy, and later
by his own tremendous rage.

    After stumbling upon a land mine in Vietnam, the injured
Tony Stark fell into the hands of Red Terrorists.    Working with a
captive physicist, elderly Professor Yinsen, together they built an
iron suit to keep his damaged heart beating.    Clad in a helmet and
his suit of invincible armor, "Iron Man" was another creation of
Lee's, written by his brother Larry Lieber and illustrated by Don
Heck.    As with Johnston McCulley's Zorro* (q. v. ), no one suspected
that the foppish playboy Stark, a wealthy industrialist and munitions
expert, was the super-steelman who contended with Communist villains and a Fu Manchu style criminal called The Mandarin, his arch
foe.    Stark was partnered with Happy Hogan, his young sidekick,
and sometimes Pepper Potts, his secretary.

    Frail Dr. Donald Blake became the legendary Norse god of
thunder when he pounded a magical walking stick on the ground.
Instantly, the cane converted into an "uru" hammer and Blake became the super-muscled, blond "Mighty Thor. "   Written by Lee
and his brother and drawn by Kirby, the adventure fantasy was
freely adapted from Norse mythology and also featured the stunning
Lady Sif, the omnipotent Odin, Heimdall and Balder the Brave.
Speaking in Shakespearean phraseology with "thou shalts" and "so
be its, " Thor was involved in epic struggles with the Asgards, who
would occasionally invade Earth, and a super-race called The In-
humans.

    The son of American Navy Commander McKenzie and Prin-
cess Fen of Atlantis, "Sub-Mariner" was the nom de guerre of a
super-amphibian also known as Prince Namor.   Created by Bill
Everett and somewhat resembling Mercury, the wing-footed hybrid
had Dr. Spock's ears and slanty eyebrows.    Equally effective on
land or sea, among his extraordinary powers were the ability to

fly and consult with sea creatures. Taken to fighting crooks and
criminals in the TV cartoons, Sub-Mariner was sometimes partnered
with another underwater inhabitant, Namora, a distaff crusader.


MATTY'S FUNDAY FUNNIES

Component Series
    CASPER, THE FRIENDLY GHOST and other HARVEYTOONS,
    BEANY AND CECIL

Network History
    Premiere:  October 11, 1959
    ABC/Oct 1959-Sep 1960/Sunday 5:00-5:30 PM
    ABC/Sep 1960-Sep 1961/Friday 7:30-8:00 PM
    ABC/Oct 1961-Dec 1962/Saturday 7:00-7:30 PM
    Last Program:  December 29, 1962
Sponsor:  Mattel Toys

Syndicated History

HARVEY CARTOONS

Distributor:  ABC Films/1963-1972; Worldvision Enterprises/1972-
Company:  Harvey Films/244 films, 6-8 minutes (1959-1961); Bob
    Clampett Productions/78 films (1962)

Cartoon Hosts
    Matty
    Sisterbelle

Principal Characters and Voices

HARVEYTOONS (1959-1961)  See  CASPER, THE FRIENDLY GHOST

BEANY AND CECIL (1962)  See  BEANY AND CECIL SHOW, THE

    Matty's Funday Funnies, a packaged program from Mattel,
initially presented cartoons produced by Famous Studios, retitled
Harveytoons after they were sold to the Harvey Publishing Company.  Produced for Paramount Pictures release between 1942 and
1958, the films were introduced by a set of cartoon hosts, a young
boy Matty, and his Sisterbelle.  Making their first TV appearance
were some of the best known Famous/Harvey characters, her friend
Melvin and the sweet tyke Little Audrey, introduced in Butterscotch
and Soda (Jun 4, 1948), Baby Huey, a naive husky duckling usually
prey for a hungry fox, that debuted in One Quack Mind (Jan 12,
1951), and Herman and Katnip, a slick mouse and oafish cat, first
seen in Mice Meeting You (Nov 10, 1950).  Later starred in his
own TV series was the meek four-fingered apparition, Casper, The
Friendly Ghost (q.v.).  Also presented were former "Noveltoons"
with the cartoonery's minor animal stars, Buzzy the Crow, Hector
Dog, Owly the Owl, Danny Dinosaur, Finny the Goldfish, Inchy the

Worm, Tommy Tortoise and Moe Hare, and Waxey the Weasel and Wishbone the Little Chicken.   On September 30, 1960, the program moved to prime time, an hour before The Flintstones (q. v. ).

The Harveytoons were replaced in January 1962 by Bob Clampett's animated gang from his syndicated puppet show, Time for Beany* (q. v. ).   Simply placed in the existing format, the series was retitled Matty's Funnies with Beany and Cecil to accommodate the new stars.   In April 1962, the Mattel cartoon hosts were dropped and the program renamed Beany and Cecil.   After the show ended, Clampett's series returned on January 5, 1963 as the long-running ABC weekend morning program, The Beany and Cecil Show (q. v. ).   One of the foremost toy companies, Mattel revolutionized its industry in the fifties, inaugurating year-around instead of sea-sonal TV advertising with such network programs as Matty's Fun-day Funnies and syndicated shows like The Funny Company (q. v. ).


MAX, THE 2000 YEAR OLD MOUSE

Syndicated History
     Premiere:   1969
Distributor:   Quality Entertainment/1969-1979; ARP Films/1979-
Executive Producer:   Steve Krantz
Company:   Krantz Animation/104 films, 5 minutes

Principal Character
     Max

     Max, the 2000 Year Old Mouse, appeared in scenes from famous moments in history.   Superimposed on live action educational films, Max joined Marco Polo, sailed with Farragut and Magellan, watched Michelangelo paint the Sistine Chapel and rode with Paul Revere.


METRIC MARVELS

Network History
     Premiere:   September 2, 1978
     NBC/Sep 1978-Sep 1979/Saturday, Various AM
     Last Program:   September 15, 1979
Producers:   George Newhall, Tom Yohe
Company:   Newall-Yohe Productions/12 films, 2 minutes

Principal Characters

     Meter Man
     Wonder Gram
     Liter Leader
     Super Celsius

     Metric Marvels, whose purpose was to stamp out metric ignorance, appeared in brief animated public service films.   Each of the instructional superheroes, Meter Man, Wonder Gram, Liter

Leader and Super Celsius, explained in understandable fashion the equivalents of a meter, a gram, a liter, and the temperature readings in Celsius degrees. The educational spots were interwoven three times during the network's Saturday morning children's programs.

## MGM CARTOONS

Component Series
BARNEY BEAR, BOSKO, CAPTAIN AND THE KIDS, HAPPY
HARMONIES, others

Syndicated History
Premiere: September 12, 1960
WABC, New York/Monday-Friday 6:15-6:30 PM
Distributor: United Artists Television/1960-
Producers: Hugh Harman, Rudolf Ising, Fred Quimby
Company: Metro-Goldwyn-Mayer Pictures (UA-TV)/135 films, 120
color, 7-9 minutes (1934-1948)

Principal Characters and Voices

| | | |
|---|---|---|
| Barney Bear/Captain | (1939-1945) | Billy Bletcher |
| Bosko | (1934-1938) | Carmen Maxwell |
| Little Cheezer | (1936-1938) | Bernice Hansen |
| George | (1946-1948) | Frank Graham |
| Junior | (1946-1948) | Tex Avery |
| Screwy Squirrel | (1944-1946) | |

MGM Cartoons were the last of the major studios' pre-1948 animated films released to television, first syndicated in 1960. The shorts package was sold to United Artists Television but excluded the popular films of Tom and Jerry (q.v.) and later cartoons seen on CBS in 1965. Leased to local stations, the comedies were simply dropped into existing children's shows or programmed under their various titles, most frequently as Barney Bear (1939-1954), because the package contained the first fifteen color films in that series. In this manner, Barney Bear debuted on WABC, New York and was seen weekday evenings on Tommy 7, hosted by Ed Bakey who appeared as the program's namesake clown. A likeable droopy-eyed character with thick layers of fur, introduced in The Bear That Couldn't Sleep (Jun 10, 1939), the bruin typified the double-takes and slow-moving theatrics of movie actor Wallace Beery. The early series was noted for its realistic treatment of the animals, for instance in The Bear and the Beavers (Mar 28, 1942), and was pleasantly humorous but virtually gagless. Although he never became a major cartoon star, Barney was first voiced by Billy Bletcher and later by Paul Frees, when the character was modernized in the fifties.
Among the others were thirteen starring Bosko (1934-1938), redesigned as a caricatured black boy, created by Hugh Harman and Ising for the first "Looney Tunes," titled Sinkin' in the Bathtub

(WB 1930). Bosko moved with the producers from Warner Brothers to MGM. The Library contained their "Happy Harmonies" (1934-1938), a diverse musical series which also starred a pair of playful young canines, first seen in Two Little Pups (Apr 4, 1936), and separate shorts featuring Ising's cute mouse with a curious nature, brought to life in Little Cheezer (Nov 1, 1936). Included were director Tex Avery's five films starring the brash Screwy Squirrel (1944-1946) and the bears George and Junior (1946-1948), that appeared in four satires drawn from the characters George and Lenny in John Steinbeck's filmed novel, Of Mice and Men (UA, 1939).

The package also contained fifteen films based on Rudolph Dirks' comic strip characters, The Captain and The Kids, first published June 14, 1916 as Hans and Fritz in The New York World. The studio bought the rights from United Features Syndicate and Fred Quimby produced the dismal series in 1938-1939, premiering with Cleaning House (Feb 19, 1938), one of the new MGM cartoonery's biggest flops. The series was revived with similar results in the seventies for The Fabulous Funnies (q. v. ).


MIGHTY HERCULES, THE

Syndicated History
    Premiere: September 3, 1963
    WPIX, New York/Monday-Friday 4:30-5:30 PM
Theme: "The Mighty Hercules," sung by Johnny Nash
Distributor: Trans-Lux/1963-1973; Alan Enterprises/1973-
Producer: Joe Oriolo
Company: Adventure Cartoons with Trans-Lux Productions/130
    films, 5 1/2 minutes

Principal Characters and Voices

| | |
|---|---|
| Hercules | Jerry Bascome |
| Newton/Tewt/Daedalius | Jimmy Tapp |
| Helena | Helene Nickerson |

The Mighty Hercules gained his superhuman powers through exposure of a magic ring to lightning in these films based loosely on Greek mythology. Probably the most popular of the Greek heroes and famed for great physical strength, Hercules was the bastard son of Zeus, the king of gods, and Alceme, his mortal mother. In the stories he resided on Mount Olympus, the traditional home of the Greek gods, and was summoned frequently to aid the mortals in the Learien Valley, in particular the most beautiful woman in Calydon, Helena, and young King Dorian at Calydon Castle. Sometimes the messenger was Tewt, a young Centaur who communicated by playing on his Syrinx, but more often it was Newton, also half-boy and half-horse. The brawny strongman's friend Newton's favorite expression was "Suffering Psyche!," which signaled imminent danger, and he was a passive companion relying on his powerful protector, who on occasion was armed with a common bow and arrow. When not involved in defending Dorian's kingdom or rescuing Helena and Newton, Hercules was pitted against such beastly adversaries as the Many-Headed Hydra, Neamean Lion, Miros Monster, Charon Beast and the Minotaur, and human foes like Omar, the Sultan's champion and the Evil Magician. But his arch enemies were an even more wicked threesome, the Defiant Mask of Vulcan, Wilamene, a sea witch, her vulturous flunkie Elvira, who once turned Helena into an ugly hag, and the clever wizard Daedalius, who kept Hercules busy with his Rod of Belarathon, which could make any object light as a feather, including the muscled superhero. The episodes were capped by a rousing song finale,

> Join us at his side,
> standing there with pride.
> Victory is here!
> Raise a mighty cheer,
> Hercules is here!

Although the series gave cursory treatment to some of the twelve tasks of Hercules, it ignored his other wondrous legendary exploits in favor of a science fiction approach which had little redeeming educational or entertainment value. The short episodic cartoons were programmed differently on local stations. WPIX, New York used them as a weekday strip-show hosted by John Zacherley.

## MIGHTY HEROES

Network History
    Premiere: October 29, 1966
    CBS/Oct 1966-Sep 1967/Saturday 9:00-9:30 AM
    Last Program: September 2, 1967

Syndicated History

THE MIGHTY MOUSE SHOW

Distributor: CBS Films/1967-1971; Viacom International/1971-
Executive Producer: Bill Weiss
Director: Ralph Bakshi
Company: CBS Terrytoons/26 films

Principal Characters
    Diaper Man
    Cuckoo Man
    Rope Man
    Strong Man
    Tornado Man

Voices
    Herschel Bernardi
    Lionel Wilson

    Mighty Heroes presented an astonishing quintet of strange

crime-fighters led by Diaper Man, a bottle-wielding, swaddling-clothed infant. An adaptation of the superhuman transformation theme, the tiny crusader worked out of a crib, packed a powerful right-hand punch and had a startling deep bass voice supplied by Herschel Bernardi. The stories depicted the talents of the superbabe and his caped companions, Cuckoo Man, Rope Man, Strong Man and Tornado Man, who all had a large "H" emblazoned on their costumes. Together they used their extraordinary skills against such self-descriptive arch criminals as The Ghost Monster, Enlarger, Frog, Toy Man, Shocker, Shrinker and Scarecrow. An original example of the combined superhero formula, interpreted and created by Ralph Bakshi, Mighty Heroes was a satire on a comic book approach whose origins lay in the "Justice Society of America," which appeared in All-Star Comics (Winter 1940) and later transferred to television as the Superfriends (q.v.).

With component cartoons from the CBS Terrytoons library, the show premiered immediately after the cancellation of the long-running Mighty Mouse Playhouse (q.v.), which it replaced for one season. The repackaged concept was instigated by Fred Silverman, CBS daytime programming chief, who recognized in Bakshi a potential for creative ideas and engineered his appointment in 1966 as the supervising director for CBS Terrytoons. Including Mighty Heroes, Silverman block-programmed six super-champion fantasies in 1966-1967 to replace vintage reruns and launched the Saturday morning superhero proliferation. After completing the cartoons, Bakshi became director for a brief period of the Paramount Cartoon Studio in New York and later achieved notoriety with the theatrical animated films Fritz the Cat (Cinemation, 1972), the screen's first X-rated cartoon, and The Lord of the Rings (UA, 1978).


MIGHTY MOUSE

Network History

MIGHTY MOUSE PLAYHOUSE
    Premiere: December 10, 1955
    CBS/Dec 1955-Mar 1956/Saturday 11:00-11:30 AM
    CBS/Mar 1956-Sep 1960/Saturday 10:30-11:00 AM
    CBS/Sep 1960-Sep 1961/Saturday 11:30-12:00 AM
    CBS/Sep 1961-Sep 1965/Saturday 10:30-11:00 AM
    CBS/Sep 1965-Sep 1966/Saturday 10:00-10:30 AM
    CBS/Sep 1966-Oct 1966/Saturday 9:00-9:30 AM
    Last Program: October 22, 1966

THE NEW ADVENTURES OF MIGHTY MOUSE AND
    HECKLE AND JECKLE
    Premiere: September 8, 1979
    CBS/Sep 1979-Sep 1980/Saturday 8:00-9:00 AM
    CBS/Sep 1980-Mar 1981/Saturday 8:00-8:30 AM
    CBS/Mar 1981-   /Sunday 8:00-8:30 AM

Syndicated History

THE MIGHTY MOUSE SHOW

Distributor: CBS Films/1966-1971; Viacom International/1971-
Executive Producers: Bill Weiss (1955-1966), Louis Scheimer,
    Norman Prescott (1979- )
Producer: Don Christensen (1979- )
Directors: Art Bartsch, Bob Kuwahara, Connie Rasinski, Dave
    Tendlar (1955-1966)
Company: CBS Terrytoons/150 films (1955-1966); Filmation Pro-
    ductions/16 films, 60 minutes (1979-1980) 30 minutes (1980-1981)

Principal Characters and Voices

| Mighty Mouse | (1955-1966) Tom Morrison |
| | (1979- ) Alan Oppenheimer |
| Pearl Pureheart | (1979- ) Diane Pershing |
| Oil Can Harry | (1979- ) Dom DeLuise |

HECKLE AND JECKLE (1979- ) See HECKLE AND JECKLE

QUACULA (1979-1980)

    Mighty Mouse, the savior of rodent brethren and mice
maidens in distress, innocently generated what has been described
as the Saturday morning cartoon ghetto.  For $3.5 million in 1955,
CBS purchased Paul Terry's studio and assets and starred its new
hero on Mighty Mouse Playhouse.  It was the pioneer all-cartoon
show seen regularly on Saturday and the genesis of network morning animated programming for children.  One of the longest tenured graphic series in TV annals, it was seen for over ten years
between 1955 and 1966.  The phenomenal popularity of the super-
mouse went unchallenged until 1958, when NBC countered with Ruff
and Reddy (q.v.), and unsurpassed until 1962, when ABC introduced
Bugs Bunny (q.v.).  Fostering the concept and vogue, CBS led the
way in animation programming between 1962 and 1965, a period
when more than half the network Saturday morning programs were
cartoons.
    Mighty Mouse was a propitious and astutely concocted attempt
to combine the wide appeal of two famed progenitors, Mickey Mouse
and Superman.  Artist Isidore Klein ignited the character's creation
with an idea for an anthropomorphic parody on Superman (q.v.),
introduced in theatrical animated films in 1941.  His concept involved a super fly, as he had read that the insect, for its size,
possessed super strength.  Instead, producer Terry decided to
make him a mouse; he had been partial to mice since his silent
"Farmer Al Falfa" series, and was undoubtedly influenced by the
success of Mickey, to whom the character bore more than a passing resemblance at first.  Premiering in The Mouse of Tomorrow
(Oct 16, 1942), the diminutive hero escaped from a brutal battle
between cats and mice, fled to a supermarket where he bathed in

Super Soap, dined on Super Soup, dove into an enormous hunk of
Super Cheese and emerged as the red-caped Super Mouse. He had
bulging biceps, a powerful chest that could repel bullets, and could
fly like Superman. The all-powerful mite walked upright as a humanized rodent, rescued his friends and Terry's studio as well.
The renewal of Terrytoons' releasing contract with Twentieth
Century-Fox Films looked bleak until the release of this cartoon,
which rekindled their interest and led to a new pact.

After seven films, Super Mouse became Mighty Mouse, debuting in an adaptation of Longfellow's poem, The Wreck of the
Hesperus (Feb 11, 1944). According to Bill Weiss, then Terrytoons' business manager, an employee left the studio and created
his version of Super Mouse for Nedor Publishing; it appeared in
Coo Coo Comics (Oct 1942), copyrighted the same month as the
first cartoon was released to theaters. After a year, instead of
continuing to promote the same character, Terry made the name
change. Subsequently, Mighty Mouse had several different origins,
gaining his super powers through vitamins in Pandora's Box (Jun
11, 1943) and a drink from a jug labeled "atomic energy" in The
Johnstown Flood (Jul 26, 1947). He adopted a disguise as "The
Mysterious Stranger," wearing a porkpie hat and trenchcoat, in
Mighty Mouse Meets Deadeye Dick (May 30, 1947), and was headquartered any place from the moon "to right here in this very
room!"

The plots were based on the mouse's amazing powers to effect dramatic rescues and engage a host of ingenious enemies, mainly cats and wolves, particularly Powerful Puss and, later, Oil Can
Harry, who became his arch foe. A blackguard of the old school
with a handle-bar mustache, the rotter was resurrected from Silk
Hat Harry, seen in eight "mellerdrammer" spoofs made between
1933 and 1937, with heroine Fanny Zilch and a hero named Strong-
heart. Harry appeared in an ongoing series with a new heroine,
Pearl Pureheart, beginning in A Fight to the Finish (Nov 14, 1947).
They were action-packed melodramas and near cliff-hangers in the
tradition of The Perils of Pauline (Pathé, 1914), and became the
most popular films of the series. Apart from routine stories about
nasty cats and endangered mice, the films included parodies on
folklore and fairy tales such as Aladdin's Lamp (Mar 28, 1947) and
Hansel and Gretel (June 1952), on classics like The Trojan Horse
(Jul 26, 1946), natural disasters, and a new operetta breed with
original scores, for example Gypsy Life (Aug 3, 1945). Between
1959 and 1961, several new cartoons were produced under Weiss,
with three released to theaters.

Four cartoons aired during the half-hour show; at first one
or two Mighty Mouse films and other "Terry Toons," and lastly all
starring the supermite. Seen in the premiere were Gandy Goose,
inspired by comedian Ed Wynn (1886-1966) and first starred in the
Goose Flies High (Sep 9, 1938); Dinky Duck, who debuted in The
Orphan Duck (Oct 6, 1939), and the mischievous magpies Heckle
and Jeckle (q. v.), soon lifted for their own series. New wraparound animation was produced for the show, featuring the tenor
voice of Roy Halee as Mighty Mouse singing the theme:

Mr. Trouble never hangs around
When he hears this mighty sound
Here I come to save the day!
Which means that Mighty Mouse is on the way.
Yes sir, when there is a wrong to right
Mighty Mouse will lead the fight
On the sea or on the land,
He gets the situation well in hand.

    Revived by CBS in 1979-1980 in The New Adventures of Mighty Mouse and Heckle and Jeckle, the cape-clad rodent again defended mice minions everywhere, and in particular extricated the beautiful Pearl Pureheart from the evil clutches of the conniving Oil Can Harry and Swifty, his new bumbling henchman. The supermouse appeared in two episodic adventures in the hour-long format, and a sixteen-chapter serial, "The Great Space Race," featuring his arch foe and the southern-accented heroine. Presented in a forties' deco-art style and drenched in campy dialogue, the films occasionally had the hero speak in heroic couplets, as in Underdog (q. v. ): "Pearl Pureheart is in distress, this is no time to digress." Between segments the cartoon star, in "Mighty Mouse Environmental Bulletins," provided cautions on wasting resources and littering. Heckle and Jeckle (q. v. ) continued their magpie madness in a pair of supporting comedies, and a vampire mallard, "Quacula," made his debut in another. A cross between Daffy and Donald with fangs, the bloodthirsty duck slept in an egg-shaped coffin in the basement of a castle owned by a bear, and terrorized his landlord and others. The show was reduced to half an hour in 1980-1981.

    The original Playhouse cartoons were syndicated as 150 half-hours starting in 1966. With the dissolution of CBS Films in 1971, Viacom International inherited the property, which was repackaged as 75 half-hours of The Mighty Mouse Show, 49 starring the little rodent and 26 with The Mighty Heroes (q. v. ). The later CBS Terrytoons theatrical cartoons were added as components, including Gene Deitch's new characters, Clint Clobber, the bombastic superintendent of the Flamboyant Arms apartments, who debuted in Clint Clobber's Cat (Jul 1957); the French artist, Gaston Le Crayon, who first made objects come to life in Gaston Is Here (May 1957); and the frustrated suburbanite, John Doormat, who bowed in Topsy TV (Jan 1957).

MIGHTY THOR   See   MARVEL SUPERHEROES


MILTON THE MONSTER

Component Series
    FEARLESS FLY, FLUKEY LUKE, MUGGY DOO, PENNY PENGUIN, STUFFY DURMA

Network History
    Premiere:   October 9, 1965

ABC/Oct 1965-Sep 1967/Saturday 12:30-1:00 PM
ABC/Sep 1967-Sep 1968/Sunday 9:30-10:00 AM
Last Program: September 8, 1968

## Syndicated History

Distributor: ABC Films/1968-1972; Worldvision Enterprises/1972-
Executive Producer: Hal Seeger
Director: Shamus Culhane
Company: Hal Seeger Productions/26 films

## Principal Characters and Voices

| | |
|---|---|
| Milton the Monster | Bob McFadden |
| Professor Weirdo/Fearless Fly/ | |
| Flukey Luke/Stuffy Derma | Dayton Allen |
| Count Kook/Muggy Doo/Two | |
| Feathers | Larry Best |
| Penny Penguin | Beverly Arnold |

Milton the Monster was an amiable oaf who befriended everyone he met, to the displeasure of his unhappy creators, Professor
Weirdo and his confederate, Count Kook. The most lovable fright
on Transylvania's Horror Hill, the eerie home of the demented pair,
Milton was a concoction of three drops of essence of terror, five
drops of sinister sauce and a tincture too much of tenderness. Although he could puff an occasional smoke plume from his flat head,
more to the freak-makers liking were Milton's scary brothers, a
white-faced ghoul named Heebie and a green one-eyed blob named
Jeebie, who could frighten the socks off any citizen in town. The
gentle Milton was such a disgrace to his kin that they barred him
from membership in The Secret Brotherhood of Monsters. Of little help to his surrogate fathers, Milton did not have the heart for
fierce battle with the Professor's arch enemies, Fangenstein or
Professor Fruitcake and his crazy creations, Abercrombie and
Zelda, a pair of Zombies. Embarrassed by Milton's disgusting
goodness, the Professor raffled him off at a Magic Show, sold him
to Hector the Protector as a collection agent, enlisted him in the
army and attempted to marry him to Miss Peaches, a hideous
spinster. But like a lovesick puppy, Milton kept returning to the
cob-webbed castle where he was not welcome, except once when
his pet crocodile discovered a sunken treasure in the moat.

In the principal supporting series, Fearless Fly's unending
war against injustice put him in some pretty sticky situations. A
meek and mild little insect known as Hyram, he retired to a match
box to don his crusader's costume and a pair of glasses which generated millions of megatons of energy through sensitive muscles in
his head. At first, Fearless tangled with the spider monsters of
Professor Weirdo, and sundry wild beasts created by his Atom Enlarger Ray Machine. But thereafter the superfly became enmeshed
in the schemes of a sinister Tibetan, the arch fiend Dr. Goo Fee
and his henchman Gung Ho, and frequently had to rescue his girlfriend, Florrie, and Horsie, a pal.

A cowpoke turned semi-private eye, "Flukey Luke," and his faithful Irish-Indian companion, Two Feathers, on his trusty horse Pronto, foiled the crafty Spider Webb, the daring robber of the Hopeless Diamond and museum treasures. A sly-as-a-fox fox, "Muggy Doo" was a wise-cracking hustler who managed to fast-talk his way out of predicaments involving a bakery shop, the Paranoid Pictures publicity department, and a money-making Chimpanzee artist. With a polka-dot hair ribbon, "Penny Penguin" was a precocious child whose hapless good deeds tried the patience of her indulgent parents. And "Stuffy Durma" was a hobo who inherited a fortune but reverted to his habitual pleasures with Stu Mulligan and Ashcan Annie, despite the efforts of Mr. Brinkly, the frustrated business manager of Durma, Inc. One of these four comedies was rotated in each program.

Written by Kin Platt and Jack Mercer, the voice of Popeye the Sailor (q. v.), the New York production, despite all its absurdities, was the pioneer "lovable monster" cartoon series, a network formula later used for both live-action and animated situation comedies.


MISSION: MAGIC!

Network History
    Premiere: September 8, 1973
    ABC/Sep 1973-Aug 1974/Saturday 11:30-12:00 AM
    Last Program: August 31, 1974
Executive Producers: Louis Scheimer, Norman Prescott
Director: Don Christensen
Company: Filmation Productions/13 films

Principal Characters and Voices

Rick Springfield     Rick Springfield
Miss Tickle       Erica Scheimer
Vinnie/Franklin     Lane Scheimer
Carol/Kim       Lola Fisher
Socks/Harvey/Mr. Samuels Howard Morris
Tolamy (Rick's owl)
Tut Tut (Tickle's Egyptian cat)


Mission: Magic! took a look at historic fact and fiction through the mysticism of a schoolmarm who transported her six teenage students to a different time continuum each week, using a premise borrowed from H. G. Wells' first book, The Time Machine (1895). Probably no other novel has been used more to establish the basic plot structure for science fiction animated cartoons. The theme has been used for such series as Hector Heathcote (q. v.), Peter Potamus and His Magic Flying Balloon (q. v.), The Brady Kids (q. v.), Fonz and the Happy Days Gang (q. v.) and dozens of other episodes with both human caricatures and anthropomorphic adaptations of every conceivable kind.

Called The Adventurers Club, Vinnie, Carol, Kim, Socks, Harvey and Franklin moved back and forth to exciting events with the help of singer Rick Springfield, one of whose songs was featured in each program. With his pet owl Tolamy, Rick was sort of an advance man who contacted Miss Tickle through a magic gramophone, advising her on skullduggery in ancient Rome or the twenty-first-century. Forewarned, Miss Tickle then approached a statue of her Egyptian cat, repeated the incantation "Tut, Tut, a cat of ancient lore, it's time to draw the magic door," and the feline would spring to life. As the enchantress drew a "Magic Chalk Circle" on the blackboard, the portal widened to engulf the teacher and her pupils in a new adventure. Joining Rick, the time-travelers jumped right in to make sure that the incident ended as chronicled, with the aid of course of Miss Tickle's unflagging magical powers. In the first show, the club visited a convoluted fantasyland, somewhat like Alice's trip through the mirror, where everything was backwards.

## MOBY DICK AND THE MIGHTY MIGHTOR

Network History
    Premiere: September 9, 1967
    CBS/Sep 1967-Sep 1968/Saturday 11:00-11:30 AM
    CBS/Sep 1968-Sep 1969/Saturday 1:00-1:30 PM
    Last Program: September 6, 1969

Syndicated History

CAPTAIN INVENTORY

Distributor: Taft H-B Program Sales/1973-1979; Worldvision Enterprises/1979-
Executive Producers: William Hanna, Joseph Barbera
Company: Hanna-Barbera Productions/18 films

Principal Characters and Voices

| | |
|---|---|
| Tom | Bobby Resnick |
| Tub | Barry Balkin |
| Scooby | Don Messick |
| Mightor | Paul Stewart |
| Tor | Bobby Diamond |
| Sheera | Patsy Garrett |
| Pondo/Ork/Tog/Rollo | John Stephenson |
| Li'l Rok | Norma McMillan |

Moby Dick and the Mighty Mightor, a pair of superheroes, a whale and a caveman, alternated in three eight-minute episodes. In his finny role, the namesake of Herman Melville's cunning and ferocious Moby Dick (1851) was recast as a substitute fatherly guardian. Swept into uncharted waters by a sudden typhoon, miles away from their uncle's ship, "The Sea Explorer," a pair of youngsters in aquasuits, menaced by man-eating sharks, were saved by the white whale. Together with Moby Dick and their pet seal Scooby, black-haired Tom and blond Tub faced the perils of an underwater world. Reaching new highs in menacing science fiction, in the premiere the coolheaded lads were trapped by an underwater earthquake, threatened by a giant Sea Spider, caught in a Giant Clam, enmeshed in cannibal seaweed and surrounded by giant electric eels. But when they were really frightened by the Crab Creatures, Shark Men, Aqua-Bats and Iceberg Monster in subsequent episodes, they sought safety by hiding in Moby's mouth. Always in on the rescue, the friendly mammal used his formidable hulk and aquatic skills to save the pair from a succession of bizarre watery terrors.

Also created by comic book artist Alexander Toth and Joe Barbera, Mighty Mightor was set in a Stone Age world. Pondo was the leader of a clan of cave-dwellers, the eldest a daughter Sheera, a teenage boy Tor, who had a pet winged-dinosaur named Tog, and Li'l Rok, a small lad who had a parrot-like pet bird called Ork. A small woolly mammoth named Rollo also trotted in and out as a clan pet. The adventures began during a hunting trip, when Tor and Tog rescued an ancient hermit and the grateful old man gave Tor a club which possessed great powers. Raising the club to the heavens, Tor was transformed into Mightor, a super-strong, loin-clothed, masked titan with steer horns protruding from the sides of his cowl, and his pet Tog became a fire-breathing dragon. As champions of good and the nemesis of evil they battled "The Scorpion Men," "The Sea Slavers," "The Plant People" and "The Serpent Queen." The pair constantly plucked Sheera from some horrible fate, with complications supplied by the over-enthusiastic actions of an imitative Li'l Rok, dressed as a midget facsimile of his brother and flying about on Ork. Overcoming his troublesome interventions, Mightor saved his sister from a fiery sacrifice to the lava pit demon by Toga, chief of the Bird People, from imprisonment by Kragor and the Cavern Creatures as a tasty meal for their Century Lizards, and from a hungry, hyperthyroid dinosaur named Tyrannor, commanded by Grok. Two episodes of Mighty Mightor served as the program's wraparound cartoons.


MOST IMPORTANT PERSON, THE

Network History

CAPTAIN KANGAROO
    Premiere: April 3, 1972
    CBS/Apr 1972-May 1973/Monday-Friday 8:00-9:00 AM
    Last Program: May 18, 1973

Syndicated History

Distributor: Viacom International/1973-
Producer: John Sutherland
Company: Sutherland Learning Associates/66 films, 5 & 3 1/2
    minutes

Principal Characters
  Mike
  Nicola
  Fumble
  Hairy
  Bird

   The Most Important Person was a bright little educational
series with topics important to a child growing up, built around a
general theme of physical and mental health.   Funded by a grant
of half a million dollars by the Office of Child Development, Department of Health, Education and Welfare, the films reached millions of preschool children with messages contributing to their
sound growth and well-being.   Among the subjects covered were
the need to eat breakfast, loneliness, playing with friends, check-
ups with a dentist, and understanding young bodies--for example,
how muscles work.   Leading authorities in psychology, education
and communication served as consultants for the films, which featured both cartooned and real children.   The main cartoon characters were Mike, a little baseball-capped boy, and Nicola, a young
black girl with pigtails.   They were augmented by Fumble, an
ostrich-like creature with a large nose, that served as an adult
image and philosopher with a wealth of knowledge.   A bell-ringing
mop-like character, Hairy was the comic relief, always popping
into a scene or climbing down a rope, tacitly representing something strange or new.   And Bird was a flustery fowl that overre-
acted to various situations and got upset a lot.   The films incorporated simple song-and-dance instruction with music and lyrics
by Elaine Simone.
   Before entering syndication, the series was seen daily for
one year on Captain Kangaroo* (q. v. ).


MOTORMOUSE AND AUTOCAT

Component Series
  IT'S THE WOLF

Network History

THE CATTANOOGA CATS/AUTOCAT AND MOTORMOUSE
  Premiere:   September 6, 1969
  ABC/Sep 1969-Sep 1970/Saturday 9:00-10:00 AM
  Last Program:   September 5, 1970

MOTORMOUSE AND AUTOCAT
  Return:   September 12, 1970
  ABC/Sep 1970-Dec 1970/Saturday 8:30-9:00 AM
  ABC/Jan 1971-Sep 1971/Saturday 12:00-12:30 PM
  Last Program:   September 4, 1971
Executive Producers/Directors:   William Hanna, Joseph Barbera
Company:   Hanna-Barbera Productions/17 films

Principal Characters and Voices

| | |
|---|---|
| Motormouse | Dick Curtis |
| Autocat | Marty Ingels |
| Mildew Wolf | Paul Lynde |
| Lambsy | Daws Butler |
| Bristol Hound | Allan Melvin |

Motormouse and Autocat were competitors in a speedy cat-and-mouse game on wheels. Determined to beat the little rodent that operated the Spin Your Wheels Garage, the feline sportscar maniac repeatedly goaded Motormouse into madcap contests in episodes with such titles as "Catch as Cat Can," "Crash Course," "Wild Wheelin' Wheels," "Match Making Mouse" and "Fueling Around." Sort of a freewheeling Tom and Jerry (q. v.), the series debuted in 1969 as "Autocat and Motormouse," one of three comedies in an hour-long show with cartoon hosts, entitled The Cattanooga Cats (q. v.). Retitled in 1970-1971, the cartoons were given their own half-hour timeslot supported by "It's the Wolf," which was reminiscent of the Warner Brothers films that included a lamb and a predator introduced in Friz Freleng's The Sheepish Wolf (Oct 17, 1942). Resolved to filch a decent meal, Mildew the Wolf preyed upon the defenseless, beguiling Lambsy, only to be foiled in his every attempt by a shaggy English sheepdog that reminded everyone, "Bristol Hound's my name, and saving sheep's my game!" The voice of Mildew was supplied by the prissy funny-man and star of The Paul Lynde Show (ABC, 1972-1973), in such episodes as "Super Sheep Sitting Service," "Pow-Wow-Wolf," "I Never Met a Lamb I Didn't Like" and "When My Sheep Comes In." The forerunners of the characters were Sam, a sheepdog, and Ralph, a wolf, introduced in Chuck Jones' "Looney Tunes" film, Don't Give Up the Sheep (Jan 3, 1953).


MR. MAGOO

Syndicated History
    Premiere: November 7, 1960
    KTTV, Los Angeles/Monday-Friday 6:30-7:00 PM PST
Distributor: UPA Productions of America/1960-

Network History

THE FAMOUS ADVENTURES OF MR. MAGOO

    Premiere: September 19, 1964
    NBC/Sep 1964-Dec 1964/Saturday 8:00-9:00 PM
    NBC/Jan 1965-Aug 1965/Saturday 8:30-9:30 PM
    Last Program: August 21, 1965

WHAT'S NEW, MISTER MAGOO?
    Premiere: September 10, 1977
    CBS/Sep 1977-Oct 1977/Saturday 9:00-9:30 AM

CBS/Oct 1977-Nov 1977/Saturday 8:00-8:30 AM
CBS/Nov 1977-Sep 1978/Saturday 1:00-1:30 PM
CBS/Sep 1978-Sep 1979/Sunday 9:00-9:30 AM
Last Program: September 9, 1979
Executive Producers: Henry G. Saperstein (1960 & 1964), David
DePatie, Friz Freleng (1977-1979)
Directors: Abe Levitow (1960 & 1964), Sid Marcus, Robert McKim-
son, Spencer Peel (1977-1979)
Company: UPA Pictures/155 films, 5 minutes (1960-1962), 13
films, 60 minutes (1964-1965); DePatie-Freleng Enterprises with
UPA Pictures/13 films (1977-1979)

Principal Characters and Voices

| | |
|---|---|
| Quincy Magoo | Jim Backus |
| Waldo | (1960-1962) Jerry Hausner/Daws Butler |
| | (1977-1979) Frank Welker |
| Millie | (1960-1962) Julie Bennett |
| Prezley/Uncle Waldo | (1960-1962) Daws Butler |
| Mother Magoo/ | (1960-1962/ |
| McBaker | 1977-1979) Jim Backus |

Mr. Magoo, virtually blind yet always involved in some
dynamic adventure, doggedly maintained his unshakeable aplomb
through three television series. The catastrophically near-sighted
oldster mistook animals, humans and innate objects for something
else, often to a point just short of self-destruction. Querulous
and sometimes irritable, he began his TV career in a syndicated
series produced between 1960 and 1962 after UPA Studios and its
assets were sold to Henry G. Saperstein by producer Steve Bosustow. The five-minute cartoons utilized the earlier theatrical format, faulty-sighted gags plotted on mistaken identities in improbable situations, in such stories as "Go West Magoo," "Lion Hearted
Magoo," "Magoo Meets Frankenstein" and "Magoo Meets McBoing-
Boing." Along with his oafish nephew Waldo, who starred in seventeen episodes, frequently with his girlfriend Millie, Quincy Magoo
was supported by several other relatives--an English nephew Prez-
ley, Uncle Waldo and Mother Magoo. Cheaply made for the juvenile
market, in Fall 1960 Mr. Magoo was stripped weekdays on KTTV,
Los Angeles and seen weekly on WNEW, New York at 6:30-7:00 PM,
Thursday, debuting February 16, 1961. The voice of the squinty-
eyed character was Jim Backus, who moved from New York radio
to Hollywood television as Hubert Updyke, the richest man in the
world, on The Alan Young Show (CBS, 1950-1953). The crinkle-
voiced characterization was based on his earlier radio creation,
"The Man in the Club Car," a misinformed, loudmouthed business-
man on a commuter train. Backus's throaty chuckle became identified with Magoo and his favorite exclamation, "By George!," the
catch-words of the films.
     The brainchild of animator-director John Hubley, the life-
like character's avowed purpose was to counter the cute animal
anthropomorphism dominating the animated screen in such series
as Tom and Jerry (q. v.). Allegedly patterned after Harry

Woodruff, Hubley's uncle, Magoo, right down to his bulbous red nose, had a lot in common with W. C. Fields. Indomitable, he first stumbled through Ragtime Bear (Sep 29, 1949), unable to distinguish a goofy grizzly from his fur-coated nephew. Leading an amazing, charmed life in Trouble Indemnity (Sep 14, 1950), the crotchety survivor starred in the first of fifty-two cartoons between 1950 and 1959 in the Mr. Magoo series, the UPA theatrical films released by Columbia Pictures. As the character metamorphosed under Bobe Cannon and particularly Pete Burness, director of the Oscar-winning When Magoo Flew (Jan 5, 1955) and Mister Magoo's Puddle Jumper (Jul 26, 1956), the cranky oldtimer loved people, was kindly and even Victorian courtly. As Fields hated children Magoo disliked dogs; in a running gag he would lash out with his cane at a fireplug or something else, shouting "Down, down!" His myopic affliction was the core of the comedy, abetted by his stubborn rigidity; nothing could convince him he was wrong. Several stories circulated regarding the origins of the name, but it seems more than a passing coincidence that Fields often used a similar pseudonym, Primrose Magoo, when registering incognito at prominent hotels like the New York Waldorf-Astoria.

Commissioned and sponsored by Timex, Magoo's network debut was an hour-long NBC musical special of Charles Dickens' perennial holiday classic, retitled Mr. Magoo's Christmas Carol (Dec 18, 1962), and with a score by Jule Styne and Bob Merrill. Backus was heard in the double role of Magoo and Scrooge, with Jack Cassidy as Bob Cratchit, Joan Gardner as Tiny Tim and Christmas Past, Jane Kean as Belle Fezzlwig, Royal Dano as Marley's Ghost and Les Tremayne as Christmas Present. Buoyed by the favorable reception and ratings, the dim-sighted old fogy was brought back to the network in 1964-1965 on a prime time show, The Famous Adventures of Mr. Magoo. Each week portraying a different literary or historical character, sometimes in two half-hour stories in the hour program, the myopic star played the trusty Swiss archer, William Tell, Friar Tuck in a four-part serialization of Robin Hood, Long John Silver in two episodes, Cyrano, Rip Van Winkle, Don Quixote, Puck in Shakespeare's Midsummer Night's Dream, the faithful Dr. Watson to Sherlock Holmes, and others. The cartoons were syndicated later as animated specials under such titles as Mr. Magoo's Storybook. Also, the feature-length cartoon 1001 Arabian Nights (UPA, 1959), starring Magoo, and a historic look at the United States, Uncle Sam Magoo (UPA, 1969) were televised as specials.

The personification of yesterday's self-made man, Magoo was resurrected in 1977-1978 on CBS in What's New, Mister Magoo? In a return to the initial format, the cane-carrying old geezer again drove his ancient flivver like a demon-possessed blind man. While looking for a new car, Magoo nearly destroyed a bulldozer and steamroller, test-driving the rigs at an old mine in the belief that the place was a used car lot. Each half-hour combined two episodic stories such as "Motorcycle Magoo" and "Magoo's Yacht Party." The premiere depicted Magoo's attendance at his 1928 Rutgers' class reunion, actually the "Roger's Animal Preserve and Zoo," and followed his frustrated attempt to find a suitable birthday present for his Great Aunt Priscilla at the local museum. Living with Magoo were Waldo and a nearsighted, white talking-dog, McBaker, a pairing the inimitable W. C. Fields probably would have abhorred.


MUMBLY  See  TOM AND JERRY/GRAPE APE/MUMBLY


MY FAVORITE MARTIANS

Network History
    Premiere:  September 8, 1973
    CBS/Sep 1973-Sep 1974/Saturday 10:00-10:30 AM
    CBS/Sep 1974-Jan 1975/Sunday 7:00-7:30 AM
    CBS/Jan 1975-Aug 1975/Saturday 8:00-8:30 AM
    Last Program:  August 30, 1975

Syndicated History

THE GROOVIE GOOLIES AND FRIENDS

Distributor:  Metromedia Producers Corporation/1978-
Executive Producers:  Louis Scheimer, Norman Prescott
Producer:  Hal Sutherland
Directors:  Don Towsley, Rudy Larriva, Bill Reed, Lou Zukor, Ed
    Solomon
Company:  Filmation Productions with Jack Chertog Television/16
    films

Principal Characters and Voices

Uncle Martin                          Jonathan Harris
Tim O'Hara/Andromeda ("Andy")         Howard Morris
Katy                                  Jane Webb
Brad Brennan                          Lane Scheimer
Chump (Brad's pet chimpanzee)
Okie ("Andy's" Martian dog)


    My Favorite Martians, a pair of aliens befriended by magazine
writer Tim O'Hara and his niece Katy, were the passengers aboard a
Mars spaceship which had to crash-land on Earth.  Convincing
O'Hara that revealing their true identity would cause worldwide
panic, they assumed the identities of his Uncle Martin and Andromeda as his nephew "Andy."  They concealed their damaged
spacecraft in Tim's garage.  Also from the red planet was Andy's
dog Okie, a white shaggy creature with antennae whose bark defied
description.  Passing them off as "normal," Tim's problems began
when the Martians displayed their extra-terrestrial powers.  Andy
was enrolled in Katy's high school, where his superior intellect
made him suspect.  One day while playing tennis the little retract-
able antennae in his skull were noticed by Brad, a neighbor's boy

who had a pet chimp named Chump.  Brad knew something was amiss, but no one would believe him, except his father Brennan, a security officer who had noticed the strange goings-on at O'Hara's house and garage.  In the "Check Up," the plot was thickened when Andy lost his strength due to a new alignment of Mars and Earth. Since he had a heartbeat of three, green blood, and no blood pressure, complications arose when he had to undergo a medical checkup.  In a similar vein, other episodes derived comedy from Andy's experiences at school and Uncle Martin's wacky inventions, among them a time machine, which he used to visit Cleopatra, a robot, and a personality-reverser ray.

The series lacked the original cast voices and added some new characters, but was a rather faithful adaptation of My Favorite Martian (NBC, 1963-1966), a prime time situation comedy starring Ray Walston and Bill Bixby.  A landmark show, the live-action program was the progenitor of the science fiction TV comedies, featuring other-worldly humans endowed with special powers, created and produced by Jack Chertog, who also participated in the animated concept.

NBC COMICS  See  TELECOMICS


NEW ADVENTURES OF BATMAN, THE  See  BATMAN AND
    ROBIN; TARZAN, LORD OF THE JUNGLE


NEW ADVENTURES OF CASPER, THE  See  CASPER, THE
    FRIENDLY GHOST


NEW ADVENTURES OF FLASH GORDON, THE

Network History
    Premiere:  September 8, 1979
    NBC/Sep 1979-Nov 1979/Saturday 11:00-11:30 AM
    NBC/Nov 1979-Dec 1979/Saturday 11:30-12:00 AM
    NBC/Apr 1980-Sep 1980/Saturday 12:30-1:00 PM
    Last Program:  September 20, 1980
Executive Producers:  Louis Scheimer, Norman Prescott
Producer:  Don Christensen
Directors:  Hal Sutherland, Don Towsley, Lou Zukor
Company:  Filmation Productions/16 films

Principal Characters and Voices

Flash Gordon/Prince Barin        Bob Ridgely
Dale Arden                       Diane Pershing
Dr. Hans Zarkov/Ming the
    Merciless                    Alan Oppenheimer
Princess Aura/Queen Fria         Melendy Britt
Thun/Vultan                      Allan Melvin

The New Adventures of Flash Gordon were animated with
large doses of the romanticism and imagery of the original newspaper comics saga.  A hero of towering strength and virtue, the
twentieth-century spaceman was created January 7, 1934 as a Sunday comic for King Features Syndicate by Raymond Chandler (1909-
1956), inspired in part by the Philip Wylie and Edwin Balmer novel,
When Worlds Collide (Stokes, 1932).  The continued serial, which
was surprisingly faithful to Chandler's premise, began with "A
Planet in Peril" and found three Earthlings marooned when their
spaceship crashed on a mission to the planet Mongo, which threatened to destroy Earth.  Aboard were the golden-haired Flash, initially described by Chandler as the son of a famous scientist, renowned polo player and Yale graduate; his peril-prone companion,
Dale Arden, a beautiful heroine; and Dr. Hans Zarkov, a scientific
genius who invented the Earth spaceship.  In the alien land of fore-
saken regions and futuristic cities they befriended the headstrong,
arrogant Prince Barin from the planet Aboria, and Thun, leader of
the Lion People, but found themselves locked in a deadly struggle
with the dreaded Emperor, Ming the Merciless.  With courage and
resourcefulness, Flash and his friends overcame the forces of evil
incarnate in such chapters as "The Monster of Mongo," "Tournament of Death" and "The Beast Birds Prey."  Among their foes
were Vultan, the King of the Hawkmen, Princess Aura, the Emper-
or's daughter and the witch warrior, and Queen Fria of the Ice
World, Fridgia.

Produced as a full-length animated feature and originally
picked up by NBC on a two-year contract for a TV special, the
elements were chopped up and new scenes added to provide the
sixteen-chapter cliff-hanger.  Although released in theaters in
Europe the movie was barred domestically by part-owner Dino De
Laurentiis to protect his own live-action version released in 1980
by Universal Pictures.  Graphically, Flash Gordon appeared also
between 1930 and 1970 in comic books published by King, Harvey,
Charlton and others.  It was regarded as the supreme feature of
the science fiction genre.  Two volumes of the strips were published by Nostalgia Press: Flash Gordon in the Ice Kingdom of
Mongo (1967) and Flash Gordon--Into the Water World of Mongo
(1971).  Widely imitated, but never equalled, Chandler's comic
spawned a radio show, three Universal movie serials and a 1954
live-action TV series, Flash Gordon* (q. v. ).


NEW ADVENTURES OF GILLIGAN, THE

Network History
    Premiere:  September 7, 1974
    ABC/Sep 1974-Aug 1975/Saturday 9:30-10:00 AM
    ABC/Sep 1975-Feb 1976/Saturday 10:00-10:30 AM
    ABC/Feb 1976-Sep 1976/Saturday 9:30-10:00 AM
    ABC/Sep 1976-Jan 1977/Sunday 10:30-11:00 AM
    ABC/Jan 1977-Sep 1977/Sunday 11:00-11:30 AM
    Last Program:  September 4, 1977

Syndicated History

THE GROOVIE GOOLIES AND FRIENDS

Distributor: Metromedia Producers Corporation/1978-
Executive Producers: Louis Scheimer, Norman Prescott
Producer: Don Christensen
Directors: Don Towsley, Lou Zukor, Rudy Larriva, Bill Reed
Company: Filmation Productions/24 films

Principal Characters and Voices

| | |
|---|---|
| Gilligan | Bob Denver |
| Jonas Grumby (The Skipper) | Alan Hale |
| Thurston Howell III | Jim Backus |
| Mrs. Lovey Howell III | Natalie Schafer |
| Roy Hinkley (The Professor) | Russell Johnson |
| Ginger Grant | Jane Webb |
| Maryann Summers | Jane Edwards |
| Snubby (Gilligan's pet monkey) | |

The New Adventures of Gilligan told the story of the "Minnow," five passengers and crew, a shipwrecked clan lost on a South Pacific Isle. Adapted from the prime-time situation comedy Gilligan's Island (CBS, 1964-1967), with the exception of Tina Louise, who played the alluring Hollywood starlet Ginger Grant, the original cast voiced their own caricatures. Marooned on the uncharted palm-treed speck were the good-natured Jonas, the flustery Skipper, and his first mate Gilligan, a clumsy buffoon who adopted a pet monkey named Snubby. Members of the party included the pompous millionaire Thurston Howell III, his empty-headed and pretentious wife, Lovey, the sweet Kansas farm girl Maryann, and Ginger, the sexy movie actress. There was also a high school science teacher, Roy Hinkley, called the Professor, who used his knowledge of nature and ingenious inventions to aid the castaways.

Under the scrutiny of educational consultant Dr. Nathan Cohen of UCLA, the scenarios demonstrated the need for teamwork and the necessity for tolerance of others while under duress, in an effort to interject positive social values for young viewers. Seldom did these morsels intrude on the plots, which were built around wacky visitors and native creatures, and riddles and mysteries they encountered on Gilligan's Isle. One day Gilligan discovered an ancient outrigger while building a bowling alley in "Marooned Again!," but the island's heartbroken animals destroyed the canoe so he staged a tournament and bowled against a Gorilla. After being bussed on the cheek by a Kissing Flower, "Super Gilligan" was endowed temporarily with super power by this botanical wonder that bloomed only once in a thousand years. And when a pirate's etheric double invaded the island in "Looney Moon," Gilligan led the ghost on a madcap hunt for buried treasure. Throughout it all the main hazard was being conked on the head by a coconut.

The program lasted three years on ABC, since 1965 the

pioneer and foremost network in adapting personalities and prime-
time comedies for Saturday morning cartoons. Distributed to local
stations on The Groovie Goolies and Friends, its history as a children's entry was overshadowed greatly by the original live-action
films. Strongly appealing to youngsters for its broad comedy, Gilligan's Island sustained high ratings in daytime reruns for over ten
years after its syndication in 1967. Created and produced by Sherwood Schwartz for Gladasya Productions in association with United
Artists Television, the films have been listed by Neilsen as the top
off-web children's situation comedy, ranked among the ten top favorites for twelve years. In 1977, for example, Gilligan's Island
was programmed on ninety-two stations, over twice as many as
televised the syndicated Bugs Bunny (q. v. ).

Also without St. John, the original cast was reassembled for
a pair of NBC TV movies, Rescue from Gilligan's Island (Oct 14 &
21, 1978) and The Castaways on Gilligan's Island (May 3, 1979) that
fared well in the ratings. The initial series enchanced the career
of its co-star Bob Denver, who later appeared in the title role of
the abysmal comedy western, Dusty's Trail (SYN, 1973-  ) and as
Junior in the children's program Far Out Space Nuts* (q. v. ).


NEW ADVENTURES OF HUCKLEBERRY FINN, THE

Network History
    Premiere: September 15, 1968
    NBC/Sep 1968-Sep 1969/Sunday 7:00-7:30 PM
    Last Program: September 7, 1969

Syndicated History

THE BANANA SPLITS AND FRIENDS

Distributor: Taft H-B Program Sales/1976-1979; Worldvision Enter-
    prises/1979-
Executive Producers: William Hanna, Joseph Barbera
Animation Director: Charles A. Nichols
Company: Hanna-Barbera Productions/20 films

Cast

| | |
|---|---|
| Huckleberry Finn | Michael Shea |
| Tom Sawyer | Kevin Schultz |
| Becky Thatcher | Lu Ann Haslam |
| Injun Joe | Ted Cassidy |

The New Adventures of Huckleberry Finn rejected Mark
Twain's traditional Mississippi River setting for make-believe fan-
tasy worlds in which to showcase his timeless spirited juveniles.
Owing nothing at all to The Adventures of Huckleberry Finn (Chatto
& Windus, 1884), written under his famous pseudonym by Samuel
L. Clemens (1835-1910), the characters were borrowed from his
earlier book, The Adventures of Tom Sawyer (American, 1876).
The series superimposed young actors as Huckleberry Finn, Tom

Sawyer and Becky Thatcher against hand-drawn backgrounds and with cartoon characters, using a combination live-action and animated film technique. Pursued in the prologue by the vengeful Injun Joe, yelling "I'll find you no matter where you go!," the youngsters sought refuge in a convenient cave. As the surroundings changed from verisimilar to graphics form, they discovered an underground stream and boarded a raft, which was soon engulfed by a fierce turbulence that swept them through a time warp to their far-fetched adventures, adapted largely from classic literature.

The premiere found the youngsters in a Swiftian Lilliputian land, where they aided a bumbling leprechaun named Grogan, voiced by Irish singer-actor Dennis Day, who had lost "The Magic Shillelah." During their search, Huck and Tom were kidnapped by the evil gypsy Zarko, a dead-ringer for their old nemesis Injun Joe, who also coveted the talisman. In "Huck of La Mancha," the plucky adventurers rescued Don Quixote and Sancho Panza from the sinister Don Jose D'Indio. Another time they took on virtually the whole Arabian Nights, meeting Sinbad and Ali Baba and finally lifting from the Scheherazade the idea of having Becky tell a Khaleef stories to keep him from killing her. Of course the Khaleef was a masquerading incarnation of Injun Joe as were all the arch villains. As narrator Huck said in the prologue, "I had a funny feeling that we'd see him again."

Twain's celebrated children appeared in one later animated cartoon, Tom Sawyer, seen in 1973 on the Festival of Family Classics (q.v.) and Huckleberry Finn (1976) was also animated in Japan. In American films, Robert Gordon was the first to portray Twain's carefree, pipe-smoking rebel in the silent version of Tom Sawyer (Oliver Morosco Photoplay 1917) and Huck and Tom (1918) followed by Lewis Sargent (1920), and in sound movies, Junior Durkin (1930 & 1931) followed by Donald O'Connor (1938), Mickey Rooney (1939), Eddie Hodges (1960) and Jeff East in the musical adaptations Tom Sawyer (1973) and Huckleberry Finn (1974).

The shrewd Missouri lad also starred in three TV specials; on CBS in The Ballad of Huck Finn (1959); José Ferrer's adaptation for Westinghouse Broadcasting, The Adventures of Huckleberry Finn (1960); and ABC's Huckleberry Finn (Mar 25, 1975), with Ron Howard as the freckle-faced boy. The subject of a New York play, Huckleberry (1962), the enduring property has been reprinted in numerous editions and excerpts have been made for recordings.


NEW ADVENTURES OF MIGHTY MOUSE AND HECKLE AND JECKLE, THE  See  MIGHTY MOUSE; HECKLE AND JECKLE


NEW ADVENTURES OF SUPERMAN, THE  See  SUPERMAN


NEW ADVENTURES OF THE LONE RANGER, THE  See  LONE RANGER, THE; TARZEN, LORD OF THE JUNGLE

NEW ARCHIE/SABRINA HOUR, THE   See   ARCHIES, THE;
SABRINA, THE TEENAGE WITCH


NEW CASPER CARTOON SHOW, THE   See   CASPER, THE
FRIENDLY GHOST


NEW FRED AND BARNEY SHOW, THE   See   FLINTSTONES, THE


NEW PINK PANTHER SHOW, THE   See   PINK PANTHER


NEW SATURDAY SUPERSTAR MOVIE, THE   See   ABC SATURDAY
SUPERSTAR MOVIE, THE


NEW SCOOBY-DOO COMEDY MOVIES, THE   See   SCOOBY-DOO


NEW SHMOO, THE

Network History
    Premiere:  September 22, 1979
    NBC/Sep 1979-Dec 1979/Saturday 10:30-11:00 AM
    Last Program:  December 1, 1979

FRED AND BARNEY MEET THE SHMOO
    Return:  December 8, 1979
    NBC/Dec 1979-Nov 1980/Saturday 9:00-10:30 AM
    Last Program:  November 15, 1980
Executive Producers:  William Hanna, Joseph Barbera
Producer:  Art Scott
Directors:  Ray Patterson, George Gordon
Company:  Hanna-Barbera Productions/16 films

Principal Characters and Voices

Shmoo                          Frank Welker
Nita                           Dolores Cantu-Primo
Billy Joe                      Chuck McCann
Mickey                         Bill Edelson

    The New Shmoo was a benevolent pear-shaped creature,
resurrected from the newspaper comic page for a protean role.
Capable of assuming different shapes and forms, the Shmoo's
gimmickry was helpful particularly to his new friends, a trio of
investigative reporters who published Mighty Mystery Comics.
The aggressive, nominal leader was Nita, a black-haired girl
whose companions were a shaggy blond, Billy Joe, a sound-alike
of Goober Pyle as personified by George Lindsey, and bespectacled, brainy-looking, auburn-haired Mickey, whose voice was

reminiscent of comic Pat Buttram's. The stories involved the teenagers in puzzling mysteries, with the falsetto-voiced Shmoo frequently their savior or in at the crux of the denouement. The cute blob once aided his friends to escape from a hidden room, becoming a shute which allowed the youngsters to slide from the gabled window to safety. Driving a three-wheeled car marked by a large "M" on the door, the spunky journalists tracked down Big Momma Malonna, a jewel thief who masqueraded as Madam Natasha, a fortune-telling gypsy in "The Crystal Ball of Fear." In other episodes they exposed "The Terror of the Trolls," "The Beast of Black Lake" and a scheming lawyer who haunted a house inherited by Angus Dalton from his seafaring father, supposedly cursed by "The Wail of a Banshee."

The invention of cartoonist Al Capp (1907-1979), born Alfred Gerald Caplin, the Shmoo was introduced in August 1948 in the famed comic strip Li'l Abner (UFS, 1934-1977), and quickly achieved international popularity. In the unveiling, the Shmoos were shaped like bowling-pins and described as quick-breeding animals that yielded milk, eggs and cheese-cake, tasted like chicken or steak, depending on how they were cooked, and could be anything else Capp dreamed up. The funny critters created a brief national mania in the late forties and by January 1949 there were 173 Shmoo Clubs happily promoting the Shmoo Rumba or Polka, Shmoo cocktails and Shmooffle. A merchandising flurry included Shmoo greeting cards, dolls, fountain pens, soap and sundry clothing items.

The New Shmoo episodes were serialized in two parts in December 1979, sandwiching The New Fred and Barney with repeats of The Thing (q.v.) to round out the ninety-minute package, Fred and Barney Meet the Shmoo. In 1980-1981, the character was featured with Fred Flintstone and Barney Rubble in "The Bedrock Cops," a segment of The Flintstones Comedy Show, a continuation of The Flintstones (q.v.).


NEW THREE STOOGES, THE   See   THREE STOOGES, THE


NEW TOM AND JERRY/GRAPE APE SHOW, THE   See   TOM AND
   JERRY; GREAT GRAPE APE, THE


NTA CARTOON CARNIVAL LIBRARY

Component Series
   ANIMATED ANTICS, COLOR CLASSICS, GABBY, GEORGE PAL
   PUPPETOONS, NOVELTOONS, SCREEN SONGS, SPEAKING OF
   ANIMALS, STONE AGE, TALKATOONS, INKWELL IMPS (1927-1929)

Syndicated History
   Premiere:  1956
Distributor:  UM&M-TV/1956-c1966; National Telefilm Associates/
   c1966-
Producers:  Max Fleischer, Jerry Fairbanks, George Pal, Sam

Buchwald, Seymour Kneitel, Isadore Sparber
Company: Fleischer Studios, Famous Studios, Jerry Fairbanks
Productions, George Pal Productions for Paramount Pictures/
211 B&W & 154 color films, 6-12 minutes (1927-1955)

NTA Cartoon Carnival Library made available for local programs the Paramount Pictures animated films produced by Max
Fleischer and Famous Studios between 1927-1955.  With the exception of the films sold later to Harvey Publishing that included
Casper, The Friendly Ghost (q. v. ), and the popular series starring
Popeye The Sailor (q. v. ), the package was syndicated to television
in 1956 after it was sold to UM&M-TV, which was bought out in the
sixties by NTA.  The Fleischer cartoons were made between 1927-
1942 and included 38 silent "Inkwell Imps" (1927-1929), a continuation of his Koko the Clown series, Out of the Inkwell (q. v. ); 39
"Talkatoons" (1929-1932); 97 B&W and 128 color "Screen Songs"
(1929-1938), the bouncing-ball sing-a-long films; 36 "Color Classics" (1934-1940); 12 "Animated Antics" (1940-1941), which featured Twinkletoes the carrier pidgeon and the furtive spies, Sneak,
Snoop and Snitch; eight starring "Gabby" (1940-1941), the town
crier from Fleischer's feature Gulliver's Travels (Dec 22,  1939);
and 12 "Stone Age" (1940-1941) comedies, which utilized modern devices in prehistoric settings and were the precursors of The Flintstones (q. v. ).  Usually programmed separately were The Adventures
of Superman (q. v. ), Little Lulu (q. v. ), and the films starring Betty
Boop (q. v. ), that were later hand-colored in Korea and re-issued by
NTA in 1971 as The Betty Boop Show.
Labelled racist and banned by many stations were 18 of the
38 "Puppetoons" (1941-1947) featuring Jasper, a wide-eyed little
black boy.  Produced by George Pal, who considered Jasper "the
Huckleberry Finn of American folklore, " black critics thought he
perpetuated the myth of black childishness and laziness and especially objected to Professor Scarecrow and Blackbird and their
typical "Amos 'n' Andy" dialogue.  For Chuck Jones in 1971, Pal
produced a special Puppetoon, "Tool Box, " choreographing various
implements as a ballet, which appeared on the ABC Saturday morning series, Curiosity Shop* (q. v. ).
Also included were 39 of Jerry Fairbanks' Oscar-winning
comedies, "Speaking of Animals" (1941-1950), twelve-minute films
which combined live animals and their witty sayings that ballooned
from their animated mouths.  Widely programmed through the late
fifties, "Speaking of Animals" was seen at 7:15-7:30 PM weekdays
on WABD, New York, beginning September 10, 1956, hosted by
Herb Sheldon.  Also from Famous Studios, 26 "Noveltoons" (1944-1955).
One of the larger packages of theatrical cartoons, the time-
worn shorts were virtually retired by the seventies, replaced by
later color films.


ODDBALL COUPLE, THE

Network History
     Premiere:  September 6,  1975

ABC/Sep 1975-Sep 1976/Saturday 11:30-12:00 AM
ABC/Sep 1976-Jan 1977/Sunday 11:00-11:30 AM
ABC/Jan 1977-Sep 1977/Saturday 12:00-12:30 PM
Last Program: September 3, 1977
Executive Producers: David DePatie, Friz Freleng
Director: Lewis Marshall
Company: DePatie-Freleng Enterprises/16 films

Principal Characters and Voices

| | |
|---|---|
| Fleabag | Paul Winchell |
| Spiffy | Frank Nelson |
| Goldie | Joan Gerber |

The Oddball Couple partnered a fastidious cat and a slovenly
dog as contrasting free-lance magazine writers who were the best
of friends and shared the same office. The meticulous feline was
named Spiffy and the messy canine Fleabag; both were loaded with
a psychologist's case book of peculiar idiosyncrasies. They made
life miserable for their shared secretary, Goldie, in their humorous attempts to outwit each other. Constantly at odds, the pair's
conflicts and cunning competiveness surfaced in such episodes as
"Who's Afraid of Virginia Werewolf?," "A Royal Mixup," "Do or
Diet" and "To Heir Is Human." Originally intended by the network's programming strategists for the Saturday morning lead-off
spot, the situation comedy turned out to have more appeal to children aged ten and up, so consequently the cartoons were slotted
later. They were a bit too sophisticated, and much of the context
of the battling dog and cat was lost upon the younger child.
    The genesis was Neil Simon's hit broadway play, The Odd
Couple (1965), filmed by Paramount Pictures in 1968 and starring
Jack Lemmon and Walter Matthau as the ambivalent cohabitants of
a shared apartment. The animated adaptation was a spin-off of
the network's successful Paramount Television prime time series,
The Odd Couple (ABC, 1970-1975) with Tony Randall and Jack
Klugman.


OFFICIAL FILMS CARTOONS

Component Series
    BROWNIE BEAR, DICK AND LARRY, JUNGLE JINKS, THE
    LITTLE KING, MERRY TOONS, others

Syndicated History
    Premiere: c1950
Distributor/Owner: Official Films/c1950-
Producer: Amédée J. Van Beuren
Directors: James Tyer, Steve Muffati, George Stallings, Burt
    Gillett, Ted Eshbaugh, Tom Palmer
Company: Van Beuren Studios-RKO/44 B&W films, 5-6 minutes
    (1933-1936)

Official Films Cartoons became a staple of local hosted
children's shows in the early fifties and comprised films made by
Van Beuren Studios (1928-1936), released by RKO (Radio-Keith-
Orpheum).   A strange set of circumstances surrounded the syndication of the cartoons produced by Amédée J. Van Beuren (1879-
1937), all of which found their way to television with perhaps the
exception of two color revivals of Felix the Cat (q. v.).   In the
forties, RKO sold forty-four of the later black-and-white negatives
to Official Films, a distributor of home-movies and rentals, and
the earlier films to Unity Pictures.   The company also sold the
Technicolor negatives, a series called "Rainbow Parades" (1934-
1936), those in two-colors to Library Films and the fifteen three-
color to Commonwealth Films, which were distributed in the Commonwealth Cartoon Package (q. v.).   There were some duplications
and additionally Commonwealth and Official retitled some of the
series.   Seven starring Cubby Bear were renamed "Brownie Bear,"
six with Tom and Jerry as "Dick and Larry," out of deference to
MGM's "Gold-Dust Twins," and eight "Aesop's Fables" were distributed as "Jungle Jinks."   Most of the films in these series,
however, were syndicated under their original titles in the Unity
Pictures Theatrical Cartoon Package (q. v.).
     The Official package also included six with "The Little King"
(1933-1934), first seen in the Fatal Note (Sep 29, 1933), an adaptation from the New Yorker and subsequent King Features Sunday
comic which debuted September 9, 1934, drawn by Otto Soglow
(1900-1975).   Directed by Burt Gillett, who won his first Oscar
while with Walt Disney for the Three Little Pigs (May 27, 1933),
the ten black-and-white versions of the "Rainbow Parades" sold to
Library Films were retitled by Official as "Merry Toons."   A
jumble of thematic comedies and stories with standardized characters, the "Parades" contained several cartoons set in Parrotville,
the adventures of "Molly Moo-Cow" and the Toonerville Folks
(Wheeler 1915), created by Fontaine Fox (1884-1964), which were
first animated for the Toonerville Trolley (Jan 17, 1936).
     One of the earliest syndicated cartoon series, Official Films
Cartoons were seen beginning in 1950 on TV Tot's Time (q. v.), a
local and network show on ABC stations and televised at least into
1953 on Ray Forrest's Saturday morning local series, Children's
Theatre (WNBT/WRCA/WNBC 1949-1961).


OSMONDS, THE

Network History
     Premiere:   September 9, 1972
     ABC/Sep 1972-Sep 1973/Saturday 9:00-9:30 AM
     ABC/Sep 1973-Sep 1974/Sunday 10:30-11:00 AM
     Last Program:   September 1, 1974
Executive Producers:   Arthur Rankin, Jr., Jules Bass
Producers:   John Halas, Joy Batchelor
Company:   Halas and Batchelor, London for Rankin-Bass Produc-
     tions/17 films

Principal Characters and Voices

| | |
|---|---|
| Alan | Alan Ralph Osmond |
| Wayne | Melvin Wayne Osmond |
| Merrill | Merrill Davis Osmond |
| Donny | Donald Clark Osmond |
| Jay | Jay Wesley Osmond |
| Jimmy | James Arthur Osmond |
| Fugi | Paul Frees |

The Osmonds, the always smiling and zesty young singing brothers of the sixties, were caricatured for their own program. Spotlighting the performances of Alan, Melvin, Merrill, Donny, Jay, and Jimmy Osmond, while on a global concert tour for the United States Music Committee, the stories were set in such different locales as "Paris," "Australia," "Transylvania," "Yukon," "Black Forest," "London" and "Rio." On a mission to promote better worldwide relations between young people, off-stage the brothers stumbled into local intrigues, which they helped to resolve while demonstrating justice, compassion and understanding. Several of the episodes focused on the younger members, Jimmy and Jay, abetted by their comical canine, Fugi. Continuing the network's pioneering tradition of personality animation, which began with The Beatles (q. v. ), the Osmonds were one of five musical groups animated for the ABC Saturday line-up between 1965 and 1973, but the overexposed formula did not prove as propitious for them as it did for The Brady Kids (q. v. ).

Discovered by Andy Williams while performing at Disneyland, and billed as a "youthful barbershop quartet from Ogden, Utah," the Osmonds made their TV debut December 20, 1962 on ABC, singing "I'm a Ding Dong Daddy from Dumas" and "Side by Side." The cartoon series followed nine years of regular appearances on The Andy Williams Show (ABC/CBS/NBC, 1958-1971). The quartet was augmented during its run by their other brothers and a sister, with six-year-old Donny Osmond introduced on December 10, 1963 singing "You Are My Sunshine." When he was eighteen, he headlined a family variety hour with his sister, The Donny and Marie Show (ABC, 1976-1978), and starred in a number of specials with the Osmond family. Starting with their 1977 Christmas program, all the shows were taped at the new Osmond Studios, built at a cost of $2.5 million in Orem, Utah, as headquarters for their various TV, film, recording and related enterprises.


OSWALD THE RABBIT

Component Series
  MEANY, MINY AND MOE, POOCH THE PUP

Syndicated History
    Premiere: February 28, 1955

KNXT, Los Angeles/Monday-Friday 6:00-6:20 PM PST
Distributor: Revue Productions (MCA-TV)/1955-1965
Executive Producers: Walter Lantz, William C. Nolan (1929-1935)
Directors: Walter Lantz, William C. Nolan, Friz Freleng, Alex
    Lovy, Fred Kopietz, Lester Kline, Rudy Zamora, Elmer Perkins
Company: Universal Pictures-Walter Lantz Cartoons/c200 B&W
    films, 6-8 minutes (1929-1938)

Principal Characters and Voices

Oswald                    (1929-1938) Bernice Hansen/Mickey Rooney

        Oswald the Rabbit was the pioneer bunny in early silent and
sound theatrical series. Walt Disney created Oswald in 1927, his
first cartoon star of any significance, one year before the creation
of Mickey Mouse. A floppy-eared caricature, like Disney's enduring star Oswald wore only a pair of short pants but without the two
front buttons, and his name was literally picked out of a hat. Released through Universal Pictures, which controlled the character
rights, "Oswald the Lucky Rabbit" (1927-1928) debuted in Trolley
Troubles (Sep 5, 1927) and appeared in twenty-six silent films for
entrepreneur Charles Mintz. When Disney tried to get more money
for the cartoons, the middleman decided to hire someone else.
Mintz's brother-in-law, George Winkler, established a studio and
hired away some of Disney's staff. They had half-finished six
films when Carl Laemmle announced on April 9, 1929 the estab-
lishment of a Universal cartoon department under Walter Lantz
and William C. Nolan. Their first job was to add sound to the
unreleased Winkler films. Retitled Oswald the Rabbit (1929-1938),
their first production was Weary Willies (Jul 22, 1929) and over
one hundred fifty films were made at the rate of about eighteen
per year. Before the advent of storymen, they featured music,
comic situations and gags in hit-or-miss fashion. As Lantz once
said, "Our only object was to turn out five or six hundred feet of
film." Seen in thirteen films, the pair's second star was another
happy animal, "Pooch the Pup" (1932-1933), that first cavorted as
The Athlete (Aug 29, 1932).
        A year after Lantz and Nolan went their own ways, Walter
established his own studio at Universal in 1936 as an independent
producer and in the forties bought the former Hollywood building
that housed Columbia Pictures' cartoonery. At the same time, he
redesigned the Mickey Mouse-like hare into a cute, round-faced,
long-eared bunny and began developing new characters. The first
were a trio of monkeys, "Meany, Miny and Moe" (1936-1937), first
seen in The Turkey Dinner (Nov 23, 1936). A menagerie followed,
including Snuffy the Skunk and Baby Face Mouse (aka Willie Mouse),
that first filched a meal in Cheese Nappers (Jul 4, 1938), directed
by Alex Lovy. Like Oswald, most of the animals resembled other
early cartoon characters and failed to establish any lasting identity
before the arrival in the forties of Andy Pandy and the star of The
Woody Woodpecker Show (q.v.).
        In 1955, Revue (MCA-TV) syndicated the black-and-white
Universal-Walter Lantz cartoons, which were used largely on local
hosted children's shows.

OUT OF THE INKWELL

Syndicated History
    Premiere: c1952 and 1956

(NEW) OUT OF THE INKWELL
    Premiere: September 10, 1962
    WPIX, New York/Monday-Friday 4:25-4:30 PM
    Distributor: Filmvideo Releasing/c1952-1959; UM&M-TV, National
        Telefilm Associates/1956-  ; Warner Brothers Television (New)/
        1962-
    Producers: Max Fleischer (1915-1929), Hal Seeger (1961-1962)
    Company: Out of the Inkwell Films/78 B&W silent films, 6-7 1/2
        minutes (1920-1929); Video House Productions/100 films, 5 min-
        utes (1961-1962)

Principal Characters and Voices

Koko/Kokete/Mean Moe  (1961-1962)  Larry Storch
Kokonut (Koko's dog)

    Out of the Inkwell starred Koko the Clown, reviving the
character from silent cartoons made between 1915 and 1929, one
of the greatest technical achievements in graphic film annals.  A
former Fleischer Studios animator, Hal Seeger formed Video House
with his ex-boss, Max Fleischer (1883-1972), to produce the series
for television.  Although he had little to do with the actual production, the pilot film used the standard formula with Max on screen,
drawing at his desk, as the character came to life from his pen.
A conventional clown in a pointed hat, Koko was supported by his
feminine counterpart, Kokete, and his dog Kokonut, and was supplied with an antagonist, the long-haired Mean Moe.  Produced in
1961-1962, the subsequent films reverted to an ordinary format,
abandoning the classic opening.  Drawing on fictional and classical
literary stories, the characters were involved in such plots as
"Bluebeard's Treasure," "Koko Meets Barney Beatnik," "Mummy's
the Word," "Musketeer Moe," "Mean Moe's Fairy Tale" and "Koko
Meets Robin Hood," five-minute episodic films that were programmed separately or strung together for longer shows.  Venting
his disappointment with the series several times in the press,
Fleischer complained about the quality of the artwork.
    The creation of the Fleischer brothers, Max and Dave, and
originally photographed by Joe, the silent Inkwell films used the
rotoscope, invented by Max, which enabled an artist to trace live-
action film movement and create realistic animated motion.  Dave
posed for the first live-action film in a clown suit and was the
model for the character, first named Koko in 1923.  In 1915, Max
interested John R. Bray in their pilot film and after the First
World War his clown cartoons became a monthly feature of the
Bray Pictograph, a weekly screen magazine released by Paramount
Pictures and beginning in 1919 by Goldwyn.  The silent Inkwell
cartoons were unsurpassed for accuracy of action, surprises and
imaginative visual gags.
    After the Fleischers opened their own studio in 1921, the

films were distributed independently until 1927-1929 when 38 were again released by Paramount retitled Inkwell Imps. In 1955, Paramount sold the cartoons with others for television to UM&M-TV (NTA) and they were syndicated beginning in 1956 and later as part of the NTA Cartoon Carnival Library (q. v. ). Forty prior silent films from "Out of the Inkwell" (1920-1927) were among several vintage series acquired and syndicated by Filmvideo Releasing Corporation in the early fifties. The silent comedies soon became obsolete due to the demand for color and sound films.

PADDINGTON BEAR

Network History
  Premiere: April 13, 1981
  PBS/Apr 1981-May 1981/Monday 6:00-6:30 PM
  Last Program: May 18, 1981
  Executive Producer: Pepper Weiss (KERA)
  Producers: Graham Clutterbuck (Film Fair), Renate Cole (KERA)
  Director: Barry Leith
  Company: Film Fair, London/6 films

Host
  Joel Grey

Narrator/Voices
  Michael Hordern

Principal Characters
  Paddington Bear
  Mr. and Mrs. Brown
  Mr. Gruber
  Mr. Curry
  Aunt Lucy

     Paddington Bear was a child-like honey-bear from South America with a passion for marmalade sandwiches and could talk to humans. Written and created by Michael Bond, the animal personality was first brought to life in A Bear Called Paddington (1958) as a blend of three worlds. He represented a child trying to grow up in adult surroundings, a foreigner attempting to accustom himself to life in a new home, and an animal striving to be human. Animated in London and presented on PBS by KERA, Dallas/Fort Worth through a grant by the Corporation for Public Broadcasting, the narrated films featured an innovative combination of two- and three-dimensional cartoons. The programs were introduced by Oscar-winning entertainer Joel Grey, each containing five vignettes based on chapters from Bond's popular books.
     Adopted by Mr. and Mrs. Brown when they found him sitting on his suitcase at Paddington Station, the bear was animal in appearance but walked on two legs. His Aunt Lucy, before she entered a home for retired bears in Peru, had advised him to stow away on a boat bound for England. Rather like another child in

the Brown's household, all naiveté, well-meaning and yet woefully clumsy, Paddington was excused his mischievous peccadilloes because he was different. Apart from the Browns, the central characters were his best friend, Mr. Gruber, an antique dealer, the selfish and cross Mr. Curry, a next door neighbor, and Aunt Lucy, who arrived for a short visit. Incongruity was the moving force of the stories--bears seldom read or plant gardens--and the plots detailed his troubles adapting to life as an Englishman. Among his adventures, Paddington was involved in a rugby match, an archaeological dig, body-building, and phony shares in an oil company; he also volunteered as a sound-effects engineer in a theatrical production, visited a wax museum, the beach, a concert and a department store's bargain basement, and had dinner out at a fancy restaurant. Occasionally wearing a duffle coat or a yellow macintosh, Paddington's trademark was his disgraceful, shabby bush hat.

## PARTRIDGE FAMILY: 2200 A. D.

### Network History
Premiere: September 7, 1974
CBS/Sep 1974-Mar 1975/Saturday 9:30-10:00 AM
Last Program: March 8, 1975

### Syndicated History

FRED FLINTSTONE AND FRIENDS

Distributor: Claster TV Productions/1977-1979
Executive Producers: William Hanna, Joseph Barbera
Producer: Iwao Takamoto
Director: Charles A. Nichols
Company: Hanna-Barbera Productions/16 films

### Principal Characters and Voices

| | |
|---|---|
| Connie Partridge | Joan Gerber |
| Keith Partridge | Chuck McClendon |
| Laurie Partridge | Susan Dey |
| Danny Partridge | Danny Bonaduce |
| Christopher Partridge | Brian Forster |
| Tracy Partridge | Suzanne Crough |
| Reuben Kinkaid | David Madden |
| Marion | Julie McWhirter |
| Veenie | Frank Welker |
| Orbit (Danny's robot dog) | |

Partridge Family: 2200 A. D. placed the popular professional rock group in an ultra-futuristic world where they performed with some imaginative space-age instruments. Reprising one of their recordings in each episode, such as "I Think I Love You," which sold four million singles, the singing Partridges played Mars, Venus, and other far-out gigs. A spin-off from the prime time situation

comedy The Partridge Family (ABC, 1970-1974), the series retained the original characterizations of the widowed mother and her
talented offspring, who hit it big in show business.  Missing were
the voices of the two principal stars, Shirley Jones as Connie
Partridge, and her step-son David Cassidy as the eldest boy Keith.
But they were animated in near likeness, as were the other children, Susan Dey as Laurie, Danny Bonaduce as Danny, Brian
Forster as Christopher, and Suzanne Crough as Tracy.  Also,
Dave Madden voiced his role as their wheeler-dealer manager,
Reuben Kinkaid, who booked them on their interplanetary concert
tour.  Along the way the youngsters made friends with a pair of
teenage aliens, a pointy-eared lad named Veenie from Venus, and
Marion, a half-light and half-dark lass from Mars.  Off-stage,
the stories involved the Partridges in the schemes of comical evil-
doers and scoundrels, such as a pair of crooks who stole their
automated likenesses from "The Wax Museum," planning to promote
the mannequins as the real musicians on another planetoid.  Among
the other episodes were "Laurie's Computer Date," "Incredible
Shrinking Keith," "Orbit the Genius" and "Danny the Invisible Man."
The freckle-faced, red-headed young Danny and his all-purpose
robot dog, Orbit, often were at the hub of the plots and helped
resolve the mishaps which befell the group.
     The Partridge Family was inspired by the experiences of the
real-life musical clan, The Cowsills, and became a successful recording group in the early seventies, due to their television exposure.  Shirley and David did most of the vocals, with the instrumental back-up provided by professionals.  The show made David
Cassidy a teeny-bopper idol and launched his career as a film star.
After a stint as a singles act he returned in the TV series, David
Cassidy--Man Undercover (NBC, 1978-1979).  The four younger
children had been animated before, as recurring guests on Goober
and the Ghost Chasers (q. v. ).


PEANUTS

Network History
     Premiere:  December 9, 1965
     CBS/Dec 1965-  /Periodic/Various PM

Executive Producer:  Lee Mendelson
Producer:  Bill Melendez
Directors:  Bill Melendez, Phil Roman (1973-  )
Company:  Bill Melendez Productions/21 films

Principal Characters and Voices

Charlie Brown            (1965-1969) Peter Robbins
                         (1971) Chris Inglis
                         (1972-1973) Chad Webber
                         (1973-1974) Todd Barbee
                         (1975-1976) Duncan Watson
                         (1976) Dylan Beach

| | |
|---|---|
| | (1977-1980) Arrin Skelley |
| | (1978) Liam Sullivan |
| | (1980-1981) Michael Mandy |
| Snoopy | Bill Melendez |
| Lucy Van Pelt | (1965) Tracy Stratford |
| | (1966-1968) Sally Dryer |
| | (1969-1971) Pamelyn Ferdin |
| | (1972-1973) Robin Kohn |
| | (1974-1975) Melanie Kohn |
| | (1976) Lynn Mortensen |
| | (1976) Sarah Beach |
| | (1977-1979) Michelle Muller |
| | (1980) Kristen Fullerton |
| | (1981) Cindi Reilly |
| Linus | (1965-1968) Christopher Shea |
| | (1969) Glenn Lelger |
| | (1971-1975) Stephen Shea |
| | (1975-1976) Liam Martin |
| | (1977-1979) Daniel Anderson |
| | (1980-1981) Earl Reilly |
| Schroeder | (1965) Chris Doran |
| | (1966-1967) Glenn Mendelson |
| | (1971) Danny Hjeim |
| | (1972) Brian Kazanjian |
| | (1975-1976) Greg Felton |
| | (1977) Daniel Anderson |
| | (1980-1981) Christopher Donohue |
| Peppermint Patty | (1965) Sally Dryer |
| | (1966) Lisa DeFaria |
| | (1967-1968) Gail DeFaria |
| | (1971-1973) Christopher DeFaria |
| | (1974) Donna Forman |
| | (1974) Linda Ercoli |
| | (1975-1976) Stuart Brotman |
| | (1977) Laura Planting |
| | (1979-1980) Patricia Patts |
| | (1980-1981) Brent Hauer |
| Sally | (1965-1968) Kathy Steinberg |
| | (1969-1973) Hillary Momberger |
| | (1974-1975) Lynn Mortensen |
| | (1975-1976) Gail Davis |
| | (1981) Cindi Reilly |
| Freida | (1965-1967) Ann Altieri |
| | (1971) Linda Mendelson |
| | (1976-1977) Michelle Muller |
| Pig Pen | (1966) Chris Doran |
| | (1967) Jeff Ornstein |
| | (1977) Ronald Hendrix |
| Russell | (1972) Todd Barbee |
| Violet | (1972) Linda Ercoli |
| Franklin | (1973) Todd Barbee |
| | (1977) Ronald Hendrix |
| Marcie | (1973-1975) James Ahrens |

|                        |                            |
|------------------------|----------------------------|
|                        | (1979-1980) Casey Carlson  |
|                        | (1980-1981) Shannon Cohn   |
| Rerun                  | (1976) Vinnie Dow          |
| Freddie                | (1979) Tim Hall            |
| Woodstock (whistling)  | (1980) Jason Serinus       |
| Paula                  | (1980-1981) Casey Carlson  |

Peanuts, with the exception of Bob Hope, became the longest-running, highest-rated series of specials in television history.  Far more than just a collection of youngsters and animals dispensing simple wisdom, the characters reasoned and acted like adults while grappling with the changing complexities of daily life.  They arrived in gentle and sensitive stories from the sparkling faculties of Charles Monroe Schulz, a self-taught, correspondence course artist who went to work as an instructor for the school.  He was born November 22, 1922 in Minneapolis, Minnesota.  His characters have always been children and the genesis of his strip was "Li'l Folks," appearing in the late forties in the St. Paul Pioneer Press; it was rechristened Peanuts by the editors for its United Feature Syndicate debut, October 2, 1950.  The most successful comic strip of all times, the world-renowned feature built slowly from eight American newspapers to 1,800 worldwide, published in more than sixty foreign countries. In the sixties, its popularity became phenomenal.  In 1969, when NASA's "Apollo 10" mother ship was named Charlie Brown and its lunar module, Snoopy, the total income reached $50 million per year, with twenty-one licensed subsidiaries and Peanuts reprint books handled by no less than seven publishers.  After some highly regarded TV commercials for Ford, produced by Playhouse Pictures, Schulz formed an association with Burlingame producer Lee Mendelson and Hollywood animator-director Bill Melendez in 1964 and his characters were incorporated in a TV pilot.  But the biggest names in television and advertising wanted no part of it.

For more than a year, one of the hottest cartoon properties languished until John Allen of McCann-Erickson, looking for a holiday show for Coca-Cola, thought the Peanuts folks would do just fine.  Rushed to completion in three months, a preview of the Yuletide film pleased the sponsor but CBS executives predicted an inked disaster.  Like their colleagues, they underestimated the impact of the comic strip and its loyal following.  One of the highest rated prime time animated specials of all time, "A Charlie Brown Christmas" (Dec 9, 1965) captured nearly half of all the sets turned on. The show received excellent reviews, thousands of appreciative letters, a Peabody award for "Outstanding Children's and Youth Program" and an Emmy as the "Best Children's Program" for 1965. Schulz's little morality story about the commercialism of Christmas launched the periodic series by the three-way partnership, who picked up four additional Television Academy awards between 1965 and 1981.  In the next five years they produced "Charlie Brown's All-Stars" (Jun 8, 1966), "It's the Great Pumpkin, Charlie Brown" (Oct 27, 1966), "You're in Love, Charlie Brown" (Jun 12, 1967), "He's Your Dog, Charlie Brown" (Feb 14, 1968) and "It Was a Short Summer, Charlie Brown" (Sep 27, 1969).  Including repeats, the eighteen telecasts averaged a 47 per cent share, with an estimated 40 million viewers per program. While later programs would gradually dip to half that audience in the late seventies, comparatively the shows lost little of their drawing power, usually outrating their competition and ranked in the top ten.

At least part of the appeal was the wistful cast, whose fitting ability to capture human follies allowed viewers to laugh at themselves. Schulz's meek "Everyman" in knee-pants, moon-faced Charlie Brown was the eternal loser, finding triumph as elusive as catching snowflakes on the tongue. So far, he has proved himself unable to kick a football, fly a kite or win a baseball game, to name but a few of his more conspicuous failings. His chief tormentor was Lucy Van Pelt, a vulnerable, sarcastic playmate and a fuss-budget, dispensing five-cent doses of psychology. Linus was Lucy's well-informed brother, often bamboozled by his sister, a fragile intellectual who spouted theology and went to pieces without his security blanket. Forthright Peppermint Patty was a doggedly loyal Tomboy and Schroeder, disdainful of girls, had only a passion to play Beethoven on his toy piano. Snoopy, Charlie Brown's beagle, was the complete antithesis of the suffering hero, a great lover, great athlete, great writer and the most celebrated ace pilot in the First World War, if not all history, doing battle in a Sopwith Camel with the Red Baron. A fantasizing, bulb-nosed hound, the sophisticate replaced the Van Gogh in his palatial dog house with an Andrew Wyeth. Actually, twenty characters comprised the Peanuts clan; among the others were Charlie's younger sister, Sally, Russell, Violet, Marcie, baby Rerun, Pig Pen, Freida with the naturally curly hair, Franklin, the bespectacled black boy, and Woodstock the bird. Much of their attraction rested on a deeply sentimental attachment to the idyllic childhood of small town America and the values of a seemingly happier past.

Several of the cast were named for Schulz's artist friends in the fifties, the namesake characters for Charlie Francis Brown and Freida Rich, both of Minneapolis, and Linus Maurer, a cartoonist in California. Snoopy's balloon-likeness was first seen in Macy's 1968 Thanksgiving Day Parade.

Subsequent specials appeared yearly: "Play It Again, Charlie Brown" (Mar 28, 1971), "You're Elected, Charlie Brown" (Oct 29, 1972), "There's No Time for Love, Charlie Brown" (Mar 11, 1973), "A Charlie Brown Thanksgiving" (Nov 20, 1973), "It's a Mystery, Charlie Brown" (Feb 1, 1974), "It's the Easter Beagle, Charlie Brown" (Apr 9, 1974), "Be My Valentine, Charlie Brown" (Jan 28, 1975), "You're a Good Sport, Charlie Brown" (Oct 28, 1975), "It's Arbor Day, Charlie Brown" (Mar 16, 1976), "It's Your First Kiss, Charlie Brown" (Oct 24, 1977), "What a Nightmare, Charlie Brown" (Feb 23, 1978), "You're the Greatest, Charlie Brown" (Mar 19, 1979), "She's a Good Skate, Charlie Brown" (Feb 25, 1980), "Life Is a Circus, Charlie Brown" (Oct 24, 1980), and "It's Magic, Charlie Brown" (Apr 28, 1981). Two hour-long programs, "Happy Anniversary, Charlie Brown" (Jan 9, 1976), celebrating Peanuts' 25th anniversary, and "Happy Birthday, Charlie Brown" (Jan 5, 1979), saluting the beginning of the comic strip's 30th year, also were broadcast, with sixteen years of Peanuts specials thus far.

Between the new shows and four or five repeats each season,

there were documentaries like "The World of Charlie Brown and
Charles Schulz" (May 24, 1969) on CBS, a PBS discussion with
evangelist-author Robert L. Short of "The Gospel According to
Peanuts" (May 30, 1967), a number of ice specials featuring a
costumed Snoopy, and an NBC presentation of the off-Broadway
hit musical, "You're a Good Man, Charlie Brown" (Feb 9, 1973),
starring Wendell Burton in the title role. Made for National
General Pictures, three of four animated feature-length films have
been televised on CBS, "A Boy Named Charlie Brown" (Apr 16,
1969), "Snoopy, Come Home" (Nov 5, 1972) and "Run for Your
Life, Charlie Brown" (Apr 26, 1981). A fourth movie, Bon Voyage,
Charlie Brown, was released to theaters at Christmastime 1980.
Contributing to the enduring success were artists Bernie Gruver,
Frank Smith, Bill Littlejohn, and Al Pabian among others.


PEBBLES AND BAMM BAMM

Network History
   Premiere:  September 11, 1971
   CBS/Sep 1971-Sep 1972/Saturday 10:00-10:30 AM
   CBS/May 1973-Sep 1973/Sunday 7:30-8:00 AM
   CBS/Feb 1974-Sep 1974/Saturday 12:00-12:30 PM
   CBS/Mar 1975-Aug 1975/Saturday 9:30-10:00 AM
   CBS/Sep 1975-Sep 1976/Saturday 8:00-8:30 AM
   Last Program:  September 4, 1976

Syndicated History

FRED FLINTSTONE AND FRIENDS

Distributor:  Claster Television Productions/1977-1979
Executive Producers:  William Hanna, Joseph Barbera
Director:  Charles A. Nichols
Company:  Hanna-Barbera Productions/27 films (1971-1974)

Principal Characters and Voices

| | | |
|---|---|---|
| Pebbles Flintstone | (1971-1972) | Sally Struthers |
| | (1972-1974) | Mickey Stevens |
| Bamm Bamm Rubble | | Jay North |
| Moonrock | | Lennie Weinrib |
| Penny | | Mitzi McCall |
| Wiggy/Cindy | | Gay Hartwig |
| Fabian | | Carl Esser |

     Pebbles and Bamm Bamm, the progeny of Fred and Wilma
Flintstone and their friends, Barney and Betty Rubble, starred in
their own satiric comedies about middle-class youth in suburban
Bedrock, circa 10,000 B.C.  Born February 22, 1963 on The
Flintstones (q. v.), the prime time cartoon hit, Pebbles was conceived nine months earlier in an atmosphere as tension-filled as
a summit conference.  A top team of Screen Gems officials were

closeted with executive producers Bill Hanna and Joe Barbera for two days to ponder the momentous problem of the baby's sex. Riding on the decision was over $50 million in merchandising tie-ins including Ideal's new Pebbles doll and Post's Pebbles Cereals. In Fall 1963, Bamm Bamm became the adopted son of the Rubbles, providing a convenient boy-next-door, which in this case was a split-level cave on Stone Cave Road. Dramatic license accelerated their puberty and in 1971-1972 the teenagers were involved with their friends at Bedrock High School and such typical activities as fixing up Bamm Bamm's "Cave Buggy," finding jobs, earning money and dating, as well as coping with the ever-present parent problems. The bespectacled, young inventor Moonrock and muscular, towheaded Bamm Bamm were inseparable buddies, as were Pebbles and her girlfriends, the sensible brunette Penny and the blond, star-gazing, astrology buff, Wiggy, whose characterization otherwise was reminiscent of comedienne Jo Anne Worley. A snobbish pair of smart-aleck brats, Fabian and Cindy were their contrasting antagonists in such episodes as "Pebbles' Big Boast," "Beauty and the Best," "Unfunny Valentine," "Gridiron Girl Trouble" and "Daddy's Little Helper." The teenagers were provided singing voices for an occasional song with their rock group, The Bedrock Rollers. Sort of a paleolithic version of The Archies (q. v.), sixteen comedies were produced in 1971-1972.

The films were rerun on The Flintstones Comedy Hour (q.v.) with eleven new 1972-1973 episodes featuring The Bronto Bunch, a rock-cycle gang. The two series were repackaged and repeated on CBS between 1974 and 1976. And in 1980-1981, Pebbles and Bamm Bamm returned on NBC as teenagers in combined family and separate comedies on The Flintstones Comedy Show (q. v.).

The pair's baby-talk was recorded by Jean VanderPyl and Don Messick on The Flintstones (q. v.), but underwent an adolescent change. Remembered as Gloria Bunker on All in the Family (CBS, 1971-1975), Sally Struthers was the first voice of the teenage Pebbles, followed by Mickey Stevens and Russi Taylor (1980-1981). The former cherub-faced Dennis the Menace* (q. v.), Jay North, and then Michael Sheehan (1980-1981) voiced Bamm Bamm.


PERILS OF PENELOPE PITSTOP, THE

Network History
    Premiere: September 13, 1969
    CBS/Sep 1969-Feb 1970/Saturday 10:00-10:30 AM
    CBS/Feb 1970-Sep 1970/Saturday 12:30-1:00 PM
    CBS/Sep 1970-Sep 1971/Sunday 7:30-8:00 AM
    Last Program: September 5, 1971

Syndicated History

THE FUN WORLD OF HANNA-BARBERA

Distributor: Taft H-B Program Sales/1977-1979; DFS Program Exchange/1979-

Executive Producers: William Hanna, Joseph Barbera
Company: Hanna-Barbera Productions/17 films

Narrator
  Gary Owens

Principal Characters and Voices

| | |
|---|---|
| Penelope Pitstop | Janet Waldo |
| Sylvester Sneekly/The Hooded Claw | Paul Lynde |
| Bully Brothers/Yak Yak/ | |
|   "Chugaboom" | Mel Blanc |
| Clyde/Softly | Paul Winchell |
| Zippy/Pockets/Dum Dum/ | |
|   Snoozy | Don Messick |

The Perils of Penelope Pitstop were provided by her fortune-seeking guardian in this comedy adventure that might have been titled "Pearl White and the Seven Dwarfs." A spin-off from the 1968-1970 CBS series, The Wacky Races (q. v.), the idea to star the plucky, pulchritudinous heroine was encouraged by Fred Silverman, CBS daytime programming chief. Driving her racer "The Compact Pussycat" in international competition around the world, Penelope was the heiress to a vast fortune doggedly pursued by The Hooded Claw, the alias of Sylvester Sneekly, who planned to do her in. Aided by his henchmen, the bumbling Bully Brothers, the cloaked-and-masked fiend slipped Penelope bon-bon bombs and left her trussed to roller-coaster tracks in such stories as "The Terrible Trolley Trap," "North Pole Peril," "Arabian Desert Danger," "London Town Treachery" and "Hair Raising Harness Race." Foiling her covetous guardian's foul schemes were her ever-present godfathers, The Ant Hill Mob, sort of a combination of the Keystone Kops and the Seven Dwarfs, named Clyde, Softly, Zippy, Pockets, Dum Dum, Snoozy and Yak Yak. The rollicking rescuers always arrived in the nick-of-time to save the innocent, wide-eyed Penelope, usually in their courageous "Chugaboom," an all-purpose black limousine that numbered among its convertibilities, wings, boat propellers and wheels that could become buzz-saws. Doused with Paul Lynde's villainous dialogue, "I'll get you yet, Penelope Pitstop!," the episodes opened to the sinister laugh of Sneekly, whose favorite expletive was "Blast!" Gary Owens supplied the campy-toned narration.

With background chase music and sight gags lifted from the silent screen, the concept owed a large debt to the serial, The Perils of Pauline (Pathé, 1914), produced by E. A. McManus, and revived first in a 1947 Paramount movie starring Betty Hutton and then by United Artists in 1967 with Pamela Austin, Pat Boone and Terry-Thomas. The cartoons were scripted by veteran writer Mike Maltese and the new team of Joe Ruby and Ken Spears.

PETER POTAMUS AND HIS MAGIC FLYING BALLOON

Component Series
    BREEZLY AND SNEEZLY, YIPPEE, YAPPEE AND YAHOOEY

Syndicated History
    Premiere: September 16, 1964
    WABC, New York/Wednesday 7:30-8:00 PM
    Distributor: Screen Gems-Columbia Pictures Television/1964-

Network History

THE PETER POTAMUS SHOW
    Return: January 2, 1966
    ABC/Jan 1966-Dec 1967/Sunday 10:30-11:00 AM
    Last Program: December 24, 1967
    Executive Producers/Directors: William Hanna, Joseph Barbera
    Company: Hanna-Barbera Productions with Screen Gems (CPT)/24
    films

Principal Characters and Voices

| | |
|---|---|
| Peter Potamus/Yahooey | Daws Butler |
| So So | Don Messick |
| Breezly Bruin | Howard Morris |
| Sneezly Seal | Mel Blanc |
| Colonel Fusby | John Stephenson |
| Yappee/The King | Hal Smith |
| Yippee | Doug Young |

Peter Potamus and His Magic Flying Balloon made trips
back in time, in his episodic Wellsian adventures. Comprising
three eight-minute cartoons featuring comical animals, the series
took its title from the lead-off comedy starring a purple hippo-
potamus with a voice borrowed from comedian Joe E. Brown
(1892-1973). Paired with the clowning So So the monkey, Peter
helped make history happen everywhere. Time-warped in his
balloon-ship, it conveniently provided an escape from brushes
with bandits, cutthroats and rogues in such stories as "What a
Knight," "Monotony on the Bounty," "Pilgrim's Regress," "Big
Red Riding Hood" and "The Reform of Clankenstein."
    The components included "Breezly and Sneezly," that
debuted on The Magilla Gorilla Show (q.v.), an oafish polar bear
and a level-headed arctic seal that made life miserable for the
men at Camp Frostbite, an Alaskan Army outpost commanded by
Colonel Fusby. In a new comedy, "Yippee, Yappee and Yahooey"
were a canine trio of goofy palace guards serving his majesty,
The King, borrowed from Alexandre Dumas's The Three Musketeers (1844). They foiled usurpers and more often themselves
in such comic swashbucklers as "Throne for a Loss," "Double
Dragon," "Palace Pals Picnic" and "Royal Rhubarb."
    The sixth syndicated package produced by Hanna-Barbera
with Screen Gems (CPT) for the juvenile market, the program

was picked up by ABC in January 1966 for its weekend children's
schedule under the title The Peter Potamus Show. Returned to
syndication, the segments were packaged by Screen Gems as The
Magilla Gorilla/Peter Potamus Show, providing fifty half-hours
for local programming.


PINK PANTHER, THE

Component Series
THE INSPECTOR, THE ANT AND THE AARDVARK, THE TEXAS
TOADS, MISTERJAWS, CRAZYLEGS CRANE

Network History

THE PINK PANTHER SHOW
    Premiere: September 6, 1969
    NBC/Sep 1969-Sep 1970/Saturday 9:30-10:00 AM
    NBC/Sep 1970-Sep 1971/Saturday 10:30-11:00 AM
    Last Program: September 4, 1971

THE NEW PINK PANTHER SHOW
    Premiere: September 11, 1971
    NBC/Sep 1971-Sep 1972/Saturday 9:30-10:00 AM
    NBC/Sep 1972-Dec 1972/Saturday 9:00-9:30 AM
    NBC/Dec 1972-Sep 1973/Saturday 9:30-10:00 AM
    NBC/Sep 1973-Dec 1973/Saturday 11:30-12:00 AM
    NBC/Jan 1974-Aug 1974/Saturday 10:30-11:00 AM
    NBC/Sep 1974-Sep 1975/Saturday 11:00-11:30 AM
    NBC/Sep 1975-Sep 1976/Saturday 9:30-10:00 AM
    Last Program: September 4, 1976

THE PINK PANTHER LAUGH & 1/2 HOUR & 1/2 SHOW
    Premiere: September 11, 1976
    NBC/Sep 1976-Sep 1977/Saturday 8:30-10:00 AM
    Last Program: September 3, 1977

THINK PINK PANTHER!
    Return: February 4, 1978
    NBC/Feb 1978-Sep 1978/Saturday 10:30-11:00 AM
    Last Program: September 2, 1978

THE ALL-NEW PINK PANTHER SHOW
    Premiere: September 9, 1978
    ABC/Sep 1978-May 1979/Saturday 11:30-12:00 AM
    ABC/Jun 1979-Sep 1979/Saturday 12:00-12:30 PM
    Last Program: September 1, 1979
Theme: "The Pink Panther Theme" by Henry Mancini

Syndicated History

Distributor (52 films): United Artists Television/1980-
Executive Producers: David DePatie, Friz Freleng

Directors: Hawley Pratt, Gerry Chiniquy, Arthur Davis, Robert McKimson, Art Leonardi, Sid Marcus
Company: DePatie-Freleng Enterprises/24 films (1971-1976), 17 films, 90 minutes (1976-1977), 16 films (1978-1979)

Hosts
Lenny Schultz (1969-1971)
Paul and Mary Ritts (1969-1971)

Principal Characters and Voices

| | | |
|---|---|---|
| Pink Panther (non-speaking) | | |
| The Inspector | (1969-1978) | Pat Harrington, Jr. |
| Ant/Aardvark | (1971-1978) | John Byner |
| Fatso | (1976-1978) | Don Diamond |
| Banjo | (1976-1978) | Tom Holland |
| Misterjaws | (1976-1978) | Arte Johnson |
| Catfish | (1976-1978) | Arnold Stang |
| Crazylegs Crane | (1978-1979) | Larry Mann |
| Crane Jr./Dragonfly | (1978-1979) | Frank Welker |

The Pink Panther was a mindless but headstrong do-gooder, whose help usually spelled disaster to those in need and around him. Amusing Saturday morning viewers for ten consecutive years, nine seasons on NBC, the happy-go-lucky cat starred in the longest running cartoon series on the network. The show arrived in Fall 1969 with some other tamer programs, after the web junked its superhero-versus-supermonster cartoons except for Underdog (q.v.). Strictly mute, the unflappable feline that walked upright was a departure from his competitors, who were increasingly adventure-oriented, dialogue-bound and backed with raucous sound effects. Relying solely on a pantomime concept with visual gags, but incorporating a laugh track, the lanky Panther was cute and sometimes funny, appearing in harmless comedies made for theaters between 1964 and 1977. Released by United Artists, his debut was The Pink Phink (Dec 18, 1964), an Oscar-winning performance. Backed by Henry Mancini's popular "Pink Panther Theme," the character was created initially for the movie titles of The Pink Panther (UA, 1964), Blake Edwards' slapstick comedy hit starring Peter Sellers as the French police bumbler, Inspector Henri Clouseau. The film had nothing to do with big cats, but rather a priceless diamond, the "Pink Panther," owned by Princess Dala and sought by The Phantom, a jewel thief sought by the lawman. The film's success prompted five sequels featuring the pink title character and over ninety cartoons. They were produced by a new studio organized in 1963 by David H. DePatie and Friz Freleng, a former Warner Brothers executive and animator who directed many of the Bugs Bunny and Sylvester cartoons, disbanded in 1980 when Freleng returned to Warners.

Hosted between 1969 and 1971 by Lenny Schultz with the comical antics of the Paul and Mary Ritts puppets, The Pink Panther Show presented two adventures of the charming rascal drawn from such colorful titles as "Pink Pajamas," "Pink,

Plunk, Plink," "Super Pink," "Pink Paradise" and "Put-Put Pink."
The standard component was "The Inspector" (1965-1969) and his
Latino lackey, Judo, who appeared in thirty-three theatrical cartoons. The blunderheaded policeman tried his hand at solving such
pseudo-French-titled mysteries as "Tolouse La Trick," "Les
Miserbots," "Crow de Guerre" and his premiere case, The Great
de Gaulle Stone Operation (Dec 21, 1965), the theft of a family
jewel by the notorious crooks, Max O'Riley and Wong.

Beginning in Fall 1971, the program was entirely animated
as The New Pink Panther Show, adding another theatrical series,
"The Ant and the Aardvark" (1966-1971), which premiered with
Never Bug an Ant (Feb 2, 1966). In such stories as "Dune Bug"
and "Odd Ant Out," a hose-nosed, purple aardvark was constantly
hot on the scent of a tasty meal, a little red ant that outwitted
him and sounded like Joey Bishop. To promote the program, in
June 1972 General Foods bankrolled Pink Panther Cartoon Festivals throughout the country and a line of merchandising novelties
were licensed.

Network television's first animated ninety-minute series,
The Pink Panther Laugh & 1/2 Hour & 1/2 Show in 1976-1977
was NBC's second packaged program of repeated and new elements.
The Atom Ant/Secret Squirrel Show (q.v.) inaugurated the raw
concept in 1965 before it was refined in the mid-seventies. Introduced with a cornball western music track, Fatso and Banjo were
hillbilly-like dudes called "The Texas Toads." At their pond, the
lazy frogs protected themselves from predators, particularly a
goofy, long-legged crane that acted and sounded like Red Skelton's
Clem Kadiddlehopper. Redubbed and retitled, it was a former
theatrical series between 1969 and 1972 with a pair of Mexican
jumping frogs named Poncho and Toro, originated as The Tijuana
Toads (Aug 6, 1969). Capitalizing on the popularity of the box-
office hit Jaws (UP, 1975), a new underwater comedy debuted as
"Misterjaws." Partnered with his obsequious flunky, Catfish the
Hunter, who always called him "Chief," Misterjaws was a near-
sighted shark with a voice borrowed from Walter Klemperer's in-
competent Colonel Wilhelm Klink on Hogan's Heroes (CBS, 1965-
1971). Along with prior cartoons the format included new vignettes with the colorful Panther, narrated by Richard Deacon, and
quickies and two-liners sent in by children.

The NBC run ended with Think Pink Panther!, a half-hour
of repeated episodes of the feline star, "Misterjaws" and "The
Texas Toads," telecast in Fall 1977 at local station option and
seen on WNBC, New York at 7:30-8:00 AM, Saturday before the
network return in February 1978.

Made for television, The All-New Pink Panther Show on
ABC in 1978-1979 continued the pantomime premise and the hued
theme with titles like "Pink Lightning," "The Pinkologist," "Pink-
tails for Two," "Yankee Doodle Pink" and "The Pink of Bagdad."
Two of the cartoons sandwiched another one starring "Crazylegs
Crane," a spin-off from "The Texas Toads," who tried haplessly
to teach his son Crane, Jr. how to catch the elusive Dragonfly.

The Pink Panther made TV commercials for SAFECO insurance and a half-hour ABC Special Pink Panther's Christmas

(Dec 7, 1978) which was expanded to an hour for A Pink Christmas
(Dec 16, 1979), followed by the Pink Panther in Olym-Pinks (Feb 22,
1980). Off-network, fifty-two half-hours were repackaged for the local
markets by UA-TV and dressed up with fresh Henry Mancini music.

## PLASTICMAN COMEDY-ADVENTURE SHOW, THE

Component Series
    FANGFACE AND FANGPUSS, MIGHTY MAN AND YUKK,
    RICKETY ROCKET

Network History
    Premiere: September 22, 1979
    ABC/Sep 1979-Dec 1979/Saturday 9:00-11:00 AM
    ABC/Dec 1979-Sep 1980/Saturday 9:00-10:30 AM
    Last Program: September 27, 1980

THE PLASTICMAN, BABY PLAS SUPER COMEDY
    Premiere: October 4, 1980
    ABC/Oct 1980-Sep 1981/Saturday 11:30-12:00 AM
    Last Program: September 5, 1981
Executive Producers: Joe Ruby, Ken Spears
Producer: Jerry Eisenberg
Directors: Rudy Larriva, Charles A. Nichols, Manny Perez
Company: Ruby-Spears Enterprises/16 films, 120 & 90 minutes
    (1979-1980), 13 films (1980-1981)

Principal Characters and Voices

| | |
|---|---|
| Plasticman/Baby Plas | Mike Bell |
| Penny/The Chief | Melendy Britt |
| Hula Hula | Joe Baker |
| Brandon Brucester/ | |
| Mighty Man | (1979-1980) Peter Cullen |
| Yukk | (1979-1980) Frank Welker |
| The Mayor | (1979-1980) John Stephenson |
| Rickety Rocket | (1979-1980) Al Fann |
| Sunstroke | (1979-1980) John Anthony Bailey |
| Splashdown | (1979-1980) Johnny Brown |
| Cosmo | (1979-1980) Bobbey Ellerbee |
| Venus | (1979-1980) Dee Timberlake |

FANGFACE AND FANGPUSS (1979-1980)  See  FANGFACE

The Plasticman Comedy-Adventure Show, ABC's second
two-hour package with four different cartoons, animated Jack Cole's
highly tensile comic book hero. A former criminal named Eel
O'Brien, the red-costumed, sunglassed character debuted in Police
Comics Number 1 (Quality, Aug 1941) and acquired his elasticity
in a strange quirk of fate while attempting to rob a chemical factory. A new person morally and physically after his accident,
Plasticman could stretch himself like a rubber band, extend his

limbs to infinity through drains or flatten himself as thin as a sheet of paper, and twist his body into any shape then quickly spring back into human form again. In the TV series he worked for a distaff law official called The Chief and was teamed with Penny, a romantically inclined blond with a southern fried accent, and an olive-skinned Hawaiian named Hula Hula, a Lou Costello sound-alike, among whose favorite expressions were "Leapin' Lava" and "Jumpin' Papayas." Called simply "Plas," the hero roared off with his pals in his "Plasticar" or frequently the "Plastijet," to battle malefactors worldwide. The superhero stretched himself to the limit against such evil-doers as Baron Von S. Stein, Hugefoot, Toyman, Highbrow, Moonraider, Honeybee, the diabolical Dr. Dome and a gang of little hoodlums called The Miniscule Seven. Two episodes were seen in each show and the cast also delivered sage advice on brief "Plasticman Consumer Tips."

The jocular lycanthrope Fangface (q. v.), introduced in 1978, was repeated with new episodes featuring his baby brother Fangpuss, along with two new elements. A pile of junk turned into a scientific marvel by a group of black teenagers, "Rickety Rocket" had a voice and mind of its own. Sort of a futuristic celestial Speed Buggy (q. v.), the spaceship transported the four youthful sleuths of the Far Out Detective Agency, whose motto was "felons foiled, burglars bagged, and pilferers positively pinched." Led by the fast-talking Cosmo, the self-described best detective in the whole universe, the quartet included the highly individualistic Venus, Sunstroke and Splashdown. Undertaking assignments for their clients, they "Blasted Off" in far-fetched "Capers" to bust up a gang of hijackers led by the Cosmic Claw, to throttle the Zombie Monster and Count Draculon and to return the Cosmic Crown stolen by the sinister Mr. Eclipse and his partner-in-crime, The Hood.

The other segment starred "Mighty Man and Yukk," the world's smallest hero and the world's ugliest dog, whose head was permanently hidden in a dog house. A hot line from The Mayor summoned the team into action and after stepping into the "Mighty Machine" or chanting "Mighty, Mighty, Mighty Man!," millionaire playboy Brandon Brucester became the tiny blue-caped crusader. With a voice like Red Skelton's Clem Kadiddlehopper, the dim-witted Yukk and the Lilliputian superhero sped into action on a motorcycle and sidecar. Among their assignments they captured the notorious jewel thief Miss Make-up, a sound- and look-alike of Mae West, got stuck with the Glue Man in an armored truck robbery, tangled with gold thieves Dr. Decay and Goldteeth, and foiled the crimes of the Mindreader, Catman and Glutinous Glop. Just the threat to remove the structure covering Yukk's ugly face was enough to drive most crooks voluntarily to the big house. The series was cut to ninety-minutes, December 22, 1979.

In 1980-1981 only the pliable hero returned in The Plasticman, Baby Plas Super Comedy. The revamped entry found Plasticman and Penny as man and wife with a new offspring, Baby Plas, a junior edition of the crime-fighter who inherited his stretchable powers. Baby Plas was seen in his own short comedies, like "Haircut Headache" and "Tiger Trouble," and with his parents and Hula Hula subdued a host of bizarre criminals such as The Abominable Snow

Spott in another. A repeat of the older episodes rounded out the half-hour show, during which the cast presented "Plasticman Safety Tips."


POPEYE THE SAILOR

Component Series
  DINKY DOG (1978-1981)

Syndicated History
  Premiere: September 10, 1956
  WPIX, New York/Monday-Friday 6:00-6:30 PM
  WBBM, Chicago/Monday-Friday 4:00-4:30 PM CST

(NEW) POPEYE
  Premiere: Fall 1961
Distributor: AAP-United Artists Television/1956-  ; Firestone
  Program Syndication (New)/1961-1979; Gold Key Entertainment
  (New)/1979-


Network History

THE ALL-NEW POPEYE HOUR

  Premiere: September 9, 1978
  CBS/Sep 1978-Sep 1979/Saturday 8:00-9:00 AM
  CBS/Sep 1979-Feb 1981/Saturday 10:30-11:30 AM
  CBS/Mar 1981-Jun 1981/Saturday 11:00-12:00 AM
  CBS/Jun 1981-Sep 1981/Saturday 10:00-11:00 AM
  Last Program: September 5, 1981
Executive Producers: Max Fleischer (1933-1942), Seymour Kneitel
  (1942-1956), Al Brodax (1961-1962), William Hanna, Joseph
  Barbera (1978-  )
Producer: Doug Wildey (1978-  )
Directors: Ray Patterson, Carl Urbano (1978-  )
Company: Fleischer Studios-Famous Studios for Paramount Pic-
  tures/234 B&W and color films, 5-7 minutes (1933-1956); Para-
  mount Cartoon Studios, Jack Kinney Productions, others for
  King Features Syndicate Television/220 films, 5 1/2 minutes
  (1961-1962); Hanna-Barbera Productions with KFS/26 films, 60
  minutes (1978-1981)

Principal Characters and Voices

| | |
|---|---|
| Popeye | (1933-1934) William Costello |
| | (1934-  ) Jack Mercer |
| Olive Oyl | (1933-1956/ |
| | 1961-1962) Mae Questel |
| | (1978-  ) Marilyn Schreffler |
| Bluto | (1933-1956) Gus Wickie/Pinto Colvig/ |
| | William Pennell |
| | (1978-  ) Allan Melvin |

| J. Wellington Wimpy | (1933-1956) Jack Mercer/Lou Fleischer/ Frank Matalone |
| | (1961-1962) Charles Lawrence/Jack Mercer |
| | (1978-    ) Daws Butler |
| Swee'pea | (1933-1956/ |
| | 1961-1962) Mae Questel |
| Brutus | (1961-1962) Jackson Beck |
| Shorty | (1961-1962) Arnold Stang |

DINKY DOG (1978-1981)

| Dinky | Frank Welker |
| Sandy | Jackie Joseph |
| Monica | Julie Bennett |
| Uncle Dudley | Frank Nelson |

Popeye the Sailor, the funny pages' wise-cracking, fist-swinging old salt, starred in more televised films than any other animated character. Popeye's continuous video exposure in more than 550 cartoons since 1956 contributed greatly to his enduring fame. Introduced over fifty years ago by Elzie Crisler Segar (1894-1938), in his strip Thimble Theater for The New York Journal (Jan 17, 1929), the feisty character appeared when Olive Oyl's brother, Castor Oyl, bought a ship and went down to the docks to hire a crew. There he met a pipe-smoking, one-eyed squinty seaman with an anchor tattooed on his muscular forearms. "Hey, there! Are you a sailor?," he asked. "Ja' think I was a cowboy?," were quick-tempered Popeye's first words. Continuing to mangle the English language, the crusty mariner soon became the principal character in the strip, which was created December 19, 1919 for the William Randolph Hearst chain. Popeye was already a worldwide favorite when Max Fleischer contracted with Segar and King Features Syndicate to transfer him to the screen for Paramount Pictures. The event was announced by a newspaper banner in Popeye the Sailor (Jul 14, 1933), one of Fleischer's popular cartoons starring Betty Boop (q.v.), in which a two-column picture began to animate as he sang, "I'm Popeye the Sailor Man," his expository song written by Sammy Lerner and Sammy Timberg. Two months later, the first official Popeye cartoon proclaimed his often repeated philosophy, I Yam What I Yam (Sep 29, 1933). With the exception of a handful of films retained by the studio for reissue as Popeye's Champions, the pre-1943 cartoons made by Fleischer and afterwards by Famous Studios under Seymour Kneitel were sold by Paramount in 1955 for $3 million to Associated Artists Productions (UA-TV) for television.

Premiering in New York and Chicago on September 10, 1956, the 234 syndicated Popeye cartoons were stripped weekdays on WPIX (hosted by "Captain" Allen Swift) and programmed by WBBM on Susie's Show (hosted by eleven-year-old Susan Heinkel), which was later transferred to CBS as Susan's Show* (q.v.). On KTLA, Los Angeles, Tom Hatten presented the comedies on October 8, 1956, initially at 7:00-7:30 PM PST weekdays and later in the afternoons until 1964 in a "peanut gallery" show, which was revived without

the youngsters on Sunday morning in 1976.  Usually introduced by
local station personalities, Popeye the Sailor was a smash hit during
the late fifties on such programs as Captain Bob in Buffalo, Popeye
Theater in Dayton and S. S. Popeye in Boston, with a 15.1 average
Neilsen rating.  During the first five years, the cartoons recouped
over ten times their purchase cost.

Characterized as an on-going battle between love-hungry sail-
ors, Popeye and Bluto, over the affections of the fickle, toothpick-
thin Olive Oyl, actually the stories were far more varied.  Ignoring
the eternal triangle format, many films were built around songs or
supporting characters and Bluto and Olive did not appear in every
film.  Although the cartoons were labeled as the classic model of
"hitting violence, " in one respect they adhered to a basic formula.
Popeye did not initiate the conflict, but was always attacked by a
Goliath, the devious, bearded bully Bluto, who was often depicted
as a sinister if not evil character.  Usually mauled in unfair tac-
tics, Popeye fought back valiantly, using the strength he derived
from spinach.  In the time-frame of the early animated concept,
the fantastic chase scenes and fisticuffs action were commonplace,
but the sole goal was laughter.  Even the pair's constant fights
were given a good ribbing in It's the Natural Thing to Do (Jul 30,
1939) and in one of the best, Brotherly Love (Mar 6, 1936).  In
Protek the Weakerist (Nov 19, 1937), which introduced Olive's pet
dog Fluffy, Popeye reminded youngsters through new lyrics to his
song, "Just because you're taller, don't hit someone smaller, says
Popeye the Sailor Man. "

Known in vaudeville as Red Pepper Sam, banjo musician-
singer William Costello, who played Gus Gorilla on the children's
radio show, Betty Boop Fables, established Popeye's gravel-voiced
characterization in the first year.  Then studio artist Jack Mercer
began his long career as Popeye's film voice.  Mercer's gruff
whiskey-baritone was not only distinctive but perfectly matched the
cartoon personality and his ad-lib mutterings were an integral part
of the series' success.  The skinny, flustery Olive Oyl reminded
Mae Questel of actress Zasu Pitts (1898-1963), whose high, whiny
voice she incorporated in the part.  A singer, Gus Wickie was the
original Bluto, followed by Pinto Colvig, who for a time voiced
Walt Disney's Goofy.  J. Wellington Wimpy, whose fondness for
hamburgers became as much a part of American folklore as Popeye's penchant for spinach, had several voices.  Several of Popeye's nephews, Peepeye, Pipeye, Pupeye and Poopeye, were recorded by Questel, and Poopdeck Pappy, Popeye's father, by Mercer.  But the visible-invisible Eugene the Jeep remained speechless
in the original films.

By 1960, Popeye was appearing on 150 stations and was the
most popular syndicated cartoon show in the country.  Since King
Features still owned the property, the Syndicate decided to hop
aboard the financial bandwagon.  In 1961-1962, Al Brodax cranked
out 220 more episodic Popeye films with several studios, featuring
the voices of Mercer and Questel.  Recorded by Jackson Beck, the
radio and TV cartoon announcer for Superman (q. v. ), Brutus became Popeye's antagonist in these versions.  Originally Brutus in
the newspaper comics, the name was changed to Bluto by Paramount

because of a conflict with a similar studio-owned name. The unimaginative series included the familiar supporting characters including Sea Hag and Alice the Goon and added Shorty, Popeye's sailor buddy, in such labored stories as "Li'l Olive Riding Hood," "Popeye and the Magic Hat" and "Private Eye Popeye." Hastily manufactured and marketed, the cartoons never enjoyed the popularity of the orignals. Under the umbrella title Popeye and Friends, the films headed a later package of syndicated cartoons.

In a salute to his stamina derived from spinach, the sailor's network bow came in 1978-1979 as The All-New Popeye Hour on CBS, with new voice characterizations except for the star. Comprised of five segments, the hour-long program featured three episodes of "The Adventures of Popeye" with Olive Oyl, Swee'pea, Wimpy sporting a new voice like that of W. C. Fields (1879-1946), and the return of Bluto. Violence was taboo in such standard stories as "A Day at the Rodeo" and "Popeye Snags the Sea Hag," and the sailor and his arch foe were portrayed as competitors in such tales as "Popeye and the Beanstalk," in which Bluto was the giant. "Popeye's Treasure Hunt" was a special feature pitting the seafarer and Olive Oyl against Bluto, who usually fell victim to his own devious schemes, in a race to find "The Dalmonica Diamond," "The Treasure of Werner Schnitzel" and "Captain Nemo's Sunken Treasure." An occasional new villain was presented, such as Goldfinger and Odd Clod, his robot henchman, who used a freeze ray to capture the Clyde satellite, the object of the hunt. In 1979-1980, "Popeye's Sports Parade" was added as an occasional component, with such fun and games as "Water Ya' Doing?," "King of the Rodeo" and "The Great Decathalon Championship."

Included was an original comedy, "Dinky Dog," the largest pup in the world, whose exploits complicated the lives of his distaff owners, roommates Monica and Sandy. Though they tried to keep their pet under control, Dinky always managed to upset the life of their Uncle Dudley, who hated dogs, but somehow the enormous pooch helped right matters in the end. Tying the elements together, Popeye and the cast appeared in short pro-social messages on health and safety: "Don't play with sharp things like knives" and "Wash your hands to keep the germs away." Between 1978 and 1980, Hanna-Barbera produced 102 cartoons with the Popeye characters for the show, many of the scripts being written by Mercer.

During the Depression, Popeye's yen for spinach increased sales of the vegetable and earned him immortality from grateful farmers who erected a large statue of the sailor in Crystal City, Texas. The super-strong scrapper contributed the catch-phrase, "Well, blow me down!" to American slang in the thirties, became a legend and folk hero, and a merchandising bonanza in virtually all media. Between 1935 and 1937, Detmar Poppen on NBC and Floyd Buckley on CBS voiced radio's Popeye the Sailor, with Olive La Moy as Olive Oyl, Charles Lawrence as Wimpy and Jimmy Donnelly as his adopted son. CBS re-edited some TV episodes for a half-hour prime time special program, The Popeye Show (Sep 13, 1978), followed by Popeye: Sweethearts at Sea (Feb 14, 1979), in which Eugene the Jeep was given a voice by Ginny McSwain. And

the star of Mork and Mindy (ABC, 1978-   ), Robin Williams, portrayed the inimitable sailor in the first movie for his old studio,
Popeye (PAR, 1980), perpetuating his forty-eight-year career in
films.


POP-UPS

Network History
    Premiere:  January 23, 1971
    NBC/Jan 1971-Aug 1971/Saturday, Various AM
    Last Program:  August 28, 1971
    Producer:  Paul Klein
    Company:  Educational Solutions/12 films, 1 minute

        Pop-Ups were brief lessons for preschoolers covering all
the conventions of reading except punctuation and capitalization.
The educational TV spots were devised by Dr. Caleb Cattegno, an
Egyptian-born educator and author, and based on a system which he
developed called "Words in Color," designed to teach children to
read within three weeks.   Produced by his own company, Educational Solutions, the one-minute messages were dropped at random
among the Saturday morning cartoons without explanation.   Dispensing with the "ABC" routine, previously presented by the "Letter"
commercials on Sesame Street* (q. v. ), the films went right into the
use of letters and employed phonetics and color to teach vowels,
consonants and simple sentences.   Bursting upon a blank screen,
the letters spread from left to right and top to bottom, illustrating
written style, with a feminine voice pronouncing their sounds.   The
Pop-Ups displayed how letters are often pronounced in different
words, with color used to differentiate sounds; for example, "a" in
the word "ate" was in Red.   Vowels were shown in combination with
consonants ("e" as in "pep"), consonants were illustrated ("i" as in
"pit"), then three-word sentences were introduced ("tap at it").   The
final spot emphasized intonation, with "stop-pat-stop" voiced in different ways.
        Although the Pop-Ups had been successfully tested earlier,
largely in black schools in New York City's Harlem in 1968 and on
the NBC O&O stations in New York and Cleveland in Fall 1970, the
full network experiment proved disappointing and the series was
dropped after about six months.   In the early seventies, the spots
were in use in about 7,000 classrooms on ETV systems and a
series of Spanish Pop-Ups was also developed.


PORKY PIG SHOW, THE

Component Series
    DAFFY DUCK, FOGHORN LEGHORN, THE GOOFY GOPHERS,
    SAM THE SHEEPDOG, others

Network History
    Premiere:  September 20, 1964

ABC/Sep 1964-Dec 1964/Sunday 10:30-11:00 AM
ABC/Dec 1964-Dec 1965/Saturday 11:30-12:00 AM
ABC/Dec 1965-Sep 1966/Saturday 10:00-10:30 AM
ABC/Sep 1966-Dec 1966/Sunday 4:00-4:30 PM
ABC/Dec 1966-Sep 1967/Saturday 9:30-10:00 AM
Last Program: September 2, 1967

Syndicated History

PORKY PIG AND HIS FRIENDS

Distributor: Warner Brothers Television/1971-
Producer: Hal Geer
Directors: Art Davis, Chuck Jones, Friz Freleng, Robert McKimson, Irv Spector (1948-1965)
Company: Warner Brothers Television/26 films (1964-1967);
Warner Brothers Television/156 films, 5-6 minutes (1971- )

Principal Characters and Voices

Porky Pig/Daffy Duck                Mel Blanc

The Porky Pig Show was repackaged from the post-1948 Warner Brothers theatrical cartoon library, first released to television in 1960 as The Bugs Bunny Show (q. v. ). A cute little porker that stuttered, Porky was probably the most famous pig in show business, not to mention comic books and merchandising novelties, until the 1976 arrival of Miss Piggy on The Muppets* (q. v. ). No newcomer to home screens, his pre-1948 black-and-white films were syndicated beginning in 1955 and 1956 as part of Looney Tunes (q. v. ) and the UA-TV Warner Brothers Cartoon package. Searching for a new character to replace Buddy, a weak imitation of Hugh Harman and Rudolph Ising's Bosko, who migrated with the team to MGM in 1934, Leon Schlesinger's "Termite Terrace" artists on Warner's Sunset lot launched the unsuspecting pig on his road to stardom. Director Tex Avery and animators Robert "Bobe" Cannon, Bob Clampett, and Chuck Jones screened one of Friz Freleng's musical cartoons, I Haven't Got a Hat (Jul 1, 1935), which included Porky and Beans, a saucy young cat, with a barnyard of animals emulating a Hal Roach Our Gang comedy. A big hog who stammered while trying to recite "The Midnight Ride of Paul Revere, " Porky struck their fancy. "It was funny as heck, " Avery said, "and on the basis of that we talked Schlesinger into it, and we designed Porky Pig. " He made his featured debut, as a giant fat hog with a slit down his back like a piggy-bank, in the gold-rush spoof, Golddiggers of '49 (Jan 6, 1936).

In his earlier cartoons, Porky was a submissive and somewhat naive character, the fall-guy subjected to crude pranks and the victim of smart-aleck adversaries both human and animal. In Milk and Money (Oct 3, 1936), he was a big-nosed, puffy-faced hog in his father's barnyard and saved the farm when his milk-wagon nag, Hank Horsefly, won the big race. A country rube, dressed in coveralls and appearing in hayseed settings, Porky was

down on the farm when he met his girlfriend Petunia, created by
Frank Tashlin in Porky's Romance (Apr 17, 1937). Clampett re-
vitalized the character that year and made him more appealing for
Porky's Badtime Story (Jul 24, 1937) and Rover's Rival (Oct 9,
1937), with a small snout, a pleasant smile on his round face, and
later a bow-tie. From 1938 to 1940, the series became virtually
Clampett's own and Porky was at his best when teamed with the
arch con-man Daffy Duck or matched with Sylvester the cat. Immortalized by the voice of the inimitable Mel Blanc, Porky Pig will
always be remembered for his "Bee-Bee-B-Ba ... Bee-Bee-B-Ba
... Tha ... Tha ... That's All Folks!," the Warner's circle signature over the theme "The Merry-Go-Round Broke Down," the most
mimicked and renowned of all cartoon endings.
    The Porky Pig comedies were seen as the lead-off cartoon
on the show, which included such components as Sam the Sheepdog,
The Goofy Gophers, Henery Hawk, Daffy Duck, Granny, Tweety Pie
and Sylvester, Foghorn Leghorn and Pepé le Pew. In 1969, after
the black-and-white Looney Tunes were withdrawn from syndication,
78 cartoons, largely with Porky Pig, were rotoscoped and hand-
colored in Korea to fill out a post-1948 color series, distributed to
local stations in 1971 as Porky Pig and His Friends.


PRINCE PLANET

Syndicated History
    Premiere: September 1966
    Distributor: American International Television/1966-1979; Filmways
        Enterprises/1979-
    Producer: Mitsuteru Yokoyama
    Company: TCJ Animation Center, Japan/52 B&W films

Principal Characters
    Prince Planet/Bobby
    Diana
    Hadji Baba
    Dynamo


    Prince Planet, a royal scion from the planet Radion, ar-
rived on Earth in the twenty-first century. A member of the Universal Peace Corps, working in the city of New Metropolis, the
youngster was given the earthly name Bobby, and tackled tasks
with his superhuman powers and the assistance of two other Corps
members, Hadji Baba and Dynamo. Together with Bobby's girlfriend Diana, who was forever in the clutches of some reprobate,
the foursome battled against the evil machinations of criminal con-
spirators like Warlock, a sinister Martian. Dubbed in English, the
series was imported from TCJ Animation, Japan, which changed its
name to Eiken Studios in the seventies, and earlier produced two
other syndicated series, 8th Man (q. v. ) and Gigantor (q. v. ).

Q. T. HUSH

Syndicated History
    Premiere: September 24, 1960
    WABC, New York/Monday-Friday 6:30-7:00 PM
    Distributor: National Telefilm Associates/1960-
    Producer: M. and A. Alexander
    Company: Animation Associates/100 films, 3 1/2 minutes

Principal Characters
    Q. T. Hush
    Shamus
    Quincy
    Police Chief Muldoon

    Q. T. Hush, private eye, and his bloodhound, Shamus,
private nose, solved baffling mysteries using their extraordinary
abilities and Sherlockian deduction. Able to transform himself into
a shadow named Quincy, who could operate independently as another
sleuth, Q. T. assisted the perplexed Police Chief Muldoon in jailing
a string of colorfully named criminals. In this non-violent animated
"Who-dun-it?," ten cliff-hanging episodes formed a complete story,
with ten "Capers" comprising the syndicated package. In "The Big
Masquerade Caper," Q. T. and Shamus followed the tire tracks of
the Scavenger Hill Mob's truck, after they had robbed the Sphinx
Packing Company wearing Halloween masks. They located the gang's
hideout and unmasked one member posing as Mother Macushla, a
sweet old lady, and persevered through the "to be continued" scrapes
to recover the money. In other "Capers," the diminutive heroes
captured the kidnappers Yo Yo and Ping Pong; the elusive international jewel thief Baffles; the oriental art thief One Ton; Professor
Zappo and his stooge, Gootch, who stole a nuclear energy capsule
from the Goatridge Atomic Plant; the hood Al Cologne and his
henchman, Looie, a pair of protection racketeers; and manacled
the magician Dr. Tickle, who invented Meany-Mix, a drink that
changed him into the evil Mr. Snide.


QUICK DRAW McGRAW

Component Series
    AUGIE DOGGIE AND DOGGIE DADDY, SNOOPER AND BLABBER

Syndicated History
    Premiere: September 29, 1959
    WPIX, New York/Tuesday 6:30-7:00 PM
    Sponsor: Kellogg's Cereals (1959-1962)
    Distributor: Screen Gems-Columbia Pictures Television/1959-

Network History
    Return: September 28, 1963
    CBS/Sep 1963-Sep 1965/Saturday 10:00-10:30 AM
    CBS/Sep 1965-Sep 1966/Saturday 11:30-12:00 AM

Last Program: September 3, 1966
Executive Producers/Directors: William Hanna, Joseph Barbera
Company: Hanna-Barbera Productions with Screen Gems (CPT)/45
films

Principal Characters and Voices

| | |
|---|---|
| Quick Draw McGraw/Baba Looey/<br>Snuffles/Injun Joe/Augie Dog-<br>gie/Snooper/Blabber | Daws Butler |
| Doggie Daddy | Doug Young |
| Sagebrush Sal | Julie Bennett |

Quick Draw McGraw, a lanky Stetson-wearing mustang, headlined this trilogy which satirized TV westerns, private-eyes and situation comedies. Snail-paced of wit and tongue, Quick Draw was a
luckless U.S. Marshal who had difficulty even getting his Colt out of
its holster, and when he did he invariably shot the wrong man. A
silly-looking bronc that walked upright and had a mule's stupidity
and a voice to match, borrowed from Red Skelton's witless boob
Clem Kadiddlehopper, McGraw persistently courted disaster by ignoring the wise advice of his diminutive partner, the Mexican burro
Baba Looey. In typical cowboy-hero fashion, McGraw was largely
indifferent to his girlfriend, a romantically inclined, flustery filly
named Sagebrush Sal. Snuffles and Injun Joe regularly provided additional problems for the most moronic lawman ever to don a badge
in New Mexico Territory, who plodded resolutely from crisis to
catastrophe in such sagas as "Six Gun Spook," "Bullet Proof Galoot,"
"Scarey Prairie" and "Dizzy Desperado." Equally inept as the
rapier-armed El Kabong, Quick Draw also appeared as a swashbuckling avenger spoofing Walt Disney's Zorro* (q.v.), in such
titles as "Who is El Kabong?," "El Kabong Strikes Again" and
"Kabong Kabongs Kabong." Cloaked in a disguise, the klutzy lawman was continually stymied because his mask had not come back
from the laundry.
    Always dimly sensing some foul play, "Snooper and Blabber"
were private investigators tracking public enemies and a menagerie
of missing animals. A cat named Super Snooper and a mouse,
Blabber Mouse, that talked as if he had a mouth full of marbles,
like Howdy Doody* (q.v.), they were involved in such cases as the
"Purloined Parrot," "Bear-ly Able," "Real Gone Ghosts," "Puss
and Booty" and "Bronco Bluster." Operating out of the Super
Snooper Detective Agency, one of their toughest assignments was
locating the world's greatest trained flea at a dog pound.
    An overly affectionate pup and his father, "Augie Doggie
and Doggie Daddy" mocked the wise and paternal family comedy,
Father Knows Best (NBC/CBS, 1954-1962). A Jimmy Durante
sound-alike, Doggie Daddy was the repeated victim of his mindless offspring's good deeds which backfired in such stories as
"Good Mouse Keeping," "Augie the Watch Dog," "Pop's Nature
Pup," "Peck o' Trouble" and "High and Flighty." Constantly trying to please, Augie Doggie addressed his paternal sire in overly
flowery phrases like "Dear old bone-provider Dad."

The second syndicated package produced by Hanna-Barbera with Screen Gems (CPT) for the juvenile market following the success of Huckleberry Hound (q.v.), the show was sponsored by the Kellogg's Company for three years on a spot market basis. The cartoons were repeated by CBS between 1963 and 1966 before ongoing syndication.

## RELUCTANT DRAGON AND MR. TOAD, THE

Network History
    Premiere: September 12, 1970
    ABC/Sep 1970-Dec 1970/Saturday 8:00-8:30 AM
    ABC/Sep 1971-Sep 1972/Sunday 10:00-10:30 AM
    Last Program: September 17, 1972

Syndicated History

Distributor: Worldvision Enterprises/1972-
Executive Producers: Arthur Rankin, Jr., Jules Bass
Company: Rankin-Bass Productions/17 films

Principal Characters
    Tobias Dragon
    J. Thaddeus Toad

The Reluctant Dragon and Mr. Toad were separate animated features drawn from the pen of the English author of children's books, Kenneth Grahame (1859-1932). Nicknamed Tobias, "The Reluctant Dragon" first appeared in a collection of Grahame stories entitled Dream Days (John Lane, 1898). A lazy but well-meaning and kind-hearted brontosaurus, Tobias was cursed with a fiery affliction, breathing flames which he despised. The affliction was brought on by a whiff of daisies, which caused the four-hundred-year-old reptile to sneeze, and Tobias was often the victim of a little girl, who delighted in presenting him bouquets. Alarmed over his torch-like breath, a nuisance which disrupted life in Willowmarsh Village, Sir Malcolm Giles attempted to protect the dragon from the whims of the little girl and his ancient curse. Two episodes were seen in each show, with such titles as "National Daisy Week," "The Campscout Girls," "A Cold Day in Willowmarsh," "The Tobias Touch" and "Tobias, The Reluctant Viking."
    The middle cartoon starred J. Thaddeus Toad, a carefree gadabout playboy. Wearing unsightly garments, the good-looking frog became an object of ridicule among his friends, the introverted Mole, the extroverted Water Rat and the Badger, a philosophical recluse. Based on the humorous characterizations in Grahame's allegorical novel The Wind in the Willows (Scribner, 1907), Mr. Toad and the inhabitants of The Wild Wood and surrounding country were seen in such stories as "Ghost of Toad Hall," "Micemaster Road," "Build a Better Bungalow," "Polo Panic" and "Jove! What a Day."
    The subject of numerous book reprints, children's record-

ings and adaptations as juvenile stage plays, both properties achieved worldwide acclaim. But the TV cartoons did not translate well and some stories, for instance the encounters of Tobias with "Wretched Robin Hood" and "Merlin the Magician, Jr.," were feeble inventions. In theatrical versions filmed by Walt Disney Productions, a musical adaptation with Barnett Parker as the voice of The Reluctant Dragon (RKO, 1941) starred Robert Benchley in the live-action and cartoon film, which introduced the song "I'm a Reluctant Dragon" by Charles Wolcott and Larry Morey; and Wind in the Willows (Feb 2, 1955) was telecast as one-half of The Adventures of Ichabod and Mr. Toad (RKO, 1949) on the studio's weekly omnibus, Walt Disney* (q. v.), with the resident of Toad Hall voiced by Eric Blore.

## RETURN TO THE PLANET OF THE APES

### Network History
Premiere: September 6, 1975
NBC/Sep 1975-Sep 1976/Saturday 11:00-11:30 AM
Last Program: September 4, 1976
Executive Producers: David DePatie, Friz Freleng
Director: Doug Wildey
Company: DePatie-Freleng Enterprises/13 films

### Principal Characters and Voices

| | |
|---|---|
| Bill Hudson/Dr. Zaius | Richard Blackburn |
| Jeff Carter | Austin Stoker |
| Judy Franklin/Nova | Claudette Nevins |
| Cornelius | Edwin Mills |
| Zira | Phillippa Harris |
| General Urko | Henry Corden |

Return to the Planet of the Apes incorporated a pair of youngsters for the animated sequel to the modern, near-classic science fiction story. It was about a stranded party on a simian-controlled Earth some two thousand years in the future. Hurled through a space warp to a different time continuum while aboard their spacecraft, Bill Hudson and his young passengers, Jeff and Judy, crash-landed in the austere and shocking alternate world, where orangutans were rulers and gorillas were warriors. The cartoons were based on the 1963 novel by Pierre Boulle, which was adapted closely for the feature Planet of the Apes (TCF, 1968), starring Charlton Heston as one of the astronaut survivors in a land where apes were masters and humans their slaves. Its success generated two further screenplays and a short-lived prime time TV series, Planet of the Apes (CBS, 1974), with only Roddy McDowall recreating his role as the curious chimpanzee named Galen. As in the initial film, the cartoon version portrayed Dr. Zaius as the scientific ruler of the planet, with General Urko as the military commander. Another difference was the casting of Cornelius and Nova as young chimpanzee friends and the simian counterparts of Jeff and Judy. Eliminating the tyrannical wickedness of the earlier filmed adaptations, the more benign juvenile stories saw the party menaced more often by the strange natural elements of their exotic world in such episodes as "Lagoon of Peril," "Tunnel of Fear," "Terror on Ice Mountain" and "Trail to the Unknown." Faithful to the original, however, were the monkey caricatures, based on the ingenious facial and body make-up created by John Chambers for the theatrical and TV films.

## RICHIE RICH/SCOOBY-DOO SHOW, THE

### Network History
Premiere: November 8, 1980
ABC/Nov 1980-Sep 1981/Saturday 9:30-10:30 AM

Executive Producers: William Hanna, Joseph Barbera
Producer: Oscar Dufau
Directors: Ray Patterson, George Gordon
Company: Hanna-Barbera Productions with Paramount Television/ 13 films, 60 minutes

### Principal Characters and Voices

| | |
|---|---|
| Richie Rich | Sparky Marcus |
| Freckles | Christian Hoff |
| Gloria | Nancy Cartwright |
| Irona/Mrs. Rich | Joan Gerber |
| Dollar | Frank Welker |
| Professor Keenbean | Bill Callaway |
| Cadbury/Mr. Rich | Stan Jones |
| Reggie Van Goh | Dick Beals |

SCOOBY AND SCRAPPY-DOO  See  SCOOBY-DOO

The Richie Rich/Scooby-Doo Show coupled repeats starring the cowardly Great Dane and his feisty cousin Scrappy-Doo with cartoons introducing the world's richest boy. With a bank account as rich as his name, Richie Rich lived in a fabulous estate and had all the conveniences money could buy, including a jet plane, a yacht and his own Jungleland. The tow-headed youngster favored blue bow ties, red sweaters, peanut butter and jelly sandwiches and anything with a dollar sign, which his enormous swimming pool resembled. Created as a feature for Harvey Publications' Little Dot Number 6 (1956) and a separate comic after November 1957, the main characters were Richie and his parents, Mr. and Mrs. Rich, his dog Dollar and close pals, Freckles and Gloria, whose favorite expression was "Neat O," and the envious, young, blueblood spoilsport, Reggie Van Goh. Cadbury was the efficient and proper family butler and Irona, a robot maid. Whatever the problem it was never too late when Master Richie was in trouble and Irona was around. Far from a functional idiot, the electronic servant could become almost anything in a crisis from a rocket powered jet to a powerful vacuum cleaner. Professor Keenbean, head of the Rich

Science Center, was the inventor of chopper-helmets, rocket-skates and futuristic gadgets of every description, which Richie used in his far-flung fantasy exploits.

Alternating with the escapades of Scooby and Scrappy-Doo (q. v. ), the hour-long show included short humorous vignettes titled "Richie Rich Gem$" and four- to six-minute stories on "Richie Rich Riche$, " "Richie Riche$' Treasure Chest" and "Richie Riche$' Zillion Dollar Adventure. " In the stories Richie and his friends foiled Eluso the Master Magician, who kidnapped all the world's leading dignitaries; the Shocking Lady with her Electric Bolts, who tried to rob the U. S. Mint; and Barnum Bullwhip, who stole African animals with his giant robot vulture and was perfecting a doomsday ray. Traveling to wherever skullduggery was rampant, with the aid of Professor Keenbean's gadgetry, and an occasional hand from Irona, Cadbury and his friends, Richie thwarted the evil plans of such arch fiends as Mr. Dirty, The Blurr, The Pickpocket, Dr. Kingum, who was looting his father's Australian Diamond Mine, and two crooks who discovered oil on the land of his destitute hillbilly cousins, Alfalfa and Cecil Rich, in Pigsville Hollow, Tennessee.


ROAD RUNNER SHOW, THE

Component Series
    DAFFY DUCK, FOGHORN LEGHORN, PORKY PIG, SYLVESTER, JR. , others

Network History
    Premiere: September 10, 1966
    CBS/Sep 1966-Sep 1967/Saturday 12:00-12:30 PM
    CBS/Sep 1967-Sep 1968/Saturday 1:30-2:00 PM
    ABC/Sep 1971-Sep 1972/Saturday 8:30-9:00 AM
    Last Program: September 2, 1972

THE BUGS BUNNY/ROAD RUNNER HOUR AND SHOW See BUGS BUNNY

Producers: Bill Hendricks (1966-1972), Hal Geer (1972-    )
Directors: Chuck Jones, Maurice Noble, Rudy Larriva, Abe Levitow, Robert McKimson (1949-1966)
Company: Warner Brothers Television/26 films (1949-1966)

Principal Characters
    Road Runner (non-speaking)
    Wile E. Coyote (non-speaking)


    The Road Runner Show featured a continuing contest between a bemused cuckoo-like bird who was a whiz at outrunning and outsmarting a wheezy coyote who was driven insanely inventive by hunger. Repackaged from the post-1948 Warner Brothers library, the program included theatrical cartoons made between 1949 and 1966, seven produced by DePatie-Freleng Enterprises in the midsixties. Modeled on the reddish, plume-headed Geococcyx californianus, the actual formal designation of the largely terrestrial birds noted for their great speed, the title character was conceived by animator-director Chuck Jones and storyman Michael Maltese for Fast and Furry-ous (Sep 16, 1949). From the outset, the pair intended to parody the animated chase films, the most popular Hollywood format in the forties, exemplified by MGM's Oscar-winning cat-and-mouse, Tom and Jerry (q. v. ). With only minimal concern for a storyline, the artists placed their "Accelerati Incredibulis" in a stark but boulder-strewn desert with the ravenous Wile E. Coyote, created ten or more gags and let the fun begin. The comedy developed out of the frustrated coyote's flawed schemes and escalating trauma. Obsessed with catching the swift, non-flying bird to sate his appetite, the "Carnivorus Vulgaris" devised a series of increasingly maniacal traps that backfired. No matter what sort of complicated gadgets he created, he never caught the maddeningly oblivious bird. Simply a catalyst, the unperturbed, red-crested fowl watched, safe and sound, while the brown coyote over-ran the sharp edge of a cliff, plummeting to the depths below, or erringly catapulted himself into walls of rock. Both characters were non-speaking, although the Road Runner voiced his familiar "Beep, Beep," the catch-call of the series. The best customer of the "Acme" company, Wile E. Coyote was also an adversary for Bugs Bunny (q. v. ).

The components featured Daffy Duck, Porky Pig, Sylvester, Jr. , Foghorn Leghorn and others drawn from the Warner library. The Road Runner films were first telecast as a filler on The Bugs Bunny Show, which debuted October 11, 1960 on ABC, before being packaged separately. In tandem with the laid-back hare, the cartoons were programmed on CBS between 1968 and 1971 as The Bugs Bunny/Road Runner Hour and subsequently from September 6, 1975. On September 11, 1971, ABC picked up The Road Runner Show, but it was dropped after one season because of its "excessively aggressive action." As a result, the network also lost the Bugs Bunny series when Warner's sold both shows again to CBS. On the air alone or in combined form for twelve years by 1980-1981, the Road Runner is one of the longer running network cartoon shows, off only between 1972-1975. Re-edited and sanitized by CBS, the films' interpersonal non-violent formula has consistently provided good humor, high ratings and profits, and has inspired several TV imitators, including "Blast Off Buzzard" seen on the C. B. Bears (q. v. ).

Some of the cartoons were spliced together as a featurette, The Adventures of the Road Runner (WB, 1962), and were incorporated in the animated feature, The Bugs Bunny/Road Runner Movie (WB, 1980). While there was some conjecture, the Road Runner emerged clearly as a male in his comic books, published successively by Western, Gold Key and Dell since the forties. Renamed Beep Beep the Road Runner, he was given a wife named Matilda and three identical sons who followed him about. He was slickly merchandised in novelties and toys, and the crowning achievement came when the Plymouth Division of Chrysler Motors named one of its models "The Road Runner."

ROCKET ROBIN HOOD AND HIS MERRY SPACEMEN

Syndicated History
  Premiere:  1969
  Producer:  Steve Krantz
  Distributor:  Quality Entertainment/1969-1979; ARP Films/1979-
  Company:  Trillium Productions/52 films

Principal Characters
  Rocket Robin Hood
  Will Scarlet
  Little John
  Friar Tuck
  Maid Marian

      Rocket Robin Hood and His Merry Spacemen, a whole new gener-
ation of direct descendants of the twelfth-century British outlaw gang--
Will Scarlet, Little John, Friar Tuck and Maid Marian--floated about
the universe on a solar-powered asteroid, New Sherwood Forest. They
battled tyranny in 3000 A. D. , in particular the Sheriff of N. O. T. , in
such episodes as "Prince of the Plotters, " "Robin vs. the Robot Knight,"
"Dinosaur Go Home" and "The Strange Castle, " with three segments
seen in each half-hour show.


ROCKY AND HIS FRIENDS

Component Series
  AESOP AND SON, FRACTURED FAIRY TALES, PEABODY'S
  IMPROBABLE HISTORY, MR. KNOW IT ALL

Network History
  Premiere:  November 19, 1959
  ABC/Nov 1959-Mar 1960/Thursday 5:30-6:00 PM
  ABC/Mar 1960-Sep 1960/Tuesday, Thursday 5:30-6:00 PM
  ABC/May 1960-Oct 1960/Saturday 11:00-11:30 AM
  ABC/Sep 1960-Dec 1960/Thursday 5:30-6:00 PM
  ABC/Oct 1960-Jun 1961/Saturday 9:30-10:00 AM
  ABC/Sep 1960-Dec 1960/Sunday 12:30-1:00 PM
  ABC/Nov 1960-Sep 1961/Sunday 9:30-10:00 AM
  ABC/Dec 1960-Sep 1961/Sunday 5:30-6:00 PM
  ABC/Jan 1961-Sep 1961/Tuesday, Thursday 5:30-6:00 PM
  ABC/Jul 1961-Sep 1961/Saturday 10:30-11:00 AM
  Last Program:  September 23, 1961

Syndicated History

Distributor:  Filmtel International/1961-1979; DFS Program Ex-
  change/1979-
Producers:  Jay Ward, Bill Scott
Directors:  Bill Hurtz, Ted Parmelee, Pete Burness
Company:  Jay Ward Productions with Producers Associates for
  Television/52 films

Narrators
> Paul Frees/"Rocky and Bullwinkle"
> Edward Everett Horton/"Fractured Fairy Tales"
> Charles Ruggles/"Aesop and Son"

Principal Characters and Voices

Rocket J. Squirrel/Natasha
  Fatale                    June Foray
Bullwinkle B. Moose/Mr.
  Peabody                Bill Scott
Boris Badenov          Paul Frees
Sherman                Walter Tetley

    Rocky and His Friends was the second all-new, network TV
cartoon program, featuring the serialized stories of Rocket J.
Squirrel and Bullwinkle B. Moose. Similar to the animal formula
devised for Jay Ward's earlier syndicated series, Crusader Rabbit
(q. v. ), the comedies paired a smart, diminutive hero and a loutish,
larger companion, unusual four-footed pals that walked upright in
their adventures. A put-down on cute critters in fairyland stories,
"Rocky and Bullwinkle" were up-home boys from Frostbite Falls,
Koochiching County, Minnesota, developed by Ward's former partner, Alexander Anderson, for a proposed pilot, "Frostbite Falls
Review. " A rakish flying squirrel, Rocky was smartly decked out
in a First World War leather helmet with goggles and a scarf, and
Bullwinkle sounded like Red Skelton's Willie Lump Lump, a punch-
drunk fighter. Endless wanderers, they were involved with such
flamboyant figures of high comedy as Mal Content, an egotistical
actor, Captain Peter "Wrongway" Peachfuzz, owner of the ship
"USS Pennsyltucky, " and Gidney and Cloid, two fun-seeking Moon
Men. In most of the installments their arch foes were an odious
pair of Pottsylvania agents directed by Mr. Big, a midget located
in the Krumlin, and his aide-de-noncompetent, Fearless Leader, a
dueling-scarred Teutonic type. Continually involved in some ex-
plosive intrigue, Rocky and Bullwinkle struggled valiantly to thwart
the subversive plots of the artless Boris Badenov and the venomous
Natasha Fatale, two good-old-fashioned spies with heavy Slavic accents like Bert Gordon's Mad Russian and Zsa Zsa Gabor. Scripted
mainly by Bill Scott, the razor-sharp satire provided ample action
and comic exaggeration for younger viewers and delightful double-
entendre for adults.
    Sandwiched between the two cliff-hanging segments were sev-
eral rotated components. Edward Everett Horton (1886-1970), the
screen's nervous flibbertigibbet, narrated "Fractured Fairy Tales, "
written principally by artist-scripter Chris Jenkyns, which always
provided an unexpected snapper. The story of "Sleeping Beauty"
starred a caricature of Walt Disney as the handsome prince, who
withheld his magic kiss, allowed the girl to sleep and built an
amusement park around her called Sleeping Beautyland. Borrowed
from H. G. Wells's The Time Machine (1895), each episode of
"Peabody's Improbable History" had a punned closing. A wealthy,
pedantic and bespectacled dog, Mr. Peabody and his young friend

Sherman were transported by the "Wayback Machine" to venerated
events where they reshaped history.   Sherman was voiced by Walter
Tetley, a radio veteran heard as Elroy on The Great Gildersleeve
(NBC, 1941-1954).   In a short segment titled "Mr. Know It All, "
the befuddled Bullwinkle gave inane answers to commonplace queries
posed by Rocky.   On "Aesop and Son, " narrated by low-key, dim-
pled actor Charles Ruggles (1886-1970), the bearded philosopher told
twisted contemporary animal fables to his offspring.   One evening
he related the tale of a lion that preferred to sing instead of roar,
because every time he bellowed, he sneezed.   "You need help, Leo
baby, " said his agent friend, the fox.   So Leo became a celebrated
pop artist, cranking out albums with titles like "You're Lion to Me"
and "Lion Goes Latin. "   The sneeze vanished, but in its place the
big cat developed a psychosomatic pain in the mane.

Arriving in Fall 1959, after The Ruff and Reddy Show (q. v. )
and before The Flintstones (q. v. ), the series was the most imaginative of all the new cartoon shows in the fifties.   Rocky and His
Friends jarred the public funnybone, attracted a cult following and
helped revolutionize and accelerate animated programming on all the
webs.   It also set a pattern for subsequent Ward and Scott programs
like George of the Jungle (q. v. ) and The Dudley Do-Right Show (q.v.),
among the most verbally entertaining cartoons ever produced for
television.

After the first season, ABC programmed the older episodes
concurrently on Saturday and Sunday mornings.   Following its run,
the program was expanded with new episodes for NBC in 1961 and
retitled The Bullwinkle Show (q. v. ).


ROD ROCKET

Syndicated History
   Premiere:  1963
Distributor:  Victor Corporation/1963-
Producers:  Louis Scheimer, Mark Lipsky
Company:  Jiro Enterprises/130 films, 5 minutes

Principal Characters
   Rod Rocket
   Joey
   Professor Argus

Rod Rocket was an aptly named celestial adventurer in this
animated space saga, accompanied on his missions by a young pro-
tégé, Joey, and the scientific genius, Professor Argus.   A science
fiction cliff-hanger, five episodes comprised a complete story and
the films could be programmed singly or strung together as twenty-
six half-hour shows.   The cartoons were produced in 1962-1963 by
Louis Scheimer who formed Filmation Studios with Norman Prescott about the time they were syndicated.

## ROGER RAMJET AND THE AMERICAN EAGLES

Syndicated History
  Premiere: September 1965
  Theme: "Yankee Doodle" (Special lyrics)
  Sponsors: Wen-Mac Toy Division of AMF, Sweets Company (1965-1968)
  Distributor: CBS Films/1965-1971; Winter-Rosen/1971-1975; Bloom Film Group/1975-
  Executive Producer: Ken Snyder
  Producer/Director: Fred Crippen
  Company: Snyder-Koren Productions/156 films, 5 minutes

Principal Characters and Voices

| | |
|---|---|
| Roger Ramjet | Gary Owens |
| Yank/Dan | Dick Beals |
| Doodle/Noodles Romanoff | Gene Moss |
| Dee/Lotta Love | Joan Gerber |
| General G. I. Brassbottom/ Ma Ramjet | Bob Arbogast |
| Lance Crossfire/Red Dog | Paul Shively |
| The Announcer | Dave Ketchum |

Roger Ramjet and the American Eagles were hundred-per
cent all-Americans, a private group of jet jockeys on call to defend the nation's freedom in the skies or outer space. An inter-
nationally famous good guy, and a daring and competent pilot,
Roger received his assignments via a hot line from General G. I.
Brassbottom in the Pentagon and was armed with a secret weapon.
When in a jam he would swallow a Proton Energy Pill which transformed him for twenty seconds into a superpatriot with the strength
of twenty atom bombs. Whenever his supply of pills was exhausted
or out of reach, the American Eagle Squadron invariably came wing-
ing to the rescue. A quartet of bright and brave youngsters, the
Eagles included Yank, the nominal leader and an idolizing junior
version of the hero, Doodle, a short, chubby lad whose love for
food repeatedly got him into trouble, Dan, a bespectacled mathe-
matician and electronic engineering genius whose weapon was a
slide rule, and everybody's sister, Dee. Called "Ma" as well by
the Eagles was Roger's sweet, little old mother, the rowdy and
rambunctious Ma Ramjet. Lotta Love was Roger's sweetheart; it
was a lukewarm romance that had lingered for fifteen years.
Roger's principal rival for Lotta's hand was Lance Crossfire, an
ace test pilot and playboy, who flashed a lot of teeth and sounded
like Burt Lancaster. The cartoon announcer was ever-present and
interacted with the other characters, describing the action.
  In the stories, Ramjet protected law-abiding citizens on
Earth from the dastardly plans of Noodles Romanoff, head of the
National Association of Spies, Traitors and Yahoos, an evil organization known as N. A. S. T. Y. A hood in hood's clothing,
Noodles was handicapped by his henchmen, the No-Goods, five
nameless, klutzy stooges who scared easily, talked at the same

time and were constantly stumbling over each other. Sometimes Roger was assigned space missions, where he tangled with the dreaded Solonoid Robots, a gang of mechanical villains trying to enslave the human race. But no matter the opposition, the pill-popping Ramjet always triumphed dramatically. As one stanza of the theme song put it,

> Roger Ramjet he's our man
> Hero of our nation
> For his adventures just be sure
> And stay tuned to this station.

A popular cartoon mascot chosen by several military air squadrons, Roger Ramjet was also selected as the favorite son of Lompoc, California. Scripted by Gene Moss and Jim Thurman, the series was placed in barter syndication for the sponsors between 1965 and 1968, appearing on 83 stations in first run.


## ROMAN HOLIDAYS

Network History
   Premiere: September 9, 1972
   NBC/Sep 1972-Dec 1972/Saturday 10:00-10:30 AM
   NBC/Dec 1972-Sep 1973/Saturday 8:30-9:00 AM
   Last Program: September 1, 1973
Executive Producers: William Hanna, Joseph Barbera
Producer: Iwao Takamoto
Director: Charles A. Nichols
Company: Hanna-Barbera Productions/13 films

Principal Characters and Voices

| | |
|---|---|
| Gus Holiday | Dave Willock |
| Laurie Holiday | Shirley Mitchell |
| Precocia Holiday | Pamelyn Ferdin |
| Happius Holiday | Stanley Livingston |
| Mr. Evictus | Dom DeLuise |
| Mr. Tycoonius | Hal Smith |
| Herman | Hal Peary |
| Henrietta | Janet Waldo |
| Groovia | Judy Strangis |
| Brutus | Daws Butler |

Roman Holidays presented a toga-clad family who lived in Nero's capital, circa A.D. 63, beset by twentieth-century everyday concerns. The pseudo-historical household at the Venus DiMillo Arms, 4960 Terrace Drive, Pastafasullo, Rome, included Gus and his wife Laurie, their daughter Precocia and young son Happius, nicknamed "Happy." Together with their playful pet lion Brutus, the Holidays' rambunctious offspring were the particular exasperation of Mr. Evictus, their nagging landlord. Frustrated at traffic jams and chariot hot rodders in the bustling metropolis and badgered by exponents of women's lib at his job, the hard working Gus was an engineer with the Forum Construction Company owned by Mr. Tycoonius. The stories, also involving Herman and Henrietta, the Holidays' best friends and neighbors, and "Happy's" girlfriend Groovia, their teenage daughter, had such titles as "Hectic Holiday," "Lion's Share," "Cyrano De Happius" and "A Funny Thing Happened on the Way to the Chariot."

A domestic comedy cartoon formula developed by Hanna-Barbera, Roman Holidays was set sort of midway between two of the studio's better known animated series, the Stone Age trials of The Flintstones (q. v.) and the Space Age tribulations of The Jetsons (q. v.), but lacked the imaginative inventiveness of the forerunners.


## RUFF AND REDDY SHOW, THE

Network History
    Premiere:  December 14, 1957
    NBC/Dec 1957-Oct 1960/Saturday 10:30-11:00 AM
    NBC/Sep 1962-Sep 1964/Saturday 9:30-10:00 AM
    Last Program:  September 26, 1964

Syndicated History

Distributor:  Screen Gems-Columbia Pictures Television/1964-
Executive Producers/Directors:  William Hanna, Joseph Barbera
Company:  Hanna-Barbera Productions with Screen Gems (CPT)/
    156 films, 6 minutes

Hosts
    Jimmy Blaine (1957-1960)
    Bob Cottle (1962-1964)

Principal Characters and Voices

Ruff                            Don Messick
Reddy                           Daws Butler

The Ruff and Reddy Show was the pioneer, all-new, network cartoon series, telecast in black-and-white until June 1959. The brainy cat and brainless dog were the first TV creations of William Hanna and Joseph Barbera, the Oscar-winning producers of Tom and Jerry (q. v.), who owed a great debt not only to their MGM animal stars but as well to the format of Crusader Rabbit (q. v.). As with that pioneer, made-for-TV cartoon program, the episodes were serialized, with ten or more six-minute installments comprising a complete story. And like Crusader and Rags the Tiger, who walked upright instead of on all fours, the pair were anthropomorphic characters, united instead of natural enemies, and engaged in madcap fantasy adventures.

Sort of a throwback to vaudeville comedy teams with a straight man and a foil, Ruff and Reddy were involved with such comedic antagonists as Captain Greedy and Salt Water Daffy, the terrible twins from Texas, Killer and Diller, the chicken-hearted

Chickasaurus, Scarey Harry Safari, the Mastermind of the planet
Muni Mula, and the Goon of Glocca Morra.  Packaged by Screen
Gems (CPT), the serials were programmed between 1957 and 1960
as wraparound segments for cartoons from the Columbia Pictures
library, including the "Color Rhapsodies" (1934-1949) introduced
with Holiday Land (Nov 9, 1934) and the "Fox and the Crow" (1941-
1950) and "Li'l Abner" (1944-1945), two series which debuted with
The Fox and the Grapes (Dec 5, 1941) and Amoozin' but Confoozin'
(Mar 3, 1944).  Emanating live from WNBC, New York, Ruff and
Reddy was hosted for the first three seasons by Jimmy Blaine with
his puppet-bird companions, Rhubarb the Parrot and Jose the Tucan.
When the show returned on the network, September 29, 1962, the
emcee chores were handled by Captain Bob Cottle and his puppets,
Jasper, Gramps and Mr. Answer, who introduced three consecutive
cliff-hanging installments in each show.

Produced between 1957 and 1964 on a budget of $2,700 per
episode, Ruff and Reddy was the third limited animation series made
for television, following Crusader Rabbit and Gerald McBoing-Boing
(q.v.).  A budget- and time-shaving device perfected by Hanna-
Barbera, which allowed mass production of their films, the technique repeated specific body and limb motions against moving
backgrounds to simulate movement and dialogue was expressed by
a simplified numbered system of lip-synchronization.

When Ruff and Reddy was aired in Fall 1957, its only major
competition was endless reruns of about one thousand faded movie
cartoons, programmed on various hosted children's shows.  NBC
opted to use the new films in the same way, dropping them in between live segments where the hosts sold the sponsor's product.
Playing second banana to the live actors, Ruff and Reddy consequently never reached superstardom and Hanna and Barbera soon
realized that if they were going to make a name in TV's formu-
lized world they would have to come up with a new idea.  The result was The Flintstones (q.v.), which sprang forth in 1960 as
an all-cartoon half-hour series.  One of the major contributions of
Ruff and Reddy, however, was to prove the feasibility of low-budget
manufactured animation to fill children's viewing hours, a technique
which launched the studio on its way to become the world's largest
producer of animated entertainment.


SABRINA, THE TEENAGE WITCH

Network History

THE ARCHIE COMEDY HOUR WITH SABRINA, THE TEENAGE
WITCH
Premiere:  September 13, 1969
CBS/Sep 1969-Sep 1970/Saturday 11:00-12:00 AM
Last Program:  September 5, 1970

SABRINA AND THE GROOVIE GOOLIES
Premiere:  September 12, 1970
CBS/Sep 1970-Sep 1971/Saturday 9:00-10:00 AM
Last Program:  September 4, 1971

SABRINA, THE TEENAGE WITCH
Premiere: September 11, 1971
CBS/Sep 1971-Sep 1972/Saturday 11:00-11:30 AM
CBS/Sep 1972-Sep 1973/Saturday 8:30-9:00 AM
CBS/Feb 1974-Sep 1974/Saturday 8:30-9:00 AM
Last Program: August 31, 1974

THE NEW ARCHIE/SABRINA HOUR
Return: September 10, 1977
NBC/Sep 1977-Nov 1977/Saturday 9:30-10:30 AM
Last Program: November 19, 1977

SUPERWITCH
Return: November 26, 1977
NBC/Nov 1977-Jan 1978/Saturday 9:30-10:00 AM
Last Program: January 28, 1978

Syndicated History

THE ARCHIES

Distributor: Vitt Media International/1977-
Executive Producers: Louis Scheimer, Norman Prescott
Producer: Hal Sutherland
Directors: Don Towsley, Lou Zukor, Rudy Larriva, Bill Reed
Company: Filmation Productions/49 films (1969-1972)

Principal Character and Voice

Sabrina                                    Jane Webb

Additional Characters
    Aunt Hilda
    Aunt Zelda
    Cousin Ambrose
    Salem (Sabrina's cat)

THE ARCHIES (1969-1970) See ARCHIES, THE

GROOVIE GOOLIES (1970-1971) See GROOVIE GOOLIES, THE

        Sabrina, the Teenage Witch cast a potent spell for CBS, not
only over her intended juvenile audience, but over the rival networks
as well.  Utilizing the prime time practice of integrating, promoting
and spinning-off new characters from a hit show, the head of daytime programming, Fred Silverman, carefully planned the debut of
the sixteen-year-old sorceress on The Archies (q. v. ).  Introduced
in 1969-1970 on The Archie Comedy Hour, Sabrina was an apprentice wonder-worker who struggled to conceal her magical powers in
order to be just another member of the Riverdale High School gang.
The perky teenager was patterned after the winsome witch from the
hit ABC comedy series, Bewitched* (q. v. ), played by Elizabeth
Montgomery, and was targeted to headline her own series in subsequent seasons.

In the hour-long comedy-variety format, Sabrina appeared
with the Riverdale regulars, Archie, Jughead, Veronica, Betty,
Reggie and Moose, in two of the four eleven-minute cartoons. In
some of her comedies, the young sorceress was supported by a
pair of spell-casting aunts, Hilda and Zelda, a warlock cousin,
Ambrose, and a cat named Salem, that could also summon up an
uncanny trick or two. In "Witch Picnic," Sabrina had a frantic
time at a convention of witches, warlocks and weirdos in Riverdale
Park, also the site of the gang outing. Dematerializing and reap-
pearing at each function, she used her powers to keep the two
groups from meeting. Her attempts to keep her sorcery secret
were the crux of such stories as "Teenage Grundy," "Moose on the
Loose" and "Party Pooper," and Sabrina frequently had to put a
spell on her friends with the incantation, "Fly back and heed this
law, forget everything you saw." Sabrina also appeared as a member of the bubblegum rock group, The Archies, which presented a
big-beat tune and dance-of-the-week between segments.

In 1970-1971, two episodes were coupled with The Groovie
Goolies (q. v.), a new series featuring a group of merry monsters,
tied together with vignettes as Sabrina and the Groovie Goolies.
In new comedies made for 1971-1972, the teenage sorceress starred
in her own half-hour show for three years, one of the most successful Saturday morning series ever. The highest rated children's program in its premiere season, receiving a 54 per cent audience
share, Sabrina spelled a death knell for its highly touted educational
competition, ABC's Curiosity Shop* (q. v.) and NBC's Take a Giant
Step* (q. v.).

NBC tried to bolster its sagging 1977-1978 ratings with
thirteen repeated episodes, initially titled The New Archie/Sabrina
Hour and two months later with the teenager renamed Superwitch,
but the spell was long broken.


## SAMSON AND GOLIATH

Network History
   Premiere:  September 9, 1967
   NBC/Sep 1967-Mar 1968/Saturday 10:30-11:00 AM

YOUNG SAMSON
   NBC/Apr 1968-Aug 1968/Saturday 10:30-11:00 AM
   Last Program:  August 31, 1968

Syndicated History

Distributor:  Taft H-B Program Sales/1969-1979; DFS Program
   Exchange/1979-
Executive Producers/Directors:  William Hanna, Joseph Barbera
Company:  Hanna-Barbera Productions/20 films

Principal Character and Voice

Young Samson                        Tim Matthieson

Samson and Goliath, a teenage lad and his pet dog, contended with despotic fiends and beastly creatures in the comics' tradition of the superhuman transformation formula. Whenever trouble threatened, young Sam raised his wrists, rubbed two gold bracelets together and declared, "I need Samson Power!" Quick as lightning, the namesake of the Hebrew Hercules became the golden-haired titan, Samson, a superhero endowed with great physical strength, and Goliath became a ferocious lion. The stories owed nothing to the Biblical tales; together the pair vanquished such oddball off-shoots of vivid imagination as "The Aurora Borealis Creature," "The Terrible Dr. Desto," "The Idol Rama-Keesh," "The Colossal Coral Creature," "Baron Von Skull" and the "Thing from the Black Mountains."

The program was retitled Young Samson, April 6, 1968, probably because of the analogous series, Davey and Goliath* (q.v.), the syndicated puppet morality plays filmed by Lutheran Television. Along with several other super fantasies, most notably The Birdman/Galaxy Trio (q.v.), the program was dropped after one season when NBC banished its hard-action superheroes in favor of comedy-variety entertainment and replaced by The Banana Splits (q.v.).

## SCHOOLHOUSE ROCK

Network History
   Premiere: January 6, 1973
   ABC/Jan 1973-   /Saturday, Sunday Various AM

Sponsors: General Foods, Nabisco, Kenner Fun Group, others
Executive Producer: Tom Yohe
Producers: Radford Stone, George Russell
Company: Kim & Gifford Animation for Newall & Yohe Productions/37 films, 3 minutes

Schoolhouse Rock began as "Multiplication Rock," a series of short, bouncy educational cartoons designed to supplement elementary school math. Set to toe-tapping music, each film dealt with a separate personality number from "Zero, My Hero" to "Little Twelve-Toes," and turned addition, subtraction, multiplication and division into an easily remembered rhythmic good time. The series was originated by David R. McCall, President of the McCaffrey and McCall advertising agency, New York, because his ten-year-old son could memorize rock-song lyrics readily but was unable to remember the multiplication tables. Similar in concept to the letter and number commercials on Sesame Street* (q.v.), the initial cartoons taught through repetition set to a musical score and vocal by Grady Tate, a sometimes drummer on The Tonight Show (NBC 1954-  ).

Under the umbrella title Schoolhouse Rock a series titled "Grammar Rock" was added September 8, 1973, and on September 7, 1974 came "America Rock," bicentennial-oriented history and government segments developed in consultation with Dr. John A. Garraty. Premiering September 10, 1977, further spots, like

"Rufus Xavier Sarsaparilla," designed to explain graphically the parts of speech, and "Mother Necessity," to illustrate old adages such as "Necessity is the mother of invention," were added. "Science Rock" debuted March 11, 1978 and in 1978-1979 "Body Rock," later changed to "Body Machine," was added.  Many of the series were expanded with new films after their inaugural season, and the segments received over three hundred airings each year.

The spots were seen five times before the hour or half-hour on Saturday morning and twice on Sunday.  A 1975-1976 and 1977-1978 daytime Emmy winner for "Children's Instructional Series," the films were produced by Newall & Yohe Productions, a joint venture with McCaffrey and McCall, owner of Scholastic Rock.  The catchy songs were merchandised by Capitol Records.

## SCOOBY-DOO

### Network History

SCOOBY-DOO, WHERE ARE YOU?
  Premiere:  September 13, 1969
  CBS/Sep 1969-Sep 1970/Saturday 10:30-11:00 AM
  CBS/Sep 1970-Sep 1971/Saturday 12:00-12:30 PM
  CBS/Sep 1971-Sep 1972/Saturday 8:30-9:00 AM
  CBS/Sep 1974-Jan 1975/Saturday 8:30-9:00 AM
  CBS/Jan 1975-Aug 1975/Saturday 10:00-10:30 AM
  CBS/Sep 1975-Aug 1976/Saturday 9:30-10:00 AM
  ABC/Sep 1978-Nov 1978/Saturday 8:00-8:30 AM
  Last Program:  November 4, 1978

THE NEW SCOOBY-DOO COMEDY MOVIES
  Premiere:  September 9, 1972
  CBS/Sep 1972-Sep 1973/Saturday 9:30-10:30 AM
  CBS/Sep 1973-Aug 1974/Saturday 9:00-10:00 AM
  Last Program:  August 31, 1974

THE SCOOBY-DOO/DYNOMUTT HOUR
  Premiere:  September 11, 1976
  ABC/Sep 1976-Nov 1976/Saturday 9:30-10:30 AM

THE SCOOBY-DOO/DYNOMUTT SHOW
  ABC/Dec 1976-Sep 1977/Saturday 9:00-10:30 AM
  Last Program:  September 3, 1977

SCOOBY'S ALL-STAR LAFF-A-LYMPICS
  Premiere:  September 10, 1977
  ABC/Sep 1977-Jul 1978/Saturday 9:00-11:00 AM
  ABC/Jul 1978-Sep 1978/Saturday 9:30-11:30 AM
  Last Program:  September 2, 1978

SCOOBY'S ALL-STARS
  Return:  September 9, 1978
  ABC/Sep 1978-Nov 1978/Saturday 10:00-11:30 AM
  ABC/Nov 1978-May 1979/Saturday 8:00-9:30 AM

ABC/Jun 1979-Sep 1979/Saturday 8:30-10:00 AM
Last Program: September 8, 1979

SCOOBY AND SCRAPPY-DOO
Premiere: September 22, 1979
ABC/Sep 1979-Dec 1979/Saturday 11:30-12:00 AM
ABC/Dec 1979-Sep 1980/Saturday 10:30-11:30 AM
ABC/Sep 1980-Nov 1980/Saturday 9:00-10:00 AM
Last Program: November 1, 1980

SCOOBY'S LAFF-A-LYMPICS
Return: June 21, 1980
ABC/Jun 1980-Sep 1980/Saturday 11:30-12:00 AM
ABC/Sep 1980-Nov 1980/Saturday 10:00-10:30 AM
Last Program: November 1, 1980

THE RICHIE RICH/SCOOBY-DOO SHOW
Premiere: November 8, 1980
ABC/Nov 1980-Sep 1981/Saturday 9:30-10:30 AM

Syndicated History

Distributor (110 films): DFS Program Exchange/1979-
Executive Producers: William Hanna, Joseph Barbera
Producers: Iwao Takamoto (1969-1974), Alex Lovy, Don Jurwich (1976-1980)
Directors: Oscar Dufau, George Gordon, Charles A. Nichols, Ray Patterson, Carl Urbano
Company: Hanna-Barbera Productions/25 films (1969-1971), 24 films, 60 minutes (1972-1974), 32 films, 12 minutes (1976-1977), 48 films, 12 minutes (1977-1979), 17 films (1978-1979), 16 films (1979-1980).

Principal Characters and Voices

| | | |
|---|---|---|
| Scooby-Doo | | Don Messick |
| Shaggy | | Casey Kasem |
| Freddy | (1969-1979) | Frank Welker |
| Daphne Blake | (1969-1979) | Heather North |
| Velma | (1969-1977) | Nicole Jaffe |
| | (1978-1979) | Patricia Stevens |
| | (1979) | Maria Frumkin |
| Scooby-Dum | (1976-1979) | Daws Butler |
| Scrappy-Doo | (1979-    ) | Lennie Weinrib |

LAFF-A-LYMPICS (1977-1978/1980)

Announcers
  Snagglepuss                 Daws Butler
  Mildew Wolf                 Frank Welker

"The Yogi Yahooeys"

Yogi Bear/Huckleberry Hound/

| Hokey Wolf/Blabber/Snooper/ Wally Gator/Augie Doggie/ Quick Draw McGraw/Dixie/ Jinks | Daws Butler |
|---|---|
| Doggie Daddy | John Stephenson |
| Boo Boo/Pixie | Don Messick |
| Grape Ape | Bob Holt |
| Yakky Doodle | Frank Welker |
| Cindy | Julie Bennett |

"The Scooby-Doobys"

| Scooby-Doo | Don Messick |
|---|---|
| Scooby-Dum | Daws Butler |
| Shaggy | Casey Kasem |
| Hong Kong Phooey | Scatman Crothers |
| Jeannie | Julie McWhirter |
| Babu | Joe Besser |
| Dynomutt/Tinker | Frank Welker |
| Blue Falcon | Gary Owens |
| Captain Caveman/Speed Buggy | Mel Blanc |
| Brenda Chance | Marilyn Schreffler |
| Dee Dee Sykes | Verneé Watson |
| Taffy Dare | Laurel Page |

"The Really Rottens"

| Mumbly/Dastardly Dalton | Don Messick |
|---|---|
| Daisy Mayhem | Marilyn Schreffler |
| Sooey Pig/Magic Rabbit | Frank Welker |
| Dread Baron/The Great Fondoo | John Stephenson |
| Orful Octopus/Dinky | Bob Holt |
| Dirty Dalton | Daws Butler |
| The Creeplys | Laurel Page/Don Messick |

DYNOMUTT, DOG WONDER (1976-1978) See DYNOMUTT, DOG WONDER

CAPTAIN CAVEMAN AND THE TEEN ANGELS (1977-1979) See CAPTAIN CAVEMAN AND THE TEEN ANGELS

Scooby-Doo was a chicken-hearted but humorous Great Dane introduced in eerie comedy-mysteries during the superhero purge in the late sixties. In one of the longer-running network cartoon series, the cowardly canine was seen for seven seasons on CBS between 1969 and 1976, and since then regularly on ABC. The premise was enriched by a pair of film editors turned writers, Joe Ruby and Ken Spears, who previously helped launch The Adventures of Gulliver (q. v. ) and The Perils of Penelope Pitstop (q. v. ). A consistent winner in its timeslot, boasting an 11. 6 rating the first season, Scooby-Doo, Where Are You? involved the black-spotted brown dog and four teenage sleuths in supernatural whodunits while traveling throughout the country in their van, "The Mystery Machine."

All-Americanish blond Freddy was the nominal leader, bespectacled brunette Velma was the brains, red-haired Daphne was trouble's target, and unruly brown-haired Shaggy was the bumbling buddy. Afraid even of his own shadow, Scooby-Doo was partnered with the similarly afflicted, squeaky-voiced Shaggy, whose wry comment, "Here we go again!," usually signaled the beginning of some incredible dilemma. Perpetually ravenous, both of them continually consumed copious quantities of food. Reluctant to venture into any spooky setting, the scaredy-cat pooch with the pussy-cat personality had to be summoned by Shaggy's catch-cry "Scooby-Doo, Where Are You?" and bribed with promises of a tasty "Scooby snack."

Typical of the "Let's get out of here" adventure genre, the episodes concerned assorted wrongdoers posing as spectres in foreboding locales and featured humorous chase scenes. Scattered with clues, the mysteries were unraveled through deductive reasoning by Freddy and Velma, with the denouement of the culprit at the close. Scooby and the teenagers unmasked shipping magnate C. L. Magnus, who as Red Beard the Pirate raided his own ships for the insurance money, and the scientist-head of the weather-eye project, Dr. Grimsley, who hijacked experimental planes in the ghostly Bermuda Triangle. In such other episodes as "A Highland Fling with a Monstrous Thing," "Scooby's Chinese Fortune Kooky Caper" and "A Night of Fright Is No Delight," Freddy's repeated aside, "Well gang, that wraps up the mystery," capped the explanation of the clues and the story. The series ended August 7, 1976 on CBS and returned on ABC beginning September 9, 1978.

Between 1972 and 1974, The New Scooby-Doo Comedy Movies continued the format, incorporating caricatured guest stars like Sandy Duncan and Tim Conway, who voiced their own parts in hourlong shows. Don Knotts appeared in a spoof on Mayberry RFD (CBS, 1968-1971), as a policeman who enlisted the gang in solving the mystery of "The Spooky Fog" (Nov 4, 1972). David Jones of The Monkees* (q. v.) was caricatured in "The Haunted Horseman of Haggelthorn Hall" (Dec 2, 1972), about a Scottish Castle whose ghost was scaring away tourists. The Harlem Globetrotters turned up with Scooby-Doo to solve the puzzle of a pirate ship in "Ghostly Group from the Deep" (Nov 25, 1972) and country-western star Jerry Reed appeared in "The Phantom of the Country Music Hall" (Dec 9, 1972). In "Scooby-Doo Meets Laurel and Hardy" (Nov 11, 1972), the comedians were bumbling bellhops, and The Three Stooges were animated in "The Ghost of the Red Baron" (Nov 18, 1972), about an airport haunted by a mysterious plane. Batman and Robin did their schtick in "The Caped Crusader Caper" (Dec 16, 1972), the genie "Jeannie" was featured in "Mystery in Persia" (Sep 15, 1973), the teenage quartet from Speedy Buggy (q. v.) in "Weird Winds of Winona" (Sep 29, 1973), and Josie and the Pussycats (q. v.) in "Haunted Showboat" (Sep 22, 1973).

A new pair of Great Danes was added in the 1976-1977 mysteries for ABC on The Scooby-Doo/Dynomutt Hour, retitled Show when the program was lengthened to ninety minutes. With a voice like Edgar Bergen's Mortimer Snerd, Scooby-Dum was Scooby-Doo's country cousin, whose ineptness helped complicate the action. A flirtatious female, the snow-white Scooby-Dee made her debut as a glamorous movie actress and Scooby-Doo's smitten puppy-love.  Separate segments introduced Dynomutt, Dog Wonder (q. v. ), a fumbling robot sidekick of the superhero, Blue Falcon, that headlined his own program in summer 1978.

The first two-hour Saturday morning cartoon show in network history, Scooby's All-Star Laff-A-Lympics in 1977-1978 contained five components, with twelve-minute reruns of Scooby-Doo from 1976-1977 as the wraparound segments.  Also repeated were the adventures of Dynomutt and a new feature presenting the Stone Age superhero, Captain Caveman and the Teen Angels (q. v. ), another spin-off in March 1980.  A separate half-hour introduced the Laff-A-Lympics, featuring forty-five Hanna-Barbera cartoon characters in comedic athletic competition around the world.  The crazy contests were staged between three teams, "The Yogi Yahooeys" headed by Yogi Bear and Boo Boo, "The Scooby-Doobys" directed by the timid canine and Shaggy, and "The Really Rottens, " a dirty-tricks bunch led by the Dread Baron and shaggy dog, Mumbly.  Sportscasters Snagglepuss the lion and Mildew the wolf described such zany events as air-boat races in swampy Florida and pulling rickshaws in Hong Kong, which awarded the winners points.  The episodes were repeated on Scooby's All-Stars in 1978-1979, trimmed to ninety-minutes with the deletion of Dynomutt and Scooby-Doo repeats and the addition of some new episodes of Captain Caveman. New exploits of Scooby-Doo, Where Are You? were programmed separately between September and November 1978 and thereafter seen on Scooby's All-Stars.

Scooby and Scrappy-Doo premiered in 1979-1980 in a slightly different format, featuring Shaggy partnered with Scooby-Doo and a new doggie cousin, a zealous and feisty little pup.  The instigator of all manner of trouble for the pair in their supernatural mysteries, Scrappy-Doo recklessly attacked all-comers while vocalizing "charge" and howling his catch-phrase, "Puppy Power." In 1980-1981, the episodes were repeated, coupled with the comedies about the world's richest boy and his problems on The Richie Rich/ Scooby-Doo Show (q. v. ).  A turning point, it marked the first time in twelve years that TV's perennial, highly rated canine was reduced to second billing on a Saturday morning show.


SCREEN GEMS THEATRICAL CARTOON PACKAGE

Component Series
    KRAZY KAT, PHANTASIES, SCRAPPY and AESOP'S FABLES,
    CUBBY BEAR, TOM AND JERRY

Syndicated History
    Premire: 1956
Distributor:  Screen Gems--Columbia Pictures Television/1956-
Producers:  Charles Mintz (1931-1940), George Winkler, Frank
    Tashlin, Dave Fleischer, Paul Worth, Hugh McCollum, Henry
    Binder, Ray Katz (1940-1948)
Directors:  Ben Harrison, Manny Gould, Dick Huemer, Sid Marcus,
    Art Davis, Allen Rose, Harry Love, Howard Swift, Bob Wicker-

sham, Alex Lovy, Paul Sommer, Alec Geiss, Frank Tashlin,
Ub Iwerks
Company: Charles Mintz Studios, Screen Gems--Columbia Pictures/
227 B&W films, 5-6 minutes (1930-1946); Van Beuren Studios--
RKO/126 B&W films, 5-6 minutes (1929-1934)

Principal Characters
    Krazy Kat
    Scrappy
    Betty
    Yippy (Scrappy's pet dog)

    Screen Gems Theatrical Cartoon Package included over 350
black-and-white films which were distributed for local programming
into the mid-sixties.  Among the cartoons were two series produced
by Charles Mintz Studios released by Columbia Pictures.  A distributor and entrepreneur, Mintz acquired the rights to the interna-
tionally acclaimed Krazy Kat (Oct 28, 1913), the Hearst newspaper
comic created by George Herriman (1880-1944), and after a silent
series between 1927-1929 he secured distribution through Columbia
at the beginning of the sound era.  Screen Gems syndicated seventy-
five of his films starring "Krazy Kat" (1930-1940), supervised by
Ben Harrison and Manny Gould, redesigned into a cute, round upright character and given a falsetto voice.  An assembly-line series, gags were the main feature of the formula stories, which did
not include Ignatz the mouse or Offissa Pupp except for one film,
Li'l Anjil (Mar 19, 1936), as did the made-for-TV series in the
King Features Trilogy (q. v.).  Instead, Krazy Kat was provided
with a girlfriend and a pet dog, straight from the mold of the early
thirties' hit cartoons starring Walt Disney's Mickey Mouse.  Lacking any identifiable personality traits, the renowned feline's twelve-
year sound career was an exercise in mediocrity.  Mintz's other
cartoon star was a human caricature, "Scrappy" (1931-1941), a
young boy in short pants fathered by Dick Huemer, Sid Marcus
and Art Davis.  Reminiscent of the young curbstone philosopher
Skippy Skinner (KFS, 1920-1943), a newspaper comic conceived by
Percy Crosby (1891-1964), Scrappy appeared in eighty-one films
with childhood themes depicting small children.  A young lad with
rounded features and a disproportionately large head capped by a
forelock, he was paired with his dog, Yippy, and supplied a girlfriend, Betty, and several antagonists, the tots Oopie and Vonsey.
In his premiere, Yelp Wanted (Jul 16, 1931), Scrappy's diagnosis
of his rescued sick Yippy proved false when she delivered a litter
of pups.  An assortment of comedies produced by Screen Gems
like The Gullible Canary (Sep 18, 1942), the seventy-one "Phan-
tasies" (1939-1946) included among the films also featured Scrappy
and Krazy Kat in some of the earlier cartoons.
    The package also contained "Aesop's Fables," "Cubby Bear"
and "Tom and Jerry," two life-like caricatures, distributed since
1947 in the Unity Pictures Theatrical Cartoon Package (q. v.), which
was bought by Screen Gems in 1956.  The in-house cartoon branch
of Columbia between Mintz (1929-1940) and UPA (1948-1959), which
also supplied the studios' theatrical cartoons along with Disney

(1929-1932), Screen Gems was revived in the fifties as the corporation's TV syndication arm. In the late fifties, it became one of the major program suppliers to the networks and the company name was changed in 1974 to Columbia Pictures Television (CPT).

## SEALAB 2020

### Network History
Premiere: September 9, 1972
NBC/Sep 1972-Sep 1973/Saturday 11:00-11:30 AM
Last Program: September 1, 1973
Executive Producers: William Hanna, Joseph Barbera
Producer: Iwao Takamoto
Director: Charles A. Nichols
Company: Hanna-Barbera Productions/13 films

### Principal Characters and Voices

| | |
|---|---|
| Dr. Paul Williams | Ross Martin |
| Captain Mike Murphy | John Stephenson |
| Bobby Murphy | Josh Albee |
| Sallie Murphy | Pamelyn Ferdin |
| Sparks | Bill Callaway |
| Hal | Jerry Dexter |
| Gail | Ann Jillian |
| Ed | Ron Pinckard |
| Mrs. Thomas | Olga James |
| Jamie | Gary Shapiro |
| Tuffy (Gail's pet dolphin) | |

Sealab 2020 was a self-contained city on the ocean floor, an experimental scientific complex in the twenty-first century. The two-hundred and fifty volunteers populating the colony were led by Dr. Paul Williams, a Chinook Indian graduate of the Scripps Institute of Oceanography. Adding to his problems were some unexpected guests: Captain Mike Murphy, his niece and nephew, Sallie and Bobby, and radioman Sparks, who when their ship floundered were rescued by three Sealab aquanauts, Hal, Ed and Gail, and her pet dolphin, Tuffy. Among the newcomers' friends were Mrs. Thomas and her young son, Jamie. Based on current underwater research, the cartoons depicted living conditions and menacing dangers in the futuristic underwater city and stressed marine ecology in such episodes as "The Singing Whale," "The Basking Shark," "The Arctic Story" and "The Deepest Dive."

## SECRET LIVES OF WALDO KITTY, THE

### Network History
Premiere: September 6, 1975
NBC/Sep 1975-Sep 1976/Saturday 9:00-9:30 AM
Last Program: September 4, 1976

Syndicated History

THE GROOVIE GOOLIES AND FRIENDS/THE NEW ADVENTURES
OF WALDO KITTY

Distributor: Metromedia Producers Corporation/1978-
Executive Producers: Louis Scheimer, Norman Prescott
Producer: Richard Rosenbloom
Directors: Don Christensen, Rudy Larriva
Company: Filmation Productions/13 films

Principal Characters and Voices

Waldo/Wetzel/Lone Hench Dog          Howard Morris
Felicia/Pronto/Sparrow               Jane Webb
Tyrone/Mr. Crock/Ping/
   Brennan Hench Dog                  Allan Melvin

The Secret Lives of Waldo Kitty featured a timid cat that
scored derring-do triumphs as a superhero in his animated dream
fantasies. The principals were Waldo and Felicia, a tomcat and
his feline girlfriend, both continually threatened by Tyrone, a bullying bulldog, and his henchdogs. Each week Waldo became one of
five fantasized saviors: that all-around good guy and champion of
justice, Cat Man; the jungle-savvy Catzan of the Apes; the renowned
English folk-hero, Robin Cat; the famous masked rider of the Old
West, Lone Kitty; or Captain Herc of the Starship "Second-prise."
Live animals with voice-overs were used in the opening and closing
scenes, to establish the particular settings in such stories as "The
Lone Kitty Rides Again," "Dr. Livingstone, I Perfume?," "Cat Man
Meets the Puzzler," "Robin Cat" and "Cat Trek."
    The concept and title pun were lifted from James Thurber's
The Secret Lives of Walter Mitty (Mar 18, 1939), published originally in the New Yorker and reprinted by the magazine by specific
request in the writer's last will. A would-be Conradian figure hiding in a three-button suit, Thurber's Mitty was an emasculated,
day-dreaming little man who used the attraction of fantasy as a
release from reality. The story was the subject of a gimmick-
embellished motion picture, The Secret Lives of Walter Mitty
(1947), produced by Samuel Goldwyn and starring Danny Kaye.
Also, the property was loosely adapted for the situation comedy,
My World and Welcome to It (NBC, 1969-1970/CBS, 1972), starring William Windom, which utilized Thurber-like cartoons for the
fantasy sequences.


SECRET SQUIRREL See ATOM ANT/SECRET SQUIRREL SHOW,
   THE

SHAZZAN!

Network History
    Premiere:  September 9, 1967
    CBS/Sep 1967-Sep 1968/Saturday 10:00-10:30 AM
    CBS/Sep 1968-Sep 1969/Saturday 12:00-12:30 PM
    Last Program:  September 6, 1969

Syndicated History

CAPTAIN INVENTORY

Distributor:  Taft H-B Program Sales/1973-1979; Worldvision Enter-
    prises/1979-
Executive Producers:  William Hanna, Joseph Barbera
Producer:  Iwao Takamoto
Director:  Charles A. Nichols
Company:  Hanna-Barbera Productions/18 films

Principal Characters and Voices

| | |
|---|---|
| Shazzan | Barney Phillips |
| Nancy | Janet Waldo |
| Chuck | Jerry Dexter |
| Kaboobie | Don Messick |

    Shazzan! was the magical command that summoned a 60-foot
genie of the same name, who materialized in a cartoon flourish to
serve his young masters.  It began in a cave off the Maine coast
where the young twins, black-haired Chuck and blond-headed Nancy,
found a mysterious chest containing the halves of a strange ring.
When joined, the ring formed the word "Shaz-zan!"  At the mention of the word, the twins were transported back to the fabled land
of the Arabian Nights, to appear in stories based in part on the
Book of the Thousand Nights and a Night (1885-1888) by Sir Richard
Burton.  There they met their giant servant, who presented them
with Kaboobie, a magical flying camel.  The bald-and-bearded
Shazzan was at their beck-and-call whenever they needed him, but
he would not return them home until they delivered the ring to its
rightful owner.  Protected by the genie's wizardry, the teenagers
began their search in the ancient land of Araby on the back of
Kaboobie, the camel muttering expressively and emitting an occasional "arrfle!" or two.  Several club-swinging, one-eyed, green
ogres threatened the youngsters in the "Valley of the Giants," the
gargantuans toying with them like trapped mice.  With the aid of
Shazzan, they also triumphed over the black magic and devil-like
red birds of "The Black Sultan," who had turned Prince Omar into
a green boar.  In "Demon in the Bottle," the twins were imprisoned
in the cavern of Basim, by the sneering turbaned keeper of the
Wazir's ancient curse, before the etheric Shazzan could be conjured
up to recork the Demon in his glass dungeon.  Constantly being
chased or captured in such episodes as "The City of Tombs" and

"The Forest of Fear," the plucky youngsters were menaced by sinister sultans and hideous monsters alike, designed by comic book artist Alexander Toth. Two eleven-minute stories were seen in each program.


## SINBAD JR., THE SAILOR

Syndicated History
   Premiere: 1965
Distributor: American International Television/1965-1979; Film-
   ways Enterprises/1979-
Executive Producers: William Hanna, Joseph Barbera
Producer: Sam Singer
Company: Hanna-Barbera Studios for AIT/130 films, 5 minutes

Principal Characters and Voices

Sinbad Jr.                          Tim Matthieson
Salty                               Mel Blanc

   Sinbad Jr., the Sailor detailed the fanciful exploits of a young boy and his first mate, Salty, a comical talking parrot. Cast as the son of the legendary seafarer, Sinbad Jr., became a superboy through use of a magic belt. The character and stories were freely based on the tall tales of magical adventures spun by Sinbad the Sailor, a merchant seaman in the prodigious Book of a Thousand Nights and a Night (1885-1888) by Sir Richard Burton. Originally titled "The Adventures of Sinbad, Jr.," the series was renamed out of deference to a Japanese feature length cartoon, Adventures of Sinbad ("Shindbad no Boken") produced in 1962 by Taiji Yabushita, Toei Studios, probably the best of the theatrical animated adaptations. A separate made-for-TV series, Adventures of Sinbad (1975-1976) also was produced by Nippon Anima-tion and aired in Japan, which presented some of the Arabian Nights tales and a little hero on a flying carpet. Max Fleischer adapted the character for his first animated Technicolor featur-ette, Popeye the Sailor Meets Sinbad the Sailor (Nov 27, 1936) with Bluto as Sinbad ruling over a remote island. Gene Kelly danced to the music of Rimsky-Korsakov in the animated Sinbad the Sailor sequence from The Magic Lamp (1956), a British film.


## SKATEBIRDS, THE

Component Series
   MYSTERY ISLAND, THE ROBONIC STOOGES, WONDER
   WHEELS, WOOFER AND WIMPER, DOG DETECTIVES

Network History
   Premiere: September 10, 1977
   CBS/Sep 1977-Nov 1977/Saturday 9:30-10:30 AM
   CBS/Nov 1977-Jan 1978/Saturday 8:00-9:00 AM

CBS/Sep 1979-Mar 1980/Sunday 7:30-8:00 AM
CBS/Mar 1980-Aug 1980/Sunday 7:00-7:30 AM
CBS/Sep 1980-Jan 1981/Sunday 8:00-8:30 AM
Last Program: January 25, 1981
Executive Producers: William Hanna, Joseph Barbera
Producer, "Mystery Island": Terry Morse, Jr.
Directors: Hollingsworth Morse, Sidney Miller
Animation Director: Charles A. Nichols
Company: Hanna-Barbera Productions/16 films, 60 & 30 minutes

Principal Characters and Voices

| | |
|---|---|
| Knock Knock | Lennie Weinrib |
| Satchel | Bob Holt |
| Scooter | Don Messick |
| Scat Cat | Scatman Crothers |
| Chester | (non-speaking) |
| Willie Sheeler | Mickey Dolenz |
| Dooley Lawrence | Susan Davis |

Cast

MYSTERY ISLAND

| | |
|---|---|
| Chuck Kelly | Stephen Parr |
| Sue Corwin | Lynn Marie Johnston |
| Sandy Corwin | Larry Volk |
| Dr. Strange | Michael Kermoyan |
| P. A. U. P. S. (voice) | Frank Welker |

THE THREE ROBONIC STOOGES (1977-1978) See THREE
    STOOGES CARTOONS, THE

WOOFER AND WIMPER, DOG DETECTIVES (1977-1981) See
    CLUE CLUB, THE

   The Skatebirds served as wraparound hosts for this packaged
program, binding the elements together with their short sketches,
nonsense and pro-social messages. The costumed feathered friends
were Knock Knock, a colorful woodpecker and jokester, Satch, a
pouch-billed pelican, and a cute little penguin, Scooter, the three
portrayed by Bruce Hoy, Ken Means and Joe Giamalva, who mimed
their roles to a pre-recorded voice track. On roller skates and
sometimes skateboards, the flock cavorted onstage and outdoors
like their forerunners, a quartet of animals known as The Banana
Splits (q. v.). Their particular nemesis was Scat Cat and their occasional champion, Chester, a dumb dog, likewise costumed actors.
Apart from their silly slapstick and two-liners, the Skatebirds delivered various warnings against littering and pollution, ending with
a catchy song stanza, "It's a beautiful world. The solution to pollution ... is keep it clean!"
   Among the cartoon components were a pair of canines who
talked to each other when no one was around, "Woofer and Wimper,

Dog Detectives," the retitled repeats of the Clue Club (q. v.). Also, Larry, Moe and Curly, who operated a junk yard as secret crime-fighters, "The Robonic Stooges," a January 1978 spin-off renamed The Three Robonic Stooges (q. v.).

In the new animated adventures of "Wonder Wheels," two high school newspaper journalists, Willie Sheeler and his girlfriend, Dooley Lawrence, joined an unbelievable motorcycle that had a heroic character all its own. In episodes laced with dialogue straight out of Superman (q. v.), the wall-climbing, soaring super-bike sprang into action at Willie's words, "This looks like a job for Wonder Wheels!" In furious and sometimes comic motorized chase scenes, the remarkable cycle captured escaped convicts and foiled other lawbreakers in the "Gold Train Robbery," "Air Race," "Hermits Horde" and "Vanishing Prince," all to the delight of Dooley, who believed Willie always missed the story because of his absence.

A throw-back to science fiction chapter-plays, "Mystery Island" was the haven of power-mad Dr. Strange in a live action serial. To further his plot to dominate the world, the scientific genius was determined to obtain the memory bank from P. A. U. P. S., a talented computer-robot. Using his "Projector Beam Ray," he forced down the "Nimbus," a small jet piloted by Chuck Kelly which was transporting the electronic brain, the clipped voice of which sounded like William Buckley's. Aboard were an attractive com-puter expert, Sue Corwin, and Sandy, her young brother. The in-stallments involved the efforts of the youngsters to keep themselves and the robot out of the clutches of the malevolent scientist and his thugs, and their narrow escapes from such perils as the "Golden Birds of Prey," "Valley of Fire" and the "Visitors from Falconia."

Trimmed to a half-hour, The Skatebirds was repeated on the Sunday schedule beginning September 9, 1979 with the "Wonder Wheels" and "Mystery Island" segments.


SKYHAWKS

Network History
    Premiere: September 6, 1969
    ABC/Sep 1969-Sep 1970/Saturday 11:00-11:30 AM
    ABC/Sep 1970-Sep 1971/Saturday 11:30-12:00 AM
    Last Program: September 4, 1971
Theme: "The Skyhawks," by Mike Curb and the Curbstones
Executive Producer: Ken Snyder
Producers: Fred Crippen, Ed Smarden
Director: George Singer
Company: Ken Snyder Productions/17 films

Principal Characters and Voices

| | |
|---|---|
| Captain Mike Wilson | Michael Rye |
| Steve Wilson/Joe Conway | Casey Kasem |
| Caroline Wilson | Iris Rainer |
| Baron "Red" Hughes/Pappy | |

| | |
|---|---|
| Wilson | Dick Curtis |
| Cynthia "Mugs" Hughes | Melinda Casey |
| Maggie McNalley | Joan Gerber |
| Buck Devlin | Bob Arbogast |

Skyhawks, Incorporated, offered "wings for hire," an all-purpose air service equipped to handle any lawful task. Owned by widower Cap Wilson, a retired U.S. Air Force pilot, the charter outfit operated out of San Marcos Field, also the home base of his unprincipled rival, Buck Devlin's Air Service. Helping Cap to run the business were his seventeen-year-old twins, Steve and Caroline, who held commercial pilots' licenses, and his two wards, fourteen-year-old Baron "Red" Hughes, an accomplished glider pilot, and nine-year-old Cynthia "Mugs" Hughes, the apple of Pappy's eye. A spry septuagenarian, Pappy Wilson liked to fly his British Sopwith Camel, stubbornly maintaining that old planes were better and safer. A wealthy southern belle, teenager Maggie McNally, had a crush on Steve and took flying lessons from him, hoping to spark a romance. Joe Conway was the Skyhawks' chief mechanic, a retired veteran who had served in the Air Force with Cap and was his close friend.

The airborne adventures emphasized the coordinated and skillful piloting of the trustworthy and reliable Skyhawks, who adroitly handled any emergency in such episodes as "Mercy Flight," "The Search" and "Runaway Ride." The action involved their diverse operations including crop dusting, oil exploration, aerial photography, transporting sky divers, flying dangerous cargo and a daring helicopter rescue at sea. Envious of their success, and in an effort to force the Skyhawks out of business, Devlin stirred up trouble whenever he could, through crafty plots and sabotage, usually after the loss of a lucrative contract to his rivals because of his irresponsible actions. A continuing mystery the suspicious Devlin was unable to unravel was Cap's secret government missions, transporting materials to a hidden research and development site for a national defense project.

Script consultant Clark Howat monitored the technical accuracy for the series, which depicted a variety of actual aircraft drawn to scale.


SMOKEY BEAR SHOW, THE

Network History
   Premiere: September 6, 1969
   ABC/Sep 1969-Sep 1970/Saturday 8:30-9:00 AM
   ABC/Sep 1970-Sep 1971/Sunday 9:30-10:00 AM
   Last Program: September 12, 1971

Syndicated History

Distributor: Worldvision Enterprises/1972-
Executive Producers: Arthur Rankin, Jr., Jules Bass
Company: Rankin-Bass Productions with Toei Animation, Japan/17 films

Principal Characters
  Smokey the Bear
  Smokey the Cub

The Smokey Bear Show starred America's number one fire-
fighter in three sets of sermon-like adventures, two as a grown-up
sandwiching one as a cub.  Toting his trusty shovel over his shoul-
der, the Ranger-hatted bruin preached the need for conservation to
his forest friends, an assortment of smartly dressed and cute animals that appeared in such stories as "Hare versus Cougar," "Ancient Caleb Coyote" and "Hobo Jackal."  The episodes stressed the
importance of wildlife and natural resources to children and demonstrated the do's and don'ts of outings in the wilderness.  The
"Smokey the Cub" segments depicted the fun and hazards encountered when young, as in the "Old Club House" and "High Divin',"
and how the bear became the protector of trees and a symbol of
the U.S. Forest Service.  Each program concluded with an appropriate homily or warning:  "Remember, Smokey's friends don't
play with matches."
     Between 1942 and 1979, Jim Felton served as volunteer
director of the save-the-forests campaign, when the government
turned to Foote, Cone and Belding advertising agency to develop a
public service program.  In 1945, Robert Stahle, a Washington
illustrator, came up with a painting of a scrubby-looking bear that
matured into Smokey.  Later, Felton's fire protection program was
directed at children aged five to twelve, and beginning in 1950
Smokey appeared as its TV spokesman.  It was the only advertising symbol protected by an act of Congress and a royalty was required to use the character, which helped finance other promotions
like the "Give a Hoot, Don't Pollute" campaign championed by
Woodsy Owl.  The live Smokey was a bear cub discovered in 1950
in a burnt out forest of New Mexico's El Capitan Mountains and
was kept at the National Zoo in Washington, D.C., where he died
of old age in the seventies.  His mate was Goldie, but they issued
no heir to continue the living role.  In Macy's 1968 Thanksgiving
Day Parade, Smokey was introduced as a featured balloon.
     As a mechanical puppet, the brown bear was starred in an
hour-long Thanksgiving special on NBC narrated by James Cagney,
named for the title tune, The Ballad of Smokey the Bear (Nov 24,
1966).  Barry Pearl was heard as the voice of Smokey in the General Electric-sponsored musical.  Between 1950 and 1976, Jackson
Weaver was the official voice of Smokey in his radio and TV spots
and on MGM's Leo the Lion album, "Smokey and His Friends."


SPACE ANGEL

Syndicated History
    Premiere:  February 6, 1962
Distributor: TV Comic Strips/1962-1978; ZIV International/1978-
Producer/Director:  Dick Brown
Company:  Cambria Studios/260 films, 5 minutes

Principal Character and Voice

Scott McCloud/Space Angel        Ned Lefebver

       Space Angel was the code name for Scott McCloud, agent for the Interplanetary Space Force, an organization devoted to the security and welfare of the solar system. The science fiction stories were serialized with five installments in each adventure so that they could be stripped on weekdays or strung together for fifty-two weekly half-hour programs. A former National Comics artist, Alexander Toth, served as art director for the films, composed mainly of panel drawings and figures animated by camera movement. Produced between 1961-1964, the series was created by Dik Darley and Dick Brown. The films were combined with a live-action process, Syncro-Vox, invented by Ed Gillette, which superimposed actual moving lips reading the dialogue over the mouth of the characters. The innovation was somewhat distracting and not particularly appealing. It was introduced in Cambria Studios' 1959 series, Clutch Cargo (q. v. ).

## SPACE GHOST AND DINO BOY, THE

Network History
       Premiere: September 10, 1966
       CBS/Sep 1966-Sep 1968/Saturday 10:30-11:00 AM
       Last Program: September 7, 1968

THE SPACE GHOST/FRANKENSTEIN, JR.
       Return: November 27, 1976
       NBC/Nov 1976-Sep 1977/Saturday 11:00-11:30 AM
       Last Program: September 3, 1977

Syndicated History

CAPTAIN INVENTORY

Distributor: Taft H-B Program Sales/1973-1979; Worldvision
     Enterprises/1979-
Executive Producers/Directors: William Hanna, Joseph Barbera
Company: Hanna-Barbera Productions/18 films

Principal Characters and Voices

| | |
|---|---|
| Space Ghost/Narrator | Gary Owens |
| Jayce | Tim Matthieson |
| Jan | Ginny Tyler |
| Dino Boy | (1966-1968) Johnny Carson |
| Ugh | (1966-1968) Mike Road |
| Bronto | (1966-1968) Don Messick |
| Blip (Jayce and Jan's pet monkey) | |

       The Space Ghost and Dino Boy roamed the far-out reaches

of the universe and a mysterious hidden prehistoric valley in three alternating adventures. A black-hooded, yellow-caped, galactic gadabout, Space Ghost's gimmick was "Inviso-power," produced by his "Invisabelt," and his favorite exclamation was "Great Galaxies!" Based on his own ghost planetoid, he rocketed to fearless exploits in his spaceship, "The Phantom Cruiser," could also soar through the heavens independently, and was armed with stun and force rays, and heat, magnetic and energy lasers controlled by "Power Bands" clipped to his wrists. For companions there were a pair of masked-and-caped teenagers, blond-haired Jan and red-headed Jayce, who sometimes flew their own small "Space Coupe" and were accompanied by their pet monkey, Blip. Endlessly, Space Ghost rescued his young friends from hyperthyroid killer creatures of every species and from the clutches of maniacal rulers on alien planets. Constantly in peril, the youngsters braved a giant, green-eyed, red scaly primate controlled by the Creature King, Lokar's hungry space locusts and the Molten Monsters of Moltor. The power-mad Cyclo trapped them in his Maze of Terror with the ferocious Cyclo Terror and threatened the destruction of a helpless planet with his army of Cyclo Sentinels. Together, the trio battled such evil despots as Metallis, the metal monster, the Sorcerer, Iceman, and Space Ghost's arch enemy, the webspinning Black Widow. Sort of a celestial cross between King Features' The Phantom (Feb 17, 1936) and The Spectre, who debuted in More Fun Comics, Number 52 (Feb 1940), the cosmic crusader was created by Alexander Toth, a former National Comics' artist and art director of Space Angel (q.v.). Two episodes of Space Ghost sandwiched Dino Boy in each show.

Called Dino Boy because he rode about on top of a brown-spotted Brontosaurus, nicknamed "Bronto," young Tod was forced to parachute from a disabled plane. Landing in an isolated Stone Age world, the red-headed lad almost became a tasty tidbit for a sabre-tooth tiger. He was saved by an Alley Oop-like giant named Ugh, a caveman who became his friend and protector. Facing frightful danger and in-the-nick-of-time rescue until the scenarios were changed to straight adventure, Dino Boy was captured by the Treemen and offered as sacrifice to a flock of prehistoric vultures, trapped in Horror Swamp and imprisoned by the slimy Worm People, and encountered the Ant Warriors, Wolf People and the Mighty Snow Creature. Also menaced by more human villains, Dino and Ugh were nearly sacrificed by the High Priest of the Sun People, and also fought the Rock Pygmies and the Bird Riders.

From the start, The Space Ghost made a substantial impact on Saturday morning programming and had surprisingly high ratings. Fathered by CBS head of daytime programming, Fred Silverman, and telecast back-to-back with five other superhero cartoons in 1966-1967, the super spectre helped set the new vogue and, predictably, the rival networks joined the parade. With the proliferation between 1966 and 1969 came a flood of protests over the horrific content aimed at tots. Reacting to the second great wave of clamor over children's programs, both CBS and NBC inaugurated a comedy-variety line-up in 1969-1970 in a major readjustment of their schedules. In November 1976, however, NBC reintroduced The Space

Ghost with Frankenstein, Jr. (q. v. ) to replace Land of the Lost*
(q. v. ), abandoning its revised philosophy because of poor ratings.

SPACE GHOST/FRANKENSTEIN, JR., THE See SPACE GHOST
AND DINO BOY, THE and FRANKENSTEIN JR. AND THE
IMPOSSIBLES

SPACE KIDETTES

Network History
 Premiere: September 10, 1966
 NBC/Sep 1966-Sep 1967/Saturday 10:30-11:00 AM
 Last Program: September 2, 1967

Syndicated History

Distributor: DFS Program Exchange/1979-
Executive Producers/Directors: William Hanna, Joseph Barbera
Company: Hanna-Barbera Productions/20 films

Principal Characters and Voices

| | |
|---|---|
| Scooter | Chris Allen |
| Snoopy | Lucille Bliss |
| Jenny | Janet Waldo |
| Countdown/Pupstar | Don Messick |
| Captain Skyhook | Daws Butler |

Space Kidettes joined the race to extraterrestrial adventure
a quartet of junior rangers exploring the cosmic world from their
space-capsule clubhouse. Accompanied by their comical pet dog,
Pupstar, the Kidettes were Snoopy, Jenny, Countdown and Scooter,
their nominal leader. Not unlike those pioneering live-action explorers on Space Patrol* (q. v. ) and Tom Corbett, Space Cadet*
(q. v. ), the youngsters continually ran afoul of menacing phenomena, creatures and humans. During their missions the Kidettes
were threatened by the Cosmic Condors, a laser-breathing Space
Dragon, Moleman and a Space Giant, Mermaid, Witch and Indians
between their visits to the "Space Carnival, " "Haunted Planet" and
"Planet of the Creeps." Surviving it all required the use of stun
guns and laser rays of every sort, plus the cool head and quick
wits of Scooter and his crew. Known as the meanest pirate in the
universe, Captain Skyhook was the arch villain whose cockney voice
characterization by Daws Butler predated his popular swashbuckler,
Cap'n Crunch, the TV cartoon spokesman for Quaker Oats cereal.

SPACE SENTINELS See YOUNG SENTINELS, THE

SPEED BUGGY

Network History
    Premiere: September 8, 1973
    CBS/Sep 1973-Aug 1974/Saturday 11:00-11:30 AM
    CBS/Sep 1974-Jan 1975/Saturday 8:00-8:30 AM
    CBS/Jan 1975-Aug 1975/Saturday 8:30-9:00 AM
    ABC/Sep 1975-Sep 1976/Saturday 11:00-11:30 AM
    NBC/Nov 1976-Sep 1977/Saturday 10:00-10:30 AM
    CBS/Jan 1978-Sep 1978/Saturday 8:00-8:30 AM
    Last Program: September 2, 1978
Executive Producers: William Hanna, Joseph Barbera
Producer: Iwao Takamoto
Director: Charles A. Nichols
Company: Hanna-Barbera Productions/16 films

Principal Characters and Voices

| | |
|---|---|
| Speed Buggy | Mel Blanc |
| Tinker | Phil Luther, Jr. |
| Debbie | Arlene Golonka |
| Mark | Mike Bell |

Speed Buggy behaved like an oversized St. Bernard, in stories that followed the on-and-off-track escapades of a talking supercar. In their anthropomorphic auto, whose mode of expression included such phrases as "who put the anti-freeze in my carburetor, yuk!," teenagers Tinker, Debbie and Mark motored to mystery and adventure throughout the country and in exotic foreign locales. Sputtering his catch-phrase, "Roger-dodger, putt putt," Speed Buggy was driven by red-headed Tinker, whose voice characterization and frequent "Gol-lee" were borrowed from Jim Nabors' popular Private, Gomer Pyle, U.S.M.C. (CBS, 1964-1970). Mark was the cool-headed brain of the trio and Debbie his sometimes brash counterpart who managed a disastrous faux pas or two in each segment. Another animated series in the "Let's get out of here!" genre, "Speedy" and his friends were continually chased by the henchpersons of some diabolical fanatic in a quick-panned slapstick escape scene. In a parody on Ian Fleming's famous character, they tangled on Forbidden Island with Gold Fever, who operated a satellite that was methodically looting the world's gold supply. Reminiscent of Herbie the Volkswagen in Walt Disney's fantasy-comedy, The Love Bug (BV, 1969), but a jeepster style vehicle in a comic book premise, "Speedy" always had a trick or two up his fenders when he ran into "Kingzilla," "Professor Snow and Madame Ice" or "The Incredible Changing Man." When the need arose, the supercar would perform all manner of feats, including flying or cruising beneath the sea to tackle "Captain Schemo and the Underwater City," and with predictability always saved the day. Speed Buggy was the only cartoon series telecast for five consecutive years on all three networks' Saturday schedule, where it was a ratings leader in its time-slot for the first three years.

After the first CBS run ended on August 30, 1975 the program appeared on ABC between September 6, 1975 and September 4, 1976 and on NBC between November 27, 1976 and September 3, 1977, before returning to the original network on January 28, 1978.

## SPEED RACER

Syndicated History
      Premiere:  September 28, 1967
      WPIX, New York/Thursday 6:00-6:30 PM
Distributor:  Alan Enterprises/1967-
Executive Producer:  Tatsuo Yoshida
Producer:  J. Fujita
Director:  Peter Fernandez
Company:  Tatsunoko Productions, Japan/52 films

Principal Characters and Voices

Speed Racer                          Jack Grimes
Spridal/Trixie                       Corinne Orr
Rex Racer/Racer X                    Jack Curtis
Chim Chim (Spridal's pet moneky)

      Speed Racer was a wide-eyed young race-car enthusiast who enjoyed exciting competition around the world.   With the support of his girlfriend, Trixie, his kid brother, Spridal, and his pet monkey, Chim Chim, the youngster entered contests of speed in his "Special Formula Mark Five."  The stories emphasized his driving skills in such exotic locations as the near East, where Speed Racer and his companions fended off plots to steal the one-of-a-kind car and attempts at sabotage by unsavory challengers.   Racer X was Speed's older brother who participated occasionally in the match races, driving "The Shooting Star #9."   The series, one of the more successful Japanese cartoon imports, was dubbed in English for syndication by Zavala-Riss Productions for Trans-Lux Productions.

## SPIDER-MAN

Network History
      Premiere:  September 9, 1967
      ABC/Sep 1967-Aug 1969/Saturday 10:00-10:30 AM
      ABC/Mar 1970-Sep 1970/Sunday 10:30-11:00 AM
      Last Program:  September 6, 1970
Theme:  "Spider-Man," by Bob Harris

Syndicated History

Distributor:  ARP Films/1970-
Executive Producers:  Robert L. Lawrence, Ralph Bakshi
Producer:  Ray Patterson
Directors:  Ralph Bakshi, Ray Patterson, Sid Marcus, Grant Simmons
Company:  Grantray-Lawrence Animation, Krantz Animation for
      National Periodicals/52 films

268 / Spider-Woman

## Principal Characters and Voices

| | |
|---|---|
| Peter Parker/Spider Man | (1967-1968) Bernard Cowan |
| | (1968-1969) Paul Sols |
| Betty Brandt | Peg Dixon |
| J. Jonah Jameson | Paul Kligman |

Spider-Man had the sticky distinction of catching criminals just as a spider does, in a web.  The costumed crusader was the alter ego of orphaned Peter Parker, who lived with his cloying Aunt May.  Peter was an average hung-up college bookworm until he was bitten accidentally by a radioactive arthropod in a physics lab.  Noting that his body had become charged with some fantastic energy, he soon discovered he had super reflexes and strength, could easily climb walls and had the porportionate power and ability of an arachnid.  Deciding to become a crime-fighter and benefit mankind, Parker designed his own red-and-blue, hooded-and-caped outfit with a spider on the chest and his special web weapon.  Then he acquired a position as a freelance newspaper photographer working for J. Jonah Jameson, the irascible publisher of the New York Daily Bugle, where he worked with reporter Betty Brandt.  His job allowed him to be on the scene when danger threatened and to use his secret arachnidal powers to combat such formidable opponents as Voltan and his lightning bolts, Dr. Zap, the Phantom from Space, The Sorcerer, One-eyed Idol, Blotto, Boomer and Nitro, Scorpion, Golden Rhino, the Winged Thing and a howling host of others.  One of the segments introduced "Skyboy," the alter-identity of Jan Caldwell, a professor's son, who derived his superpowers from his father's invention, an "Astro-wave Helmet."

Writer-editor Stan Lee's third feature, Spider-Man debuted in Amazing Fantasy Number 15 (Marvel, Aug 1962), as illustrated by Steve Ditko.  The best known comics' creation of the sixties, the web-slinging superhero soon appeared in his own books, The Amazing Spider-Man, and became Marvel's best-selling title for over a decade.  Conceived as an embodiment of the publisher's philosophy, Spider-Man was a superhuman beset with personal problems, battling for truth, justice and the American way, an anti-hero questioning his motives and the institutions he upheld.

Starring Nicholas Hammond, The Amazing Spider-Man (Sep 14, 1977) was a ninety-minute CBS TV movie, in which the hero helped the police snare a mind-controlling extortionist.  A five-week, prime time series was telecast April 5 through May 3, 1978, followed by some new hour-long episodes and repeats on an irregular basis.

## SPIDER-WOMAN

### Network History
Premiere:  September 22, 1979
ABC/Sep 1979-Dec 1979/Saturday 11:00-11:30 AM
ABC/Dec 1979-Mar 1980/Saturday 11:30-12:00 AM
Last Program:  March 1, 1980

Executive Producers: David DePatie, Friz Freleng
Producer: Lee Gunther
Director: Bob Richardson
Company: DePatie-Freleng Enterprises with National Periodicals/
13 films

## Principal Characters and Voices

| | |
|---|---|
| Jessica Drew/Spider-Woman | Joan Van Ark |
| Jeff | Bruce Miller |
| Billy | Bryan Scott |
| Police Chief | Lou Krugman |
| Detective Miller | Larry Carroll |

Spider-Woman was dedicated to fighting evil and could sling a mean web of justice to ensnare her supernatural foes. Jessica Drew, a reporter for Justice Magazine, was bitten by a poisonous spider in her father's lab and injected with an experimental serum, which saved her life and endowed her with arachnidal superpowers. Like her comic book and TV ancestor Spider-Man (q. v. ), she could cast a strong silk line to swing from tall buildings, but additionally she was armed with a "venom blast" and had an ultra-high arthropod shriek with which she could signal for help. Spinning like a top, Jessica was transformed into the red-masked superwoman in form-fitting red tights with a yellow hour-glass design on her stomach, yellow boots and gloves. Only Jeff, a reporter on the magazine, knew of her secret, which they managed to hide from Billy, her young nephew. Trundling about in the "Justice Jet-Copter, " Spider-Woman was enmeshed with such diabolical fiends as Tomand, ruler of the Realm of Darkness, Dormamu, a hideous green flaming-mask, the Great Magini, the Ghost Vikings, and The Fly.

A product of the seventies' women's movement, Spider-Woman was produced in cooperation with Stan Lee of Marvel Comics, creator of The Amazing Spider-Man.


## SPUNKY AND TADPOLE

### Syndicated History
Premiere: September 6, 1958
WPIX, New York/Monday-Friday 5:30-6:00 PM
Distributor: TV Cinema Sales/1958-1978; ZIV International/1978-
Producer: Beverly Hills Film Corporation
Company: Barrett Films (owner)/150 films, 3 1/2 minutes

### Principal Characters and Voices

| | |
|---|---|
| Spunky | Joan Gardner |
| Tadpole | Don Messick/Ed Janis |

Spunky and Tadpole, a little boy and his come-to-life Teddy Bear, were the central characters in serialized fantasy adventures. The bright young lad and the upright-walking Teddy found excitement

as "Counterspies in Secret Guise" and "The Private Eyes," unraveled the "Secret of Cactus Corners" and the "London Mystery,"
and made a "Moon Trip" and a search for "Buried Treasure."
Ten episodes comprised a complete story and the films could be
programmed also as fifty quarter-hours. Most frequently, the cartoons were stripped weekdays in existing shows and premiered in
this manner on Fun House, hosted by "Officer" Joe Bolton on
WPIX, New York.


STAR BLAZERS

Syndicated History
    Premiere: September 10, 1979
    WNEW, New York/Monday-Friday 7:00-7:30 AM
Distributor: Claster TV Productions/1979-
Producer: Yoshinobu Nishizaki
Director: Reiji Matsumoto
Company: Office Academy, Japan and Sunwagon Productions/52
    films

Principal Characters
    Captain Avatar
    Cadet Derek Wildstar
    Cadet Mark Venture
    Nova
    Dr. Sane
    IQ-9
    Desslok
    Prince Zordar

    Star Blazers was a continuing story about a group of patriots
in the year 2199, on a mission to save Earth from destruction.
While Earth was threatened with extinction by the evil Gamilons,
an alien race led by Desslok, hope existed on Iscandar, a friendly
planet across the galaxy where Queen Starsha promised a device
that would save the world. All Earth had to do was get there.
What resources remained were diverted to build a super spaceship, "Argo," and an elite band of scientists and adventurers was
put together for the flight. Called Star Force, the team was
headed by courageous Captain Avatar ("Admiral Jyuzo Okita" in
the Japanese version), and his idealistic second-in-command,
Derek Wildstar ("Sosumu Kodai"), devoted to the cause and out
to avenge his older brother, Alex, who had been killed by the
Gamilons. On board were his love interest, Nova ("Yuki Moro"),
a pretty radar operator; Mark Venture ("Daisuke Shima"), Chief
of Operations; IQ-9, a robot nicknamed "Tin-Wit" for its sense of
humor; the cyborg Sandor, the Chief Mechanic; and the enigmatic
Dr. Sane ("Dr. Sado"), a physician tending the ailing Captain.
Later allies included Nox, a rescued space marine; Gideon, Captain of the "Andromeda," the flagship of the Earth Defense Fleet;
and Trelaina, Venture's romantic interest who lived on the planet
Telezart. During their perilous journey, Star Force battled the

forces of Desslok and his various henchmen, Krypt, Volgar, Bane and General Lysis, his top commander and a cunning opponent. In the last twenty-six episodes, Desslok was joined in the fight against Star Force by Prince Zordar, satanic ruler of Empire City, which was constructed to resemble a comet; Princess Invidia, his daughter; Dira, the second-in-command; and Naska, commander of Zordar's reconnaissance squadron. Featuring elaborate animation, intricate plots and romantic sub-plots, the space saga was notable for its imaginative spaceships, cosmic conflicts and effects.

Originally appearing in a comic book by artist Reiji Matsumoto titled Space Battleship Yamato, ("uchū senkan yamato"), the spacecraft was based on the Japanese Navy ship "Yamato," built before the Second World War. The stories transferred the Pacific to outer space as the battleship gunned its way through enemy fleets to Iskandar. The cartoon version debuted in 1974 and became one of the most popular animated series ever shown on Japanese television. It was revived on Nippon TV after the success of Star Wars (TCF, 1977), and a second series followed with the re-edited feature film, Space Cruiser Yamato, distributed in the United States in 1978. A third series, Yamato: The New Voyage, began Japanese TV serialization in 1980. The prior TV films were purchased by the Westchester Corporation, re-edited and redubbed and leased to Claster TV Productions for American distribution. Seen in first run in 1979-1980 in about thirty markets, Star Blazers was not particularly successful.


STAR TREK

Network History
    Premiere:  September 8, 1973
    NBC/Sep 1973-Dec 1973/Saturday 10:30-11:00 AM
    NBC/Jan 1974-Aug 1974/Saturday 11:00-11:30 AM
    NBC/Sep 1974-Aug 1975/Saturday 11:30-12:00 AM
    Last Program:  August 30, 1975

Syndicated History

Distributor:  Paramount TV Sales/1977-
Producers:  Louis Scheimer, Norman Prescott
Director:  Hal Sutherland
Company:  Filmation Productions with Norway Productions and
    PAR-TV/22 films

Principal Characters and Voices

| | |
|---|---|
| Captain James T. Kirk | William Shatner |
| Science Officer Spock | Leonard Nimoy |
| Dr. Leonard McCoy | DeForest Kelley |
| Chief Engineer Montgomery | |
|    Scott | James Doohan |
| Nurse Christine Chapel | Majel Barrett |
| Lieutenant Uhura | Nichelle Nichols |
| Mr. Sulu | George Takei |

Star Trek continued the intergalactic journey of the Federation Starship "U.S.S. Enterprise" in graphic form, featuring the familiar likenesses and voices of the original crew. The cartoons were adapted from the prime time space adventure, Star Trek (NBC, 1966-1969), created and produced by Gene Roddenberry in association with Paramount Television, the first adult science fiction series with continuing characters. Captain James T. Kirk commanded the spaceship, supported by Vulcan Science Officer, Mr. Spock, Chief Medical Officer Leonard "Bones" McCoy, Engineering Officer Montgomery "Scottie" Scott, Nurse Christine Chapel, Communications Officer Uhura, and Helmsman Sulu. With a complement of over four hundred the huge battle cruiser traveled in various "warp drives" at speeds in excess of light, and was armed with Phasers and Photon Torpedoes. Crew members were "beamed down" from the spacecraft's transporter room to their planetary adventures through "dematerialization" and "re-materialization."

The stories took place two hundred years in the future, during a five-year interstellar voyage of the "Enterprise," assigned to explore strange new worlds and seek out new life and new civilizations--"to boldly go where no man has gone before." The exceptional scripting was supervised by associate director Dorothy Fontana, Roddenberry's story editor, who selected some of the original writers, Stephen Kandel, Margaret Armen, David P. Harmon and Paul Schneider. Fontana penned the premiere, "Yesteryear," in which Spock had to return to Vulcan before his "death" to reweave the threads of history. Walter Koenig, seen as Ensign Pavel Chekov in the live-action films, wrote "The Infinite Vulcan," also featuring Spock, who was cloned into an immortal giant by Dr. Keniclius 5. The warlike Romulians and Klingons were still the arch enemies of The Federation. Millionaire space trader Carter Wilson was actually a treacherous reincarnated Vendorian and Romulian spy, capable of assuming any shape or identity. As Captain Kirk he ordered the Starship into The Federation-Romulian neutral zone, thereby inviting an attack. The devious Klingons aboard their battle cruiser "Klothos," led by the Romulian Xerius, once succeeded in planting a bomb on the "Enterprise."

The crew was involved with the seductive women from Taurean and the pirates from Orion and became victims of the deadly Saurian virus on Dramia. In alternate world themes they visited the Lilliputian city on Terratin in the Cepheus system and the demon-hunting Puritan-like civilization of the Megans on Megas-Tu. And there were the usual bug-eyed monsters designed by artists Bob Kline and Herb Hazelton. On the largely water-covered planet Argo, they were attacked by an enormous sea creature and imprisoned by the Aquans, captured and put in a zoo by the wormlike slugs on Lactra VII, and with Ensign Dawson Walking Bear placed in a private menagerie by the Mayan-Aztec god Kulkukan, a winged serpent. Additional anthropomorphic encounters occurred with the cat-like people on Kzin in the Beta Lyrae system and the lizard men on Delta Theta III, in the company of Commander Ari bn Bem, the green rascal from Pandro. The interstellar con-man, Harvey Mudd, voiced by Roger C. Carmel, hawked a fake love potion, necessitating his rescue from some angry miners in the

Acadian star system.   In "More Tribbles, More Troubles," sales-
man Cyrano Jones reappeared, transporting more furry purring
critters.   But this time they did not rapidly proliferate; they just
enlarged themselves to 200 pounds.

"Trekkie" fan-zines by the dozen and clubs by the score
still revel in the enchantment of both programs.   One of the very
few animated series so recognized, Star Trek received a daytime
Emmy in 1975 as an outstanding children's entertainment series.
It was produced on a budget of $75,000 per episode, and the con-
flicting schedules of the actors required that segments of the sound
track be recorded in locations all over and later re-edited together.
Don Christensen served as art director.   There was lavish merchandising of spin-off gadgetry and paraphernalia, the items ranging
from model kits of the "U.S.S. Enterprise" to Tribbles, the furry
round extraterrestrials that purred until their batteries died.   Roddenberry produced the movie Star Trek (PAR, 1979), based on the
live-action TV series, and the first re-usable orbiting spacecraft,
used for atmospheric testing in 1981, was named the "Enterprise"
by President Gerald Ford.

The series found legion acceptance and high ratings after its
syndication in 1977.


SUPER GLOBETROTTERS  See  HARLEM GLOBETROTTERS, THE


SUPER PRESIDENT AND SPY SHADOW

Network History
    Premiere:   September 9, 1967
    NBC/Sep 1967-Sep 1968/Saturday 9:30-10:00 AM
    NBC/Sep 1968-Dec 1968/Saturday 12:30-1:00 PM
    Last Program:   December 28, 1968
Executive Producers:  David DePatie, Friz Freleng
Company:  DePatie-Freleng Enterprises/15 films

Principal Characters
    James Norcross/Super President
    Richard Vance/Spy Shadow

Voices
    Ted Cassidy
    June Foray
    Paul Frees
    Shepard Menken
    Don Menken
    Don Messick
    Lorrie Scott
    Mark Skor


Super President and Spy Shadow were the contrived efforts of
insipid imaginations, a pair of superheroes in three adventures drawn
from the human transformation comic book formula.   In the episodic

wraparound cartoons, Super President was the alter-identity of James Norcross, Chief Justice of the United States, who secretly possessed incredible mental and protean powers. Showered with mysterious chemical particles during a cosmic storm, Norcross discovered he was able to change his molecular structure at will into any gaseous or solid form. In his guise as the crusading patriot, Super President, he battled enemies of the country too tough for regular law enforcement or military agencies, ranging from "The Electronic Spy," "Toys of Death" and the "Red Ray Raiders" to the "Monster of the Atoll," "Birds of Terror" and "The Cosmic Gladiators."

The sandwiched feature was Spy Shadow, a reworked theme borrowed from the earlier syndicated TV cartoon series, Q. T. Hush (q.v.). A private detective, Richard Vance was sometimes at odds with his own shadow, which operated independently, when out to solve such mysteries as "The Kilowatt Killer Caper," "The Mystery Rustler Caper," "The Aurora Borealis Business" and "The Case of the Treacherous Tugboat."

Arriving during the avalanche of superhero shows, Super President was a denigrating concept and in questionable taste for a children's audience. The focus of particularly sharp criticism, the program was terminated by NBC in mid-season of the second year, along with The Birdman/Galaxy Trio (q.v.), despite the fact that it cost more than $750,000 to junk them. In the purification prompted by the public clamor, the network switched its Saturday programming largely to a comedy-variety format in 1969-1970.


SUPER SIX, THE

Component Series
    SUPER BWOING, SUPER SERVICES, INC.

Network History
    Premiere:  September 10, 1966
    NBC/Sep 1966-Aug 1969/Saturday 9:00-9:30 AM
    Last Program:  August 31, 1969
Executive Producers:  David DePatie, Friz Freleng
Directors:  Hawley Pratt, Art Davis, Art Leonardi, Dave Detiege
Company:  DePatie-Freleng Enterprises with Mirisch-Rich TV
    Productions/26 films

Principal Characters
    Elevator Man
    Granite Man
    Magneto Man
    Super Stretch
    Brothers Matzoriley
    Super Bwoing

Voices
    Daws Butler
    Pat Carroll

June Foray
Paul Frees
Joan Gerber
Arte Johnson
Lynn Johnson
Diana Maddox
Charles Smith
Paul Stewart

The Super Six were a half-dozen crime-fighters for hire, working for The Super Services Incorporated.   In their assignments, each of the heroes applied his own transformable talents to the task at hand.   Making up the agency complement were Elevator Man, Granite Man, Magneto Man, Super Stretch and the Brothers Matzoriley.   Disguised as a guitar-playing performer, Super Bwoing was a gumshoe hero in the tradition of Don Adam's Maxwell Smart in Get Smart (NBC/CBS 1965-1970), appearing in his own separate action adventures.

## SUPERFRIENDS

Network History
    Premiere:   September 8, 1973
    ABC/Sep 1973-Sep 1974/Saturday 9:00-10:00 AM
    ABC/Sep 1974-Aug 1975/Saturday 11:00-12:00 AM
    ABC/Feb 1976-Sep 1976/Saturday 10:00-11:00 AM
    ABC/Dec 1976-Sep 1977/Saturday 11:30-12:00 AM
    Last Program:   September 3, 1977

THE ALL-NEW SUPERFRIENDS HOUR
    Premiere:   September 10, 1977
    ABC/Sep 1977-Jul 1978/Saturday 8:00-9:00 AM
    ABC/Jul 1978-Sep 1978/Saturday 8:30-9:30 AM
    Last Program:   September 2, 1978

CHALLENGE OF THE SUPERFRIENDS
    Premiere:   September 9, 1978
    ABC/Sep 1978-Nov 1978/Saturday 9:00-10:00 AM
    ABC/Nov 1978-May 1979/Saturday 9:30-11:00 AM
    ABC/Jun 1979-Sep 1979/Saturday 10:00-11:30 AM
    Last Program:   September 15, 1979

THE WORLD'S GREATEST SUPERFRIENDS
    Return:   September 22, 1979
    ABC/Sep 1979-Sep 1980/Saturday 8:00-9:00 AM
    Last Program:   September 27, 1980

THE SUPERFRIENDS HOUR
    Return:   October 4, 1980
    ABC/Oct 1980-Sep 1981/Saturday 8:00-9:00 AM

Executive Producers:   William Hanna, Joseph Barbera

Producers: Iwao Takamoto (1973-1975), Don Jurwich (1977-1980)
Directors: Charles A. Nichols, Ray Patterson, Carl Urbano
Company: Hanna-Barbera Productions/16 films, 60 minutes (1973-1975), 15 films, 60 minutes (1977-1978), 16 films, 60 & 90 minutes (1978-1979), 8 films, 60 minutes (1979-1980).

Narrators
Ted Knight (1973-1977)
Bob Lloyd (1977-1978)
Bill Woodson (1977-1978/1979-1980)
Stanley Ross (1978-1979)

Principal Characters and Voices

| | | |
|---|---|---|
| Superman | | Danny Dark |
| Batman | | Olan Soulé |
| Robin | | Casey Kasem |
| Wonder Woman | | Shannon Farnon |
| Aquaman | (1973-1978) | Norman Alden |
| | (1978-1980) | Bill Callaway |
| Marvin/Wonder Dog | (1973-1975) | Frank Welker |
| Wendy | (1973-1975) | Sherry Alberoni |
| Zan/Gleek | (1977-1980) | Mike Bell |
| Jayna | (1977-1980) | Louise Williams |
| Computer | (1978-1979) | Casey Kasem |
| Black Vulcan | (1978-1979) | Buster Jones |
| Samurai/Flash/ Hawkman | (1978-1979) | Jack Angel |
| Apache Chief/Green Lantern | (1978-1979) | Michael Rye |

LEGION OF DOOM (1978-1979)

| | |
|---|---|
| Luthor | Stan Jones |
| Brainiac/Black Manta | Ted Cassidy |
| Toyman | Frank Welker |
| Giganta | Ruth Forman |
| Cheeta | Marlene Aragon |
| Riddler | Mike Bell |
| Captain Cold | Dick Ryal |
| Sinestro | Vic Perrin |
| Scarecrow | Don Messick |
| Bizzaro | Bill Callaway |
| Solomon Grundy | Jimmy Weldon |
| Grodd the Gorilla | Stanley Moss |

Superfriends donned their gaudy costumes as colleagues against crime, engaged in derring-do battles with hideous crackpots and supernatural creatures. A revolutionary comic book concept, the innovative approach was introduced by D. C. Comics (NP), which pioneered the superhuman fantasy with Superman (q. v. ) and followed with Batman and Robin (q. v. ). Assembling an all-star team of the publisher's characters, artist Sheldon Mayer and writer

Gardner Fox put eight superheroes in a single adventure as the
"Justice Society of America" for All-Star Comics (Winter 1940),
dropping some and adding others before the feature died in February 1951.  In February 1960, the idea was revived by Fox as
the "Justice League of America" in Brave and Bold Number 28.
While the members changed frequently, the regulars became
Superman, Batman and Robin, Wonder Woman, The Flash and
Aquaman (q.v.), who made their animated "Justice League" debut
in 1967-1968 on CBS on The Superman/Aquaman Hour of Adventure (q.v.).  With the exception of The Flash, the five characters
formed the initial Superfriends on ABC between 1973 and 1975,
adding the teenagers, Marvin and Wendy, The Wonder Twins, and
their canine marvel, Wonder Dog.  United at the Hall of Justice,
Washington, D.C., the Superfriends were called upon "to fight injustice, right that which is wrong and serve all mankind."

Out of necessity, the plotting for so many characters adhered to a basic formula.  Each episodic half-hour of the sixty-
minute show found the Superfriends gathered for an introductory
scene at the great Hall, then singly or teamed sent out on a specific mission, sometimes temporarily incapacitated by their foes,
but finally reunited to triumph in the finale.  In "Dr. Pelagian's
War," built around pollution, Superman, Batman and Robin with
Wonder Woman flew off separately to admonish three industrial-
ists who were poisoning the seas in their concern over the threats
of Pelagian, the alias of Professor Ansel Hilbrand, a marine biologist and engineer.  Aquaman swam off to locate the fanatic's
headquarters, but meantime Marvin and Wendy were accidentally
trapped aboard his submarine, "The Sprite," and sent Wonder Dog
for help.  In the climax, the superheroes each destroyed a tidal
wave aimed at a seashore factory created by Pelagian, and with
Aquaman rallied to save The Wonder Twins and resolve the crisis.
Other arch villains included "The Weather Maker," "The Fantastic
Frerts," "The Watermen," "The Androids" and "The Balloon People," whose stories also incorporated pro-social values approved
by psychologist Dr. Haim Ginott, an educational advisor.  The
sixteen shows were repeated in 1976-1977, re-edited with different
episode combinations.

Revived as "the most powerful forces of good ever assem-
bled, dedicated to truth, justice and peace for all mankind," The
All-New Superfriends Hour in 1977-1978 included four stories in
each hour-long program.  The regular champions returned with
Zan and Jayna as The Wonder Twins, a new pair who looked sus-
piciously like the Osmonds, the network's Donny and Marie (ABC,
1976-1979).  Accompanied by their pet monkey, Gleek, the teenagers, endowed with protean powers, were able to assume any form
by placing their magic rings together.  Several minority members
also made guest appearances:  Black Vulcan, who stunned his enemies with electric charges; Samurai, an oriental muscle-man;
Apache Chief and, in single episodes, El Dorado and Rima, the
Jungle Queen.  These newcomers were teamed with the regulars;
for instance, Rima and Wonder Woman rescued a missing scientist
in "The River of Doom."  Three episodes of the teamed Superfriends were augmented by one with the League of Justice, which

added The Flash, Hawkman and Green Lantern. Different combinations of the superheroes were involved with such supernatural foes as the "Mysterious Time Creatures," "The Water Beast," "The Lion Men," "The Mummy of Nazca" and "The Mind Maidens." Between components the regulars dispensed health and safety tips, simple craft ideas and "Superfriends Decoder Clues," which invited viewers to participate in the solution through deductive reasoning.

Thirteen of the most sinister villains dedicated to conquering the universe appeared in half-hour episodes in 1979-1980 on Challenge of the Superfriends. Drawn from the comic book pages, the League of Justice adversaries were gathered from remote galaxies at the Hall of Doom, located beneath a primeval swamp. Led by the brilliant evil genius Luthor, Superman's particular nemesis, the Legion of Doom included The Riddler, Captain Cold, Sinestro, Bizarro, Solomon Grundy, Cheeta, Black Manta, Toyman, Scarecrow, Grodd the Gorilla, the computer-android Brainiac and the feminine but ferocious Giganta. The League regulars with Black Vulcan, Hawkman, Green Lantern, Samurai, Apache Chief and The Flash dared to challenge their schemes of despotic domination, two of more members becoming involved with several of the Legion's arch fiends in each show. Among their heroic feats they destroyed Luthor's "Dream Machine" and "Growth Ray," that created the Giants of Doom, and triumphed over his surrogates, the three-headed Thirian invaders from Venus and Lord Darcon and his Demons from the planet Exxor. Repeats of the old and New Superfriends episodes expanded the program to sixty and ninety minutes. Reruns and eight new episodes constituted The World's Greatest Superfriends in 1979-1980 and The Superfriends Hour in 1980-1981 repeated the 1977-1980 episodes, also incorporating safety tips.

Posing the real challenge for tots was the horde of characters, which made it difficult to keep up with the rotated good-guys and bad-guys. And if the large cast was not confusing enough, while Batman and Robin were active in the League of Justice on ABC, their earlier cartoons with Batgirl were rerun on Saturday morning on CBS between 1978 and 1980 as part of Tarzan and the Super 7 (q.v.) and in 1980-1981 on NBC as Batman and the Super 7 (q.v.).


SUPERMAN

Syndicated History

THE ADVENTURES OF SUPERMAN
    Premiere: March 26, 1956
    WABD, New York/Monday-Friday 6:00-6:30 PM

SUPERMAN/AQUAMAN/BATMAN

Distributor: UM&M-TV, Flamingo Telefilm Sales/1956-c1966; Warner Brothers Television (New)/1970-

Network History

THE NEW ADVENTURES OF SUPERMAN
  Premiere: September 10, 1966
  CBS/Sep 1966-Sep 1967/Saturday 11:00-11:30 AM
  CBS/Sep 1969-Sep 1970/Saturday 1:00-1:30 PM
  Last Program: September 5, 1970

THE SUPERMAN/AQUAMAN HOUR OF ADVENTURE
  Return: September 9, 1967
  CBS/Sep 1967-Sep 1968/Saturday 11:30-12:30 PM
  Last Program: September 7, 1968

THE BATMAN/SUPERMAN HOUR
  Return: September 14, 1968
  CBS/Sep 1968-Sep 1969/Saturday 10:30-11:00 AM
  Last Program: September 6, 1969
Executive Producers: Max Fleischer (1941-1942), Seymour Kneitel
  (1942-1943), Allen Ducovny (1966-1968)
Producers: Louis Scheimer, Norman Prescott (1966-1968)
Directors: Dave Fleischer (1941-1942), Isadore Sparber, Dan Gor-
  don (1942-1943), Hal Sutherland (1966-1968)
Company: Fleischer-Famous Studios for Paramount Pictures/17
  films, 6 minutes (1941-1943); Filmation Studios for Ducovny
  Productions and National Periodicals/26 films (1966-1968)

Narrator
  Jackson Beck

Principal Characters and Voices

Clark Kent/Superman                              Bud Collyer
Lois Lane                                      Joan Alexander
Superboy                            (1966-1968) Bob Hastings
Krypto (Superboy's superdog)

       Superman, the king and father of the comic book super-
heroes, made his TV cartoon debut in a syndicated series, ten
years before his CBS shows.  The local station appearances were
over-shadowed by the widely popular live-action series, The Adventures of Superman* (q. v. ), which was introduced in 1953 and
by 1956 had become one of the favorite programs in the nation.
Striking a balance between realistic animation and graphic fantasy,
the films were six-minute shorts made by Fleischer and Famous
Studios for Paramount Pictures between 1941 and 1943, adapted
just a few years after writer Jerry Siegel and artist Joe Shuster
penned their first D. C. Comics' adventure for Action Comics Number 11 (Jun 1938).  Portions of the embryo legend story were presented in the first film, Superman (Sep 26, 1941), about an orphan
from the planet Krypton who rocketed to Earth as a babe endowed
with an awesome array of superhuman powers.  As an adult he
battled crackpots, criminals and injustice, masking his true identity in the guise of Clark Kent, mild-mannered reporter for the

Metropolis Daily Planet, where his co-worker was Lois Lane.
Hewing to the familiar formula, emphasizing weird, larger-than-
life foes and futuristic equipment, in The Billion Dollar Limited
(Jan 9, 1942) Superman rescued a passenger train as it plummeted
off a trestle, grabbed both ends of a disconnected wire to let electrical power flow through his body in Magnetic Telescope (Apr 24,
1942), and used his X-Ray vision to find Lois trapped inside one of
the Mechanical Monsters (Nov 21, 1941).  Subsequent entries during
the Second World War concentrated largely on foreign saboteurs,
secret agents and underground activities, and themes like The Mummy Strikes (Feb 19, 1943) and Jungle Drums (Mar 26, 1943).  The
seventeen films were part of a short-subject package sold by Paramount in 1955.  They first appeared in Spring 1956 on Captain
Video's Cartoons (WABD, 1956-1957), hosted weekday evenings by
the Master of the Universe, Al Hodge.  By that Fall they were
telecast in about fifty cities, beginning September 6, 1956 on KHJ,
Los Angeles at 8:15-8:30 PM PST, Thursday, and were withdrawn
before the new episodes premiered.
    Promoted by Fred Silverman, head of CBS daytime program-
ming, The New Adventures of Superman arrived in 1966-1967 as one
of six superhero cartoons slotted back-to-back on Saturday mornings,
launching the super-fantasy craze.  Two episodes sandwiched another
featuring "Superboy," which introduced a teenage version of the all-
powerful human and his caped, flying superhound, Krypto.  Constantly falling into the clutches of some evil-doer, Lois Lane was on
hand to provide grist for the plots.  Among the new foes were Merlin, the malevolent Mummy, an abominable Ice Man, the Black
Knight, Mr. Mist and Image Maker, assorted aliens from distant
planets like the Tree Men from Abora, Mermen from Enos and
Luminians, and such hypertrophied animals as the Octopod, killer
bees, a deep sea dragon and various simians.  Drawn from the
comics were some of Superman's more renowned antagonists, Toyman, the computer-android Brainiac, the impish prankster from
the fifth dimension, Mr. Mxyzptlk, and the warped scientific genius
and arch fiend, Lex Luthor, who was seen in six episodes.
    The last segments were created in 1967-1968 for The Super-
man/Aquaman Hour of Adventure, which alternated four components
and introduced other National Comics' characters and Aquaman
(q. v. ).  The cartoons were repeated in 1968-1969 on The Batman/
Superman Hour (q. v. ) and rerun again separately in 1969-1970.
Lasting for twenty-eight years as the newspaper comic Superman
(McClure Syndicate, 1939-1967), the adventures were continued in
eight different comic books on sale in thirty countries and written
in fifteen languages.  Also continuing in both live-action and animated films in syndication, Superman is the most enduring of all
comic book superheroes, in print and on television.  As a cartoon
star, Superman also guested on The Brady Kids (q. v. ) and appeared as one of the Superfriends (q. v. ).


SUPERWITCH  See  SABRINA, THE TEENAGE WITCH

## SYLVESTER AND TWEETY

Component Series
FOGHORN LEGHORN, PORKY PIG, SPEEDY GONZALES, others

Network History
    Premiere: September 11, 1976
    CBS/Sep 1976-Sep 1977/Saturday 8:00-8:30 AM
    Last Program: September 3, 1977
Executive Producer: Hal Geer
Directors: Bob Clampett, Friz Freleng (1942-1962)
Company: Warner Brothers Television/13 films (1949-1962)

Principal Characters and Voices

Sylvester P. Pussycat/
    Tweety Pie                          Mel Blanc
Granny                                  Bea Benaderet/June Foray

    Sylvester and Tweety, the classic cartoon cat and canary,
were repackaged from the post-1948 Warner Brothers theatrical
film library.  Previously relegated to supporting roles, actually
Sylvester P. Pussycat and Tweetie Pie had provided fun and hilar-
ity for viewers since 1960 as components of series starring Bugs
Bunny (q. v. ).  Later recognized for his acclaimed puppet show,
Time for Beany* (q. v. ), and its animated spin-off, Cecil and Beany
(q. v. ), director Bob Clampett was one of the prime creative minds
behind the birth of the pair.  He first featured the babyish yellow
bird in several films, including A Tale of Two Kitties (Nov 21,
1942) and Birdie and the Beast (Aug 19, 1944), followed by the
oafish lisping tomcat in Kitty Kornered (Jun 8, 1946).  Helping to
mold their distinct comic personalities, Clampett contributed the
catch lines "Sufferin' Succotash!" and the near immortal "I tawt I
taw a putty tat!, " the signature cry of the series and title of a
popular record by Mel Blanc, the common voice of the characters.
Director Friz Freleng resurrected Tweety, changed his design and
paired him with Sylvester in Tweety Pie (May 3, 1947), a 1947
Oscar-winner.  With occasional exceptions, thereafter Tweety was
seen exclusively with Sylvester, although the cat was paired with
other characters and in one series Robert McKimson gave him a
pint-size son named Junior, beginning with Pop 'im Pop (Oct 28,
1950).
    Based on a standard format, developed to its zenith by
Chuck Jones for The Road Runner (q. v. ), the cartoons followed the
progressive maniacal determination of the spluttering Sylvester,
ever obsessed with hopes of a tasty meal, with a half-dozen funny
plots topping each other in intensity and ingenuity in his hapless
attempts to devour the tempting caged canary.  Often the brunt of
his own schemes, the black-and-white tomcat was always outwitted
by the prissy bird, sometimes with the aid of Butch the Bulldog.
And the addition of a kindly old woman named Granny provided another obstacle for the cat.  Particularly memorable was another
Oscar-winner, Birds Anonymous (Aug 10, 1957), in which Sylvester

underwent a crash course similar to the methodology of Alcoholics Anonymous and promised to swear off eating his fine feathered friends. Driven by uncontrollable hunger, which made him imagine every dish a roasted succulent bird, his primeval urge soon reasserted itself, only to be frustrated time and again by the wily Tweety Pie, whose wide-eyed innocence masked a character as resourceful and ruthless as Bugs Bunny's.

The filler cartoons for the series included Porky Pig, Foghorn Leghorn, Speedy Gonzales, Hippety Hopper, the kangaroo and other Warner Brothers characters. In 1980-1981, Sylvester appeared as the TV cartoon commercial spokesman for Nine Lives Cat Food.

## TARZAN, LORD OF THE JUNGLE

Component Series
   THE FREEDOM FORCE, MANTA AND MORAY, SUPER
   STRETCH AND MICRO WOMAN, WEBWOMAN, BATMAN AND
   ROBIN, JASON OF STAR COMMAND

Network History
   Premiere: September 11, 1976
   CBS/Sep 1976-Nov 1976/Saturday 9:30-10:00 AM
   CBS/Nov 1976-Sep 1977/Saturday 10:00-10:30 AM
   Last Program: September 3, 1977

THE BATMAN/TARZAN ADVENTURE HOUR
   Return: September 10, 1977
   CBS/Sep 1977-Nov 1977/Saturday 11:00-12:00 AM
   CBS/Nov 1977-Aug 1978/Saturday 10:30-11:30 AM
   Last Program: September 2, 1978

TARZAN AND THE SUPER 7
   Premiere: September 9, 1978
   CBS/Sep 1978-Sep 1979/Saturday 10:30-12:00 AM
   CBS/Sep 1979-Aug 1980/Saturday 12:30-1:30 PM
   Last Program: August 30, 1980

THE TARZAN/LONE RANGER ADVENTURE HOUR
   Premiere: September 6, 1980
   CBS/Sep 1980-Feb 1981/Saturday 12:30-1:30 PM
   CBS/Mar 1981-Jun 1981/Saturday 10:00-11:00 AM
   CBS/Jun 1981-Sep 1981/Saturday 11:00-12:00 AM
   Last Program: September 5, 1981
Executive Producers: Louis Scheimer, Norman Prescott
Producer: Don Christensen
Directors: Ed Friedman, Marsh Lamore, Gwen Wetzler, K.
   Wright, Lou Zukor
Company: Filmation Productions/22 films (1976-1978), 16 films,
   90 minutes (1978-1980), 16 films, 60 minutes (1980-1981)

Principal Characters and Voices

Tarzan                                     Robert Ridgely
Nkima (Tarzan's monkey)

MANTA AND MORAY (1978-1980)

Manta                                      Joan Van Ark
Moray                                      Joe Stern

SUPER STRETCH AND MICRO WOMAN (1978-1980)

Chris/Super Stretch                        Ty Henderson
Christy/Micro Woman                        Kim Hamilton
Trouble (Stretch and Micro's Dog)

WEBWOMAN (1978-1980)

Kelly Webster/Webwoman                     Linda Gray
Spinner (Webwoman's pet)

THE FREEDOM FORCE (1978-1980)

Isis                                       Diane Pershing
Hercules                                   Bob Denison
Merlin/Super Samurai/Sinbad                Mike Bell

BATMAN AND ROBIN (1978-1980)  See  BATMAN AND ROBIN

JASON OF STAR COMMAND (1978-1979)  See  JASON OF STAR
    COMMAND*

Tarzan, Lord of the Jungle, swung from the familiar vine
into fantastic civilizations in his first animated cartoons.   The
legend of the brawny hero was based on background created by
Edgar Rice Burroughs (1875-1950) and initially serialized in All
Story Magazine (Oct 1912).   Orphaned as an infant when his parents died in Africa, the animated Tarzan was native-born and
raised by a she-ape named Khala, who taught him the ways of the
wild.   Partnered only with a spider monkey, Nkima, the apeman
shared the friendship and trust of all jungle animals, summoned
his creatures with a shrill oscillating yell and used his animal
cunning and strength to protect the ecology and others who came
to the jungle.   Most of the loinclothed white man's exploits happened in lost cities and hidden empires where he championed the
cause of justice and good versus oppression.   In order to free the
Waspons, Tarzan had to solve the mystery of "The Beast in the
Iron Mask" in the lost land of Paluton, ruled by the King's evil
twin brother.   The apeman liberated the athlete slaves of Emperor
Chronos in the concealed city of Olympus, fought the crocodile,
Luxor, in the despotic land of Queen Neuvia, dethroned King Aga,
an unscrupulous ivory poacher seeking the graveyard of the elephants, and freed the Tantors from toilsome captivity in the tree-

top mines of the Spider People. With six new films, the episodes were combined with reruns of The New Adventures of Batman (q. v. ) for an hour-long show in 1977-1978.

In 1978-1979, Tarzan and the Super 7 served wherever duty called, in the jungle, city, ocean or skies and even outer space, in a ninety-minute package which was reduced to sixty minutes the following season. Eight new Tarzan episodes and reruns were mixed with some new components. A pair of finny teenagers, "Manta and Moray, Monarchs of the Deep," turned up in such super humane aquatic causes as saving whales from Japanese whalers, who in turn needed rescuing themselves. "Super Stretch and Micro Woman" were black superpersons. Chris could turn himself into rubber or any elastic form he desired and Christy could shrink herself to germ size. With their dog, Trouble, they wandered into a bayou to find the Swamp Beast, actually a Jekyll and Hyde changeabout named Professor Morris, who was conducting ecology experiments, and foiled Granny Candy's sweet caper to take over every corporate computer in the country. One of their more unsavory foes was "The Phantom of the Sewers."

Of more substance was Kelly Webster, who was endowed with the power of all insects throughout the galaxy as "Webwoman." Guided by the wisdom of Scarab, her mentor from a distant planet, and assisted by her furry little partner, Spinner, Webwoman battled evil in all its many forms. Two were the lunatic dictator of the Earth's inner core, Dr. Abyss, who nearly subjugated the surface world by activating volcanoes, and Madame Macabre, who ran the best sideshow menagerie in the universe, exhibiting grotesque denizens from other worlds. Unmasking the Madame as a hideous hag with ugliness in her heart, Webwoman spun pro-social messages like, "The only true beauty is inner beauty."

From the Valley of Time, home of "The Freedom Force," came the superheroes Isis, goddess of elements; Merlin, master of magic; Sinbad, hero of the seven seas; Super Samurai, the young boy Toshi, who became a giant of justice; and mounted on the white flying-horse Pegasus, the world's mightiest man, Hercules. They used their powers singly or combined in fantasy adventures, one time aiding Egyptian King Ros overcome the sorcerer Toth, lord of "The Plant Soldiers."

Also introduced was the space serial, Jason of Star Command* (q. v. ), a fine mix of derring-do and dastardly villains, miniatures and model-animated aliens, which was later accorded its own timeslot. The crime crusades of Batman and Robin (q. v. ) were repeated, and with the exception of Jason and Tarzan, the elements were repackaged for NBC in 1980-1981 as Batman and the Super 7 (q. v. ).

In eight new jungle adventures mixed with the old, Tarzan returned in 1980-1981 with the second series of animated tales starring The Lone Ranger (q. v. ), as the perennial swinger preserving the ecological balance of his habitat and protecting its inhabitants from interlopers, poachers and renegades.

One of the most widely known characters in English fiction, Burroughs' noble jungle savage appeared in twenty-six novels starting with Tarzan and the Apes (1914) and a long succession of continuing graphic features. In Burroughs' ape language, "white skin," Tarzan was among the first comic strips to tell a consecutive adventure story, beginning January 7, 1929 for the Metropolitan Newspaper Service (UFS), and the first to appear in modern comic books, initially under the title Tip Top (Apr 1936). The author's son-in-law, Jim Pierce, first voiced the role on radio in 1932, in what is regarded as the earliest major syndicated broadcast series, and was followed by Carlton KaDell, and in 1952 on CBS by Lamont Johnson. A licensed trademark, "Tarzan" products have multiplied rapidly, all authorized by ERB Incorporated, which owns all rights to the property. In American films, Ron Ely became the fifteenth actor to portray the adult apeman in the TV series, Tarzan (NBC 1966-1968/CBS 1969).


TELECOMICS

Syndicated History
    Premiere: 1949
Distributor: Vallee Video/1949-

Network History

NBC COMICS
    Premiere: September 18, 1950
    NBC/Sep 1950-Mar 1951/Monday-Friday 5:00-5:15 PM
    Last Program: March 30, 1951
Sponsor: Standard Brands
Company: Vallee Video

Principal Characters
    Danny March
    Eddie Hale/Kid Champion
    Johnny
    Mr. Do-Right (Johnny's dog)
    Horace "Space" Barton, Jr.

    Telecomics resembled the early practice of televising the Sunday newspaper funnies, the camera slowly panning the strip-art panels sequentially. The syndicated black-and-white film series was distributed beginning in 1949, presenting the adventures of "Joey and Jug," "Sa-Lih," "Brother Goose," and "Rick Rack, Special Agent." After the series was picked up for network telecasts as NBC Comics, four new features were created in serialized three-minute episodes for the fifteen-minute program.
    An orphaned son of a Yale man, "Danny March" was raised by his unprincipled uncle in Metro City, where he became one of the toughest kids in town. Rejected for the police force because he was too short, he built a reputation as a tenacious private eye and was hired by the Mayor as his personal detective. "Kid Champion" was a prize fighter, son of a former boxing champ, and wanted to pursue a musical career. After innocently nearly killing a gas station attendant during a holdup, he dropped his

name, Eddie Hale, called himself "Kid," and teamed up with Lucky
Skinner, a hard-luck fight manager. "Johnny and Mr. Do-Right"
followed the escapades of a young boy and his dog.

The most popular of the four features was "Space Barton."
Born Horace Barton, Jr., in a plane over Kansas, "Space" was the
son of a pilot, an all-American college football star, enlistee in the
Army Air Corps during the Second World War, and was chosen to
test the first U.S. jet plane. With Professor Dinehart, an astron-
omer, they built a rocket ship and blasted off for Mars with his kid
brother, Jackie, as a stowaway. For most of his exploits, "Space"
was engaged in a civil war on the red planet, pitted against a fac-
tion led by a deranged scientist from Earth who had preceded him.

After the network run ended, the films were again syndicated
as Telecomics to local stations, seen initially at 8:00-8:15 AM,
weekdays on WCBS, New York in 1952-1953.


TENNESSEE TUXEDO AND HIS TALES

Component Series
THE KING AND ODIE, THE HUNTER, TOOTER TURTLE, THE
WORLD OF COMMANDER McBRAGG, YAP AND BALDY

Network History
Premiere: September 28, 1963
CBS/Sep 1963-Sep 1966/Saturday 9:30-10:00 AM
ABC/Sep 1966-Dec 1966/Sunday 4:30-5:00 PM
Last Program: December 17, 1966

Syndicated History

Distributor: Filmtel International/1967-1979; DFS Program Ex-
change/1979-
Producers: Treadwell Covington, Peter Piech
Company: Leonardo TV Productions with Total TV Productions/56
films

Principal Characters and Voices

| | |
|---|---|
| Tennessee Tuxedo | Don Adams |
| Chumley | Bradley Bolke |
| Professor Phineas J. Whoopie | Larry Storch |
| Yap/Baldy/Commander McBragg | Kenny Delmar |

Tennessee Tuxedo and His Tales was one of the first humorous educational cartoons introduced in the wake of FCC Chairman
Newton R. Minow's 1961 "vast wasteland" speech. An engagingly
self-important little penguin, Tennessee, and his pal, Chumley, a
wacky walrus, busied themselves with absurd mechanical and financial projects to improve their environment at the Megalopolis Zoo.
No matter what the project, their endeavors required consultation
with their educated friend, Phineas J. Whoopie. Using elementary
illustrations on a blackboard and film clips, the Professor taught

the pair about basic scientific principles involved in the operation of
a block-and-tackle or the operation of a hot air balloon, in such
nine-minute stories as "Scuttled Sculpture," "Hot Air Heroes," "The
Bridge Builders," "Lever Levity" and "Rocket Ruckus." Continually
troublesome to Stanley Livingston, the fussy, exasperated curator,
and his oafish assistant, Flunky, their grandiose schemes, abetted
by the nincompoop, Chumley, who never fully grasped the rudimentary principles, somehow managed to go awry.

The supporting comedies were repeats from the 1960-1963
NBC series King Leonardo and His Short Subjects (q. v.). "The
King and Odie" were a lion and skunk, the ruler of Bongo Congo
and his right-hand man, fending off plots by Itchy Brother, his
blood relative and the pretender, and his treacherous accomplice
Biggy Rat. A southern bloodhound and private eye who sounded
like Kenny Delmar's Senator Beauregard Claghorn, "The Hunter"
relentlessly pursued the ace con-man, The Fox. A resident of
The Great Forest, "Tooter Turtle" continued his fantasy exploits
through the sorcery of Mr. Wizard the Lizard.

Later programs introduced several adventures of "Yap and
Baldy," a long-horned steer, and an American Eagle, partnered
in episodes like "Smilin' Yak's Sky Service." And in 1966, the
series added the ninety-second installments of "The World of Commander McBragg," a retired naval officer and graduate of H. E. X.
University. In the over-stuffed surroundings of his trophy-laden
library, McBragg spun Baron Münchausen-style yarns about his
feats in "The Himalayas," "Okefenokee Swamp," "Khyber Pass"
and at "The North Pole."

After the network run, Tennessee Tuxedo was repackaged
several times with different components for syndication, lastly
substituting "Klondike Kat" from Go Go Gophers (q. v.) for
"The Hunter."

## THESE ARE THE DAYS

Network History
    Premiere: September 7, 1974
    ABC/Sep 1974-Aug 1975/Saturday 12:00-12:30 PM
    ABC/Sep 1975-Sep 1976/Sunday 11:00-11:30 AM
    Last Program: September 5, 1976
Executive Producers: William Hanna, Joseph Barbera
Producer: Iwao Takamoto
Director: Charles A. Nichols
Company: Hanna-Barbera Productions/16 films

Principal Characters and Voices

| | |
|---|---|
| Martha Day | June Lockhart |
| Kathy Day | Pamelyn Ferdin |
| Ben Day | Andrew Parks |
| Danny Day | Jackie Haley |
| Grandpa Jeff Day | Henry Jones |
| Homer | Frank Cady |

These Are the Days chronicled the experiences of a family growing up in small-town America at the turn of the century. Owing something more than a nodding appreciation to the successful clannish drama, The Waltons (CBS, 1972-1981), the domestic comedies depicted the trials and joys of life in Elmsville, where Grandpa Jeff Day owned the Day General Store. The other Days were his daughter-in-law Martha, a widow, her three children, Kathy, Ben and young Danny, and his friend, Homer. Story consultant Myles Wilder and story editor Ed Jurist kept the scenarios void of crime or violence, concentrating on the pastimes and problems of the youngsters in such episodes as "Danny's Musical Dilemma," "Kathy's Job," "How Ben Was Cowed" and "Danny Runs Away." But the folksy homespun stories were not overly appealing to young viewers accustomed to hard-action cartoons, and the sentimental series lasted only one season on its Saturday morning schedule.

THING, THE  See  FLINTSTONES, THE/FRED AND BARNEY MEET THE THING

THINK PINK PANTHER  See  PINK PANTHER, THE

THREE ROBONIC STOOGES, THE  See  THREE STOOGES, THE

THREE STOOGES, THE

Syndicated History

THE NEW THREE STOOGES
    Premiere: December 20, 1965
    WBKB, Chicago/Monday-Friday 7:00-7:30 PM CST
Distributor: Video-Media, Peter Rodgers Organization/1965-

Network History

THE SKATEBIRDS/THE ROBONIC STOOGES
    Premiere: September 10, 1977
    CBS/Sep 1977-Nov 1977/Saturday 9:30-10:30 AM
    CBS/Nov 1977-Jan 1978/Saturday 8:00-9:00 AM
    Last Program: January 21, 1978

THE THREE ROBONIC STOOGES
    Return: January 28, 1978
    CBS/Jan 1978-Sep 1978/Saturday 8:00-8:30 AM
    CBS/Sep 1979-Mar 1980/Sunday 7:00-7:30 AM
    CBS/Feb 1981-Mar 1981/Sunday 8:00-8:30 AM
    CBS/Mar 1981-Sep 1981/Sunday 8:30-9:00 AM
    Last Program: September 6, 1981
Theme: "Three Blind Mice"
Executive Producers: William Hanna, Joseph Barbera (1977-1978)

Producers: Norman Maurer, Dick Brown (1965)
Director: Charles A. Nichols (1977-1978)
Company: Cambria Studios with Normandy III Productions/156
    films, 7 minutes (1965); Hanna-Barbera Productions with Norman
    Maurer Productions/16 films (1977-1978)

Principal Characters and Voices

| Moe | (1965) Moe Howard |
| | (1977-1981) Paul Winchell |
| Larry | (1965) Larry Fine |
| | (1977-1981) Joe Baker |
| Curly | (1965) Joe De Rita |
| | (1977-1981) Frank Welker |
| Triple O | (1977-1981) Ross Martin |

The Three Stooges were animated for two different series,
continuing the slapstick antics of the comic movie team whose two-
reelers became widely popular on television in the late fifties.  Co-
owned by producer Norman Maurer and the actors, principally Moe
Howard, who for a time survived his partners, The New Three
Stooges was produced and syndicated in 1965.  Voicing their own
self-likenesses were Moe, the chief Stooge with the Beatle haircut,
Larry Fine, with hair resembling a fright wig, and the chubby,
nearly bald Joe De Rita, the last actor to play Curly.  With an
unnerving disregard for plot, the comedies placed the Stooges in
different settings, ranging from a sunny California beach to the
Spanish Main, where they were buccaneers, utilizing their screen
personalities and interaction to provide humor.  Moe's ineffectual
leadership developed into a satire of the rough-shod dictator, Curly
suggested an oversized infant, and Larry was sort of a reality
bridge between the others.  The sight gags remained: Curly's
pratfall, Larry's pie in the face, combined with a good round-
house chase and a knock or two on the noggin.  The actors also
appeared in live-action wraparound segments, as the madcap forerunners of The Monkees* (q. v. ) and The Banana Splits (q. v. ),
racing around the beach in their "Penguin" amphibious vehicle, or
the desert in dune buggies.
    Although Moe, Larry and Curly had been slapping each other
around since Soup to Nuts (Fox, 1930), their broad comedy did not
translate as well in this cartoon format as in their short films for
Columbia Pictures.  While the films could be strung together as 52
half-hour shows, and premiered in this manner on WBKB, Chicago,
the series achieved only nominal exposure, at its peak in about
forty markets.  Yet The New Three Stooges inspired imitations of
their voices for a number of other cartoon characters, particularly
that of Curly, and were the second animated TV "personalities"
following The Beatles (q. v. ).
    Incarnated as the world's most perfect androids, The Robonic
Stooges returned in Fall 1977 on CBS as a segment of The Skatebirds (q. v. ).  Built from the world's finest electronic parts, Moe,
Larry and Curly became manufactured superheroes, faster than a
speeding locomotive, able to leap tall villains in a single spring,

and with the power to stretch their limbs to near infinity.  The
wacky trio operated out of their secret cover, a junk yard garage,
and were summoned to action by their boss, Mr. Triple "O. "
They were assigned such missions as retrieving stolen rockets and
thwarting the wicked plans of scoundrels like Mr. Toy Ploy, who
was out to filch all the toys in the world in "There's No Joy in an
Evil Toy," and were up against such meanies as "Super Kong,"
"Rip Van Wrinkle," "Mother Goose on the Loose" and "Blooper-
man. "  Beginning in January 1978, two of the fantasies were the
wraparounds for the mystery adventures of "Woofer and Wimper,
Dog Detectives," the shortened, retitled and repeated episodes of
The Clue Club (q. v. ), in their half-hour series, The Three Robonic
Stooges.
        The second cartoon series arrived two years after the death
of Moe Howard (1895-1975) and Larry Fine (1911-1975), the last
original members of the trio, whose live-action films remained in
syndication as The Three Stooges* (q. v. ).


THUNDARR, THE BARBARIAN

Network History
    Premiere:  October 4, 1980
    ABC/Oct 1980-  /Saturday 10:30-11:00 AM

Executive Producers:  Joe Ruby, Ken Spears
Producer:  Jerry Eisenberg
Director:  Rudy Larriva
Company:  Ruby-Spears Enterprises/13 films

Principal Characters and Voices

Thundarr                         Robert Ridgely
Princess Ariel                   Nellie Bellflower
Ookla the Mok                    Henry Corden


        Thundarr, the Barbarian, roamed a cataclysmic Earth two
thousand years in the future, an oppressive world of savagery,
super science and sorcery.  Born the slave of Sabian, one of the
evil wizards of the new land, Thundarr had a soul for freedom,
ran afoul of his master and was imprisoned.  Freed by the wizard's stepdaughter, Princess Ariel, an educated beauty with some
of the magic talents of her stepfather, Thundarr led his fellow
slaves in rebellion.  Ariel also provided him with the Sunsword,
an energy weapon capable of slicing through almost anything and
parrying bolts of energy.  Carried on his magnetized metal cuff,
it looked like a common sword handle, but when the force beam
leaped from the hilt it cracked like thunder, flashed like lightning,
and became an awesome weapon.  During the insurrection, Thundarr met his fast and loyal friend, the ape-like Ookla the Mok, a
powerful mutant that spoke in grunts and growls.  Near-human in
intelligence, but baffled by all things mechanical, Ookla was also
the source of comic relief.  Mounted on steeds, the three com-

panions journeyed to bizarre locales, often among familiar twentieth-
century ruins, crawling with life, strange people and beasts, mutants and monsters, and ruled by wizards using secrets of ancient
technologies, parapsychology and magic in a barbarous era.
  Time and again Thundarr rushed into the middle of some
battle to free a slave or rescue a hostage.  Pitting his strength
and courage against the forces of evil, the barbarian and his companions tangled with incredible primitive creatures, among them
hordes of rat men, lizard men and men-apes led by Simian, who
was trying to reconstruct a huge robot from the past.  In the "Den
of the Sleeping Demon," the plucky trio rescued Tork, leader of
the glider people, from Judag's mutants mounted on devil dogs, and
in the "Brotherhood of Night," saved local tribes from a pack of
werewolves led by the village chief, Zeevon, who were out to make
themselves invincible by converting the wizard, Furniss, into one of
their kind.  Adding a touch of realism in the mind-boggling world
were the grim stories, which concentrated on the dangerous situations that challenged the heroes.
  Perhaps the most accomplished of all comic book creators,
long-time National Periodicals' artist Jack Kirby, recognized as the
comic book king, served as the graphic director, with an assist
from artist Alexander Toth.  Writer Steve Gerber was story editor.
With the exception of NBC's short-lived version of Flash Gordon
(q. v.) and perhaps CBS's Tarzan, Lord of the Jungle (q. v.), the
program came closer to capturing the spirit of heroic science fiction fantasy than any TV cartoon series since the late sixties.


TIN TIN

Syndicated History
  Premiere: January 2, 1971
  WABC, New York/Saturday 8:00-9:00 AM
Distributor:  Tele-Features/1971-
Company:  Tele-Hachette, Paris/7 films, 60 minutes or 102 films,
  5 1/2 minutes

Principal Characters
  Tin Tin
  Snowy

    Tin Tin, who sported an upright tuft of hair on top of his
head, was a wandering teenage reporter engaged in fantasy-world
exploits.  An animated adaptation of the acclaimed comic strip by
Hergé, pseudonym of Georges Rémi, the most famous of all Euro-
pean cartoonists, Tintin first appeared in 1929 in Le Petit Vingtième, the weekly supplement of the Belgian daily Le Vingtième
Siècle.  Beginning with Tintin in the Land of the Soviets (1930),
twenty-two books were published between 1930 and 1976 and seven
of the works were made into animated films.  Produced in France
between 1961 and 1964, and later dubbed in English, the re-edited
five-and-one-half-minute installments were titled The Adventures
of Tin Tin and the half-hour and hour programs as Hergé's Adven-

tures of Tin Tin or simply, Tin Tin. In this latter fashion, the
series appeared in first-run syndication on WABC, New York as an
hour-long program from January through August 1971.
    Always accompanied by his faithful fox-terrier, Snowy
("Milou" in Belgian), in the American premiere, Secret of the Unicorn (1960), Tin Tin was involved with kidnappers and the irascible
rum-guzzling Captain Haddock, skipper of the old pirate ship,
"Karaboudjan." In scenarios that ranged from detective mysteries
to adventures in outer space, other memorable characters the
youngster had to deal with included the identically attired, klutzy
twin gumshoes, Thomson and Thompson ("Dupont" and "Dupond"),
the absent minded and deaf Professor Calculus, and the incurable
conspirator General Alcazar. They appeared in such films as
Crab with the Golden Claw (1961), Star of Mystery (1961), Red
Hacham's Treasure (1962), Black Island (1962), Objective Moon
(1962) and The Calculus Case (1964). Also a stage play and a pair
of live-action movies, Tin Tin's books were translated into thirty
languages, six of which were published in the United States by
Golden Press.


TOM AND JERRY

Component Series
    GRAPE APE, MUMBLY, DROOPY

Network History
    Premiere: September 25, 1965
    CBS/Sep 1965-Sep 1966/Saturday 11:00-11:30 AM
    CBS/Sep 1966-Sep 1967/Saturday 1:00-1:30 PM
    CBS/Sep 1967-Sep 1972/Sunday 7:00-7:30 AM
    Last Program: September 17, 1972

THE NEW TOM AND JERRY/GRAPE APE SHOW
    Premiere: September 6, 1975
    ABC/Sep 1975-Sep 1976/Saturday 8:30-9:30 AM
    Last Program: September 4, 1976

THE TOM AND JERRY/GRAPE APE/MUMBLY SHOW
    Premiere: September 11, 1976
    ABC/Sep 1976-Nov 1976/Saturday 8:00-9:00 AM
    Last Program: November 27, 1976

THE TOM AND JERRY/MUMBLY SHOW
    Return: December 4, 1976
    ABC/Dec 1976-Sep 1977/Saturday 8:00-8:30 AM
    Last Program: September 3, 1977

THE TOM AND JERRY COMEDY SHOW
    Premiere: September 6, 1980
    CBS/Sep 1980-Feb 1981/Saturday 8:30-9:00 AM
    CBS/Mar 1981-Sep 1981/Saturday 8:00-8:30 AM

## Syndicated History

Distributor (1940-1967 films): MGM Television/1977-
Executive Producers: Chuck Jones, Les Goldman (1965-1967);
   William Hanna, Joseph Barbera (1975-1977); Louis Scheimer,
   Norman Prescott (1980-1981)
Producers: Iwao Takamoto (1975-1977), Don Christensen (1980-
   1981)
Directors: William Hanna, Joseph Barbera, Gene Deitch, Chuck
   Jones, Ben Washam, Abe Levitow, Tom Ray, Jim Pabian (1940-
   1967), Charles A. Nichols (1975-1977)
Company: Tower 12-MGM Animation, Visual Arts/263 films, 6-8
   minutes (1940-1967); Hanna-Barbera Productions/48 films, 12
   minutes (1975-1977); Filmation Productions/11 films (1980-1981)

## Principal Characters and Voices

| | | |
|---|---|---|
| Tom/Jerry | (1940-1967/ 1980-    ) (non-speaking) | |
| | (1975-1977) John Stephenson | |
| Droopy | (1949-1958) Bill Thompson/Don Messick/ Daws Butler | |
| | (1980-    ) Frank Welker | |
| Barney Bear | (1948-1954) Billy Bletcher/Paul Frees | |
| | (1980-    ) Frank Welker | |
| Spike | (1948-1957) Bill Thompson/Daws Butler | |
| | (1980-    ) Frank Welker | |
| Slick | (1980-    ) Frank Welker | |

MUMBLY (1976-1977)

| | |
|---|---|
| Mumbly | Don Messick |
| Shnooker | John Stephenson |

THE GRAPE APE (1975-1976) <u>See</u>  GREAT GRAPE APE, THE

   Tom and Jerry, the world famous characters in a continuing
cat-and-mouse game, renewed their animated chase on television
beginning in 1965.   Perfectly matched for the fast-paced action and
ricocheting pizzazz which characterized their theatrical films, the
mute pair were dubbed as MGM's "Gold Dust Twins" in sparkling
testimony to their box-office success.   During their theatrical heyday, their continual motion and rapid-fire sight gags quickly established Tom and Jerry as the superstars of the studio's cartoon
division, where they were created and refined by artists William
Hanna and Joseph Barbera under producer Fred Quimby.   The unnamed little mouse was first afforded an opportunity to get even
with his bullying nemesis, a moon-faced cat called Jaspar, in Puss
Gets the Boot (Feb 10, 1940).   An enormous hit, the cartoon soon
mushroomed into a series and ousted Walt Disney from the Motion
Picture Academy Awards list, monopolizing the cartoon Oscars with
seven awards for Yankee Doodle Mouse (1943), Quiet, Please (1945),
The Cat Concerto (1947), The Little Orphan (1948), Two Mouseke-

teers (1951), Johann Mouse (1952) and Mouse Trouble (Dec 22, 1944), the only film in which Tom spoke, exclaiming "I don't believe it!" Apart from the 113 films directed by Hanna and Barbera and released between 1940 and 1958 by MGM, Gene Deitch made thirteen cartoons in 1961-1962 for the studio in Prague, Czechoslovakia, and between 1963 and 1967 Chuck Jones and Les Goldman produced 34 films, which were incorporated in the first of the three network series.

On CBS between 1956 and 1972, Tom and Jerry was a repackaged program with new wraparounds featuring two of their cartoons sandwiching others drawn from the MGM library. Among them were such favorites as Jerry's Cousin (Apr 7, 1951), which introduced Tuffy, the mouse's muscular relative, and Quiet, Please (Dec 22, 1945), in which the pair became involved with a new neighbor, a bulldog named Spike, joined in later films by his son, Tyke. In their new films, Tom and Jerry were redesigned by Jones and though the cartoons were slicker but not as funny as the originals, they were still some of the most impressive ever seen on television, labeled with clever titles like Much Ado About Mousing (1964), Of Feline Bondage (1965), The Cat's Me-Ouch (1965), Puss 'n' Boats (1966) and A-Tominable Snowman (1966). The constant pantomime premise was that of a gentle little mouse, minding his own business, until he was picked on by the cat and had to protect himself. The producers re-edited many of the vintage theatrical films, for instance replacing Mammy-Two-Shoes, a black stereotype, with an Irish housemaid voiced by June Foray. But the older scenarios inevitably relied on violent slapstick antics in which the characters knocked each other silly. Some included crude and brutal physical action, as when Tom tried to use a hatchet on Jerry in Hatch Up Your Troubles (May 14, 1949), or bordered on the sadistic, as when off-screen Tom lashed a baby mouse in The Little Orphan. Protests and pressure by parents' activist groups soon forced the network to eliminate the more offensive cartoons. While the series continued on CBS for seven years, the last five relegated to Sunday mornings, Tom and Jerry incurred a bad reputation for senseless violence, and were never to return to the networks in their fast-paced, cat-and-mouse mayhem of old.

The misadventures of "Droopy," a mild-mannered Basset Hound famed for the Shooting of Dan McGoo (Mar 3, 1945), made up one of the principal components of the show. The easy-going canine was created by Tex Avery for Dumb Hounded (Mar 20, 1943), built around the funny mush-mouthed voice of Bill Thompson, who initiated a similar sounding radio characterization named Wallace Wimple, the friend of Fibber McGee and Molly (NBC, 1935-1957). An admitted underdog, Droopy somehow always managed to come out on top. The cartoons rotated with other post-1948 MGM shorts featuring Barney Bear, and Spike and Tyke.

In a revival as an hour program on ABC in 1975-1976, Hanna and Barbera reunited their creations as pals instead of enemies, in three comedies alternating with two starring a thirty-foot tall gorilla on The New Tom and Jerry/Grape Ape Show. The purple primate debuted in far-out fantasies, overcoming his incredible stupidity by using his tremendous strength to help his much smaller partner, a sly canine con-artist named Beegle Beagle. Returning in a non-violent. format as loyal buddies, who walked on two legs instead of four, the much maligned Tom with Jerry, sporting a bow tie, scooted through colorless comedies. The episodes were rerun in 1976-1977 on The Tom and Jerry/Grape Ape/Mumbly Show, adding the new capers of a Sherlockian dog and his stooge, Shnooker. Dropped in November, the huge gorilla appeared in repeats during 1977-1978 as The Great Grape Ape (q. v.) and the cat and mouse ended the season sandwiching sixteen episodes of the muttering mutt, a trench-coated, slouch-hatted detective that grumbled nonsense while sleuthing on The Tom and Jerry/Mumbly Show. But no matter with whom they were coupled, Hanna and Barbera's resurrected Tom and Jerry fared miserably in the ratings.

    In another try, MGM Television leased their cartoon stars to CBS for a new series in 1980-1981, The Tom and Jerry Comedy Show, in which the cat and mouse continued to walk upright in two pantomime adventures. The middle segment featured Droopy, usually paired with Slick the Wolf, and was separated from the other portions by the heavy-lidded dog reading a poem, and a vignette with the mush-mouthed canine and Slick, Barney Bear and Spike the bulldog. Again adversaries, the Tom and Jerry plots were pegged on "To catch or not to catch" in routine stories like "Under the Big Top" and sanitized versions of the studio's vintage cartoons, such as Tom's mishaps with a ravenous gopher in the garden, a remake of Spike's film, Garden Gopher (Sep 30, 1950). Sacrificing creativity for cuteness, the third version was a flagging revival of the "Gold Dust Twins," who had lost all of their charm and pizzazz.

    In a pair of televised movies, Jerry alone danced with Gene Kelly in Anchors Aweigh (MGM, 1945) and in Dangerous When Wet (MGM, 1953) they both cavorted in an underwater ballet with Esther Williams. Eighteen re-edited cartoons were released also as a feature titled The Tom and Jerry Festival of Fun (MGM, 1962).

    Placed in syndication in 1977, the initial TV package of 263 films with Tom and Jerry appeared on more than 80 stations. They were the last of the mainly theatrically-produced big cartoon series marketed for local children's programming and commanded top dollar in the big cities, as much as $45,000 per half-hour for a five-year run. And this time around, the network-banned cartoons raised scarcely an eyebrow.


TOM TERRIFIC

Network History

CAPTAIN KANGAROO
    Premiere: June 10, 1957
    CBS/Jun 1957-Sep 1961/Monday-Friday 8:00-9:00 AM
    Last Program: September 21, 1961

Syndicated History

Distributor: CBS Films/1962-1971; Viacom International/1971-

Executive Producer: Bill Weiss
Director: Gene Deitch
Company: CBS Terrytoons/130 B&W films, 5 minutes

Principal Characters and Voices

Tom Terrific/Mighty Manfred      Lionel Wilson

Tom Terrific was the world's greatest mini-superhero,
thanks to his funnel-hat. The headgear enabled the curly-haired
youngster to assume any shape or form, a bird, a locomotive, a
rock or a window, to become anything he wanted. Tom was partnered with a droopy-eyed canine, a faint-hearted and sometimes
reluctant companion, and one time spotted two fleeing culprits.
"There they are, Mighty Manfred the Wonder Dog," said Tom,
who always spoke emphatically, "shall we go resolutely on?"
"L-let's go resolutely home!," the timid canine responded. Initially presented as a daily cliff-hanger on Captain Kangaroo* (q. v. ),
five installments comprised a complete story, usually programmed
Monday through Friday. The pair were provided with a coterie of
descriptive and comical adversaries, including "The Gravity Maker," "The Prince Frog," "Sweet Tooth Sam," "Captain Kidney
Bean," "The Flying Sorcerer," "The Silly Sandman" and an arch
foe, Crabby Appleton, who was "rotten to the core" and employed
sundry flunkies including a demented dragon. An imaginative and
rudimentary graphic series, the simple non-violent cartoons utilized
line drawings and sparse backgrounds and were full of clever visual ideas pegged on the protean premise. The starkness of the
black-and-white films was enchanced by fine personality characterization, dialogue and narration.
    Tom Terrific was one of the first projects created by Gene
Deitch and fellow artists at Terrytoons in late 1956, one year after
the studio was sold and became a division of CBS Films. After
four years of serialization on Captain Kangaroo, the episodes were
released separately and also spliced together as twenty-six half-
hour adventures in syndication. Lionel Wilson supplied the voices
for all the characters in the stories.


TOMFOOLERY

Network History
    Premiere: September 12, 1970
    NBC/Sep 1970-Jan 1971/Saturday 9:00-9:30 AM
    NBC/Jan 1971-Sep 1971/Saturday 8:00-8:30 AM
    Last Program: September 4, 1971
Executive Producers: Arthur Rankin, Jr., Jules Bass
Producers: John Halas, Joy Batchelor
Company: Halas and Batchelor, London for Rankin-Bass Produc-
    tions/17 films

    Tomfoolery called upon the imaginations of some renowned
authors in an attempt to bring elements of children's literature

with substantive content to Saturday morning. Riddles, stories, limericks and jokes were the basis of the show, an animated variety style program patterned after Rowan and Martin's Laugh-in (NBC, 1968-1973). Among the whimsical cartoon characters were several of those created by Edward Lear (1812-1888), including The Scroovy Snake, The Enthusiastic Elephant, The Fastidious Fish, The Umbrageous Umbrella Maker and the ill-starred lover, the Yonghy-Bonghy-Bo. As an English author of artful alliteration, Lear wrote for the grand-children of his patron, the Earl of Derby, The Book of Nonsense (1846), which did much to popularize the limerick. Also used was material from the nonsense works of other famous authors, the Purple Cow and Goops of Frank Gelett Burgess (1866-1951) and silly characters conceived by Ogden Nash (1902-1971) and Lewis Carroll, pseudonym of English writer Charles Lutwidge Dodgson (1832-1898), who penned the classic Alice in Wonderland (1865).

In the wake of the superhero cartoons, which were phased out on NBC beginning in 1969-1970, the series was a venture to bring "wholesome entertainment to young children." A bit too literary and lofty, Tomfoolery was a noble failure.

## TOP CAT

### Network History
Premiere: September 27, 1961
ABC/Sep 1961-Sep 1962/Wednesday 8:30-9:00 PM
ABC/Oct 1962-Dec 1962/Saturday 11:30-12:00 AM
ABC/Jan 1963-Mar 1963/Saturday 11:00-11:30 AM
NBC/Apr 1965-Sep 1965/Saturday 9:00-9:30 AM
NBC/Oct 1965-Sep 1966/Saturday 11:00-11:30 AM
NBC/Sep 1966-Dec 1966/Saturday 12:00-12:30 PM
NBC/Sep 1967-Aug 1968/Saturday 12:00-12:30 PM
NBC/Sep 1968-May 1969/Saturday 9:30-10:00 AM
Last Program: May 10, 1969

### Syndicated History

Distributor: Taft H-B Program Sales/1970-1979; Worldvision Enterprises/1979-
Executive Producers/Directors: William Hanna, Joseph Barbera
Company: Hanna-Barbera Productions/28 films

### Principal Characters and Voices

| | |
|---|---|
| Top Cat | Arnold Stang |
| Benny the Ball | Maurice Gosfield |
| Officer Dibble | Allen Jenkins |
| Choo Choo | Marvin Kaplan |
| Spook/The Brain | Leo de Lyon (pseud.) |
| Fancy-Fancy/Pierre | John Stephenson |
| Goldie | Jean VanderPyl |
| Honey Dew | Sallie Jones |

Top Cat was the opportunistic leader of a gang of sophisticated New York alley cats, living in a lane just off Mad Avenue in
the 13th Police Precinct.   A master con artist, "T. C." busied
himself manipulating his feline followers in quick-money schemes
like "The $1,000,000 Derby," "The Missing Heir" and "The Golden
Fleecing," which invariably went awry.   Living in abandoned trash
cans furnished with all the cozy conveniences of home, the cats
used a police phone on a nearby pole for unlimited calls, fresh
milk and the latest newspaper were available on nearby doorsteps,
and there was an array of appetizing tidbits waiting to be scrounged
from the local delicatessen.   Due to their proximity, the fat-cats
were often involved with three humans, the milkman, the delicatessen owner and a kindly cop.   But despite the constant threats of
Officer Dibble, voiced by the droll, long-faced Allen Jenkins (1900-
1974), they enjoyed a carefree, easy life in their comfortable
habitat.

Top Cat's dupes included a litter of tabbys with Runyonesque
names, Choo Choo, Spook, The Brain, Pierre, Fancy Fancy, Honey
Dew and Goldie.   Celebrated for his emphatic grunts, "ooh! ooh!,"
Benny the Ball was voiced by comic Maurice Gosfield, who created
the role of Private Duane Doberman, the foil of Sergeant Bilko on
You'll Never Get Rich (CBS, 1955-1959).   In many ways the cartoons and characters resembled that series and one of the episodes
titled "Sgt. Top Cat" was a parody of the prime time hit comedy.
The whiny, nasal, Brooklynese voice of "T. C." belonged to comedian Arnold Stang, heard later as another feline in Walt Disney's
animated box-office success, The Aristocats (BV, 1969).

Originated for a "Kidult" audience, Top Cat was the second
series produced by Hanna-Barbera for an evening timeslot.   The
creation of Joe Barbera, who knocked out the first two episodes
one idle afternoon, it became a ratings failure in prime time but
found new allegiance among children on the Saturday morning
schedule.   After the ABC repeats ended March 30, 1963, Top Cat
was rerun on NBC for three years, beginning April 3, 1965, before
on-going syndication.


TOUCHE TURTLE   See   HANNA-BARBERA NEW CARTOON SHOW,
     THE


TV TOTS TIME

Network History
     Premiere:   December 30, 1951
     ABC/Dec 1951-Mar 1952/Sunday 4:45-5:00 PM
     Last Program:   March 2, 1952


TV Tots Time was the umbrella title for fifteen minutes of
black-and-white films, generally animated cartoons.   Before its
network appearance, the program was scheduled locally by several
ABC stations, February 4 until April 22, 1950 at 7:15-7:30 PM,
Saturday on WJZ, New York, repeated Sunday at 4:45-5:00 PM and

weekdays at 5:15-5:30 PM between January 8 and May 11, 1951.
One of the earliest network cartoon shows, apart from Kids Kapers
(q. v. ), the program was telecast 11:00-11:15 AM CST, Sunday on
WENR, Chicago. The September 1, 1951 show presented Official
Films Cartoons (q. v. ), starring Brownie Bear in "Villain Pursues
Her" (aka Sinister Stuff, Jan 26, 1934) and "Picnic Problems" (aka
Cubby's Picnic, Oct 6, 1933), produced by Van Beuren Studios.
Also featured were "Terryland" films from the Commonwealth Car-
toon Package (q. v. ); on September 8, 1951 the cartoons Captain Kidder
(Feb 20, 1924) and Transatlantic Flight (Jan 19, 1925).


UNCLE CROC'S BLOCK

Component Series
    FRAIDY CAT, M*U*S*H, WACKY AND PACKY, SUPER FIENDS

Network History
    Premiere:  September 6, 1975
    ABC/Sep 1975-Oct 1975/Saturday 10:30-11:30 AM
    ABC/Oct 1975-Feb 1976/Saturday 12:00-12:30 PM
    Last Program:  February 14, 1976

Syndicated History

THE GROOVIE GOOLIES AND FRIENDS

Distributor:  Metromedia Producers Corporation/1978-
Executive Producers:  Louis Scheimer, Norman Prescott
Producer/Director Live Action:  Mack Bing
Producer Animation:  Don Christensen
Company:  Filmation Productions/17 films, 60 & 30 minutes

Cast

Uncle Croc                      Charles Nelson Reilly
Mr. Rabbit Ears                 Alfie Wise
Basil Bitterbottom             Jonathan Harris

Principal Characters and Voices

FRAIDY CAT

Fraidy/Tinker/Dog/Mouse/
    Hokey                       Alan Oppenheimer
Tonka/Wizard/Captain Kitt/
    Sir Walter Cat/Winston      Lennie Weinrib

M*U*S*H

Bullseye/Tricky John/Sonar/
    Hilda                       Robert Ridgely
Sideburns/Coldlips/Colonel
    Flake/General Upheaval      Ken Mars

## WACKY AND PACKY

Wacky/Packy                                    Allan Melvin

   Uncle Croc's Block was a contrived attempt to derive humor
from a spoof of the local children's show genre, but the audience
found the satire singularly unfunny.  Set in a TV studio, the hour-
long show-within-a-show presented Charles Nelson Reilly as Uncle
Croc, the recalcitrant host of a small-fry video program, dressed
in an idiotic crocodile costume and engaged in banter with Mr. Rabbit Ears, his buffoonish assistant who was attired in a bunny suit.
Far from happy in his job, the irritable Uncle Croc was constantly
bickering with Basil Bitterbottom, the TV show's director, played
by prissy Jonathan Harris.  Between times, he introduced the animated cartoons "Fraidy Cat," "M*U*S*H" and "Wacky and Packy,"
and a live-action sketch, "Super Fiends," featuring some actors
costumed as familiar monsters in a parody on the combined superhero concept, with Robert Ridgely as the $6.95 Man.
   The animated "Fraidy Cat" was a felinized, pussy-footed Don
Knotts, living on his luck in the streets and alleys of a large city,
a timid tabby troubled by his eight ghostly former selves.  Each
had a distinct personality and the mischievous phantom felines tried
to entice Fraidy Cat into relinquishing his ninth and last life to join
them.  For example when one snatched a bone from under the nose
of a hungry bulldog, visible only to Fraidy, it seemed to the furious
dog that the cat did it himself.  The ghosts were summoned inad-
vertently through mention of their name or number, and a simple
exclamation, "Me, too!," was sure to bring Ghost Number Two.
The etheric doubles were cave-cat, called Elafunt (One), the magician, Kitty Wizard (Two), a swashbuckler, Captain Kitt (Three),
Sir Walter Cat (Four), Billy the Kitt (Five), the undertaker, Jasper
Catdaver (Six), the barnstorming aviator, Captain Eddie Kittenbacker
(Seven) and Hep Cat (Eight).
   "M*U*S*H" was an irreverent and satiric view of the TV
situation comedy, M*A*S*H (CBS, 1972-  ), starring Bullseye and
Tricky John, a plucky pair of irrepressible pooches that despised
organization of any kind and spent their time avoiding contamination
by the "system."  As members of the Mangy Unwanted Shabby
Heroes, a unit of the Mounted Police stationed in a remote frozen
post, the pair preserved law and order against wacky wildlife--a
Polar Bear that drove a snowmobile like Evel Knievel, a Wolf with
a French lumberjack accent that loved nurses, a Coyote that thought
he was a police dog, and an overgrown Moose called Bruce, whose
well-meaning intentions always landed him in jail.  Filling out the
police pack were Coldlips and Major Sideburns, a female poodle and
her mongrel paramour; Sonar, a small, bespectacled, dachshund
radio operator; Colonel Flake, the easy-going, airedale camp commander; Lupey, a Charo-like chihuahua; Hilda, a powerful female
Great Dane; and a General Patton-style Pekingese, General Upheav-
al, an occasional visitor and military mutt of the old school.
   Also featured were the adventures of a pair of displaced
Stone Agers in New York City, "Wacky and Packy," a highly excitable not-so-bright Neanderthal type and a prehistoric pachyderm

of the woolly mammoth variety.

The ABC Vice President for Children's Programming, Squire Rushnell, said the series was "satire at the level of understanding of youngsters." But the National Association for Better Broadcasting took a different view, saying it was "a monument of junk." No matter what it was called, Uncle Croc's Block deserved its title as the biggest turkey of the ABC 1975-1976 season, if not of all time. On October 25, 1975 the show was reduced to a half-hour, retaining the cartoons, before it was jerked from the air in mid-season, February 1976.


UNCLE WALDO  See  ADVENTURES OF HOPPITTY HOOPER, THE


UNDERDOG

Component Series
   THE HUNTER, THE WORLD OF COMMANDER McBRAGG, GO GO GOPHERS, KLONDIKE KAT, others

Network History
   Premiere:  October 3, 1964
   NBC/Oct 1964-Sep 1965/Saturday 10:00-10:30 AM
   NBC/Oct 1965-Sep 1966/Saturday 10:30-11:00 AM
   CBS/Sep 1966-Sep 1967/Saturday 9:30-10:00 AM
   CBS/Sep 1967-Sep 1968/Sunday 7:30-8:00 AM
   NBC/Sep 1968-Aug 1969/Saturday 11:30-12:00 AM
   NBC/Sep 1969-Sep 1970/Saturday 12:30-1:00 PM
   NBC/Sep 1972-Dec 1972/Saturday 8:00-8:30 AM
   NBC/Dec 1972-Sep 1973/Saturday 10:00-10:30 AM
   Last Program:  September 1, 1973

Syndicated History

Distributor:  Filmtel International/1974-1979; DFS Program Exchange/1979-
Executive Producers:  Treadwell Covington, Peter Peich
Company:  Total TV Productions with Leonardo TV Productions/ 62 films

Principal Characters and Voices

Shoeshine Boy/Underdog            Wally Cox
Sweet Polly Purebred              Norma McMillan


      Underdog was the secret alter-identity of the self-proclaimed "loveable, humble" Shoeshine Boy, a durable canine crime-fighter that vanquished villains for seven years on the networks. An anti-hero of sorts, mocking that invincible surviving son of Krypton, Superman (q.v.), the lowly mutt gained limited super strength, speed and stamina by donning a magic cape. The power waned at

inopportune moments, causing the superdog all kinds of trouble until
he gained renewed vigor from an energy pill concealed in a com-
partment of his ring.  His would-be doggie girlfriend was Sweet
Polly Purebred, an ace TV reporter often in a jam, who summoned her hero with a song, "Oh where, oh where, has my Underdog gone?"  Usually her plight was at the hands of some wacko reprobate like Simon Bar Sinister, a deranged scientist with the voice
of Lionel Barrymore (1878-1954), and his assistant, Cad, who sounded
like Humphrey Bogart (1899-1957).  Simon once stole all the world's
water with the aid of his Big Dipper Machine, enslaved the citizenry
and made them do as "Simon Says" to get a drink.  Among the
plucky pooch's other ingenious foes were a sound-alike of Charles
Laughton named Captain Marblehead and his henchmen Gravel and
Crusher, and the greatest pirate in the world, Riff Raff, and his
Ghost Ship Gang, who robbed the ocean liner, "Queen May."
Those in distress frequently became hapless victims of overkill,
and one time while trying to save a child trapped in a safe, Underdog destroyed the wrong bank.  Of course, he refused to pay dam-
ages, since heroes had no obligations or responsibilities.  A Washington, D. C. -based superhero, his principal schtick was speaking
in heroic couplets: "When the country's in trouble I'm not slow,
It's Hip, Hip, Hip and away I go!"  Each program began with a
parody of Superman's famous opening: "Hey, look in the sky,
there's a plane, it's a bird, it's a frog-og-og ... a frog?"  Inter-
rupting, the canine set the record straight, "Not plane, not bird or
even frog, it's just little 'ole me, Underdog!"
      Featuring the voice of Wally Cox, television's mild-mannered
Mr. Peepers (NBC, 1952-1955), two episodes of Underdog sandwiched several rotated comedies, including the repeated capers of
the southern bloodhound, "The Hunter," first seen on King Leonardo
and His Short Subjects (q. v.) and "The World of Commander Mc-
Bragg," from Tennessee Tuxedo (q. v.).  After the series ended
September 3, 1966 on NBC, the head of CBS daytime programming,
Fred Silverman, bought the show and replaced the components with
a pair of buck-toothed gophers and a bumbling Mountie cat.  He
slotted Underdog back-to-back with five more fantasies, September
10, 1966, to launch the superhero vogue.  When the program ended
its CBS run, September 1, 1968, Silverman repackaged the comedies, featuring "Klondike Kat" with some further episodes of the
zany little Indians, Go Go Gopers (q. v.), for a separate series in 1968-1969.  Although the cartoons were simply lifted intact
with a new opening, the approach was a forerunner of Silverman's
spin-off principle, which he pioneered in 1969-1970 with characters
from The Wacky Races (q. v.).  Underdog returned to NBC, September 7, 1968 for three more seasons.
      The superdog first appeared in balloon-likeness in Macy's
1965 Thanksgiving Day Parade.  One of the more enduring cartoon
canines, in 1975 Underdog was the ninth most popular syndicated
children's show in the Neilsen ratings and in 1980 was still telecast
in twenty-eight markets.

UNITY PICTURES THEATRICAL CARTOON PACKAGE

Component Series
AESOP'S FABLES, CUBBY BEAR, TOM AND JERRY

Syndicated History
  Premiere: March 11, 1947
  WABD, New York/Tuesday 7:00-8:00 PM
Distributor/Owner: Unity Pictures/1946-1956; Screen Gems-Columbia
  Pictures Television/1956-
Producer: Amédée J. Van Beuren
Directors: John Foster, George Stallings, Steve Muffati, George
  Rufle, Frank Sherman, Harry Bailey
Company: Van Beuren Studios-RKO/126 B&W films, 5-6 minutes
  (1928-1934)

    Unity Pictures Theatrical Cartoon Package, if not the pioneer
films, were among the first to appear regularly on television. In
March 1947, they were seen on Movies for Small Fry, the first
children's TV series hosted by Big Brother Bob Emery from WABD,
New York, the flagship station of the DuMont Television Network.
Programmed at 7:00-7:30 PM from April until the end of 1947, on
the other weekdays he guided the Small Fry Club* (DTN, 1947-1951),
the first network show telecast five days a week.   Along with the
animated comedies, various educational films were dropped in the
format and before it ended the program introduced some of the
early films made by Walter Lantz.   On January 19, 1948, Emery
presented one of the thirteen Van Beuren-RKO films in the package
starring "Cubby Bear" (1933-1934), created by Mannie Davis for
Cubby's Nut Factory (Aug 11, 1933).   More like a cute doll than a
teddy bear, Cubby's round-features were reminiscent of Walt Disney's Mickey Mouse and he capered in innocuous situation comedies,
sometimes with his girlfriend.   Not the famous cat-and-mouse but
a tall-and-short life-like pair, "Tom and Jerry" (1931-1933) were
the first characters developed for Van Beuren Studios by John
Foster, George Stallings and George Rufle, and seldom spoke but
reacted to situations around them.   Their twenty Unity films ranged
from uninspired to imaginative, the first Wot a Night (Aug 1, 1931).
Although it had no continuing characters, "Aesop's Fables" (1928-
1933) featured standardized animal stars for a time and in 1930 the
morals which ended each film were dropped.   A continuation of
Fables Studio, which Paul Terry started in 1921 as a minority
partner, Amédée J. Van Beuren (1879-1937) acquired the majority
interest and added sound to the Aesop's films beginning with Dinner Time (Dec 17, 1928) and Terry left in 1929 to eventually found
Terrytoons.   Together with the other films, the ninety-three Fables
in the package were released by RKO (Radio-Keith-Orpheum), which
sold them to Unity in the forties.   During his studio's eight year
existence, Van Beuren produced several other series which were
syndicated to television as Official Films Cartoons (q. v. ) and in the
Commonwealth Cartoon Package (q. v. ).

U.S. OF ARCHIE, THE  See  ARCHIES, THE


VALLEY OF THE DINOSAURS

Network History
    Premiere: September 7, 1974
    CBS/Sep 1974-Jan 1975/Saturday 10:00-10:30 AM
    CBS/Jan 1975-Aug 1975/Saturday 11:00-11:30 AM
    CBS/Sep 1975-Sep 1976/Saturday 12:00-12:30 PM
    Last Program: September 4, 1976

Syndicated History

Distributor:  Taft H-B Program Sales/1976-1979; DFS Program
    Exchange/1979-
Executive Producers:  William Hanna, Joseph Barbera
Producer:  Iwao Takamoto
Director:  Charles A. Nichols
Company:  Hanna-Barbera Productions/16 films

Principal Characters and Voices

John Butler                          Mike Road
Kim Butler                           Shannon Farnon
Katie Butler                         Margene Fudenna
Greg Butler                          Jackie Haley
Gorok                                Alan Oppenheimer
Gara                                 Joan Gardner
Tana                                 Melanie Baker
Lok                                  Steacy Bertheau
Digger (the Butlers' dog)
Glomb (a pet stegasaurus)


    Valley of the Dinosaurs was the prehistoric home for two
families, one modern and sophisticated, the other aboriginal and
ridden with superstition.  Unexpectedly thrust into a primeval time
continuum, the Butlers were on an archaeology expedition in an uncharted Amazon River canyon when they were engulfed by a whirl-
pool and swept through an underground cavern to the lost Stone Age
world.  Stranded in a land where dinosaurs still roamed, John, a
high school science instructor, and his wife Kim, their daughter
and son, Katie and Greg, and pet dog, Digger, encountered a paral-
lel primitive family.  The skin-clad, cave-dwellers were Gorok and
his wife Gara, and their daughter and son, Tana and Lok, who had
a pet stegasaurus named Glomb.  Faced with peril everywhere,
from menacing ancient reptilian creatures to natural catastrophes,
together the two families struggled to survive in the foreboding environment.  Educational features were interwoven in the stories
through the Butlers' use of scientific principles to solve practical
problems such as their mutual everyday needs, water, food and
the conveniences of a comfortable shelter.
    The series was a cut above average for a prehistoric

science-fiction entry, despite the fact that science teachers and their students were more than surprised to see dinosaurs and hominids living in the same era.

## WACKY RACES, THE

Network History
Premiere: September 14, 1968
CBS/Sep 1968-Sep 1969/Saturday 9:30-10:00 AM
CBS/Sep 1969-Feb 1970/Saturday 12:30-1:00 PM
CBS/Feb 1970-Sep 1970/Saturday 10:00-10:30 AM
Last Program: September 5, 1970

Syndicated History

THE FUN WORLD OF HANNA-BARBERA

Distributor: Taft H-B Program Sales/1977-1979; Worldvision Enterprises/1979-
Executive Producers: William Hanna, Joseph Barbera
Director: Iwao Takamoto
Company: Hanna-Barbera Productions with Heatter-Quigley Productions/17 films

Narrator
Dave Willock

Principal Characters and Voices

| | |
|---|---|
| Peter Perfect/Sergeant/Big Gruesome/Red Max/Rufus Ruffcut/Rock and Gravel Slag | Daws Butler |
| Dick Dastardly/Clyde/Private Pinkley | Paul Winchell |
| Muttley/Sawtooth/Professor Pat Pending/"Ring-A-Ding Convert-A-Car"/Little Gruesome | Don Messick |
| Penelope Pitstop | Janet Waldo |
| Luke and Blubber Bear/General | John Stephenson |

The Wacky Races pitted eleven daredevil drivers in cross-country road competition for the title of "The World's Wackiest Racer." Driving a variety of bizarre but functional vehicles, at every turn they faced the devious mischief of the scoundrel, Dick Dastardly, and Muttley, his shaggy canine accomplice. With lunatic determination to possess the trophy, the villainous rotter resorted to sabotage, ruse and Rube Goldberg-style contraptions, which invariably backfired. A caricature not unlike British comedian Terry-Thomas, Dastardly was reminiscent of the maniacal villain portrayed by Jack Lemmon in the movie, The Great Race (WB, 1965), and the premise owed a great debt to the film as well. Crammed full of Dastardly's dirty tricks and nasty schemes, each show contained two ten-minute episodes with titles like "The Baja-Ha-Ha Race," "Rhode Island Road Race," "Dopey Dakota Derby," "The Speedy Arkansas Traveller" and "Ball Point, Penn or Bust."

The entrants included Dastardly and Muttley in the "Mean Machine" (#00) and Professor Pat Pending in his "Ring-A-Ding Convert-A-Car" (#3), a talking auto created by the zany inventor who often foiled the pair's despicable plots. Driving the "Turbo Terrific" (#9) was a John Wayne sound-alike and all-American good-guy, Peter Perfect, who frequently made a play for pretty Penelope Pitstop, the glamor girl of the gas pedal in her "Compact Pussycat" (#5). The other competitors were Rufus Ruffcut and Sawtooth in their "Buzz Wagon" (#10), the General, Sergeant and Private Pinkley in the "Army Surplus Special" (#6), the Slag brothers, Rock and Gravel, in the "Boulder Mobile" (#1), Clyde and The Ant Hill Mob in the "Bulletproof Bomb" (#7), the Red Max in his "Crimson Haybailer" (#4), the Gruesome Twosome in the "Creepy Coupe" (#2), and the hillbillies, Luke and Blubber Bear in the "Arkansas Chugabug" (#8). The series had a built-in prize contest, which provided an opportunity for young viewers to win attractive reproductions of all eleven of the crazy cars and their drivers.

Following two years of Saturday mornings saturated with hard-action superhero adventures, The Wacky Races inaugurated light comedy programming on CBS with The Archies (q. v.). At the suggestion of Fred Silverman, head of daytime programming, several of the characters were selected as spin-offs for new cartoon shows, the first time the principle had been applied to animated children's programming. Elevated to headline their own series in 1969-1970 were Dastardly and Muttley (q. v.) and the wily racing heroine in The Perils of Penelope Pitstop (q. v.), supported by The Ant Hill Mob.


## WAIT TILL YOUR FATHER GETS HOME

### Syndicated History
Premiere: September 12, 1972
WNBC, New York/Tuesday 7:30-8:00 PM
Distributor: Taft H-B Program Sales/1972-1979; Worldvision Enterprises/1979-
Executive Producers: William Hanna, Joseph Barbera
Producer: Iwao Takamoto
Director: Charles A. Nichols
Company: Hanna-Barbera Productions/24 films

### Principal Characters and Voices

| | |
|---|---|
| Harry Boyle | Tom Bosley |
| Irma Boyle | Joan Gerber |
| Chet Boyle | Lennie Weinrib |
| Alice Boyle | Tina Holland |
| Jamie Boyle | Jackie Haley |
| Ralph | Jack Burns |
| Julius (Boyle's pet dog) | |

Wait Till Your Father Gets Home addressed the ever-widening generation gap between an old-fashioned father and his modern-day children. The household was dominated by Harry Boyle, owner of the Boyle Restaurant Supply Company, and included his supportive wife, Irma, their older son Chet, teenage daughter Alice, and young Jamie. Ralph was the oustpoken Boyle's next-door neighbor and Julius was the family dog. The series focused on the interaction of characters suggestive of All in the Family (CBS, 1971-1979), the patriarch being continually at odds with the life-style of his free-spirited offspring, particularly his activist daughter who supported various social reforms including women's lib. The conflicts were developed in such stories as "The Hippie," "Chet's Fiancée," "Mama's Identity," "The Commune" and "Sweet Sixteen." In 1973-1974, several guest stars voiced their caricatures: Phyllis Diller in "The Lady Detective," Don Adams in "Don for the Defense," Jonathan Winters in "Maude Loves Papa," Monty Hall in "Mama Loves Monty," and "Don Knotts, the Beekeeper" and "Rich Little, Supersleuth." With a similar theme, All in the Family also inspired a 1972-1973 NBC anthropomorphic cartoon series, The Barkleys (q.v.).

Appearing in first run between 1972 and 1974 and achieving moderate ratings, the series was produced especially for the prime access period inaugurated in Fall 1971, which returned a half-hour of network time between 7:30 and 8:00 PM to local stations in the top fifty markets. The last cartoon series produced by Hanna-Barbera for nighttime viewing, after 1974 the episodes were scheduled mainly for children in the early afternoon and weekends. Tom Bosley, who voiced Harry Boyle, thereafter appeared as a more understanding father in his role as Howard Cunningham in the hit comedy, Happy Days (ABC, 1974-  ).


WALLY GATOR   See   HANNA-BARBERA NEW CARTOON SHOW, THE


WHAT'S NEW, MISTER MAGOO?   See   MR. MAGOO


WHEELIE AND THE CHOPPER BUNCH

Network History
    Premiere:  September 7, 1974
    NBC/Sep 1974-Aug 1975/Saturday 8:30-9:00 AM
    Last Program:  August 30, 1975

Syndicated History

Distributor:  Taft H-B Program Sales/1978-1979; DFS Program Exchange/1979-
Executive Producers:  William Hanna, Joseph Barbera
Producer:  Iwao Takamoto
Director:  Charles A. Nichols
Company:  Hanna-Barbera Productions/13 films

## Principal Characters and Voices

| | |
|---|---|
| Wheelie/Chopper | Frank Welker |
| Rota Ree | Judy Strangis |
| Scrambles | Don Messick |
| Revs | Paul Winchell |
| Hi-Riser | Lennie Weinrib |

Wheelie and the Chopper Bunch, a righteous supercar and a wild-riding motorcycle gang, gnashed gears in this personified vehicular fantasy. Wheelie was the world's greatest stunt-racing car, known as the fastest thing on wheels, a souped-up compact whose parts could extend as functional limbs. Out to foil the little auto-hero, the bully Chopper tried to win over the affections of Rota Ree, his rotary-engined girlfriend, and with his bike pals named Scrambles, Revs and Hi-Riser created mischief at every opportunity. Three episodes with such titles as "Dr. Crankenstein," "Bulldozer Buddy" and "Lennie Van Limousine" made up one program. Involved with a variety of distinct jalopies and conveyances, Wheelie met up with the bizarre Dr. Race Cycle, M.D., who used a powerful "Dr. Cycle and Mr. Ryde" gas formula, and the hard-working Two-Ton Tony, the Towing Truck, voiced in Italian dialect. Go-Go the Go-Cart, a young nephew of Rota, joined the pair on an outing in "Camping with Go-Go," which provided an opportunity for the Ranger jeepster to lecture about conservation. Interwoven in each program were instructional and safety tips for young viewers. When the Chopper Bunch plunged off the road into a patch of poison ivy, Wheelie and Rota humorously demonstrated what to do about the itchy affliction. And during a Chinatown New Year's celebration in "Carfucius Says," the Chinese Rickshaw admonished proverbially, "Joy riding is not always joyful" and "Reckless passing leads to wrecks and crashing." The series had a singular catchy and repeated theme by Hoyt Curtin.

## WHERE'S HUDDLES?

### Network History
Premiere: July 1, 1970
CBS/Jul 1970-Sep 1970/Wednesday 7:30-8:00 PM
CBS/Jul 1971-Sep 1971/Sunday 5:30-6:00 PM
Last Program: September 5, 1971
Executive Producers: William Hanna, Joseph Barbera
Producer: Iwao Takamoto
Director: Charles A. Nichols
Company: Hanna-Barbera Productions/10 films

### Principal Characters and Voices

| | |
|---|---|
| Ed Huddles | Cliff Norton |
| Marge Huddles | Jean VanderPyl |
| Bubba McCoy | Mel Blanc |
| Penny McCoy | Marie Wilson |

Claude Pertwee            Paul Lynde
Mad Dog Maloney      Alan Reed
Freight Train             Herb Jeffries
Sports Announcer       Dick Enberg
Fumbles (Huddles' pet dog)
Beverly (Pertwee's pet cat)

Where's Huddles? was an animated "Kidult" situation comedy inspired by the world of professional football. The stories concentrated mainly on the off-field family misadventures of the Rhinos' star quarterback, Ed Huddles, his wife, Marge, and their best friends, the mammoth, muscular center Bubba McCoy and Penny, his giddy wife. The Huddles lived next door to the fussy busybody Claude Pertwee, a self-caricature voiced by Paul Lynde. He was a football-hating neighbor who delighted in their professional and domestic misfortunes, and Pertwee's mischievous cat, Beverly, was a source of constant trouble to the Huddles' dog, Fumbles. Substantially underpaid by today's pro standards, Ed and Bubba engaged in wild schemes to supplement their income, one time forming "The Offsensives," a jock rock group with Freight Train. Some of the other episodes were titled "The Ramblin' Wreck," "Hot Dog Hannah" and "A Weighty Problem." NBC sports commentator Dick Enberg delivered the play-by-play commentary, describing the Rhinos' hapless hopes for a championship season. Mad Dog Maloney was the Rhinos' frustrated coach.

Originally a prime time summer replacement series, Where's Huddles? ended September 9, 1970 and was repeated on the network beginning July 11, 1971.


WILL THE REAL JERRY LEWIS PLEASE SIT DOWN?

Network History
     Premiere: September 12, 1970
     ABC/Sep 1970-Sep 1971/Saturday 10:00-10:30 AM
     ABC/Sep 1971-Sep 1972/Saturday 8:00-8:30 AM
     Last Program: September 2, 1972

Syndicated History

Distributor: Worldvision Enterprises/1972-
Executive Producers: Louis Scheimer, Norman Prescott
Producer: Hal Sutherland
Company: Filmation Productions/17 films

Principal Characters
     Jerry Lewis
     Geraldine Lewis
     Rhonda
     Mr. Blunderbuss
     Spot (Geraldine's pet frog)

Will the Real Jerry Lewis Please Sit Down? caricatured the

multi-talented comic for a series based on the actor's own premise. The stories cast Lewis as a klutzy janitor at the Odd Job Employment Agency, owned by the pompous Mr. Blunderbuss. A last choice substitute, he tackled a variety of temporary assignments in an effort to better his lot, appearing as a frantic misfit in such episodes as "Computer Suitor," "How Green Was My Valet" and "Movie Madness." Although he did not voice the cartoon character, several of the episodes were contributed by Lewis based on his roles in features like The Errand Boy (PAR, 1962), The Caddy (PAR, 1958) and The Geisha Boy (PAR, 1958). The regular supporting characters were his girlfriend Rhonda, his sister Geraldine, and Spot, her pet frog.

## WINKY DINK AND YOU

Syndicated History
  Premiere: 1969
Distributor: W. J. Seidler/1969-1975
Producer: Fred Calvert
Company: Ariel Productions with Barry & Enright Productions/52
  films, 5 minutes

Principal Characters and Voices

Winky Dink                        Mae Questel
Woofer                            Dayton Allen

    Winky Dink and You incorporated a simple problem which children could help solve at home by drawing on a transparent sheet placed over the TV screen. Dressed in a jester's outfit, quartered alternately in squares, Winky Dink was a little boy with a large head and hair that resembled a five-pointed star, and was partnered with his dog, Woofer. In the middle of their animated adventures, the pair were always confronted with some predicament--an impassable gorge that needed a bridge, a boat that needed a sail or a gloomy underground cave that needed an exit. This allowed the narrator to remind the audience to get their crayons and draw the missing object, part or outlet. Some episodes asked the viewer to connect the dots to form a picture or to "Follow the Notes." In such episodes as "Woofer's Draw-in," "U-Boat in the Moat," "The Zip Code Zipper" and "The Missing Color Mystery," youngsters were asked to summon their imaginations and provide an object to help complete the story. Easily erased with a cloth, the plastic sheet could be used for the next cartoon.
    A unique concept that involved children in self-expression and creativity, Winky Dink and You* (q.v.) was hosted by Jack Barry for over four years on CBS between 1953 and 1957, and produced by Barry and Dan Enright around the brief Winky cartoons. The team sold millions of fifty cent Winky Dink TV Kits containing a plastic sheet and some "magic crayons." The black-and-white cartoons were syndicated by CBS Films through the mid-sixties

and revived with some innovations in this color series made for flexible local programming. But the films arrived at about the time when consumer groups were concerned over TV tube radiation and were urging viewers not to get too close to their sets. The campaign adversely affected the concept and the cartoons were withdrawn.

Among the pioneers in children's programming, Barry and Enright became producers of top-rated game shows like The Joker's Wild (CBS, 1972-1975/SYN, 1976-  ), and over a dozen series including Juvenile Jury* (q. v.) and the children's game show, Joker! Joker!! Joker!!!* (q. v.).


## WINNIE-THE-POOH

Network History
    Premiere:  March 10, 1970
    NBC/Mar 1970-Nov 1977/Periodic/Various PM
    ABC/Nov 1976/Friday 8:00-8:30 PM
    Last Program:  November 25, 1977
Sponsor:  Sears, Roebuck and Company
Executive Producers:  Walt Disney (1965), Ron Miller (1968 & 1974)
Directors:  Wolfgang Reitherman, John Lounsbery
Company:  Walt Disney Productions/3 films (1965-1974)

Narrator
    Sebastian Cabot

Principal Characters and Voices

| | |
|---|---|
| Winnie-the-Pooh | Sterling Holloway |
| Eeyore | Ralph Wright |
| Wol the Owl | Hal Smith |
| Christopher Robin | Bruce Reitherman |
| Kanga | Barbara Luddy |
| Baby Roo | Clint Howard |
| Rabbit | Junius Matthews |
| Gopher | Howard Morris |
| Tigger | Paul Winchell |

Winnie-the-Pooh preserved the whimsical flavor of A. A. Milne's renowned children's stories and the sympathetic personalities of Ernest Shepard's original illustrations.  Produced as three theatrical featurettes by Walt Disney Studios between 1965 and 1974, the animated series was based on the English writer's Winnie-the-Pooh (E. P. Dutton, 1926) and The House at Pooh Corner (E. P. Dutton, 1928), which introduced young Christopher Robin, who talked with animal friends from the Hundred Acre Wood.  They were telecast as prime time specials, with the bumbling yet lovable teddy bear that was fond of eating honey making his TV bow, appropriately, in "Winnie-the-Pooh and the Honey Tree" (Mar 10, 1970).  The supporting menagerie included Milne's familiar creations:  Eeyore, the melancholy gray donkey, the marsupial Kanga and her Baby Roo, Rabbit, and Wol the Owl in his tree house, The

Wolery. In the musical fantasy, Pooh's craving for "hunny" landed him in all kinds of trouble, in particular a sticky encounter with a swarm of bees. After gorging himself silly on the sweet stuff, the bear developed a weight problem and got stuck in the entrance to the Rabbit's house. "Winnie-the-Pooh and the Blustery Day" (Nov 30, 1970), a 1968 Oscar-winner, followed the adventures of the characters during a storm that toppled the Owl's lofty house and brought a drenching rain. While the flood waters rose, the Pooh had a frightful dream about honey-stealing creatures called "heffalumps" (elephants) and "woozles." Another delightful trip into the Wood in "Winnie-the-Pooh and Tigger Too" (Nov 28, 1975) found the characters trying to "unbounce" the lively Tigger, whose overly enthusiastic greetings usually knocked his hapless friends flat on their backs. Songs for the films were by Richard and Robin Sherman, who wrote the Oscar-winning score for Disney's Mary Poppins (BV, 1964).

Winnie-the-Pooh began as Edward Bear, a teddy bear belonging to Christopher Robin, the young son of Milne (1882-1956), that made an occasional appearance in humorous domestic poems published in Punch beginning in 1924. The unforgettable film voice of the bear was supplied by Sterling Holloway, who became famous for his voice characterization of the skunk in Bambi (RKO, 1942) and the Cheshire Cat in Alice in Wonderland (RKO, 1951), and who was awarded a Grammy for his children's recordings of the Pooh stories. The films were repeated on NBC through 1977 with the exception of "Tigger Too," which was rerun on November 25, 1976 as an ABC presentation.

WONDERFUL STORIES OF PROFESSOR KITZEL, THE

Syndicated History
    Premiere: 1972
Sponsor: National Pal Vitamins (1972-1976)
Distributor: S. S. C. & B. Advertising/1972-1976; Worldvision Enterprises/1976-
Executive Producer: Shamus Culhane
Company: M. G. Animation/104 films, 4 1/2 minutes

Principal Character
    Professor Kitzel

    The Wonderful Stories of Professor Kitzel covered historic and cultural events in an educational context as viewed by the electronic wizard. Borrowing another leaf from H. G. Wells' evocative novel, The Time Machine (1895), the mustachioed little inventor carried young viewers back to different years to see for themselves discoveries, people, issues and events that helped shape the world today. Utilizing live film clips with commentary for some of the substance, each brief episode was devoted to one particular subject. The inventions ranged from the telescope and microscope to early ships, balloons, rockets and automobiles, and the inventors from James Watt and Marconi to Benjamin Franklin and Thomas Edison.

Also covered were individuals and peoples, like George Washington, Abraham Lincoln, Daniel Boone, Joan of Arc and The Vikings, life in New Amsterdam, among the Pile Dwellers and the Eskimos, and in various foreign countries. The series was based on the New York and Los Angeles city schools curriculum and came with a prepared study guide, which summarized each topic for classroom teachers. In first-run syndication, Professor Kitzel was offered as a barter program between 1972 and 1976 by Bristol and Myers for Pal Vitamins.

WOODY WOODPECKER SHOW, THE

Component Series
  MUSICAL MINIATURES, OSWALD, WALLY WALRUS,
  ANDY PANDA (1957-1958), FOOLISH FABLES, CHILLY WILLY,
  INSPECTOR WILLOUGHBY, MAW AND PAW, THE BEARY FAM-
  ILY, HICKORY, DICKORY AND DOC (1970-1977)

Network History
  Premiere: October 3, 1957
  ABC/Oct 1957-Sep 1958/Thursday 5:00-5:30 PM
  NBC/Sep 1970-Jan 1971/Saturday 8:30-9:00 AM
  NBC/Jan 1971-Sep 1971/Saturday 9:00-9:30 AM
  NBC/Sep 1971-Jan 1972/Saturday 8:30-9:00 AM
  NBC/Jan 1972-Sep 1972/Saturday 9:00-9:30 AM
  NBC/Sep 1976-Sep 1977/Saturday 8:00-8:30 AM
  Last Program: September 3, 1977

Syndicated History

WOODY WOODPECKER AND FRIENDS

Distributor: MCA-TV/1958-
Executive Producer: Walter Lantz
Directors: Alex Lovy, Shamus Culhane, Dick Lundy, Don Patter-
  son, Paul Smith, Tex Avery, Jack Hannah, others (1938-1972)
Company: Walter Lantz Productions/26 films (1957-1958), 26
  films 1970-1972), 13 films (1976-1977)

Host
  Walter Lantz (1957-1958)

Principal Characters and Voices

| | |
|---|---|
| Woody Woodpecker | (1940-1952) Mel Blanc/Ben Hardaway |
| | (1952-1972) Grace Stafford |
| Andy Panda | (1939-1949) Sara Berner/Walter Tetley |
| Wally Walrus | (1942- ??) Hans Conried/Paul Frees |
| Buzz Buzzard | (1942- ??) Dal McKennon |
| Maw and Paw | (1953-1954) Grace Stafford/Paul Frees |
| Chilly Willy/Smedley | (1953-1972/ |
| Windy/Gabby Gator | 1958-1961) Daws Butler |

| | |
|---|---|
| Space Mouse | (1959-1960) Johnny Coons |
| Doc | (1959-1962) Paul Frees |
| Hickory/Dickory | (1959-1962/ |
| Inspector Willoughby | 1960-1965) Dal McKennon |
| The Beary Family | (1962-1971) Paul Frees/Grace Stafford |

The Woody Woodpecker Show featured a hyperactive and brash little red, white, and blue bird with a staccato laugh, "ha-ha-ha-HA-ha," Walter Lantz's most popular and durable character. Comprised of three theatrical comedies, some new wraparound animation and a five-minute peek at behind-the-scenes cartoon making hosted by Lantz, the ABC series was the 1957-1958 Thursday afternoon replacement for the first half-hour of the shortened Mickey Mouse Club* (q. v.), replaced on the other weekdays by live-action films. Consisting of the Walter Lantz "Cartunes" released by Universal Pictures, the twenty-six episodes excluded all shorts that caricatured blacks and were re-edited to eliminate all drinking scenes and any material considered risqué. A raucous and visually expressive character, Woody Woodpecker was initially designed by Ben "Bugs" Hardaway, a former Schlesinger Studios director who helped develop Daffy Duck (q. v.) and his namesake, Bugs Bunny (q. v.). Mel Blanc voiced Woody for the first few films, followed by Hardaway and others until 1952 when Grace Stafford, Lantz's wife, became the permanent voice. Introduced in Knock Knock (Nov 25, 1940), Woody was a rooftop pest that annoyed Andy Panda and his Pop. Apart from Tom and Jerry (q. v.), the films were among the last of the pre-1948 cartoons from a major studio seen on network television, although some of Lantz's vintage films were syndicated in the package, Oswald the Rabbit (q. v.).
In his early years often an unwanted intruder, Woody was usually on the offensive, invading and destroying Wally Walrus' seaside amusement pier in The Beach Nut (Oct 16, 1944), being a nuisance and freeloader at Wally's Swiss Chard Lodge in Ski for Two (Nov 13, 1944), and with zest and enthusiasm disturbing the peace and quiet of Birdland in his first starring film, Woody Woodpecker (Jul 7, 1941). While it was easy to laugh at the nutty bird's antics, it was just as easy to dislike him until the characterization was toned down in the fifties and he became essentially defensive in nature. Woody's family grew to include his wife Miranda, also voiced by Grace Stafford, and his nephew and niece, Splinter and Knothead. Nominated for an Academy Award, "The Woody Woodpecker Song" was introduced in Wet Blanket Policy (Aug 27, 1948), the only musical entry from a cartoon short to make the finals for the Best Song of the Year. The pesky character also appeared in a special segment of George Pal's Destination Moon (Eagle-Lion, 1950). The TV premiere related the story of how Woody was first discovered in Who's Cooking Who (Jun 24, 1946) and Wally Walrus trying to conduct the Overture to William Tell (Jun 16, 1947). Other supporting features included the cute Chinese cub who made his debut in Life Begins for Andy Panda (Sep 9, 1939) along with Lantz's first cartoon character, "Oswald the Rabbit," inherited from the Charles Mintz-Walt Disney series. After the ABC run

ended September 25, 1958, the program was syndicated for about
eight years.

For his NBC show, which began September 12, 1970, Lantz
put together twenty-six additional episodes from his post-1948 films
featuring Woody and such other comedies as "Inspector Willoughby"
(1960-1965), "Foolish Fables" (1953), "Maw and Paw" (1953-1954),
developed from Universal's popular Ma and Pa Kettle movies,
Space Mouse, Sugarfoot the Horse and a little penguin who first appeared in Chilly Willy (Dec 21, 1953). With mostly rebound humor,
similar to that used in The Road Runner (q. v. ), Willy's antagonists
suffered largely through their own ineptness or stupidity. In another
live-action segment, "Woody's Newsreel," Lantz showed some comical scenes from vintage news films, introduced by Woody as "My
boss, Walter Lantz. " The films were repeated on the network in
1976-1977 without the newsreel and with later fillers, including
"The Beary Family" (1962-1971) and "Hickory, Dickory and Doc"
(1959-1962). Subsequently, the series were combined and with additional episodes syndicated as Woody Woodpecker and Friends.

WORLD'S GREATEST SUPERFRIENDS, THE  See  SUPERFRIENDS


YOGI BEAR

Component Series
 SNAGGLEPUSS, YAKKY DOODLE (1961-1963), THE BUFORD
 FILES, THE GALLOPING GHOST, THE GALAXY GOOF-UPS
 (1978-1979)

Syndicated History

THE YOGI BEAR SHOW
 Premiere: January 30, 1961
 WPIX, New York/Monday 6:30-7:00 PM
Sponsor: Kellogg's Cereals (1961-1963)

YOGI AND HIS FRIENDS (1967)

Distributor: Screen Gems-Columbia Pictures Television/1961-

Network History

YOGI'S GANG

 Premiere: September 8, 1973
 ABC/Sep 1973-Aug 1974/Saturday 8:30-9:00 AM
 ABC/Sep 1974-Aug 1975/Saturday 8:00-8:30 AM
 Last Program: August 30, 1975

YOGI'S SPACE RACE
 Premiere: September 9, 1978
 NBC/Sep 1978-Oct 1978/Saturday 8:00-9:30 AM

NBC/Nov 1978-Jan 1979/Saturday 11:00-12:00 AM
NBC/Feb 1979-Mar 1979/Saturday 8:00-8:30 AM
Last Program: March 3, 1979
Executive Producers: William Hanna, Joseph Barbera
Producers: Iwao Takamoto (1973-1975), Alex Lovy, Art Scott (1978-1979)
Directors: William Hanna, Joseph Barbera (1961-1963); Charles A. Nichols (1973-1975), Ray Patterson (1978-1979)
Company: Hanna-Barbera Productions/32 films (1961-1963), 17 films (1973-1975), 13 films, 90 minutes (1978-1979)

Narrator
  Gary Owens (1978-1979)

Principal Characters and Voices

| | | |
|---|---|---|
| Yogi Bear/Huckleberry Hound/Peter Potamus/ Quick Draw McGraw/ Snagglepuss/Wally Gator/Augie Doggie/ Fibber Fox | (1961-1979) | Daws Butler |
| Boo Boo/Touché Turtle/Squiddly Diddly/ Atom Ant/Ranger John Smith/Major Minor/Hunter | (1961-1979) | Don Messick |
| Yakky Doodle | (1961-1963) | Jimmy Weldon |
| Chopper | (1961-1963) | Vance Colvig |
| Doggie Daddy | (1973-1975) | John Stephenson |
| Paw Rugg | (1973-1975) | Henry Corden |
| Magilla Gorilla | (1973-1975) | Allan Melvin |
| Scarebear | (1978-1979) | Joe Besser |
| Quack-Up | (1978-1979) | Mel Blanc |
| Rita | (1978-1979) | Pat Parris |
| Wendy | (1978-1979) | Marilyn Schreffler |
| Jabberjaw/Buford Bloodhound/Nugget Nose/Captain Good/ Clean Cat/Phantom Phink/Sinister Sludge | (1978-1979) | Frank Welker |

THE BUFORD FILES AND THE GALLOPING GHOST (1978-1979)
See  BUFORD AND THE GALLOPING GHOST

THE GALAXY GOOF-UPS (1978) See  GALAXY GOOF-UPS, THE

Yogi Bear, fond of telling all comers that he was "smarter than the average bear," indeed was, and proved his point by becoming one of the few made-for-TV cartoon superstars. Making his bow in 1959-1960 on The Huckleberry Hound Show (q.v.), a smash syndicated success with sixteen million viewers on stations worldwide, Yogi soon surpassed the little blue canine to become a perennial favorite, unequalled perhaps by any other anthropomorphic member of the animated video-world with the exception of theatrical transfers like Donald Duck and Bugs Bunny (q. v.). Elevated from second banana comedies to star in The Yogi Bear Show, he appeared in the third syndicated Hanna-Barbera series for Screen Gems (CPT), between 1961 and 1963 sponsored by Kellogg's Cereals, which placed the program in early evening timeslots in markets of their choosing. Initially produced and directed by the Academy Award-winning MGM team responsible for Tom and Jerry (q. v.), many of the first stories were written by Michael Maltese and Warren Foster, former storymen for such Warner Brothers cartoons as those featuring Bugs, Daffy Duck, Porky Pig and others. One of the most surprising new stars in show business in the early sixties, Yogi Bear, together with The Flintstones (q. v.), accelerated the meteoric rise of Hanna-Barbera studios as the world's foremost producer of animated entertainment.

A non-conformist who tried to uphold the spirit of his forebears, Yogi was a gentle, friendly soul who cavorted around Jellystone Park in a tie and pork-pie hat. Bearing a startling resemblance to Art Carney's sewer-worker Ed Norton, a character popularized on The Honeymooners (CBS, 1955-1956) but developed on the DuMont network program in 1950 and later a segment of The Jackie Gleason Show (CBS, 1957-1959) and its sequels, Yogi was bright in a stupid sort of way. His name was borrowed from the colorful baseball catcher-coach, Yogi Berra, of the New York Yankees. Roaming the preserve before the advent of a rules-conscious Forest Service, Yogi was a genial panhandler and incurable filcher of visitors' picnic baskets. With Boo Boo, his faithful, small bear-buddy trailing resignedly behind him, Yogi used his knack of cheeky persuasion and masterful cunning to make life miserable for John Smith, the Park Ranger. Despite the warnings from Smith and his assistant, Ranger Anderson, and the inevitable punishment meted out for his ravenous transgressions, Yogi and Boo Boo managed to cadge food in a variety of devious ways. Among the featured supporting characters was Yogi's southern girlfriend, Cindy Bear, whose "Ah, do declare!" voiced by Julie Bennett became a much-mimicked expression among regular viewers.

The premiere, "Home Sweet Jellystone," established the background for the series, which starred the Park's notorious scavenger in such stories as "Bear on a Picnic," "Hoodwinked Bear," "Threadbare Yogi" and "Do or Diet." The supporting series included Major Minor in "Major Operation" and the flowery-speaking Augie Doggie and Doggie Daddy in "From A to Z," a component that debuted on Quick Draw McGraw (q. v.). About six months later, two new cartoons became regular features, "Snagglepuss" the Lion and "Yakky Doodle" and Chopper. A hip thespian who was always "on," Snagglepuss's favorite expression was "Heavens to Murgatroyd!," and his voice was a blatant but amusing imitation of Bert Lahr's cowardly lion in The Wizard of Oz (MGM, 1939). "Snag" was seen in such episodes as "Footlight Fright," "Fraidy-Cat Lion" and "Paws for Applause." Muttering stage directions

like "Exit Left," when he was winged by his frequent adversary, the
pith-helmeted, red-moustached Hunter, Snagglepuss gasped, "Et tu,
Brutus, and all that Shakespearean jazz." A mischievous and talka-
tive duck, Yakky Doodle, and Chopper the Bulldog, his protector
when anyone threatened the "little fella," were do-gooders and often
at odds with Fibber Fox, a sly con-artist after a tasty meal in episodes titled "Foxy Proxy," "Duck Seasoning" and "Witch Duck-ter."
Jimmy Weldon was the voice of Yakky, a ventriloquist with a duck-
dummy, Webster Webfoot, who later hosted the NBC children's game
quiz, Funny Boners* (q. v.). And Vance Colvig, who dubbed Chopper, was seen on KTTV, Los Angeles as Bozo the Clown* (q. v.).

In the first network series on ABC between 1973 and 1975,
Yogi's Gang left Jellystone Park on a crusade to protect the environ-
ment and tackle such social themes as bigotry and cheating. Realiz-
ing that their living conditions were becoming intolerable due to pollution, Yogi Bear and Boo Boo decided to do something about it and
commissioned Noah Smith to construct them a balloon ship, "Ark
Lark." Accompanied by their animal friends, Huckleberry Hound,
Snagglepuss, Quick Draw McGraw, Peter Potamus, Wally Gator,
Touché Turtle, Squiddly Diddly, Augie Doggie and Doggie Daddy,
Paw Rugg, Magilla Gorilla and Atom Ant, they traveled about the
country crusading for conservation. Later episodes found them battling the enemies of both man and nature, personified by such ad-
versaries as Mr. Waste, Mr. Bigot, Mr. Prankster, The Envy
Brothers, Lotta Litter and Mr. Cheater. The pilot was an hour-
long adventure re-edited as two episodes titled "Yogi's Ark Lark"
(Sep 16, 1972), seen on The ABC Saturday Superstar Movie (q. v.).
Dr. Tom Robischon, UCLA, served as educational advisor for
the program.

Yogi's Space Race on NBC in 1978-1979 brought together six
teams of cartoon characters vying for an all-expense-paid vacation
on sunny Mars, highlighted by a romantic gondola cruise on the
Martian Canals. With Gary Owens' robust voice urging on the action, Yogi Bear and his co-pilot, Scarebear, rocketed off from post
position number one in their "Supercharged Galactic Leader" for the
weekly interplanetary contests. In what was sort of an outer-space
Wacky Races (q. v.), they were challenged by teams in space vehicles of all kinds, Huckleberry Hound and Quack-Up (#2), Jabberjaw and Buford Bloodhound (#3), Rita and Wendy with Nugget Nose
(#5) and the unselfish sport Captain Good and Clean Cat (#4), alias
dirty trickster Phantom Phink and his henchman, Sinister Sludge.
The teams rocketed among the planets in a five-hundred lap race
around the rings of Saturn in the premiere, beset by the cheating
and alter-guises of the Phink. Some subsequent contests were
titled "The Mizar Marathon," "Race Through Oz" and "The Pongo
Tongo Classic." Jetting out of the blue with scintillating speed,
naturally Yogi and Boo Boo persevered and usually were the nip-
and-tuck winners over the fiendish Phink.

A ninety-minute packaged program trimmed to an hour in
November 1978, at first Yogi's Space Race provided the wraparound
segments for three components. A bumbling squad of outer-space
policemen headed by Captain Snerdly, Officers Yogi Bear, Scarebear,
Huck Hound and Quack-Up tackled a host of dastardly cosmic villains

as The Galaxy Goof-Ups (q. v. ).  "The Buford Files" starred a
lavender bloodhound with his Pendike County buddies, Cindy Mae
and Woody, and a pair of distaff dudes, Rita and Wendy, were
teamed with an ectoplasmic horse, Nugget Nose, known as "The
Galloping Ghost. "  Combined as Buford and The Galloping Ghost
(q. v. ), the comedies were programmed separately beginning February 3, 1979, and The Galaxy Goof-Ups on November 4, 1978.

Appearing in parades at Thanksgiving, Christmas and other
holidays, TV commercials for Kellogg's and as a child pleaser in
amusement parks, ice shows and comic books, Yogi Bear with his
Hanna-Barbera predecessors sold a merchandise miscellany that
grew to over $105 million by the mid-sixties.  Seen as a prime
time ABC special, December 23, 1972, the cagey bruin starred in
the studio's first feature length cartoon, Hey There, It's Yogi Bear
(1964), and in a two-hour syndicated 1980 holiday treat, Yogi's
First Christmas.  One of TV's most beloved and enduring cartoon
characters, for over ten years his early adventures were syndicated as Yogi and His Friends and Yogi's Gang also appeared on
Fred Flintstone and Friends between 1977 and 1979.


YOUNG SAMSON  See  SAMSON AND GOLIATH


YOUNG SENTINELS, THE

Network History
     Premiere:  September 10, 1977
     NBC/Sep 1977-Jan 1978/Saturday 9:00-9:30 AM
     NBC/Feb 1978-Sep 1978/Saturday 11:30-12:00 AM
     Last Program:  September 2, 1978
Executive Producers:  Louis Scheimer, Norman Prescott
Producer:  Don Christensen
Director:  Hal Sutherland
Company:  Filmation Productions/13 films

Principal Characters and Voices

| | |
|---|---|
| Astraea | Dee Timberlake |
| Hercules/Sentinel One | George DiCenzo |
| Mercury | Evan Kim |
| M. O. | Ross Hagen |

     The Young Sentinels were three Earthlings selected for
training by Sentinel One, an intelligent life force from another
galaxy.  Granting them extraordinary powers and eternal youth,
the omnipotent seer returned them to Earth to watch over the
human race, help the good flourish and battle those who threatened its survival.  Drawing on Greek mythology for their names,
the caped-and-costumed teenage superheroes were Astraea, Hercules and Mercury.  In early myth known as the star maiden,
Astraea in the cartoons was an African princess who had the
ability of molecular change.  The most famous of the Greek

heroes, the long-haired blond Hercules still had his bulging biceps but also the strength of one hundred men. And Mercury, the herald of the gods, bereft of his winged cap and sandals, became an Asian who moved with the speed of light. Headquartered inside a volcano, the Sentinels were directed by their mentor from outer space, a computer in the shape of a large head. One of their foes was Morpheus, the god of dreams, who could summon human shapes, and who devised a whole bank of Sentinel Ones, anxious to rule the universe. This legerdemain confused the Sentinels for a time, but the difficulty was resolved with the aid of M.O., the Maintainence Operator, a clever robot that was dedicatingly programmed to the cause. The antagonist line-up resurrected several imaginative, wicked villains from mythology like Anubis, the jackal-headed Egyptian god, and Loki, the Teutonic enfant terrible, along with such fictional contemporaries as "The Wizard of Od" and "The Time Traveler."

Incorporating style, humor and some very good animated art, the science fiction fantasy had an aura of Space Age authenticity and was a notch above the norm. For some undisclosed reason, the series was retitled The Space Sentinels as of November 19, 1977.

## ADDITIONAL TV SERIES USING ANIMATION

In addition to all-cartoon shows and syndicated packages, animated cartoons have been incorporated as elements of other children's programs on the networks and in syndication. The following series presented animated films or characters and are profiled in Children's Television: The First Thirty-Five Years, 1946-1981, Part II: Live, Film and Tape Series (Scarecrow, 1983).

| | |
|---|---|
| ABC Afterschool Specials | ABC 1972- |
| ABC Weekend Specials | ABC 1977- |
| Animals, Animals, Animals | ABC 1976- |
| Big Blue Marble | SYN 1974- |
| Brother Buzz | SYN 1963-1975 |
| CBS Library | CBS 1979- |
| Captain Kangaroo | CBS 1955-1981 |
| Curiosity Shop | ABC 1971-1973 |
| Dear Alex and Annie | ABC 1978- |
| Electric Company, The | PBS 1971- |
| Gumby | NBC 1957 |
| Hot Dog | NBC 1970-1971 |
| In the Know | CBS 1970-1971 |
| Infinity Factory | PBS 1976-1978 |
| Lancelot Link, Secret Chimp Hour, The | ABC 1970-1972 |
| Magic Land of Allakazam, The | CBS 1960-1962 ... |
| Make a Wish | ABC 1971-1976 |
| Marlo and the Magic Movie Machine | SYN 1977- |
| Mickey Mouse Club, The | ABC 1955-1959/ SYN 1962/1975 |
| Mouse Factory, The | SYN 1972-1976 |
| NBC Children's Theatre | NBC 1963-1973 |
| NBC Special Treat | NBC 1975- |
| Off to See the Wizard | ABC 1967-1968 |
| Paddy the Pelican | ABC 1950 |
| Sesame Street | PBS 1969- |
| Small Fry Club | DTN 1947-1951 |
| Susan's Show | CBS 1957-1958 |
| 3-2-1 Contact | PBS 1980- |
| Vegetable Soup | SYN 1975- |
| Villa Alegre | PBS 1974- |

| | |
|---|---|
| Vision On | SYN 1973- |
| Wally Western | SYN 1960-1969 |
| Walt Disney | ABC 1954-1961/ |
| | NBC 1961-1981 |
| Winky Dink and You | CBS 1953-1957 |

APPENDIX II

## SYNDICATED OFF-NETWORK PACKAGES

After their network run, various series were combined and packaged by production studios and distributors for weekly or daily local programming. Sometimes the packages were given new titles and wraparound animation. The following includes the major syndicated films with 52 or more half-hour episodes made available to local stations.

ALVIN AND THE CHIPMUNKS (104 films)  SYN 1966-

ARCHIES, THE (104 films)  SYN 1977-

BANANA SPLITS AND FRIENDS (125 films)  SYN 1971-
 Adventures of Gulliver, The
 Atom Ant/Secret Squirrel Show, The
  Hillbilly Bears
  Precious Pupp
  Squiddly Diddly
  Winsome Witch
 Banana Splits Adventure Hour, The
  Arabian Knights
  Micro Ventures
  Three Musketeers
 New Adventures of Huckleberry Finn, The

CAPTAIN INVENTORY (129 films)  SYN 1973-
 Birdman and The Galaxy Trio
 Fantastic Four, The
 Frankenstein Jr. and The Impossibles
 Herculoids
 Moby Dick and the Mighty Mightor
 Shazzan!
 Space Ghost and Dino Boy, The

CASPER, THE FRIENDLY GHOST AND
 COMPANY (244 films, 5-6 minutes)  SYN 1976-

FLINTSTONES, THE (116 films)  SYN 1970-

FRED FLINTSTONE AND FRIENDS
 (95 films)  SYN 1977-1979

323

Flintstones Comedy Hour, The
Goober and the Ghost Chasers
Jeannie
Partridge Family in Space, The
   (... 2200 A.D.)
Pebbles and Bamm Bamm
Yogi's Gang

FUN WORLD OF HANNA-BARBERA (84 films)   SYN 1977-
   Dastardly and Muttley
      (... in Their Flying Machines)
   Funky Phantom, The
   Perils of Penelope Pitstop, The
   Wacky Races, The

GROOVIE GOOLIES AND FRIENDS
   (104 films)   SYN 1978-
   Groovie Goolies, The
   Lassie's Rescue Rangers
   My Favorite Martians
   New Adventures of Gilligan, The
   New Adventures of Waldo Kitty, The
      (Secret Lives of ...)
   Uncle Croc's Block
      Fraidy Cat
      M*U*S*H
      Wacky and Packy

MIGHTY MOUSE SHOW, THE (75 films)   SYN 1972-
   Mighty Heroes

PINK PANTHER (52 films)   SYN 1980-

ROCKY AND HIS FRIENDS (52 films)   SYN 1961-

SCOOBY-DOO (110 films)   SYN 1980-

SPIDER-MAN (52 films)   SYN 1970-

SUPERMAN/AQUAMAN/BATMAN
   (69 films)   SYN 1970-

TENNESSEE TUXEDO AND HIS TALES
   (56 films)   SYN 1967-

TOM AND JERRY (91 films)   SYN 1977-

UNCLE WALDO (52 films)   SYN 1965-

UNDERDOG (62 films)   SYN 1974-

WOODY WOODPECKER AND FRIENDS   SYN 1958-1966/
   (52 films)   1972-

YOGI AND HIS FRIENDS (96 films)                    SYN 1967-
    Hokey Wolf
    Huckleberry Hound
    Pixie and Dixie
    Snagglepuss
    Yakky Doodle
    Yogi Bear

APPENDIX III

SYNDICATED IMPORTED SERIES

| | | |
|---|---|---|
| Amazing 3, The | Japan | 1967 |
| Astro Boy | Japan | 1963 |
| Battle of the Planets | Japan | 1978 |
| Cyborg Big "X" | Japan | 1967 |
| Do Do--The Kid from Outer Space | England | 1965 |
| 8th Man | Japan | 1965 |
| Gigantor | Japan | 1966 |
| Kimba, the White Lion | Japan | 1966 |
| Marine Boy | Japan | 1966 |
| Prince Planet | Japan | 1966 |
| Speed Racer | Japan | 1967 |
| Star Blazers | Japan | 1979 |
| Tin Tin | France | 1971 |

## LONGEST RUNNING AND MULTI-NETWORK SERIES

Continuously televised for 25 years, <u>Popeye the Sailor</u> is the longest-running syndicated series, arriving four days earlier than <u>Bugs Bunny</u>, which endures as the longest-tenured network program. Among the periodic series including repeats, <u>Peanuts</u> heads the parade of on-going animated Specials with 15 years, followed by <u>Dr. Seuss</u>, but with far fewer programs. Four animated series have been programmed on all three networks: <u>The Adventures of Jonny Quest</u>, <u>The Flintstones</u>, <u>The Jetsons</u> and <u>Speed Buggy</u>. Following are the series televised for five or more years, the premiere year, and the networks on which they appeared.

| | | | |
|---|---|---|---|
| Bugs Bunny (with The Road Runner) | 21 years | 1960 | ABC/CBS |
| Jetsons, The | 14 1/2 years | 1962 | ABC/CBS/NBC |
| Heckle and Jeckle (with Mighty Mouse) | 14 years | 1956 | CBS/NBC |
| Flintstones, The | 13 years | 1960 | ABC/CBS/NBC |
| Mighty Mouse (with Heckle and Jeckle) | 12 1/2 years | 1955 | CBS |
| Bullwinkle | 12 years | 1961 | NBC/ABC |
| Road Runner, The (with Bugs Bunny) | 12 years | 1966 | CBS/ABC |
| Scooby-Doo | 12 years | 1969 | CBS/ABC |
| Pink Panther | 10 years | 1969 | NBC/ABC |
| Tom and Jerry | 10 years | 1965 | CBS/ABC |
| Archies, The | 9 years | 1968 | CBS/NBC |
| Fat Albert | 9 years | 1972 | CBS |
| Adventures of Jonny Quest, The | 8 1/2 years | 1964 | ABC/CBS/NBC |
| Superfriends | 8 years | 1973 | ABC |
| Sabrina, the Teenage Witch | 7 years | 1969 | CBS/NBC |
| Underdog | 7 years | 1964 | NBC/CBS |
| Batman | 6 years | 1968 | CBS/NBC |

| | | | |
|---|---|---|---|
| Pebbles and Bamm Bamm | 6 years | 1971 | CBS |
| Top Cat | 6 years | 1961 | ABC/NBC |
| Beany and Cecil | 5 1/2 years | 1962 | ABC |
| Linus the Lionhearted | 5 years | 1964 | CBS/ABC |
| Speed Buggy | 5 years | 1973 | CBS/ABC/NBC |
| Tarzan, Lord of the Jungle | 5 years | 1976 | CBS |

Following are series that were programmed also on two networks.

| | |
|---|---|
| Alvin Show, The | CBS/NBC |
| Fantastic Four, The | ABC/NBC |
| Frankenstein Jr. | CBS/NBC |
| Groovie Goolies, The | CBS/ABC |
| Harlem Globetrotters, The | CBS/NBC |
| Herculoids | CBS/NBC |
| Hong Kong Phooey | ABC/NBC |
| Josie and the Pussycats in Outer Space | CBS/NBC |
| Mr. Magoo | NBC/CBS |
| Space Ghost, The | CBS/NBC |
| Tennessee Tuxedo and His Tales | CBS/ABC |
| Woody Woodpecker Show, The | ABC/NBC |
| Yogi Bear | ABC/NBC |

## WEEKLY PRIME TIME NETWORK SERIES

| | |
|---|---|
| Adventures of Jonny Quest, The | ABC 1964-1965 |
| Alvin Show, The | CBS 1961-1962 |
| Bugs Bunny Show, The | ABC 1960-1962 |
| Bullwunkle Show, The | NBC 1961-1962 |
| CBS Cartoon Theater | CBS Summer 1956 |
| Calvin and the Colonel | CBS 1961-1962 |
| Famous Adventures of Mr. Magoo, The | NBC 1964-1965 |
| Flintstones, The | ABC 1960-1966 |
| Gerald McBoing-Boing Show, The | CBS Summer 1958 |
| Jetsons, The | ABC 1962-1963 |
| Matty's Funday Funnies/Beany and Cecil | ABC 1960-1962 |
| New Adventures of Huckleberry Finn, The | NBC 1968-1969 |
| Top Cat | ABC 1961-1962 |
| Where's Huddles? | CBS Summer 1970/ Summer 1971 |

APPENDIX VI

## SERIES BASED ON COMIC BOOK SOURCES

| | |
|---|---|
| Aquaman | National Periodicals 1941-1971 |
| Archies, The | Archie Publications 1941- |
| Batman | National Periodicals 1939- |
| Fantastic Four, The | Marvel Comics Group 1961- |
| Josie and the Pussycats | Archie Publications |
| Kimba, the White Lion | Manga Shōnen 1950-1954 |
| Little Lulu | Western Publishing 1948- |
| Marvel Superheroes | Marvel Comics Group |
|    Captain America |    1941-1954/1964- |
|    Incredible Hulk |    1962- |
|    Iron Man |    1963- |
|    Mighty Thor |    1962- |
|    Sub-Mariner |    1939-1949/1962-1974 |
| Plasticman | National Periodicals 1941-1956/ 1966-1968 |
| Richie Rich | Harvey Publishing 1956- |
| Spider-Man | Marvel Comics Group 1962- |
| Spider-Woman | Marvel Comics Group |
| Star Blazers | Shōjo/Akita Shoten 1974- |
| Superfriends | National Periodicals 1940-1951/ 1960- |
| Superman | National Periodicals 1938- |
| Thing, The/ The Flintstones | Marvel Comics Group 1961- |

## SERIES BASED ON NEWSPAPER COMICS

| | |
|---|---|
| Amazing 3, The | Shōnen 1965 |
| Archies TV Funnies | |
|   Alley Oop | NEA 1933- |
|   Broom Hilda | CNS 1970- |
|   Captain and the Kids | UFS 1914- |
|   Dick Tracy | CNS 1931- |
|   Emmy Lou | UFS 1944- |
|   Moon Mullins | CNS 1923- |
|   Nancy and Sluggo | UFS 1940- |
|   Smokey Stover | CNS 1935- |
| Astro Boy | Shōnen 1951-1958 |
| Cyborg Big "X" | Shōnen 1963 |
| Dick Tracy Show, The | CNS 1931- |
| 8th Man | Shōnen 1963-1966 |
| Fabulous Funnies, The | |
|   Alley Oop | NEA 1933- |
|   Broom Hilda | CNS 1970- |
|   Captain and the Kids | UFS 1914- |
|   Emmy Lou | UFS 1944- |
|   Nancy and Sluggo | UFS 1940- |
| Gigantor | Shōnen 1958-1966 |
| Heathcliff | McNaught 1973- |
| Kid Power | Register and Tribune 1965- |
| King Features Trilogy | |
|   Barney Google and | |
|     Snuffy Smith | KFS 1919- |
|   Beetle Bailey | KFS 1950- |
|   Krazy Kat | KFS 1913-1944 |
| MGM Cartoons | |
|   Captain and the Kids | UFS 1914- |
| New Adventures of Flash | |
|   Gordon, The | KFS 1934- |
| New Shmoo, The | UFS 1948-1977 |

Official Films Cartoons

| | |
|---|---|
| Little King | KFS 1934- |
| Toonerville Folks | Wheeler 1915-1955 |

| | |
|---|---|
| Peanuts (Special series) | UFS 1950- |
| Popeye the Sailor | KFS 1929- |

Screen Gems Theatrical
    Cartoon Package

| | |
|---|---|
| Barney Google | KFS 1919- |
| Krazy Kat | KFS 1913-1944 |
| Li'l Abner | UFS 1934-1977 |

| | |
|---|---|
| Tin Tin | Le Petit Vingtième 1929- |

## SERIES BASED ON LITERARY SOURCES

| | |
|---|---|
| Aesop and Son/ Rocky and His Friends | Aesop's Fables |
| Adventures of Gulliver, The | Gulliver's Travels (1726) Jonathan Swift |
| Adventures of Sinbad | Thousand Nights and a Night (1885-1886) Sir Richard Burton |
| Amazing Chan and the Chan Clan | Charlie Chan novels (1925-1932) Earl Derr Biggers |
| Arabian Knights/ The Banana Splits | Thousand Nights and a Night (1885-1886) Sir Richard Burton |
| Around the World in 79 Days/ The Cattanooga Cats | Le Tour du monde en quatre-vingts jours (1873) Jules Verne |
| Around the World in 80 Days | Le Tour du monde en quatre-vingts jours (1873) Jules Verne |
| Book Report, The/ Drawing Power | Various |
| Dr. Seuss | Dr. Seuss books (1937-    ) Theodor Seuss Geisel |
| Family Classics Theater (Special series) | Various |
| Famous Adventures of Mr. Magoo, The | Various |
| Famous Classic Tales (Special series) | Various |
| Fangface | The Were-wolf (1890) Clemence Housman |

Festival of Family Classics      Various
  (Special series)

Fractured Fairy Tales/      Various
  Rocky and His Friends

Frankenstein Jr.      Frankenstein, or the Modern
       Prometheus (1818)
       Mary Shelley

Further Adventures of      Dr. Dolittle novels (1920-1952)
  Dr. Dolittle        Hugh Lofting

Hardy Boys, The      The Hardy Boys novels (1927-  )
       Edward L. Stratemeyer

Journey to the Center of      Voyage au centre de la
  the Earth        terre (1864)
       Jules Verne

Jungle Book, The      The Jungle Book (1894)
  (Special series)        Rudyard Kipling

Mighty Hercules, The      Greek mythology

Mighty Thor/      Norse mythology
  Marvel Superheroes

Moby Dick      Moby-Dick (1851)
       Herman Melville

New Adventures of      Various
  Huckleberry Finn

Paddington Bear      Paddington Bear books (1958-  )
       Michael Bond

Reluctant Dragon and      Dream Days (1898) and The
  Mr. Toad, The        Wind in the Willows (1907)
       Kenneth Grahame

Rocket Robin Hood and      English legend and ballads
  His Merry Spacemen

Shazzan!      Thousand Nights and a Night
       (1885-1886)
       Sir Richard Burton

Sinbad Jr., the Sailor      Thousand Nights and a Night
       (1885-1886)
       Sir Richard Burton

Tarzan, Lord of the Jungle      Tarzan of the Apes (1914)
       Edgar Rice Burroughs

Three Musketeers, The /
   The Banana Splits

Les Trois Mousquetaires (1844)
   Alexandre Dumas

Tomfoolery

Various

Winnie-the-Pooh
   (Special series)

Winnie-the-Pooh books
   (1926-1928)
   A. A. Milne

Young Sentinels, The

Greek mythology

## SERIES BASED ON TV PROGRAMS

ABC Saturday Superstar Movies

| | |
|---|---|
| The Brady Kids on Mysterious Island | The Brady Bunch<br>ABC 1969-1974 |
| Gidget Makes the Wrong Connection | Gidget*<br>ABC 1965-1966 |
| Lassie and the Spirit of Thunder Mountain | Lassie*<br>CBS 1954-1971/<br>SYN 1972-1975 |
| Lost in Space | Lost in Space*<br>CBS 1965-1968 |
| Mini-Munsters | The Munsters<br>CBS 1964-1966 |
| Nanny and the Professor | Nanny and the Professor<br>ABC 1970-1971 |
| Phantom of the Circus | Nanny and the Professor<br>ABC 1970-1971 |
| Tabitha and Adam and the Clown Family | Bewitched*<br>ABC 1964-1973 |
| That Girl in Wonderland | That Girl<br>ABC 1966-1971 |
| Addams Family, The | The Addams Family<br>ABC 1964-1966 |
| Barkleys, The | All In The Family<br>CBS 1971-1979 |
| Beany and Cecil | Time for Beany*<br>SYN 1949-1958 |
| Brady Kids, The | The Brady Bunch<br>ABC 1969-1974 |

336

| | |
|---|---|
| Captain Caveman and the Teen Angels | Charlie's Angels <br> ABC 1976-1981 |
| Emergency + 4 | Emergency <br> NBC 1972-1977 |
| Fonz and the Happy Days Gang | Happy Days <br> ABC 1974- |
| Heyyyyy, It's the King/ C. B. Bears | Happy Days <br> ABC 1974- |
| Houndcats, The | Mission: Impossible <br> CBS 1966-1973 |
| Jeannie | I Dream of Jeannie <br> NBC 1965-1970 |
| Lassie's Rescue Rangers | Lassie* <br> CBS 1954-1971/ <br> SYN 1972-1975 |
| Lone Ranger, The | The Lone Ranger* <br> ABC/CBS/NBC 1949-1969/ <br> SYN 1961- |
| M*U*S*H/ Uncle Croc's Block | M*A*S*H <br> CBS 1972- |
| My Favorite Martians | My Favorite Martian <br> CBS 1963-1966 |
| New Adventures of Gilligan, The | Gilligan's Island <br> CBS 1964-1967 |
| Oddball Couple, The | The Odd Couple <br> ABC 1970-1975 |
| Partridge Family: 2200 A. D. | The Partridge Family <br> ABC 1970-1974 |
| Return to the Planet of the Apes | The Planet of the Apes <br> CBS 1974 |
| Star Trek | Star Trek <br> NBC 1966-1969 |
| Winky Dink and You | Winky Dink and You* <br> CBS 1953-1957 |

## SERIES BASED ON OTHER SOURCES

| | |
|---|---|
| Abbott and Costello Cartoons | Movie comedians |
| Alvin Show, The | Liberty Records vocalists |
| Baggy Pants and the Nitwits | Movie comedian/TV characters |
| Beatles, The | Musicians-singing group |
| Bozo the Clown | Capitol Records character |
| Butch Cassidy and the Sun Dance Kids | 1969 TCF movie |
| Calvin and the Colonel | Radio series |
| Fantastic Voyage | 1966 TCF movie |
| Felix the Cat (New) | Silent animated cartoons |
| Godzilla | 1954 Toho movie |
| Harlem Globetrotters, The | Professional athletes |
| I Am the Greatest: The Adventures of Muhammad Ali | Professional athlete |
| Jackson 5ive, The | Singing group |
| King Kong Show, The | 1933 RKO movie |
| Laurel and Hardy Cartoons | Movie comedians |
| Osmonds, The | Singing group |
| Out of the Inkwell (New) | Silent animated cartoons |
| Smokey Bear Show, The | U. S. Forest Service symbol |
| Three Stooges, The | Movie comedians |
| Will the Real Jerry Lewis Please Sit Down? | Movie comedian |

APPENDIX XI

ANIMATED-FILM AWARDS

ANNIE AWARDS

The Annie Awards are presented for distinguished contributions to the liveliest film art by the International Animated Film Society, Hollywood. The Association internationale du Film animé (ASIFA), founded in 1959 in Annecy, France under the aegis of UNICEF, promotes animation through education, publicity and annual film festivals, in particular three major events, at Annecy; Ottawa, Canada; and Zagreb, Yugoslavia. Comprised of more than one thousand upper-echelon animation professionals in thirty-nine countries, ASIFA, Hollywood is the largest branch and established its own annual awards program in 1972. Including posthumous presentations, the Annie Award recognizes excellence by men and women in one or more of the skills and crafts which make up the animated film industry; and work for television, the theater, and other mediums is represented among the following recipients. The Windsor McCay Award* is presented for exceptional contributions and involvement, usually spanning fifty years.

1972

David Fleischer
Max Fleischer

1973

Walter Lantz

1974

Fred "Tex" Avery
Art Babbitt*
Isadore "Friz" Freleng
Chuck Jones

1975

John R. Bray*
Walt Disney
Faith Hubley

John Hubley
Norman McLaren
Grim Natwick*

1976

Robert "Bobe" Cannon
Hugh Harman
Rudolf Ising
Ward Kimball*
Mike Maltese
George Pal

1977

Joseph Barbera
Mel Blanc
Oskar Fischinger
William Hanna
Milt Kahl
Bill Scott

## 1978

Hans Conried
Dick Huemer
Ubbe "Ub" Iwerks
Carl Stalling
Jay Ward

## 1979

Clyde "Gerry" Geronomi
J. C. "Bill" Melendez
Otto Messmer*
Mae Questel

## 1980

LaVerne Harding*
Cal Howard
Oliver "Ollie" Johnston
Paul Julian
Frank Thomas

## 1981

Ken Harris*
T. Hee
Bill Peet
Vladimir "Bill" Tytla
John Whitney


## EMMY AWARDS

The Emmy Awards were founded locally in 1949 in Hollywood, which continued to administer the program after the formation of the National Academy of Television Arts and Sciences in 1957. In 1976, a dispute between the Hollywood and New York chapters resulted in the reestablishment of the Academy of Television Arts and Sciences, Hollywood, which continues to bestow Emmy Awards for prime time entertainment programs and crafts, and Los Angeles area awards. The relocated headquarters of the National Academy of Television Arts and Sciences, New York, presents Emmy Awards for daytime, sports and local programs. Since 1957, the awards have been presented on a seasonal rather than a yearly basis. The following include those garnered for animated films. A complete listing of all the Emmy Awards for Children's Television is contained in Children's Television: The First Thirty-Five Years, 1946-1981, Part II: Live, Film and Tape Series (Scarecrow, 1983).


## 1959-1960

Huckleberry Hound (SYN)

## 1965-1966

A Charlie Brown Christmas
    (CBS)

## 1973-1974

Charles Schulz, writer
A Charlie Brown Thanks-
    giving (CBS)

## 1974-1975

Yes, Virginia, There is a Santa
    Claus (ABC)
Star Trek (NBC)
Elinor Bunin, graphic design
Funshine Saturday, Sunday
    Titles (ABC)

## 1975-1976

You're a Good Sport, Charlie
    Brown (CBS)
Happy Anniversary, Charlie

Brown (CBS)
Grammar Rock (ABC)

## 1976-1977

Jean de Joux, Elizabeth Savel,
    videoanimation
Peter Pan (NBC)

## 1977-1978

Halloween Is Grinch Night
    (ABC)
Schoolhouse Rock (ABC)

## 1978-1979

The Lion, the Witch and the
    Wardrobe (CBS)
Science Rock (ABC)

## 1979-1980

Carlton, Your Doorman (CBS)
Schoolhouse Rock (ABC)
H. E. L. P. !! (ABC)

## 1980-1981

Life Is a Circus, Charlie
    Brown (CBS)


## OSCAR AWARDS

The Oscar Awards, presented by the Academy of Motion
Picture Arts and Sciences, first incorporated animated films in
1931-1932. Initially, they were added to the Short Subject category, which was divided into the cartoon, comedy, and novelty
divisions. During its evolution, the category underwent several
changes until 1957 when the divisions were standardized to en-
compass cartoon or live action films. Recognizing that not all
animated shorts are cartoons, the title "animated film" was substituted in 1971 and the category's name was changed to Short
Films in 1974. Although the Oscar Awards are presented to animated films primarily made for theaters, nearly all of the winners have been televised in various programmings.

## 1932

Flowers and Trees (Walt
    Disney)

## 1933

Three Little Pigs (Walt
    Disney)

## 1934

The Tortoise and the Hare
    (Walt Disney)

## 1935

Three Orphan Kittens (Walt
    Disney)

## 1936

The Country Cousin (Walt
    Disney)

## 1937

The Old Mill (Walt Disney)

## 1938

Ferdinand the Bull (Walt Disney)

## 1939

The Ugly Duckling (Walt Disney)

## 1940

The Milky Way (MGM)

**1941**

Lend a Paw (Walt Disney)

**1942**

Der Fuehrer's Face (Walt Disney)

**1943**

Yankee Doodle Mouse (MGM)

**1944**

Mouse Trouble (MGM)

**1945**

Quiet, Please (MGM)

**1946**

The Cat Concerto (MGM)

**1947**

Tweety Pie (Warner Brothers)

**1948**

The Little Orphan (MGM)

**1949**

For Scent-imental Reasons (Warner Brothers)

**1950**

Gerald McBoing Boing (UPA)

**1951**

The Two Mouseketeers (MGM)

**1952**

Johann Mouse (MGM)

**1953**

Toot, Whistle, Plunk and Boom (Walt Disney)

**1954**

When Magoo Flew (UPA)

**1955**

Speedy Gonzales (Warner Brothers)

**1956**

Magoo's Puddle Jumper (UPA)

**1957**

Birds Anonymous (Warner Brothers)

**1958**

Knighty Knight Bugs (Warner Brothers)

**1959**

Moonbird (Storyboard)

**1960**

Munro (Rembrandt Films)

**1961**

Ersatz (Zagreb Film, Yugoslavia)

**1962**

The Hole (Storyboard)

**1963**

The Critic (Ernest Pintoff)

**1964**

The Pink Phink (DePatie-Freleng)

**1965**

The Dot and the Line (Chuck Jones)

**1966**

Herb Alpert and the Tijuana
Brass (Storyboard)

**1967**

The Box (Brandon Films)

**1968**

Winnie-the-Pooh and the
Blustery Day (Walt Disney)

**1969**

It's Tough to Be a Bird (Walt
Disney)

**1970**

Is It Always Right to Be
Right? (Bosustow and
Adams)

**1971**

The Crunch Bird (Ted Petok)

**1972**

A Christmas Carol (Richard
Williams, England)

**1973**

Frank Film (Frank Mouris)

**1974**

Closed Mondays (Vinton and
Gardiner)

**1975**

Great (Bob Godfrey, England)

**1976**

Leisure (National Film
Board, Canada)

**1977**

Sand Castle (National Film
Board, Canada)

**1978**

Special Delivery (National Film
Board, Canada)

**1979**

Every Child (National Film
Board, Canada)

**1980**

The Fly (Pannonia, Budapest)

**1981**

CRAC (Société radio de la
Canada)

## PEABODY AWARDS

The Peabody Awards are given annually to programs, stations, networks and individuals. They are designed to recognize
distinguished achievement and the most meritorious public service
rendered by radio and television for excellence in news, entertainment, education, public service, and children's and youth programming. Administered by the School of Journalism, University of
Georgia, the television awards were inaugurated in 1948. The following Peabody Awards were made for animated cartoon series in
the Children's and Youth category. A complete listing of all Peabody Awards which have been presented for juvenile programming

is contained in <u>Children's Television:  The First Thirty-Five Years, 1946-1981, Part II:  Live, Film and Tape Series</u> (Scarecrow, 1983).

### 1965

A Charlie Brown Christmas (CBS)

### 1970

Dr. Seuss programs (CBS)

### 1977

The Hobbit (NBC)

# ANIMATED-FILM MAKERS

# ANIMATED-FILM VOICES

* indicates voice impersonation and/or caricature
† indicates Narrator/Announcer

Abbott, William "Bud"  3, *4
Adams, Don  286, 307
Adler, Cynthia  6
Ahrens, James  213
Albee, Josh  255
Alberoni, Sherry  6, 155, 276
Albert, Eddie  †83-84
Alden, Norman  80, 276
Alexander, Joan  279
Ali, Muhammad  147
Allen, Chris  10, 265
Allen, Dayton  12, 26, 60, 65, 79, 135, 137, 188, 310
Allen, Gene  154
Allen, Marty  *60
Allman, Sheldon  59
Altieri, Ann  213
Anderson, Daniel  213
Anderson, Eddie  132
Andes, Keith  46
Andrusco, Gene  5, 16, 35
Angel, Jack  276
Annabelle  115
Ann-Margret  107
Aragon, Marlene  276
Arbogast, Bob  142, 242, 261
Arnold, Beverly  188
Autterson, Gay  105
Avery, Tex  181

Backus, Jim  194-195, 199
Bagdasarian, Ross (David Seville)  14-15
Bailey, John Anthony  223
Baker, Joe  105, 223, 289
Baker, Melanie  304
Balkin, Barry  190
Bannister, Frank  147
Barbee, Todd  212, 213

Barrett, Majel  271
Barrymore, Lionel  *302
Bascome, Jerry  182
Beach, Dylan  212
Beach, Sarah  213
Beals, Dick  46, 111, 113, 236, 242
Beck, Jackson  †38, 165, 226-227, †279
Becker, Sandy  125
Beery, Wallace  *181
Begg, Jim  31, 68
Bell, Mike  6, 59, 80, 123, 223, 266, 276, 283
Bellflower, Nellie  290
Benaderet, Bea  104, 281
Bennett, Julie  32, 68, 194, 226, 233, 251, 317
Berg, Nancy  †18
Bergen, Edgar  *252
Bernardi, Herschel  183-184
Berner, Sara  313
Bertheau, Steacy  304
Besser, Joe  116, 144, 151, 251, 316
Best, Larry  188
Bishop, Joey  *222
Blackburn, Richard  235
Blanc, Mel  4, 28, 52, 55, 63, 76, 81, 104, 105, 109, 116, 130, 134, 153, 173, 175, 218, 219, 230-231, 251, 258, 266, 281, 308, 313-314, 316
Bletcher, Billy  181, 293
Bliss, Lucille  74, 265
Blocker, Dan  *60
Blondell, Gloria  61
Blore, Eric  *118, 235
Blu, Susan  95

Bly, Nellie *172
Bogart, Humphrey *302
Bolke, Bradley 286
Bonaduce, Danny 126, 211-212
Bosley, Tom 306-307
Boyer, Charles *77
Brando, Marlon *146
Brandt, Eddie 41
Braverman, Bart 95
Bravo, Danny 11
Brennan, Walter *51, *108,
 *146
Britt, Melendy 38, 197, 223
Brooks, Albert 142
Brotman, Stuart 213
Brown, Joe E. *130, *219
Brown, Johnny 223
Bryan, Arthur Q. 52
Buckley, William *260
Burke, Billie *29
Burns, Jack 306
Butler, Daws 6, 31, 32, 48,
 58, 59, 68, 112, 116, 117,
 130, 139, 144, 145, 153,
 193, 194, 219, 226, 233,
 243, 244, 250-251, 265,
 274, 293, 305, 313, 316
Buttram, Pat *202
Buxton, Frank 36
Buzzi, Ruth 30
Byner, John 221


Cabot, Sebastian †311
Cady, Frank 287
Cagney, James †262
Callaway, Bill 68, 85, 139,
 236, 255, 276
Cantu-Primo, Dolores 202
Carlson, Casey 214
Carmichael, Casey 147
Carmichael, Patrice 147
Carney, Art *106, *146,
 *317
Carr, Jack 173
Carradine, John 42
Carroll, Larry 269
Carroll, Pat 274
Cartwright, Nancy 236
Casey, Melinda 142, 261
Cassidy, Jack 195
Cassidy, Ted 8, 46, 97, 111,
 122, 123, 200, 273, 276

Chaplin, Charles *30
Charo *300
Christopher, Stefanianna 140
Clampett, Bob 41
Clampett, Bobby 41
Clampett, Sody 41
Clary, Robert 42
Cohn, Shannon 214
Collyer, Bud 38, 279
Colman, Ronald *118
Colvig, Pinto 48, 225, 227
Colvig, Vance 316, 318
Conn, DiDi 109
Conrad, William †55-56, 171
Conried, Hans 10, 56, †83-84,
 85, 87, 313
Conway, Tim 252
Coogan, Jackie 7
Cook, Tommy 32, 112, 149
Coons, Johnny 314
Corbett, Carol 72
Corden, Henry 28, 32, 35,
 50, 58, 104, 109, 235,
 290, 316
Correll, Charles J. 61-62
Cosby, Bill 99
Costello, Lou (Louis Francis
 Cristillo) *3, *4, *60, *223
Costello, William 225, 227
Cotting, Richard 70
Coughlan, Russ 74
Cowan, Bernard 268
Cox, Wally 301-302
Crawford, Jan 99
Crosby, Bing *170
Crothers, Scatman 42, 132,
 141, 251, 259
Crough, Suzanne 126, 211-212
Cullen, Peter 223
Curtis, Dick 193, 260-261
Curtis, Jack 176, 267
Curtis, Tony 107, *118


Daniell, Henry *118
Dano, Royal 195
Dark, Danny 276
David, Jeff 122
Davies, Gwen 66
Davis, Gail 213
Davis, Susan 58, 142, 259
Day, Dennis 201
Deacon, Richard †222

## OTHER PROPER NAMES

* indicates cast and production staff/live action children's series
† indicates hosts/children's series

Addams, Charles  8
Aletter, Frank  *33
Allen, John  214
Anderson, Murphy  38
Andriola, Alfred  17
Armstrong, Roger  171
Arons, Richard  151
Arrendondo, Rodrigo  *33
Asimov, Isaac  98
Austin, Pamela  218

Baker, Paul  156
Bakey, Ed  †181
Balmer, Edwin  198
Becker, Sandy  †53, †173
Begley, Ed  17
Bemelmans, Ludwig  120
Benchley, Robert  235
Bennett, Al  14
Berra, Yogi  317
Berry, Dr. Gordon L.  100
Biggers, Earl Derr  16
Bing, Mack  *299
Bixby, Bill  178, 197
Bixby, J. Lewis  98
Blaine, Jimmy  †244-245
Bolton, Joe  †82, †270
Bond, Michael  210
Boone, Pat  218
Boulle, Pierre  235
Bowen, Dennis  23
Brian, Marcel  101
Brice, Fanny (Fanny Borach)  109
Brown, Reb  178
Bryant, Ed  102
Buckley, Floyd  228

Buell, Marjorie Henderson "Marge"  171
Burgess, Frank Gelett  297
Burroughs, Edgar Rice  118, 283-285
Burton, Sir Richard  257, 258
Burton, Wendell  216
Busch, Wilhelm  92
Bushmiller, Ernie  93

Capp, Al (Alfred Gerald Caplin)  203
Carbaga, Leslie  46
Carmel, Roger C.  272
Carradine, David  142
Carroll, Lewis (Charles Lutwidge Dodgson)  103, 297
Cassidy, David  212
Chambers, John  236
Chandler, Raymond  198
Chaney, Lon, Jr.  96
Chaplin, Charles  101
Clemens, Samuel L. (Mark Twain)  200
Clement, Otto  98
Cole, Dennis  144
Cole, Jack  223
Cole, Renate  210
Collins, Max  82
Connell, Del  171
Connelly, Walter  17
Conrad, Con  163
Coons, Johnny  †114
Cooper, James Fenimore  94
Cooper, Merian C.  165
Cosby, Bill  †99
Cottle, Bob  †244-245

# ANIMATED FILMS AND SERIES MADE FOR THEATERS

# ANIMATED CARTOON SERIES MADE FOR TELEVISION